GROUP THERAPY WITH TROUBLED YOUTH

To my wife, Cindy,
without whose support
and encouragement this book
would never have been written.

Sheldon D. Rose

GROUP THERAPY WITH TROUBLED YOUTH

*A Cognitive-Behavioral
Interactive Approach*

SAGE Publications
International Educational and Professional Publisher
Thousand Oaks   London   New Delhi

For information:

SAGE Publications, Inc.
2455 Teller Road
Thousand Oaks, California 91320
E-mail: order@sagepub.com

SAGE Publications Ltd.
6 Bonhill Street
London EC2A 4PU
United Kingdom

SAGE Publications India Pvt. Ltd.
M-32 Market
Greater Kailash I
New Delhi 110 048 India

Printed in the United States of America

Library of Congress Cataloging-in-Publication Data

Rose, Sheldon D.
   Group therapy with troubled youth: A cognitive-behavioral
interactive approach / by Sheldon D. Rose.
     p. cm.
   Includes bibliographical references and index.
   ISBN 0-7619-0927-3 (cloth: acid-free paper). — ISBN
0-7619-0928-1 (pbk.: acid-free paper)
    1. Problem youth—Counseling of. 2. Group psychotherapy for
youth. 3. Cognitive therapy for teenagers. I. Title.
RJ506.P63R67 1998
616.89'152'0835—dc21   97-33797

98 99 00 01 02 03 10 9 8 7 6 5 4 3 2 1

Acquiring Editor:	Jim Nageotte
Editorial Assistant:	Kathleen Derby
Production Editor:	Diana E. Axelsen
Production Assistant:	Karen Wiley
Typesetter/Designer:	Danielle Dillahunt
Indexer:	Mary Mortensen
Cover Designer:	Candice Harman
Print Buyer:	Anna Chin

Contents

PART IV: APPLICATIONS OF COGNITIVE-BEHAVIORAL INTERACTIONAL GROUP THERAPY

List of Exercises

Preface and
Acknowledgments

There are many books on group therapy, group work, and group counseling especially with youth. Some emphasize group process. Others focus on goal setting and the achievement of goals. Still others stress various intervention approaches. This book is characterized by all of these, but with a special focus on using the group as the major tool of intervention within the structure of a cognitive and behavioral theoretical framework. The chapter titles reflect primarily the cognitive-behavioral and social support emphasis. Although a special chapter is devoted solely to group process, every chapter emphasizes process issues. Yet, in every chapter and with every behavioral and cognitive strategy employed, the ways in which the participants are involved in their own learning are described in detail, and the role of the group therapist in that involvement is specified. Highly concrete techniques for enhancing motivation and participation by the youth are identified, such as the use of subgroups and "brainstorming" or writing down reponses before giving them. Cohesion-building strategies are elucidated, such as the use of interesting and attractive group activities or techniques of teaching skills that the youth can enjoy, the use of positive interventions, and cooperative projects. Ways of preventing group problems as well as strategies for dealing with them are added to the mix. It should be noted that in this book, the term *group process,* in contrast with its use by many authors, refers primarily to patterns of interaction among the youth and between the youth and the group therapist. Intervention involves creating the kinds of processes that enhance motivation and learning. I have used primarily the term *group therapist* to designate the professional person facilitating the learning activities of the members because of the therapeutic focus of the endeavor. He or she could just as easily been called the group worker, the group counselor, the group facilitator, or the group practitioner.

This book has been written in response to the questions of practitioners who lead cognitive behavioral groups for troubled youth. But it is also written for the student or practitioner who is being introduced to this style of group therapy or group work for the first time and who seeks concrete guidelines for helping members to help each other to achieve behavioral and cognitive change. All too often, cognitive behavioral groups are conducted solely as psychoeducational groups with detailed plans as to how each session should be carried out. These is little room for the ideas of the participants. There seems to be little concern for their motivation to change. There is considerable empirical support for such groups, though significant statistically the differences are often small between the highly structured groups and the contrast groups or waitlisted controls (see pp. 37-44, this volume, for a review of that research). The clinical experience of my colleagues and coworkers suggests that these methods can be enhanced by the incorporation of various group strategies that recognize the contribution of the members and involve them actively in their own therapy.

I draw heavily for examples and illustrations from my own experience and from that of my associates, students, and practitioners in agencies to which I have provided consultation and/or for which I have provided workshops and training programs.

Because groups of the sort described in this volume draw on diverse theoretical sources, they have their foundation in many sets of ideas. These include the group work theories of Vinter (1985a), the group therapeutic theories of Yalom (1985), and the cognitive-behavioral theories of Bandura (1977a), Meichenbaum (1977), Beck (1976), and Kazdin (1989). In spite of its eclecticism, there are several consistent themes or assumptions throughout this book. Youth involvement in the change process is essential for group cohesion and behavior change; the group provides both the context and a set of intervention strategies. If youth do not enjoy the therapeutic experience, they will not be motivated to change, but enjoyment is not enough. Specific targets of change negotiated with the youth are more likely to be achieved than general targets of change. Shared and individualized interventions are used to achieve specific targets of change; the youth are taught these interventions so as to facilitate their own change and that of their peers; the therapist must help the youth to go beyond the limits of psychological interventions to the incorporation of those social and material resources available to him or her; and the focus of therapy with all interventive endeavors is on achieving changes that generalize to the real world. In spite of these diverse theoretical contributions, I have attempted to blend these assumptions as much as possible into a coherent and integrated whole.

Organization of the Book

This book is organized into four parts: In the Beginning of Groups, Assessment and Goal Setting in Groups, Interventions in and Beyond the Group, and Applications of Cognitive-Behavioral Interactional Group Therapy. Part I begins with Chapter 1, an overview in which the entire approach is set out and the major research support is identified. It is assumed that anyone reading the following chapters is familiar with the content of the introductory chapter. Also in Part I are Chapter 2, on preparation for group therapy, and Chapter 3, on starting the group— orientation, cohesion building, and motivation enhancement. In Part II, Assessment and Goal Setting in Groups, the chapters include Chapter 4, on assessment in groups—interviewing and observation strategies; Chapter 5, on measurement procedures in assessment and evaluation; and Chapter 6, on goal setting and intervention planning. Part III, Interventions In and Beyond the Group, includes Chapter 7, on solving problems and negotiating differences; Chapter 8, on reinforcement and stimulus control in groups; Chapter 9, on the modeling sequence; Chapter 10, on cognitive and relaxation coping strategies; Chapter 11, on extragroup tasks; Chapter 12, on assessing and enhancing social support (with Katherine P. Reardon); Chapter 13, on integrating socio-recreational activities into therapy; Chapter 14, on intervening in the group process; and Chapter 15, on procedures for generalization—going beyond the boundaries of the group. Part IV, Applications of Cognitive-Behavioral

Interactional Group Therapy, consists of Chapter 16, on group strategies for reducing anger and aggression (with Martin D. Martsch), and Chapter 17, on staff training and supervision for cognitive-behavioral interactive group therapy.

Acknowledgments

As in most books, this work has been the result of the effort of many people. In particular, I would like to thank the many practitioners, former students and participants in workshops, and staffs of agencies (for whom I have consulted) who provided many of the examples used in this book. In particular, I would like to mention Peter Duby, Cynthia Olenick, Martin Martsch, Kathleen Todar, and Thomas Weston, who have tried out and trained others in this approach and provided me with feedback on its merits and limitations. I would also like to express my appreciation to Dr. William Butterfield, Professor Emeritus, Washington University, St. Louis, and Dr. Charles Garvin, Professor, University of Michigan, Ann Arbor, who read early versions of this work. I would also like to thank Ruth Evans, who assisted me in typing, revising, and carrying out the multitude of administrative tasks associated with putting a book together. In spite of all these valuable contributions, it is I alone who must accept the responsibility for all that is written in this book.

PART I

In the Beginning
of Groups

CHAPTER 1

An Overview

A cognitive-behavioral approach with youth emphasizes the effects of beliefs and other cognitions on behavior (see, e.g., Reinecke, Dattilio, & Freeman, 1996, pp. 2-3). Generally, the cognitive-behavioral approach is highly structured and guided directly by the therapist. What distinguishes cognitive-behavioral interactive group therapy (CBIGT) from other cognitive approaches is twofold. First, there is a greater emphasis on modeling and operant strategies. Second, as CBIGT progresses, the youth are increasingly involved in adapting that structure to their own needs. The interaction among members of the group is as important as that between therapist and members. Group and self-management gradually replaces much (but not all) of therapist management of change. CBIGT takes particular advantage of the opportunities the group affords for mutual support, leadership, new relationships, prosocial roles, receiving peer feedback, and helping others. CBIGT goes beyond therapy by identifying social issues such as racism, sexism, or homophobia, as they arise, and it develops with youth specific ways of dealing with such issues as they arise. The behavior of youth is viewed not only as the product of their thinking and beliefs but also as the product of their immediate environment, family, community, gender, race, and ethnicity.

The aim of this chapter is to give the reader an overview of CBIGT. In the subsequent chapters, the basic concepts are exemplified in greater detail. From this overview, the reader can determine how each of the subsequent chapters fits into the whole approach. First, let us look at who these troubled youth are.

Troubled Youth

The youth who attend these groups are troubled by varied problems with which they must learn to cope. Let us look at examples of four young people who are typical of many served by CBIGT. Presented are not only their background and problem areas but also their personal interests and resources.

Chas, age 15, is a tall, slender, African American youth who wears an Afro. His mother works as a checkout person at a supermarket. The stepfather is an unemployed mechanic who overhauls motors at home and resells them. Chas has a sister, age 14, who also lives at home. Chas was convicted of breaking and entering together with three other boys. Chas said he did it for the fun of it and could use the money. His mother describes him as violent, easy to incite to anger, and uncooperative. He frequently talks back to both parents when they ask him to do anything. He cuts school often and hangs out with his friends. Chas tested positive for drugs when he was caught for the breaking and entering. He said he had been using for just a year on and off. The arresting officer said he probably was dealing but had no hard proof. Chas fights frequently with his sister, but looks out for her on the streets. He is now in group therapy as part of the program of the day treatment center that he is required to attend. Chas played basketball at a nearby school playground and now plays it at the day treatment center. He admires Michael Jordan and has souvenirs of him all over his room. Chas worked at McDonald's for 4 weeks at the beginning of the year but was fired because of chronic lateness and an "attitude" problem. He is interested in motors, but he and his stepfather have never worked together because they cannot get along. His health is good. In the group, he is a leader and often tries to compete with the therapist.

Linda, age 15, Hispanic, lives with her single mother and is now in a community treatment group to which she was referred by the school. She misses a lot of school because she cannot get up in the morning and does not feel well. She claims she has sleep problems and is tired most of the time. Her mother says she is extremely moody and mostly seems to be sad. Linda says that her mother and sister hate her, so she tries to stay away from them as much as she can. She rarely talks to either of them. Nobody will give her a job, she says, because she is too young. Linda drinks about 10 to 12 bottles of beer a week and smokes marijuana when she can get it. Her mother yells at her for drinking and being drunk. She describes herself as overweight (she is about 150 pounds) and short, and she hates all comments about her weight. She recently had a physical examination, but the doctor could find no physical cause of her depression. She has few friends. She used to like to watch TV and read love stories and walk in the mall with her one friend. But she doesn't do much of that anymore. When she attended school regularly, she did average work.

Lon, age 16, white, is a child of a single parent. He was arrested for sexually abusing a younger boy on the block and is now in an institutional group as part of treatment. He says that an uncle abused him when he was much younger but that he has not had any previous sexual encounters, and he claims that the boy initiated the contact. He has few friends and in the institution is considered by his residential worker to be a loner. He weighs 210 pounds and is 6 feet tall but not very well coordinated. He complains about being teased and called names by his peers and then getting into trouble because he fights back. His mother says that when he was at home and when he comes home on furlough, he does not do any chores, sleeps a lot, watches TV many hours a day, and wanders around a lot in the neighborhood. She says the only interaction they have is to argue. She is glad to have him out of the house. When staff ask Lon to do something or criticize him for anything, he becomes extremely angry, or he becomes passive and his affect goes flat. Lon likes to watch sports, bowl, and play the guitar, but he says he is not very good at any of these activities. He put himself down frequently in the interview and continues to do this in group meetings. When he was still at home, he did slightly below-average work at school. He attended regularly but rarely did homework, so he got low grades. His work has

improved in the institution with a lot of reinforcement for assignment completion and reminders to study.

Vaughn, age 13, lives with a single mother and his sister, age
12. He has poor social skills. He talks slowly, and kids label him
as "dumb." Actually, he does only slightly below-average work.
His sister teases him too. She turns off the TV when he is watching
it, and she will not let him play with her cat. Vaughn is a small
youth. He has diabetes but is not careful about what he eats. He
has almost no interests outside of TV. He does minimal chores
around the house. He has few friends and shows no interest in
making friends. He is being treated in a social skill training group
at the health care center as part of a health insurance program in
which his mother is enrolled.

As can be observed from the above examples, some of the youth whom
CBIGT serves are extremely angry and manifest that anger in aggression
toward others. Some have been arrested and adjudicated for serious
misdemeanors and felonies. Some are residing in treatment or correctional institutions. Some are still on the brink of being convicted or being
institutionalized because of their behavior at school and on the streets.
Others are withdrawn and have inadequate social skills. Most have poor
relationships with their families, and some have a history of running
away. Many have left school prematurely or have been suspended; many
of those remaining are doing poorly. Many either have poor relationships
with peers or have friendships primarily with antisocial youth. A large
number have problems with the abuse of alcohol and drugs. Most have
major concerns about their sexuality, and some have sexually abused
others and/or have been abused sexually. Many are at risk for acquiring
sexually transmitted diseases. Some have children of their own. Some of
the adolescent girls have been or are pregnant, and many of them are at
risk of pregnancy.

Many of these young people suffer from depression or hyperactivity,
high levels of anxiety, and other psychological problems. The psychological problems are often seen in multiple combinations. Almost all seem to
suffer from low self-esteem. Most respond to stressful situations with
distorted and illogical cognitions. Although many have limited social,
recreational, and educational skills and interests, some have such skills
and interests but have little opportunity to develop them further.

The young people whom CBIGT serves are of many races, religions, and socioeconomic levels. Many come from families with limited resources or live in deep poverty. Many live in deteriorated neighborhoods with little access to recreational facilities. But many come from moderately or even well-off families with many resources.

All of the young people described in this book were being treated in groups as well as in other treatment contexts. Some were being seen in community or outpatient groups; these were often court ordered. Others were being treated in groups in day treatment centers, and still others were treated in groups in residential facilities. Most were receiving other forms of treatment at the same time, such as family therapy or milieu therapy or individual counseling.

Although all of the case examples presented in this book are of adolescents and preadolescents, the treatment guidelines presented in this book are often applicable to both younger and older age groups. The focus has been restricted to adolescents and preadolescents because of the current rise in problem adolescents observed in the legal, school, child welfare, and mental health systems and because of the vast number of youth being placed into treatment or correctional settings.

As children develop into adolescents, they must relate to people such as parents and teachers who have greater power than they do and a great deal of control over them. At the same time, they seek to relate to peers who have, for the most part, equal power and status. If they have had successful supportive, nurturing relationships with parents and teachers, they are free to take their values with them into their relationships with their peers. As adolescence approaches, they seek greater control of their own lives. If this is not adequately provided by the adults in their world or if the adults do not offer other supports that they value, they may seek their freedom and relationships outside the approved value systems of the adults in their lives and may develop emotional disorders.

In normal development, preadolescents are characterized by growing social understanding of such concepts as fairness and equity. They begin to adjust to the demands of school. Most develop a sense of industry. Adolescents begin to form same-sex friendships and to develop loyal friendships. They can take the perspective of others and think in "as-if" terms. As major hormonal changes take place, they develop and search for romantic/sexual relationships. They struggle for emancipation and their own identity (Erikson, 1963). According to Rutter (1981), failure to achieve normal or optimal development results in emotional disorder. It should be pointed out that most children, regardless of their circumstances and parenting, do not develop serious problems. Some children seem to have a natural resiliency. It is hypothesized that this resiliency is due to genetic factors (Anthony, 1968), but although the amount of it varies from one child to the next, most children have some resiliency that can be drawn on in therapy.

The youth usually seen in group therapy are characterized by a breakdown in normal development. For both preadolescents and adolescents, the peer group is a major socialization environment. The therapy group affords a prophylactic or corrective environment that can help in the process of development. In a sense, this book aims at specifying the nature of that resocialization process.

Characteristics of CBIGT

CBIGT is characterized by several features. First, it is a small group approach; that is, it makes use of the unique characteristics of the small group as a means of enhancing the achievement of individual treatment goals. The group provides not only the context of treatment but a set of powerful means to resolve problems. This approach differs from the approach of psychoeducational cognitive-behavioral group therapy, in which the group is used primarily as a convenience. The major contribution of this book is its description of a group adaptation of cognitive, behavioral, recreational, motivational, and societal strategies to formulate and achieve individual treatment goals.

Second, CBIGT aims at teaching youth strategies for coping effectively with the anger-evoking or stressful situations that they encounter. These coping strategies are clearly defined and linked closely to the specific nature of the presenting problem. CBIGT draws mostly, but not exclusively, on cognitive and behavioral as well as group theories in the selection of interventions that facilitate the achievement of individual coping goals. These interventions include motivational techniques, the overt modeling sequence (modeling-rehearsal-coaching-feedback), operant and stimulus control, cognitive restructuring and self-instructional training, social support networking, small group intervention, socio-recreational procedures, relational procedures, and extragroup or environmental modification procedures. These various intervention methods are designed to teach those behaviors (cognitive and overt behavioral) that the client needs (a) to cope with identified anger-inducing, stress-inducing, or other problematic situations for which he or she has no adequate solution or has insufficient resources and (b) to relate more effectively with the significant persons in his or her life.

Third, CBIGT makes extensive use of systematic problem solving as the therapist leads the group through the following steps:

1. The targets of change are arrived at through careful assessment.
2. These are usually formulated as behaviors or cognitions to be produced in well-defined problematic situations.
3. Once goals are established, strategies are generated by the group, and some are selected to prepare the target person to deal with the problematic situations.
4. The preparation or training to implement the new behaviors and cognitions takes place in the group.
5. Implementation of the target behaviors is carried out, usually in the form of extragroup or home tasks.
6. Finally, the results of the attempt to carry out the target behaviors are reported back to the group, and, if necessary, the cycle is repeated.

At the same time, group members are taught the systematic problem-solving method as a coping skill.

Fourth, the goal of CBIGT is not only change of relevant coping behaviors and cognitions in significant situations by the end of therapy but stable behavior change in situations external to the treatment context and after treatment has terminated. In other words, the goal is generalization of behavior and cognitive changes, and treatment strategies are specifically employed to achieve change generalized to the extragroup world.

Finally, the practitioners of CBIGT recognize that many problems are not necessarily of young people's own making. Their socioeconomic status, their place in the family, the communities in which they are forced to live, and their race, ethnicity, and gender may exacerbate or even in part cause their problematic responses. Some of these same factors may also serve as resources on which to build a treatment program or as barriers that must be dealt with. Regardless of the contributors to the problem, young people must suffer the consequences of their actions, thinking, and strong emotions that are evoked in problem situations.

General Targets of Intervention

Almost all the targets of intervention in CBIGT are the behaviors and cognitions necessary to cope effectively with problematic situations, inducing anger, stress, or other strong emotions, that young people confront every day. In this approach, behavior, cognition, and emotional responses are seldom isolated from the situational context in which they occur or from the consequences of the responses in the real world.

One can identify at least four general categories of coping skills commonly taught in cognitive-behavioral therapy groups on the basis of their situational context: interpersonal, problem solving, cognitive and affective coping, and self-management. All of these skills are aimed either directly or indirectly at coping with specific problematic situations. The achievement of these skills mediates the attainment of specific treatment goals designed for each individual in the group. Let us examine each of these general coping skill categories in terms of its implications for CBIGT. It should be noted that these skills generally overlap with one another and are separated in this chapter solely for purposes of analysis.

Interpersonal Skills

Interpersonal (social) skills have been defined as "those responses which, within a given situation, prove effective or, in other words, maximize the probability of producing, maintaining or enhancing positive effects for the interactor" (Foster & Ritchey, 1979, p. 626). This definition stresses a situational and interactional emphasis. Interaction is the basis of group process; thus, a peer group approach as opposed to individual treatment should be the most appropriate context for teaching and learning interpersonal skills. Interpersonal skills are critical for healthy development in youth. Most of the young people who are the focus of this book are dramatically deficient in important social skills that help them to establish prosocial relationships and general social competence.

As a result of increased interpersonal skills development, a client's social status may change. The group therapist can structure opportunities for group members to play roles quite different from those assigned to them by their peers. For example, the group therapist may assist a client to assume a leadership role, allowing him or her to demonstrate a wider range of skills than previously observed by his or her age-mates. These kinds of experiences may produce increased feelings of mastery that strengthen his or her sense of self-efficacy (Bandura, 1977b).

The social skill component of CBIGT seems to be effective with both minority groups and women. La Framboise and Rowe (1983) demonstrated that it was possible to adapt social skill training in groups to the unique needs of Native Americans by involving them in the design of the program and the situations to be worked on. Native Americans rarely avail themselves of mental health services in the first place, and when they do so, they usually fail to return for the scheduled second visit. This was not the case with skills training. The authors pointed out that skills training has great promise in terms of preventive applications for Native Americans, especially because the small group setting is more compatible with commonly practiced behavior of many Indian people than is the standard therapy dyad. Finally, they noted that social skills training is applicable to a wide range of problem areas that may be particularly relevant to Native Americans. Such areas include, but are not limited to, effective assertiveness, handling stress, problem solving, job interviewing, parenting, substance abuse, leadership training, handling depression, and marital relations. In each case, however, special attention must be given to the cultural adaptation of a technology that is largely culture-blind. The authors noted that the dropout rate was much less than in any other mental health program for which Native Americans had been recruited and that the outcomes compared favorably with outcomes in white groups.

Comas-Diaz and Duncan (1985) described a social skills/assertiveness training program for Puerto Rican women who had recently come to the U.S. mainland. They pointed out that assertiveness is often devalued within Puerto Rican culture, particularly among women. Thus, they had had to adapt the program to make it consistent with Puerto Rican cultural values and practices. In particular, the women had to find ways of developing appropriate assertive responses while adhering to such cultural norms as respect for one's elders and responsibility to one's family, and discrimination among these situations was included in the training program. The authors were careful to teach women to examine the consequences of being assertive versus being nonassertive. Through specific examples taken from the women's cultural and familial contexts, the women were able to evaluate potential consequences of asserting or not asserting themselves. This provided them with the information necessary to make reasonable choices about their behavior, which is crucial, given that women, according to Fodor (1988), are sometimes more highly valued when they are passive and are often punished rather than reinforced for the behaviors encouraged by assertiveness training programs.

One study in particular stands out because it demonstrates the efficacy of group assertiveness training with African American youth. Huey and Rank (1984) not only compared the effectiveness of group assertiveness training with that of a discussion group but compared the effectiveness of peer-led and counselor-led groups. The sample, though not a clinical sample, consisted of 48 chronically disruptive African American ninth graders attending an urban high school. The subjects were randomly assigned to a peer- or a counselor-led condition of either the assertiveness training or the discussion treatment group or to an untreated control group. The groups, with the exception of the no-treatment control, met for eight 1-hour sessions over a 4-week period. Two African American male-female teams of professional counselors and trained peer counselors led both the assertiveness training and the discussion groups. Subjects were assessed at pretest and posttest by several outcome measures: (a) the Behavioral Role-Playing Test (BRPT), developed by the authors; (b) the Hand Test (Elie, 1977); and (d) the Anger and Acting-Out subscales of the Walker Problem Behavior Identification Checklist (WPBIC) (Walker, 1970).

An omnibus MANCOVA revealed a significant difference among the five conditions. Univariate ANCOVAs showed significant differences between those in the assertive training conditions and those in the comparison groups on the measure of assertiveness (BRPT). Subjects in the assertiveness training groups also exhibited less classroom aggression as measured by the WPBIC. No differences were found (a) between peer- and counselor-led groups, (b) in the felt anger and the projective anger tests, and (c) in client satisfaction.

In general, there was sufficient support to warrant the continued use of the group assertiveness training program with African American youth. The use of peers, though not having a different outcome than the use of counselors, certainly appears to represent a less expensive way than professional counselors of reducing disruptive classroom behaviors and increasing assertive behaviors of African American middle schoolers who are also disruptive in the classroom.

Problem-Solving Skills

Interventions aimed at developing problem-solving skills have been increasingly applied to child and adolescent problems. This application was initially spearheaded by Spivack and Shure's work on the assessment and teaching of interpersonal, cognitive problem-solving (ICPS) skills to youth (Spivack, Platt, & Shure, 1976; Spivack & Shure, 1974). Their research revealed consistent findings showing that subjects with ICPS abilities were better adjusted (Spivack et al., 1976). This led to their attempting to teach ICPS abilities to young children. Several studies (see Spivack et al., 1976) found that children learned the cognitive abilities, that these gains were related to adjustment, and that the results were maintained over time. However, this research was not carried out with adolescents.

Problem-solving skills are one set of key behaviors that can maximize a child's adjustment and interpersonal effectiveness. The components that have been identified by Spivack and Shure (1974) as primary skills include (a) alternative thinking, or the ability to generate multiple alternative solutions to interpersonal problem situations; (b) consequential thinking, or the ability to anticipate short- and long-term consequences of a particular alternative and then to use this in decision making; and (c) means-end thinking, or the ability to plan a series of specific means or actions necessary to carry out the solution to an interpersonal problem. This last category includes the recognition of obstacles that need to be overcome and implies that a realistic time frame is important in achieving a goal. Problem solving is an important cognitive coping skill, but other more specific cognitive skills are equally important.

Cognitive Coping Skills

Cognition refers to thoughts, images, values, thinking patterns, self-statements, or private or covert events that may be inferred from verbal or other overt behavior. Cognitive coping skills involve the use of cognitions to facilitate coping with internal and social phenomena. Examples of such skills are the ability to analyze one's own cognitions; to label appropriately one's self-defeating self-statements; to observe and rehearse new, more appropriate self-statements; and to reinforce oneself covertly. Though important skills in their own right, cognitive coping skills also mediate the attainment of the more observable social skills defined above. Thus, the goal of increasing cognitive coping skills is important as a means of correcting anxiety-inducing and behavior-inhibiting cognitions and in improving social behavior (Meichenbaum, 1977). Self-statements such as "Everyone thinks I'm weird" not only produce anxiety but promote inaction or ineffective behaviors. Changing such a statement to something such as "Sure, I'm different from other kids in many ways; some things I like and some I'll change" may reflect a more accurate appraisal, may suggest avenues of change, is more self-respecting, may reduce anxiety, and ultimately should improve social behavior. Cognition in the form of self-instruction may also be used to guide oneself through difficult situations, such as making a speech or interviewing for a job.

Another set of cognitive coping skills is moral reasoning. Delinquents, according to Arbuthnot and Gordon (1986), have consistently been shown to function at lower stages of moral reasoning than nondelinquents. The authors reasoned that adolescents at risk for juvenile delinquency would benefit both cognitively and behaviorally from an intervention designed to accelerate moral reasoning development, an assumption for which the authors found some support in their study.

Cognitive coping skills are not, however, the only coping techniques available for dealing with stressful situations. In the next subsection, we discuss targets that are not exclusively cognitive but may also require overt behavior on the part of the youth to cope with problematic or stressful events.

Cognitive procedures appear to be especially effective for women. Wolfe (1987) described the use of rational-emotive therapy (RET) in combination with other cognitive-behavioral approaches. She asserted that RET is in keeping with the guidelines of feminist therapy and provides a way of countering the "shoulds and musts" characteristic of female sex-role socialization. Other reasons cited for RET's congruence with a feminist approach are that clients are involved in setting therapy goals and choosing techniques and that RET offers women means for striving to achieve the changes necessary for an egalitarian society.

Other Active Coping Skills

Problem-solving, social, and cognitive skills can all be regarded as coping skills if they help youth to deal with a stressful or anger-inducing situation. Others are of equal importance. One of the most useful is the ability to relax in stressful situations. If youth can respond to stressful stimuli by relaxing, they will be able to access other coping skills more effectively. Furthermore, once relaxation is mastered as a general coping skill, it may enhance a child or adolescent's general quality of life.

Recreational and leisure-time skills may be regarded as coping skills as well. Although some are social in nature, they may be regarded as a separate category for coping with general life stress as well as specific situations. In groups, youth may be taught both individual and group leisure-time activities that may enhance the quality of their day-to-day experiences. The process of learning these skills presents optimal opportunities for learning such social skills as communicating positively with others, cooperating with others, handling competition, showing good winning and losing behaviors, and getting involved and involving others. The process of teaching socio-recreational skills is discussed in detail in Chapter 13.

Self-Management Skills

Self-management refers to procedures to control one's own environment as a means of controlling one's own behavior. Procedures such as the use of environmental cues, self-monitoring, self-instruction, self-evaluation, and self-reinforcement fall under this rubric. In any case, youth will still be struggling with various problems long after the group has terminated. These skills, if learned, represent a set of strategies that youth can use when only limited external support is available. Most of these skills are cognitive and are described in Chapter 10 or are operant and are described in Chapter 8. Most interventions can eventually be learned in the group and applied by youth alone in dealing with problematic situations outside the context of treatment. In this sense, they can all be promoted to self-management strategies.

Specific Targets of Intervention

The above categories of targets suggest the general areas in which the group therapist formulates the more specific targets of change in the group. The specific targets are concrete behaviors or identifiable cognitions in response to a given specified problem situation peculiar to a given client. Some of the specific problem areas for which youth in groups have been treated are controlling violent behavior when one is being criticized by peers or adults; increasing participation in social situations with peers; when having difficulty, asking adults for help; reducing anxiety in response to specific fear-inducing situations; handling impulsive behavior in a variety of social contexts; establishing nonimpositional behaviors toward the opposite sex; coping with recurring depressive responses, especially when one is alone; learning to help and share with others; carrying out chores at home; completing school homework tasks; and leading in group situations. The strategies for the identification of these and other specific change goals and their situational context are elaborated on in Chapters 4, 5, and 6.

A whole set of other specific targets do not exclusively involve changes in behaviors, cognition, or affective responses of the target person but rather involve the external environment. Such targets might be absence of food in the home, insufficient money to get to school on the bus, or abuse by or of the client in the home. Such targets may require intervention in the community, the school, or the family or, at the very least, referral to those who can better deal with these problems by virtue of resources or community sanction. Though such problems are often identified within the group, intervention to ameliorate them may fall outside the scope of intragroup interaction. In many cases, the group may be the ideal setting for training youth to deal more effectively with their own environment: For example, the group therapist may provide members with necessary information about job employment opportunities or how to get food stamps. Or the group therapist may encourage the members to accompany one member with a particular need to a given agency.

In the above two sections, we have described the major target behaviors and problems with which CBIGT is designed to deal. Let us now examine the many methods used in this approach as means of achieving those targets or resolving those problems.

The Place of the Group in Therapy

The small group is a natural and highly attractive setting for most youth. Some of the major sources of learning for youth are street groups or gangs and other informal groups with whom youth associate at people's houses, at the community center, in the playgrounds and gymnasia, and on the streets. What youth learn, however, is dependent on the norms of the group, to which adolescents are highly susceptible.

Groups provide an opportunity for frequent and varied forms of peer reinforcement, which, for the adolescent, is often far more powerful than adult reinforcement. Each member is given the chance to learn or to improve his or her ability to mediate rewards for others in social interactive situations (with acquaintances, friends, family members, group members, teachers, or employers). The group therapist can construct a situation in which each member has frequent opportunities, instructions, and rewards for reinforcing others in the group. Reinforcement is a highly valued skill in our society; as one learns to reinforce others, one is reciprocally reinforced by others, and mutual liking also increases (see Lott & Lott, 1965).

Because of its kinship with the natural peer group, the therapy group more nearly simulates the real world of most clients than the situation consisting solely of a high-status adult and a low-status youth, as one finds in the treatment dyad. Thus, the group represents an intermediate step between performing a newly learned behavior in a therapeutic setting and transferring that performance to the community.

The group also provides a large number of models, role players for behavioral rehearsal, persons to do monitoring, and partners for use in a "buddy system." The group provides multiple sources of ideas in that members can "brainstorm" goals, alternative behaviors, reinforcement, and even intervention strategies. Another important benefit is that the group provides a natural laboratory for learning discussion and leadership skills that are essential to good social relationships. Furthermore, negotiation and problem-solving skills are readily addressed in the context of the group as the members solve group problems and negotiate differences among the members.

In the process of interaction in treatment groups, norms are often established that serve to control the behavior of individual members. If these norms (informal agreements among members as to preferred modes of action and interaction in the group) are introduced and effectively maintained by the group therapist, they can be powerful therapeutic tools. The group pressures deviant members to conform to such norms as attending regularly, reinforcing peers who do well, analyzing problems systematically and specifically, and assisting peers with their problems. Of course, if the group therapist is not careful, antitherapeutic norms also can be generated. An example of such a norm was demonstrated in one group by all the youth becoming silly, off task, or silent whenever any demand was placed on them for self-disclosure.

To prevent or reduce the impact of such problems, a group therapist can use various group problem-solving techniques for modifying the norms of the group. The group therapist can also facilitate the attainment of both individual and group treatment goals by such procedures as modifying the cohesiveness, status pattern, or communication structure of the group. It is also necessary to resolve more specific group problems, such as scapegoating, interpersonal conflict, and excessive teasing, as they arise. Much of the power of group treatment to facilitate the achievement of treatment goals is lost if negative group dynamics are unrestrained or group problems remain unresolved. (See Chapter 14 for more detail on group attributes and modification of group attributes in service of achieving treatment goals.)

In groups, youth must learn to deal with the idiosyncrasies of other individuals. They must learn to tolerate minor or even major differences and in some cases to deal with them. They must learn to offer other youth feedback and advice. By helping others, they are likely to practice a set of strategies for helping themselves. Also, by helping others, they are not always relegated to the role of helpee or client, as in dyadic treatment. They become aware that they have skills and knowledge that might benefit others. Moreover, they are afforded the opportunity to learn the art and skills involved in giving and receiving both critical feedback and advice. These are frequent and important everyday transactions that most of the youth in CBIGT have difficulties in handling.

By providing additional training in giving and receiving feedback, the group gives members a major source of feedback about behaviors that are annoying or pleasing to others in the group, and probably to others outside the group, and about cognitions that appear to others to be self-defeating. This enhances the quality of assessment and the acceptance of the initial targets of intervention. Assessment is further refined by the opportunity in groups for the therapist to directly observe each person interacting with other youth.

Finally, the group also appears to be at least as effective as, and more efficient in terms of therapist cost than, dyadic treatment methods. Although there is no research comparing the treatment of youth individually and in groups, research on adult groups versus individual treatment using cognitive-behavioral procedures in the treatment of assertion, stress, phobias, and depression seems to indicate far lower costs for similar results. (See, e.g., Linahan, Walker, Bronheim, Haynes, & Yevzeroff, 1979; Teri & Lewinsohn, 1985; and Toseland & Siporin,

1986, for reviews of research comparisons between group and individual treatments.)

Of course, the group setting can have some disadvantages. Many youth are excessively susceptible to group pressure, and the group may reinforce that tendency. As mentioned above, reinforcement and modeling by group members for each other, though employed to facilitate the achievement of prosocial goals, have also the potential for supporting antisocial and antitherapeutic norms. Moreover, such phenomena as group contagion and mutual aggression can get out of hand more readily in groups than in the therapist-client dyad. Despite such complications, strategies for dealing with such dysfunctional group phenomena are available (see, e.g., Chapter 14). It is also more difficult, though not impossible, to individualize each client in the group because, for the sake of efficiency, the group therapist is continually looking for common goals to pursue. Confidentiality is more difficult to maintain in groups than in the dyad, although, in our experience, breaches of confidentiality among group members are rare, especially when the issue is dealt with in early sessions with the group members and when periodic reminders of members' responsibility in this area are provided. Finally, working with groups requires a unique and extensive repertoire of skills in which the practitioner must be trained to be minimally effective. One of the reasons for disillusionment of some therapists with groups has been their assumption that group therapy is more or less the same as individual therapy, as is clearly not the case.

If the group therapist is aware of these potential problems, they can be dealt with. Even the positive characteristics of the group become advantages only if they are opportunistically seized on by the group therapist. Throughout this book, we will point out how group therapists have dealt with the difficulties encountered in group interaction and how they have taken advantage of the group's unique and manifold assets.

For the opportunities it affords, the group not only is the context for therapy but also provides some of the central means of intervention in the approach proposed in this book. Although there are many books on cognitive and behavioral therapy for adolescents (see, e.g., Barth, 1986; Forman, 1993; Reinecke et al., 1996; Wilkes, Belsher, Rush, & Frank, 1994; Zarb, 1992), none focus on the delivery of the intervention strategies within the framework of the group. Although most of the interventions used in CBIGT have already been mentioned, they are described in more detail below.

Methods of Intervention

There has been extensive research on methods of teaching youth various coping skills. In most of these studies, the major means of intervention were limited to one or two of the following methods: problem solving, cognitive-affective, modeling-rehearsal, operant and stimulus control, socio-recreational, relational, small group, and extragroup. Even when carried out in the group, most of these studies ignored both the potential of the group and the problems that the group could create. In CBIGT, we have attempted to combine most of these methods into one integrated approach. A method was selected for inclusion if it had some independent empirical foundation; if, at least in case studies, some relationship to the above-mentioned targets could be demonstrated; and if the method could be carried out readily within the context of the group. In the following sections, we will review each of these methods in terms of its contribution to the total approach. In subsequent chapters, the brief explanation of each of these methods will be elaborated on. The first, which has been mentioned above as a set of skills to be learned, is systematic problem solving; it will be defined below as a major set of intervention strategies in CBIGT. Because of the centrality of problem solving in CBIGT, this method has been separated in this chapter from other cognitive strategies, several of which are discussed in the section "Cognitive Change Methods," later in this chapter.

Systematic Problem-Solving Method

This method involves learning and carrying out a systematic set of steps for solving a problem: (a) defining the problem, (b) generating alternative solutions and consequences, (c) selecting and implementing the best solution, and (d) evaluating the outcome. We have added an intermediate step, preparation for implementation, not commonly found in the paradigms of others (e.g., Spivack et al., 1976, or D'Zurilla, 1986) because identification of the problem and suggestions for its solution have often been insufficient to prepare the client for implementing the solution. The reader may have noted that problem solving has been identified in this chapter as (a) a set of skills, the development of which can be one of the general goals of intervention, and as (b) one of the several methods of intervention. It is in fact both. As youth identify either cognitive distortions or social skill deficiencies that prevent them from

[handwritten margin note: Help client understand problems are a part of life.]

coping effectively with a given problematic situation, the problem-solving method is invoked. In using the problem-solving method repeatedly, youth learn the skills and general problem-solving paradigm required to resolve specific problems on their own when they are no longer in the group. Social problem-solving training has been demonstrated to be effective for juvenile offenders in a study by Kazdin, Esveldt-Dawson, French, and Unis (1987a, 1987b).

It should also be noted that problem solving is inherent in all of the other methods used. For example, to determine and plan for dealing with a social skill deficiency, the problematic situation is analyzed, goals for learning specific social skills are established, specific content for employing those social skills is generated through group brainstorming, the client evaluates and selects the best of the procedures, the client prepares for implementation by having the procedure modeled and rehearsing it in the group with feedback from his or her peers, and, finally, the program is implemented via homework or performed in the real world in what is referred to in this book as an *extragroup task*. Finally, the client reports his or her experience back to the group, and, if difficulties still exist, the cycle is repeated. The same steps are used in learning cognitive responses to problematic or stressful situations. Thus, one could assert that CBIGT is also a problem-solving approach.

The Modeling Sequence

This sequence is designed to facilitate the learning of specific positive interactive behaviors (social skills and social competencies) and includes such techniques as overt modeling, behavior rehearsal, coaching, and group feedback. *Modeling* refers to learning through the observation of a model, who might be an adult, a peer, or even a puppet. Modeling is often used to demonstrate how a situation problematic to one or more youth in the group may be handled effectively. *Behavioral rehearsal* is also a simulation technique in which a client with a given problem situation practices new, more effective ways of handling that situation. *Coaching* refers to instructions or verbal cues given to the client when she or he is modeling or rehearsing a set of behaviors in a given situation. *Group feedback* is the verbal evaluation from others as to how effectively the client performed the modeled behaviors. All of the procedures in the modeling sequence are demonstrated in Chapter 9. Following the modeling sequence, the client prepares for and carries out a homework assignment or extragroup task to practice the social or other coping skill in the real world. As the reader may have observed, the modeling sequence lends itself readily to groups because of the profusion of available models, role players for significant others, and sources of feedback when each client rehearses.

Reinforcement and Stimulus Control

One particular form of modifying the consequences of a given behavior is presenting a positive reinforcer following the performance of a given behavior. Whether a particular event is a positive reinforcer is defined by its effects on the behavior (Kazdin, 1989, p. 105). If the response frequency of a given behavior increases when followed by the event, it is a positive reinforcer. A reinforcer effective in altering one response in one situation may be effective in altering other behaviors in other situations as well. In groups, youth receive many kinds of rewards that seem to function as positive reinforcers for the performance of prosocial group behavior and the completion of extragroup tasks. These potential positive reinforcers may take the form of praise, tokens, points, goods, small objects, activities, and whatever is small, manipulable, and valued by and appropriate to the given age and developmental category of the recipient. In all cases, these reinforcers are delivered according to a systematic plan called a *schedule of reinforcement*. Reinforcers such as attention or tokens can be withheld in response to undesirable behaviors (although in groups the attention of other youth is difficult to control). This is referred to as *extinction* and is a common response in groups. Occasionally, reinforcement is removed (usually in the form of tokens) following undesirable behaviors, a process known as *response cost*. Occasionally, aversive stimuli are presented in a process similar to that of punishment. Response cost and punishment are designed to reduce the frequency of the behavior that precedes them. Because CBIGT focuses on strengths wherever possible, positive reinforcement is the method of choice.

Modifying the antecedent conditions or stimulus control is exemplified in the group by the use of games that permit and encourage cooperation rather than competition when cooperation is the target behavior. Some examples of the use of this technique with individuals are a youth working on nail biting who wore thin gloves to prevent him from chewing on his nails; an adolescent trying to lose weight who permitted herself to eat only at a set table and allowed herself only food that had been cooked; and a youth with an alcohol problem who arranged with the group to stay away from bars and from his drinking friends (he substituted participating in plays, which required evening rehearsals, for "bar attending" and the friends in the play for the old "drinking buddies").

Modifying antecedent conditions involves changing the immediate environment that is conducive to or parallel with a given behavior in order to create conditions more amenable to the performance of a desired behavior. The latter is often referred to as *stimulus control.* Both reinforcement and stimulus control are discussed in more detail in Chapter 8.

Cognitive Change Methods

These strategies refer to the procedures by which youth are trained in more effective ways of thinking about or evaluating themselves or problematic situations. They also involve changing values or beliefs. In groups, many cognitive procedures are used, often in combination with each other and with other types of procedures, such as the modeling sequence and the use of reinforcement. The procedures most commonly used are cognitive restructuring, self-instructional training, and self-reinforcement.

Cognitive restructuring is characterized by a set of procedures used to replace self-defeating, illogical, or automatic patterns of thinking that interfere with social functioning with self-enhancing or logical ones. It is assumed that in a given set of circumstances, cognitions in part mediate overt behavioral responses. These cognitions include how one values oneself and one's action and how one specifically thinks or responds covertly in a given situation. Youth are trained to identify their thoughts in stress- or anger-inducing situations. They later help each other to change thoughts that are self-defeating, illogical, or damaging to self-enhancing or coping thoughts (Meichenbaum, 1977).

In self-instructional training, youth are taught to identify self-defeating statements uttered to themselves in the face of a problematic or stress-inducing situation and then to replace these statements with new, more functional self-statements. This process consists of step-by-step verbalizations concerning the problem definition. In the face of an anger- or stress-inducing situation, youth are taught to instruct themselves, among other cognitions, to remain calm, to take one step at time, to remind themselves that they have succeeded before, and to reinforce themselves if they are successful. The specific cognition depends on the situation and the *phase* in which the situation occurs. (The phases are well in advance of, immediately before, during, or just after the event.) These and other cognitive strategies are described in detail in the first half of Chapter 10.

Relaxation Methods

Relaxation methods are used to teach youth who need help in coping with stress, pain, anger, or external environmental events for which no external coping behavior is possible. This involves teaching them a modified version of the alternate tension and relaxation technique (a modified version of the system developed by Jacobsen, 1978) and then later fading the tension phases. Various alternatives uniquely suited to youth are also taught. Modest research support for the use of relaxation procedures in reducing anxiety and stress is to be found in studies by Borkovec, Mathews, Chambers, and Ebrahimi (1987) and Hillenberg and Collins (1986). However, Heide and Borkovec (1983) have also shown that for a few persons relaxation may increase anxiety. Relaxation training is seldom used as an isolated procedure. It is often combined with other strategies as a means of stress management or anger control. Details on various forms of relaxation training and alternative breathing and meditative techniques as they are used in groups and with youth are described in the second half of Chapter 10.

Socio-Recreational Methods

This method involves using active games, board games, arts, crafts, storytelling, and dramatics to facilitate the achievement of therapeutic goals and to increase group cohesion. Whittaker (1976) noted that "despite the popularity of group treatment as a mode of helping troubled youth, many clinicians underestimate the potential of program activities as a medium for growth and change in groups" (p. 459). Ross and Bernstein (1976) stated that "games and activities offer youth a workshop for discovering and developing new ways to manage obstacles" (p. 127).

Socio-recreational activities provide youth with a highly satisfying set of stimulus conditions in which concrete skills can be informally prac-ticed and reinforced. They form the initial basis for broad participation and increased group attraction. Furthermore, they provide the context for practicing social skills in a way that is more realistic and more entertaining than role playing. Chapter 13 is devoted to a description of the philosophy and specific activities used as part of the socio-recreational method. Interactive socio-recreational activities are often selected to influence the group process and as such are regarded as one procedure within the general category of small group methods.

Social Network Enhancement

Social support may be viewed as coping assistance (Thoits, 1986) that buffers the effect of stress. It may be considered as an active process in which some party attempts to provide support for the other or as a passive process that flows out of mutual relationship without any conscious plan. There are a number of ways of increasing external social support of the group members by facilitating the group members' awareness of their respective social networks and then expanding them. The group is often rich in suggestions and provides diverse models as to how fellow members might achieve a more supportive social network. The group itself becomes another source of support.

Most youth in our groups have contact with certain persons, groups, or institutions that can enhance the achievement of treatment goals or a sense of well-being or, as mentioned above, buffer the effects of stress. Such support systems will exist long after treatment has ended. Clients may cultivate new social units in which they can participate after treatment has ended. Thus, enhancing social networks that are primarily supportive is an important strategy for maintaining change in the real world.

Vinter (1985a) suggested that extragroup intervention strategies are as important as those which occur within the group. These strategies involve the group therapist in working with the family, the classroom, the school administration, and other social units whose activities and policies impinge on the outcome of specific treatment. The strategies may involve reevaluating policies and rules or simply communicating with representatives of these social units to prepare them for changes in the client and to facilitate their reinforcing any gains. Failure to address these issues often results in the failure to maintain treatment goals even if these can be achieved in the group.

One application of extragroup intervention was demonstrated by a group therapist who referred a girl in his group and her family to the county social services department. The therapist believed that the girl was being sexually abused. This referral required extensive communication with the family, the social service worker, and the school before the referral was complete. The behavioral problems, unassertiveness, and excessive anxiety that were being worked on in the group were relevant to the problem of sexual abuse to which the girl had been subjected. In Chapter 12, many other strategies of extragroup intervention are discussed.

Small Group Methods

The effective use of small group techniques is probably as important as any of the other technical procedures being used. Among these group techniques are group discussion, role playing, the buddy system, group feedback, subgrouping, leadership delegation, and group exercises, all of which are described below. The small group method is the process of using one or more of these procedures to mediate the attainment of group goals or resolution of group interactive problems. The small group method also includes delegation of responsibility to the clients themselves. Inherent in the structured approaches are barriers to the delegation of responsibility to the group members. The more responsibility clients have for running the group, the more they feel it is their group. CBIGT is characterized by a highly complex technology that may indeed require at least preliminary control by the therapist. But even then, as will be illustrated later, that control need only be partial, and over time, more and more aspects of it can be readily delegated to the group members. Clients come to the groups with a variety of useful experiences not only in the day-to-day world but in individual and group treatment. This previous experience can be harnessed early in CBIGT if the group therapist has determined the extent and nature of that experience as part of the assessment process, either in early sessions or in a pregroup interview.

Second, most of these approaches involve a heavy didactic component as well as skill development. That information, it is assumed, is usually known only to the group therapist, who then makes it available to the group. However, the assumption that the therapist is the exclusive possessor of relevant knowledge is often not valid. For example, in a weight loss group, many of the members were quite expert on various theories of eating disorders and various approaches to diet, exercise, and other aspects of the general problem. In this group, the therapist could have readily drawn on the available knowledge in the early sessions if he had made a point of becoming acquainted with the knowledge base in the area of concern of each of the members. In every group, youth are experts in the kind of situations youth must endure in school and on the street. Despite structural barriers to complete client self-determination, there are many actions a group therapist together with the group can take to correct for the imposition of structure and to enhance self-decision. These are discussed in Chapter 14.

Broad Group Discussion

Broad group discussion is youth-to-youth as well as youth-to-therapist verbal interaction in which all members participate and the direction of the interaction is largely from members to other members. It is the essential way in which problems are laid out and considered, solutions are shared and evaluated, decisions are formulated and affirmed, values are deliberated, and friendships are made. Implicit in broad group discussion is the assumption that maximum involvement of all group members is essential for high cohesion and effective treatment. Broad group discussion is enhanced in the early sessions by use of the group exercises briefly described below and the "writing down" technique. In this technique, whenever a question is asked or suggestions are sought, the therapist asks the members to write down their answers. Then the members are asked what they wrote down. This technique prevents the more assertive members from dominating the interaction.

Role Playing

In its most elementary form, *role playing* can be defined as the practice of roles in simulated conditions. The group therapist, by acting as a guide and structuring the role playing, controls the outcome of the role-playing process. If the group therapist is clear about the purposes of role playing, even through focused use, this technique can prove highly beneficial in promoting change. In the modeling sequence, role playing is used both to demonstrate specific skills and to practice them. Role playing is also used in assessment, in teaching specific treatment skills, in role reversal, and in generalization training. No matter how it is used, role playing uses to advantage the multiple persons in the group in their various simulated roles and as observers and providers of feedback.

Subgrouping

Subgrouping is a procedure of working on specific tasks in pairs, triads, or other-sized subgroups as a means of increasing interaction among the members and giving them an opportunity to work without the oversight of an adult. It creates an opportunity to practice leadership skills. Different sizes and compositions of subgroups are used throughout the history of the group.

The Buddy System

This is a special subgrouping procedure that allows youth to work together outside the group. In addition to the advantages mentioned above, it contributes to the transfer of learning occurring in the group to situations outside the group. It also affords youth the opportunity to function independently, although the results of this interaction are monitored at the following session. To avoid the formation of "cliques" (negative exclusive subgroups), the membership of the pairs is changed often.

Group Exercises

Group exercises are structured interactive activities used as ways of teaching youth the skills that mediate the achievement of treatment goals. For example, an introduction exercise is used in which youth interview at least two youth in the group and introduce them to the others in the group. Another exercise is one in which members study a case and discuss how they themselves are different from the person in that case. Other exercises involve teaching youth how to give and receive both praise and criticism; analyze problem situations; identify beliefs, expectations, and other cognitions; use role playing; look at one's social supports; and plan for generalization. Usually at least one such exercise is carried out in every session. The advantage of such exercises is that although members are monitored by the therapist, they work in small groups to carry them out. There is less opportunity for conflict with the therapist because the instructions are to be found in a manual. Throughout this book, the various exercises used in the treatment of adolescents in groups are described, and their specific purposes and rationales are given.

Relational Methods

A number of skills have been identified as crucial to any helping relationship, whether or not this relationship is dyadic or within the structure of a small group. We have noted in our work with students that even if therapists have a high level of technological skill in the other methods, their failure to possess or apply relational or clinical skills results in high dropout rates, lack of interest on the part of the clients, and disturbing group problems. In a sense, relational skills are the solution into which all the other methods are dissolved.

Many of these relational skills are to be found in the other methods described above. For example, group therapists who can comfortably and frequently provide their members with high levels of reinforcement tend to establish sound relationships with their members. Similarly, group therapists who model self-disclosure and all of the other skills that the members are expected to carry out discover that the indicators of group problems (high levels of conflict, low cohesion, low satisfaction, pairing) seldom arise. Those group therapists who create stimulating socio-recreational activities with group members also enhance their relationship to the members and the members' relationships to each other. Because of their specificity, these are highly trainable skills.

Some skills are unique to relationship building. For example, the use of humor with youth is not addressed elsewhere in the above methods. Yet to work with youth, one must be able to find pleasure in interacting with adolescents in groups, joking with them, and permitting oneself to be teased. At the same time, one must be able to draw the line between occasional teasing and playing and out-of-control or off-task patterns of behavior. The effective group therapist must also be able to set firm limits when necessary.

Involving youth in their own treatment is a skill that is essential to achieve generalization of change. Although we focus on this skill in Chapter 14, each of the intervention chapters discusses the ways in which members can gradually assume responsibility for much of their own treatment. The process by which youth are involved is a vital relationship-building skill.

Listening to youth is a skill not covered above, yet the absence of careful listening often results in wrong targets of change being pursued. Effective listening does not necessarily require seeing the underlying implications of someone's words but rather grasping the obvious meanings, sometimes a far more difficult task. Often, in the group therapist's haste to carry out the items on the session agenda, he or she interrupts or ponders on the next step while a client is still speaking. Effective listening by the therapist also models this skill for the group—a skill that, once learned, can improve the overall quality of the group members' relationships.

Attending skills are such nonverbal skills as eye contact, body posture, and a voice tone that indicates acceptance, warmth, and trust. Although these are nonspecific characteristics in that they are difficult to define, observations of group therapists in action tend to indicate to observers whether such skills are indeed operating.

Identifying and dealing with a youth's affective response to a crisis that has occurred just before a given session but that falls outside the specific purpose of the session requires following a difficult but necessary line of activity. Ignoring such crises inevitably results in passive or chaotic meetings and failure to achieve preplanned objectives.

Setting limits on disruptive or off-task behavior is another relational skill that must be considered often in the history of the group if the goals of change are to be sought in a congenial milieu (Garvin, 1987, p. 133). This is one of the more difficult of the relational skills and yet one of the most frequently required. The indications for when to set limits and when to ignore behavior are not always clear. Using the group itself to set limits is a powerful tool used often in institutional groups, although even then the therapist must watch out for an excessively tyrannical or permissive group. Skill in reinforcement and program development often protects the group therapist from frequent application of this skill of limit-setting.

The technology for dealing with these (often called) nonspecific treatment skills is not well worked out. We suggest that modeling these basic skills may be the most fundamental way of teaching them to youth. Although no one chapter in this book is devoted to the application of relationship skills, their presence permeates most of the chapters.

The Integration of Methods

No one of the above strategies appears to be adequate to achieve the varied goals pursued in the heterogenous group with which most therapists work. Several studies indicate that a combined approach may be more effective in working with youth than any approach separately (DeLange, Lanham, & Barton, 1981; Kendall & Finch, 1978; LeCroy, 1983; Lochman & Curry, 1986). Not only are the behavioral and cognitive strategies integrated into a treatment package, but socio-recreational programs need to be included so that learning can take place in an enjoyable and challenging manner. Using group procedures as an additional means for the achievement of goals potentially offers several distinct advantages, such as increased participation, broader distribution of participation, greater cohesion in the group, and greater involvement of the members in leadership.

In general, the problems of youth coming to the group are not restricted to the learning of one clearly isolated behavior or cognition or the handling of one kind of problem situation. Impulsive youth often have to learn more systematic problem-solving skills. They must often learn new ways of evaluating themselves. They may need to interact more effectively with their peers. Often, simple operant behaviors (e.g., attending to others when they are speaking to oneself) may need to be learned through reinforcement, and other behaviors (e.g., shoplifting) may need to be reduced in frequency through stimulus control. The client and the referring adult may complain of many problem situations that are not being adequately handled, and each of these situations may require a range of new or modified skills to be dealt with adequately. For this reason, broad-based treatment would appear to provide the greatest benefit.

Although the methods used are varied in this approach, this does not imply that the approach is haphazard or unsystematic. Nor does the group therapist arbitrarily bombard the client or group with an arsenal of cognitive, behavioral, and other techniques. The process by which these various methods can be selected and applied is highly systematic and is briefly outlined in the following section.

Phases of the Treatment Process in CBIGT

The treatment process can best be described in terms of the steps the therapist takes in the treatment process:

1. Planning for group treatment
2. Getting the group started, which includes orienting the members and significant others to the possibilities and limitations of group treatment, building the cohesion of the group, and increasing the motivation of its members
3. Assessing the presenting problems and client resources
4. Selecting and applying interventions to effect change
5. Identifying and dealing with group problems
6. Planning for generalization of changes to the real world and preparing for termination

These steps often overlap with each other in time and in content. Let us examine briefly the therapist activities involved in each.

Planning for Group Treatment

In planning for group treatment, the group therapist must establish the group's purposes, determine potential membership, recruit members, decide on the group structure, and create the group's physical environment. Once it is determined that a group can meet the needs of a given population, the group therapist must determine whether a population of youth exists that can be reached and served by such a group. Then the best possible structure for such a group to achieve its general purposes must be established.

Once these issues are settled, the group members need to be recruited or selected. Recruitment serves not only to obtain members who should be in a given group but also to screen members for their appropriateness for group therapy in general (see Chapter 2 for more details).

Getting the Group Started

Orientation to CBIGT

As part of recruitment and later during the group, members and their parents and/or teachers need to be oriented to the purposes of the group, the methods to be used, the goals that can be achieved, and the potential risks of the approach. Inadequate orientation often leads to high dropout rates. As part of orientation, group contracts—agreements between the group members and the therapist—are often developed. These group contracts establish what the members and their parents can expect from the group therapist and the agency and what they can be expected to do. This contract is usually in writing, and members and their parents as well as the group therapist usually sign it. All of the above issues of organization and orientation are discussed in detail in Chapter 3.

Enhancing the Cohesion of the Group

Early in therapy, the cohesion of the group (the attractiveness of members to each other, to the activities, and to the therapist) is encouraged through the timely use of socio-recreational activities, large amounts of positive reinforcement, interesting activities such as group exercises, protection from excessive confrontation, and a structure that encourages broad participation. To evaluate the level of cohesion, a postsession questionnaire is used at the end of every session. As the level of cohesion reaches a plateau toward the end of therapy, less attention is paid to enhancing or even maintaining the cohesion, and the attraction of the members to nontherapy groups is encouraged (see Chapter 3 for more details).

Establishing the Motivation of the Members

Specific actions to be taken to establish the motivation of the members involve giving maximum opportunity for choice to them, supporting their self-efficacy, expressing empathy as they relate their stories, normalizing and accepting their ambivalence toward change, helping them to weigh the advantages and disadvantages of their problematic behavior, and eliciting and reinforcing motivational statements. (See Miller & Rollnick, 1991, pp. 64-88, and Chapter 3 for more details on how these strategies are employed in groups.)

Assessing Presenting Problems and Resources

Assessment is a concept central to all empirical approaches. The purpose of assessment is to determine the specific targets of interventions in such a way as to make them amenable to intervention; to determine whether the given group or another type of therapy might be the most appropriate setting for each potential client; to determine the client's personal resources for working toward the achievement of goals; and to examine any potential barriers to participation in therapy or to achieving therapy goals. During group sessions, the assessor, usually the therapist with the help of the members, must also determine the nature of group goals and group problems, whether goals are being achieved, and whether problems are being resolved. Finally, assessment is used as the first step in determining to what degree and for whom therapy will have been effective.

To answer all these questions, data must be systematically collected before, during, immediately following, and at some time 3 to 6 months after therapy. Some of the methods of collecting data are personality inventories and checklists, role-play tests, sociometric tests, diaries, self-observation, direct observations of the group or of individuals when not in the group, postsession questionnaires, and interviews. However, the most important assessment procedure in groups is the systematic analysis of problem situations encountered by the members in their day-to-day life. Of almost equal relevance are the observations, by both members and the therapist, of each member's behavioral responses to stressful situations in the group and his or her descriptions of experiences with extragroup tasks. In Chapter 4, the basic principles of applying assessment in groups are presented in greater detail. Chapter 5 provides details of the specific measurement techniques and evaluates them in terms of their applicability to a group approach. Chapter 6 discusses the strategies of individual and group goal setting.

Selecting and Implementing
Interventions to Achieve Change

In this step, the appropriate intervention strategies are selected, the group members are oriented to and trained to use these procedures, and, with their concurrence, the actual training in new behaviors, particularly coping responses, begins. Let us examine how the various intervention strategies might be integrated. To begin with, problem situations are analyzed, solutions are generated and selected, and a plan is developed to learn the necessary skills to achieve the solution to the problem. Thus, all situations are first dealt with through problem solving. To prepare a person for carrying out the solutions decided on in the problem solving, the modeling sequence or one of the several cognitive procedures or both are used. Often a plan is established in which the target person receives reinforcement for carrying out steps in the plan. And reinforcement is distributed throughout the session for achievements within the group and for completion of behavioral tasks to be performed outside of the group. Because of the centrality of extragroup tasks in this method, an entire chapter (Chapter 11) is devoted to it.

At first, common problem situations and, with reluctant members, the problems of simulated clients are worked on. Later, individual problem situations that members have recorded in their diaries are the focus of therapy. Homework or extragroup tasks to try out new ways of coping with problem situations in the real world are designed and carried out between sessions, and results are subsequently reported back to the group.

Group procedures are used throughout therapy. Group feedback is requested after every cognitive or behavioral rehearsal. The buddy system is used between all sessions to monitor and lend support to the carrying out of homework assignments. At least one group exercise is used at every session to facilitate the teaching of such skills as reinforcing others, giving and receiving criticism, identifying self-defeating statements, listening to others, and being assertive instead of aggressive. Many of these exercises are carried out in subgroups of two or three. The integration of these multiple procedures is made possible by the highly structured nature of the group. However, as the group progresses, this structure gradually diminishes. Group procedures are elaborated on in Chapters 2 and 14.

Identifying and Resolving Group Problems

In the history of any group, problems arise that interfere with the pursuit of therapy goals. Many of these problems are momentary, but some persist, and the regular group process must be interrupted to deal with them. Although often the therapist can deal with the problem him- or herself by sitting between two "troublemakers," proposing a new, more appealing program, or adding new reinforcers, often it is more effective to allow the group to solve the problem themselves. This affords the group the opportunity to practice their problem-solving skills with coaching from the therapist. However, group problem solving is costly in time, and, if it happens too frequently, it takes away from the specific needs of many members. This step occurs at almost any time within the history of the group, although the ability of the group to deal with these problems increases as the group gains experience. Chapter 14 focuses primarily on strategies for classifying and resolving group problems.

Planning for Generalization of Change

Generalization is the process of transferring what one has learned in the group to the outside world and maintaining what one has learned beyond the end of therapy. One of the major strategies for transferring learning from the group to other situations is the extragroup task.

At the end of every meeting, the members design tasks to be carried out at home, at school, on the playground, or at any other location out of the group session. These tasks are characterized by their specificity as to what, when, where, or with whom certain behaviors and/or cognitions are to be manifested within a given time period. The purpose of extra-group tasks is to create an opportunity for members to try out in the real world what they have learned in the group. Because they are rarely monitored, the tasks provide the members with an opportunity to try out behaviors on their own and, in so doing, to lessen their dependency on the group therapist.

A portion of every meeting is devoted to the designing of new tasks and the monitoring of the results of the previous group assignments. If one views the therapy process as analogous to a problem-solving process, homework is the implementation phase of therapy, and reporting back to the group is the validation phase. In any case, the extragroup task is an essential part of the therapy process.

As part of generalization training, group members prepare for termination by developing plans for applying what they learned in the group when the group finally ends and by designing activities appropriate for practicing their newly learned skills. Possible self-referral sources are discussed, such as the school counselor or a local clinic. The group therapist identifies with each of the youth the specific behavioral and cognitive cues for seeking outside help.

To diminish the intensity of the relationship of the members to each other and to the group therapist, the therapist encourages members to establish relationships outside the group and to become involved in extragroup activities such as after-school interest or sport groups, Boy Scouts/Girl Scouts, or YMCA/YWCA groups. Furthermore, nongroup members whom they have befriended may be invited as guests to hear what they have achieved in the group. Assignments to carry out activities with these friends are encouraged.

In this phase, material reinforcement is ended for extragroup task completion and conformity to group rules. The tasks have become less structured but more extensive. Preparation is largely in the hands of the group members. Monitoring is less strict. Social, recreational, and other cohesion-building activities are held to a minimum in the group. Many of the leadership functions are gradually put in the hands of the group members. Finally, as part of this phase, a follow-up "booster" session may be held 2 or 3 months following therapy. In booster sessions, youth have an opportunity to discuss their achievements and any new problems that may have arisen. This final phase is described in detail in Chapter 15.

Research Support

There is considerable empirical support for therapy programs that have been carried out in small groups. These therapy programs are similar to or contain many of the same elements as CBIGT, though none refer to studies that completely overlap the method proposed here. In this section, we briefly review some of that research with preadolescent and adolescent youth, many of whom are similar to the youth that CBIGT therapists have served.

Hawkins, Jenson, Catalano, and Wells (1991) tested a cognitive-behavioral skills training program in small groups with 141 incarcerated juvenile delinquents (aged 11-18 years). The adolescents were randomly assigned to an experimental skills training or a normal institutional therapy group. The researchers used a randomized block design stratified by county of residence, race, and sex. A behavioral role-play inventory, the Adolescent Problem Situation Inventory, was used to assess subjects' skill levels before and after the intervention.

The intervention for the experimental subjects combined behavioral skills training with social network development and involvement in prosocial activities. It was conducted in two phases: (a) preparation for community reentry and (b) aftercare. The reentry preparation phase included a 10-week program of goal setting and skills training as well as involvement with a case manager. Skills training was conducted in group sessions that met twice weekly for 2 hours. The skills taught included consequential thinking, self-control, avoiding trouble, social networking, problem solving, negotiation and compliance, and drug and alcohol refusal skills. Training was conducted using role-play situations that were likely to be encountered once the adolescents left the institution. Training techniques included instruction, modeling, role playing, feedback, group discussion, and homework. Videotape was used for feedback in role playing.

A common skills entry step was taught for all skills. As subjects confronted each situation, they were asked to recognize signals of getting into trouble ("signal"), to stop and consider alternative courses of action ("stop"), and to question the potential consequences of various behaviors ("question"). The steps of signal, stop, and question provided cues for using skills in specific situations.

Experimental subjects had significantly higher posttest scores than did control subjects in a range of 14 situations that included avoidance of drug use, self-control, and social interaction and interpersonal problem solving. Generalization of skills to untrained role-play situations was found among experimental subjects. No evidence of interactive effects of gender, race, offense type, or pretherapy drug use on posttest skill level was found. The role-play tests were the only measures used as dependent variables. The absence of behavioral observations, rating scales, and social impact measures represents a limitation of this study. As a result, one cannot reject the alternative hypothesis that what the youth learned was role-play skills. The interpretation of the findings is further confounded by the addition of a case management program to the group therapy program, which may very well have contributed heavily to the success of the program.

Lochman and her colleagues went beyond the simple experiment to develop and test a group program for the therapy of aggression with young adolescents. First, the program was tried out and reported on in data-based case studies (Lochman, Nelson, & Sims, 1981); then it was tested using a classical experimental design. This program initially lasted 12 group sessions but in later studies was increased to 18 sessions with five 9- to 12-year-old children in each group. The children were referred by teachers, who were asked to nominate the most aggressive children in their classes. The groups were conducted by two cotherapists.

The program consisted of group discussion, modeling, and behavioral rehearsal activities and included the use of many hands-on materials and games, such as instant cameras, dominoes, puppets, decks of cards, and pictures of social problems from the Developing Understanding of Self and Others Kit (Dinkmeyer, 1973); videotape and camera equipment for modeling and role playing was also incorporated. The first session provided a general orientation to the group format and rules. Later, the group discussion turned to the practice of problem-solving elements (identifying problems, generating alternatives, and evaluating solutions by identifying consequences), strategies for increasing physiological awareness, and the use of self-talk during problem situations. In the final sessions, the therapist emphasized typical social and school-related situations. All aspects of the cognitive strategies learned during the course of the program were reviewed and practiced. Role playing and videotaped feedback were also used in these later sessions.

Once the program had been developed, Lochman and colleagues (Lochman, 1985; Lochman, Burch, Curry, & Lampron, 1984; Lochman & Curry, 1986) conducted a series of studies aimed at evaluating its effects. In a randomized pretest-posttest control group design, Lochman et al. (1984) compared the cognitive-behavioral program described above with the goal-setting condition alone, a cognitive-behavioral plus goal-setting condition, and a no-therapy condition as means of reducing disruptive aggressive off-task behavior in the classroom. Seventy-six boys in the fourth to sixth grades (53% African American, 47% white) were randomly assigned to each of the four therapy conditions. At the 1-month follow-up, testing revealed that the cognitive-behavioral plus goal-setting condition (a minimal-therapy condition in which children set daily behavioral goals that were monitored and reinforced by their teachers) resulted in greater reductions in aggressive behavior than did the cognitive intervention alone and that both cognitive-behavioral groups did better than the control group in the reduction of aggressive behavior in the classroom. Parents noted similar changes on rating scales in the home for the youth in the experimental condition. The treated youth also showed significant increases in self-esteem. Although Lochman and associates controlled many potential alternative hypotheses through the use of multiple control groups and multiple measures, including observations, they did not consider group factors such as group cohesion, the establishment of group norms, or subgrouping as contributors to outcome. The use of recreational strategies may well have increased the cohesion of the experimental conditions. As a result, group cohesion may have been confounded with the anger-coping and goal-setting interventions to produce the changes noted in the study. Although the differences between the conditions as described by the authors was large, no explicit attempt to check on therapy integrity was made.

Guerra and Slaby (1990) developed an intervention program of twelve 1-hour sessions based on a model of social-cognitive development designed to remediate cognitive factors identified as correlates of aggression in an earlier study. The subjects were 120 male and female adolescents incarcerated for having committed one or more violent criminal acts (i.e., assault and battery, robbery, rape, attempted murder, and murder). The subjects were equally divided by gender and ranged in age from 15 to 18 years. They were randomly assigned (balanced by gender) to one of three experimental groups: cognitive mediation training (CMT), attention control (AC), and no-therapy control (NTC). Subjects assigned to the CMT or AC groups were divided into small discussion groups ranging in size from 10 to 14 youth. The CMT group program focused on correcting those social problem skills deficits and changing those beliefs that supported the use of aggression. The training techniques were limited to instruction and structured discussion because these techniques were equally applicable for the two control conditions. The AC group sessions were devoted to the exercise of basic skills such as reading comprehension and basic math and the application of these skills to career preparation. The NTC group participated solely in pretesting and posttesting. Compared with subjects in both control groups, subjects in the therapy group showed increased skills in solving social problems, decreased endorsement of beliefs supporting aggression, and decreased aggressive, impulsive, and inflexible behaviors, as rated by staff. Posttest aggression was directly related to change in cognitive factors. With respect to impact measures, no group differences were detected for the number of parole violators up to 24 months after release. Of particular importance was the fact that the authors dealt with extremely difficult youth. The authors also controlled for any group attention by having an attention group control as well as a no-therapy control. As in most studies, they did not consider group factors such as group cohesion, which probably was higher in the therapy groups than in the placebo groups where the youth did schoolwork and could have provided another explanation of the findings. No attention was given to other group factors such as participation, the establishment of group norms, or subgrouping as contributors to outcome. The fact that there were only twelve 1-hour sessions may have explained why there was no difference in parole violations, which may have required more therapy time and more focus. There was no clearly developed transfer-of-change program.

However, even with the limited number of sessions, many other differences were detected.

Feindler and colleagues have developed a group anger control training program for the therapy of anger and disruptive behavior in the classroom (Feindler, Ecton, Kingsley, & Dubey, 1986; Feindler, Marriott, & Iwata, 1984). In the Feindler et al. (1984) investigation, 36 junior high school students with a history of high rates of classroom and/or community disruption were randomly assigned to the therapy program or to a no-therapy control condition. Students completed self-report measures of locus of control, means-ends problem solving, and impulsivity. Teachers completed ratings of self-control, carried out an already ongoing contingency management program, and kept daily records of fines for aggressive behavior. The groups were run for 7 weeks for ten 50-minute sessions. Students analyzed provocation cues and anger responses, provided alternative responses to provoking stimuli, and used other strategies to control their own provocative behaviors. Among control techniques that were taught and practiced were self-monitoring; self-imposed "time-out" from anger-producing stimuli; and relaxation, assertiveness, and problem solving. The therapist gave didactic instruction, modeling, behavioral rehearsal, and negotiated homework assignments as training procedures. Five weeks following the end of the program, it was noted that the students who had received anger control training performed better than the students in the no-therapy control condition, and teachers rated the treated students more highly on the self-control measure than the controls. However, no differences between conditions were found on the number of behavioral fines received or on the self-report measures. As in all the other studies, no check of therapy integrity was made. The one social impact measure, the receiving of behavioral fines, did not show a difference.

Etscheidt (1991) examined the effectiveness of a cognitive-behavioral training program in reducing aggressive behavior and increasing self-control in 30 behaviorally disordered adolescents (aged 12-18 years). Students assigned to a cognitive-behavioral group participated in a cognitive-behavioral training program adapted from the anger control program model by Lochman et al. (1981). This program assists students in modifying their aggressive behaviors by altering their cognitive processing of events and response alternatives. The 3-week adapted training program consisted of 12 structured 30- to 40-minute lessons. Program goals were identified as (a) to provide self-awareness, (b) to explore the student's reaction to peer influences, (c) to identify problematic situations, (d) to generate alternative solutions to problems, (e) to evaluate alternative solutions, (f) to increase physiological awareness of anger arousal, and (g) to integrate techniques of physiological awareness, self-talk, and social problem solving.

Students in the cognitive-behavioral plus reinforcement condition received the cognitive-behavioral training program but also received a positive consequence for using the skills taught in the program. Students assigned to a control group did not receive the cognitive-behavioral training program or positive consequences for implementing the training strategy.

Measures were taken to determine (a) whether students participating in the training program exhibited fewer aggressive behaviors than students not involved in the training program and (b) whether the addition of an incentive (i.e., an externally controlled positive consequence) would increase the effectiveness of the training program. Participating students were observed to have significantly fewer aggressive behaviors and were rated as having significantly more self-control than those students not participating. The addition of an incentive for implementing the training strategies did not appear to increase the effectiveness of the training program. Because of the small sample size, there may have been insufficient power to detect the added effect of reinforcement.

Dupper and Krishef (1993) evaluated the effects of a school-based social-cognitive skills training program for 35 sixth and seventh graders at risk for school suspension. Subjects were randomly assigned to a therapy or control group using a randomized pretest-posttest control group design. Scores from the Nowicki-Strickland Locus of Control Scale for Children (Nowicki & Strickland, 1973) and the Teachers Self-Control Rating Scale (Humphrey, 1982) were used to assess subjects' cognitive and behavioral changes before and immediately following the therapy program. There were significant differences between pretest and posttest scores from both measures for the therapy group but not for the control group. However, there were no significant differences between the two conditions. With a sample size of only 35, there may have been insufficient power to reject the null hypothesis.

A study by Larson (1992) dealt with the evaluation of a group therapy program teaching anger and aggression management for at-risk students in an urban middle school. The curriculum addressed both emotional and instrumental types of aggression by teaching anger control as well as social problem solving. The sample ($N = 37$) was selected from a larger pool of 48 students assigned to a program for children at risk. The mean age of the sample was 13.8 years. The gender composition was 22 males and 15 females. Racial composition was 24 African Americans (65%) and 13 whites (35%).

Subjects were assigned to one of two experimental conditions: (a) the "Think First" group (a cognitive problem-solving procedure) ($n = 22$) or (b) the discussion-only control group ($n = 15$), in a modified randomized groups design. Teachers were blind as to the condition to which the student was assigned. The groups met 10 times over 5 weeks for 50-minute sessions. During the group sessions, the "Think First" youth were taught behavioral analysis, self-instruction, and social problem solving. The group relied on modeling and role-play procedures to describe and teach the skills. Homework and attendance were encouraged through a token exchange program. Participants in the discussion-only group met for discussion but did not receive any skill training.

The outcome measures of interest included (a) the Incident Referral Form (IRF), (b) the Children's Inventory of Anger (Nelson & Finch, 1978), (c) the Jesness Inventory (Jesness, 1972), and (d) the Teacher's Report Form (Achenbach & Edelbrock, 1986). The TRF was a teacher-initiated report of a specific behavioral incident of aggression or disruptive behavior. A pretest baseline was established in the form of a weekly mean score. TRF data were continuously recorded for all subjects. The Children's Inventory of Anger was administered at pretest and posttest. The Jesness Inventory, also administered at pretest and posttest, assessed the subjects' self-reported attitude toward delinquency.

The TRF results were analyzed with a 2 (group) by 3 (time) repeated-measures ANOVA. A significant difference was found in the group by time interaction. No differences were found on the other measures. This study, though not without methodological flaws, provides additional evidence that a cognitive and problem-solving approach has an impact on aggressive behavior.

In general, the research reviewed above, though carried out in groups, did not concern itself with the group as a means of intervention; rather, the group was used only as the context. Although it is likely that there were differences in groups in the same condition, no group attributes were examined. In most cases, the group condition was confounded with the intervention strategies. All of these programs lend at least modest support for the use of cognitive-behavioral strategies within the context of groups for delinquent and/or aggressive youth and other behavioral problems. Although the subjects in these studies were predominantly male, treatment was equally effective for female clients. Treatment was as effective for African American as for white youth, and as effective for junior high school-aged as for high school-aged youth. The number of sessions in these studies ranged from 10 to 18, and the average length of sessions was 1 hour. There was evidence in one experimental study that, to achieve significant change, 18 sessions were more effective than 12 (Lochman et al., 1984).

Summary

In this chapter, an overview of cognitive-behavioral interactive group therapy (CBIGT) has been presented. This overview provides the reader with a brief description of all of the components of CBIGT. With this overview as background, the reader can more readily understand the relationship of any one chapter to the entire approach. Each subsequent chapter represents a more detailed description of one of the components.

The major components of CBIGT that are dealt with in this text are how to prepare for CBIGT; how to start the group, including orientation, cohesion building, and motivation enhancement; how to assess individual and group problems through interviewing and observation strategies; how to employ measurement procedures in assessment and evaluation; how to formulate goals and link them to intervention planning; how to help youth in solving problems systematically and negotiating differences; how to use reinforcement and stimulus control strategies in groups; how to carry out modeling, rehearsal, coaching, and feedback techniques in groups; how to use the group in facilitating cognitive coping skill training; how to design successful extragroup tasks for members; how to increase social support of group members; how to integrate games and other socio-recreational activities into the therapy program; how to identify and resolve group problems; and, finally, how to train youth beyond the boundaries of the group. As can be seen from the above list, each chapter stresses how to carry out the given component within the context of and by means of the group.

This chapter also reviews some of the recent research that serves, despite the noted limitations, as the empirical foundation for the cognitive-behavioral component of the approach. No one of these studies uses an approach that completely overlaps with CBIGT, which has been developed from the related research as well as from clinical experience with groups.

CHAPTER 2

Preparation for Group Therapy

Before therapy can begin, the group therapist must prepare the group environment for the members' advent. Decisions must be made for both community and institutional groups regarding the number of youth in the group, the frequency and duration of sessions, the number of group therapists, and the composition of groups in terms of personal characteristics. Also, as part of preparation, decisions must be made as to the general content of sessions and the degree and type of involvement of parents and other significant persons in the lives of the youth. In community groups, the recruitment and selection strategies of members must also be determined.

In contrast with many other group approaches, CBIGT includes careful advanced preparation as one of its salient characteristics. This advanced preparation makes it possible to explain to the youth and their parents what the group is all about and what will happen in the course of therapy. (See Chapter 3 for a description of youth and parent orientation.) Despite the detailed preparation, the final product is not rigid. As the group progresses, the members are increasingly involved in evaluating and, if necessary, modifying the decisions made earlier. Two examples of the pregroup preparation of groups follow: one of a time-limited community group, the other of an open-ended group in residential treatment.

Because of the large number of referrals to the county mental health agency of youth 14 to 16 years of age whose parents complained of their excessive aggression and poor relationships to parents, a group was developed in which the general goal was to learn how to cope more effectively with situations that led to anger and aggression. The specific goals to be worked on were reducing the incidence of aggressive outbreaks at home and in school, dealing with parents' criticism and limit setting, developing conversational skills, showing an interest in the ideas and activities of others, listening to others without interrupting, asking others for help and information, improving studying skills, and increasing the frequency of studying behavior. The group was to meet once a week after school on Friday for 16 weeks with one group therapist. An option of 4 additional weeks would be provided if the members, their parents, and the group therapist thought it necessary. In organizing the group, the therapist would write all the parents and youth on the agency waiting list for therapy. The agency would also let the local high schools know of the availability of the groups. The therapist also distributed a description of the group to all other staff members and talked to them individually about the group. Each group would be no larger than eight youth of the same gender, and care would be taken to include at least two youth who could serve as models for the others. The models would be selected from successful graduates of previous groups. The group therapist would meet with all youth who were referred before the first group meeting to tell them about the group. At the end of every session, a postsession questionnaire would be administered to evaluate ongoing group process.

The above example describes a brief plan for setting up a new community group. The following example describes the preparation for organizing an open-ended group in a residential therapy center.

In a large residential therapy center for youth referred for being adjudicated for delinquent acts, groups were organized primarily on the basis of open beds and similarity of gender. Wherever a choice was possible, youth were assigned to units in which the age was about the same. Because of the press to admit youth referred by the courts, little attention could be paid to a preferred composition. However, the size of the group was limited to 12 youth. The living group and the therapy group overlapped in membership, but the therapy group met weekly for therapeutic purposes 5 days a week for 1½ hours with one group therapist. Occasionally residential staff, the clinical supervisor, or the family therapist sat in on groups and would serve as therapists for subgroups. They also would conduct parts of or entire sessions. This would require a brief meeting of the leadership staff in advance to coordinate their efforts.

The agenda for each session was determined by the group therapist in consultation with the youth. On the 3 days a week that the focus was on behavioral change, each session had a specific theme, such as examining one's beliefs, identifying and changing cognitive distortions, dealing with group pressure, learning to interview for a job, listening to others effectively, improving study skills, or getting along with parents. In each session, one or two exercises related to the themes were carried out, extragroup tasks were reviewed, and new tasks were planned for. All sessions ended with filling out a postsession questionnaire.

Attributes of CBIGT

A number of different categories of groups lend themselves to a CBIGT approach. Two have been exemplified above, institutional and community groups. Most but not all of the community groups are also time limited; that is, they have a fixed beginning and end. In contrast, most but not all of the institutional groups are open-ended groups; as there are openings in the group, new members are added. Members leave the group when they leave the institution. Within institutions, there may be special interest groups, such as anger management or assertiveness training, that may be either open or time limited.

Preparation for group therapy is somewhat different for institutional and community groups. In particular, questions of size, treatment duration, and number of leaders require different considerations for these two types of groups. Let us examine these areas of decisions one at a time for both types of groups and make recommendations based on experience, analysis, and, where available, research.

Group Size

The size of a group depends on its purpose, the need for individualization, and practical considerations such as available space, length of stay in the institution, and available staff. Because individualization within a group context is highly valued, the community groups with which this approach has been used usually range in size from three to eight members. Generally, however, a group size of six members makes it possible to involve everyone at every session. A group with fewer than three members seems to lose many of the beneficial group attributes discussed in Chapter 1. A size larger than eight members makes it difficult to permit every member to bring in a problematic situation at every meeting. It has been noted that the satisfaction of members tends to increase until there a total of six members and then to decline slightly after that.

There are clinical reasons to modify this range. In the initial phases in adolescent groups, upward of 12 adolescents have been put into one group to permit the adolescent to explore the possibility of the group without submitting to its intimacy. Occasionally still larger "drop-in" groups of adolescents (15-30) have been organized to permit opportunities to experiment in subgroups with a variety of programs without putting too much pressure on the adolescent. Even in these cases, the goal is eventually to establish a number of small group and individual therapy possibilities. Groups of 12 have been carried out effectively when all the youth share a problem or when there are two therapists and the activities of the group are frequently carried out in subgroups.

In some cases where there have been too few referrals, group therapists start with a pair of youth and add youth as they are referred. The earlier-recruited members serve to orient the newer members; this affords the original members practice in their newly acquired abilities and a chance to try out leadership skills. Before the new members are admitted, the therapist reviews the leadership behaviors necessary to include the new members.

The size of community groups tends to change slightly over time. Illness, changing home locations, dropouts, and referrals to other services often take their toll. If the change in number is too dramatic, the cohesion and satisfaction of the group tend to go down. In some cases, the group therapist may add new members and handle it just as in the case where he or she began with a pair (see below for a discussion of modifying the existing composition).

Institutional groups tend to be larger because they often overlap with the residential group. To facilitate greater individualization, the group may be divided into two subgroups, one led by the group therapist and the other led by the residential worker or family worker or even a supervisor. Another reason that larger groups in institutions are possible is that as a rule they meet much more frequently than community groups.

Frequency, Length, and Duration of Group Sessions

Group size is also a function of the frequency, length, and duration of sessions. In institutions in which the group meets every day for an hour and a half, larger groups can be permitted without losing the opportunity in any 2-day period for a person to discuss his or her own problem. Most community groups discussed in this book are time limited and meet for approximately 1 hour a week for about 12 weeks. Regular weekly sessions rather than the more variable schedule recommended below are the general pattern, primarily because of the personal or work schedules of the families, of the youth, and of the group therapist rather than for any particular therapy rationale. Research on learning suggests that when reinforcement is reasonably continuous, newly learned behaviors will rapidly fade away if reinforcement is terminated too abruptly (Kazdin, 1989). On the basis of this hypothesis, at least two and sometimes three sessions per week during the initial phase of community group therapy are recommended, gradually fading to once a week, still later to once every 2 weeks, and eventually to once a month for the remainder of the therapy year. For practical reasons, most organizations have been unsuccessful in departing with any regularity from the weekly schedule for community groups. A few have been able to follow eight weekly sessions with four monthly ones as a way of providing the youth with more gradual fading of the intensity of treatment.

The exact number of sessions for community groups depends on the purpose of the group, its composition, and certain practical limitations.

In heterogeneous groups (with diverse presenting problems), 14 to 18 sessions are usually required to meet treatment goals. The same number of sessions is required for groups in which the therapy goals are complex and involve many diverse situations. In groups in which the goals are preventative, such as social skill training for the entire classroom, eight sessions have been demonstrated to be sufficient for the majority of youth (see, e.g., LeCroy & Rose, 1986) to attain these modest goals. When a highly specific and limited goal is pursued, still fewer sessions may suffice. For example, a number of adolescents wanted to learn how to interview for a seasonal job at a local cheese factory. Two sessions were sufficient for demonstrating and practicing simple interviewing skills and providing information about appearance. Youth groups, even in non-school settings, are usually organized in conjunction with the school semester. It is a rare community group that is carried out during the summer months, although some groups may be connected with therapeutic summer camps or residential treatment centers. In October, referrals usually begin to pour in as parents and teachers become frustrated with the response of the youth to demands at home, to social situations, and to pressures at school and on the playground or in other extraschool situations. The groups organized at this time will last until the Christmas break, April, or the end of the school year. New groups may be started in January and meet until the end of the school year. Adolescent groups in the community have a way of gradually losing their membership at the beginning of spring. Only rarely do groups carry over into a second year, although individuals have been referred to other therapy groups for periods as long as 3 years. In general, however, assuming that major goals have been achieved after one set of therapy sessions, clients are referred to nontherapy groups such as the YMCA/YWCA or Girl Scouts/Boy Scouts. Referral to individual therapy may also occur. Some groups are organized on a different time basis completely. For example, some adolescent groups may meet for a marathon three Saturdays in a row for 6 to 7 hours each Saturday. Some group therapists have organized entire weekends for as long as 10 hours a day for therapy groups. In institutions, transitional groups will meet from 1 to 3 hours daily from their onset until termination, which is usually at about 3 to 6 weeks. In one project, the entire seventh and eighth grades of the middle schools received a 1-hour social skill training session daily for 2 weeks (LeCroy & Rose, 1986). Only modest research exists to point the way to differences in the number of sessions. In adult groups undergoing therapy for social anxiety, D'Alelio and Murray (1981) demonstrated that eight 2-hour sessions were significantly more effective in reducing social anxiety than four 2-hour sessions. In adolescent anger management groups, Lochman (1985) demonstrated the greater effectiveness of 16 sessions over 8 in increasing the control of anger.

As we mentioned earlier, most community groups are closed, but some are open ended and have no set duration. When youth provide evidence that goals have been attained and that a plan for generalization (see Chapter 15) has been designed, they may plan to terminate. Of course, in such groups, termination of a given individual may also occur against the advice of the group therapist as the attraction of the group fades for that individual without concurrent achievement of treatment goals.

In residential treatment, groups tend to meet every weekday or every other day for an hour and a half as long as the members are in the institution. Occasionally, a member will miss sessions for such practical reasons as illness, doctor's appointments, court appearances, psychological testing, and special programs. Some institutions use CBIGT for only 2 or 3 of the 5 days and use the other days for more traditional methods, such as positive peer culture (PPC; see Rose, Duby, Olenick, & Weston, 1996, for an example).

Number of Group Therapists

As the number of group therapists in any one group increases, so does the cost to the parent, the agency, or the community. There is no evidence that two group therapists are more effective than one, provided that all group therapists are experienced and trained. Thus, in most cases, one group therapist is adequate and less costly than two or more. There are, however, several situations in which more than one group therapist is recommended:

1. If the second group therapist is a trainee. On-the-job tutoring is an excellent teaching strategy, especially if the experienced therapist gradually delegates responsibility to the cotherapist for leading and planning and provides supervision to the trainee.

2. If both group therapists are leading a new type of group for the first or second time. Coleadership provides an opportunity for peer group super-

vision. Cotherapists, in our experience, tend to plan more carefully than single therapists.

3. If the second group therapist alternates with the first as observer (however, having an observer is cheaper). Having a process observer in groups is helpful in identifying process issues.

4. If there are clearly demonstrated skills necessary to lead the group, and these skills are divided between the group therapists.

5. If the group is larger than eight (although, when there are 10 youth or more, it is usually more effective and easier to individualize if there are two groups).

6. If one group therapist is unlikely to be able to remain in the group until the end. Usually, in this case, one group therapist is gradually faded in, and the other is faded out.

7. In groups of highly active or aggressive youth where control is initially a major problem. If "time-out from reinforcement" (see p. 217-218) has to be used, someone needs to go with the individual when he or she is sent to some time-out place.

Cotherapists are not always beneficial. They sometimes create problems for themselves and the group by competing with each other, by both attempting to dominate the group interaction, and by frequently amplifying and repeating what the other says. If cotherapists are to be used, this issue should be examined carefully before and during the group sessions.

Recruiting Members for Community Groups

In general, it is not necessary to recruit members for institutional groups or community groups in which attendance is mandatory, such as groups of parolees. In contrast, the first prerequisite for developing a group program in community groups is to obtain an adequate number of potential members. To identify this population, a large number of people must become familiar with the group program and consider it useful for themselves, their children, their students, or their clients. A recruitment program is an essential part of any group program, despite the program's many advantages as seen by the group therapist. Below is an example of a recruitment program.

One group therapist had just entered a new high school as a psychologist and, on the basis of her observations in the classroom and on the playground and her brief interviews with a number of individuals, decided that it would be important to organize social skills and coping skills training groups. After gaining the support of the principal and several of the teachers from whose classrooms youth might be taken, she wrote letters to the parents of all the students in the 9th and 10th grades, asking which of them would be interested in having their children participate in a group. She described the group and some of the goals that had been worked on in the school where she had been previously. The response to the letter was overwhelming and yielded more youth than the group therapist could incorporate into her groups. Parents generally felt that social problems existed about which they could be quite explicit and of which the teachers were often unaware. The youth too had to be interested in the group before they were admitted. The group therapist also recruited a number of youth referred by the teachers once they understood the program. Both the applicants and their parents had to agree to the applicants' attending the group before they were admitted.

In the above example, the group therapist demonstrated a number of recruitment procedures. Having determined that there was a need, she discussed how a group program might meet this need with the teaching staff and the principal to make sure they would support her if her recruitment proved to be successful. She then wrote the parents directly, describing the program and the potential benefits to participants. The enlistment of the teachers in obtaining referrals resulted in their better understanding of the group, its purposes, and its methods; consequently, they became a source of referrals as well. In the following example, a somewhat different set of recruitment techniques is demonstrated.

In a child guidance clinic, the group therapist learned from the staff that there was no effective service available for anxious young adolescents. Following lengthy discussions with the director and colleagues, he developed a small brochure that described the kinds of groups that might be useful to that age group. He was allotted 30 minutes at a staff meeting to explain the program and to answer questions about it. At that time, he distributed the brochure to clinic staff to give out to appropriate members. He also advertised the group in the local advertising weekly as a service to be offered by the clinic. He was able to obtain spots on the public service and commercial radio stations. The director also organized an interview with a feature writer in the local paper. When this article appeared, it seemed to draw the largest number of referrals. Within several weeks, he had a large enough number of potential members so that he could begin the selection process.

In the above example, the added following procedures were exemplified: advertising the program on the radio and in the newspaper, putting a feature article in the newspaper, and distributing brochures to agency members. However, it was important once again to inform and negotiate with staff and director their support of a new program. Without this support, the recruitment program would not have gotten started.

A few other recruitment strategies not discussed in the above examples might also be considered. When the agency has a waiting list, groups become especially interesting to the potential clientele who have already committed themselves to wanting help. Posters in the school and at the agency have attracted a number of applicants. One group therapist arranged to be interviewed on a radio talk show in which she told about her program and its research foundations in great detail.

One population that is often difficult to recruit for community therapy groups is adolescents because of their struggle for independence from adults. They are often afraid that joining a treatment group may be considered "weird" by their peers. Referrals by adults, whether parents or teachers, are often ignored. One creative method by which adolescents have been recruited has been the "drop-in group," mentioned briefly earlier. Drop-in groups are large, informal groups of 15 to 40 youth, usually adolescents, who come together in an open room whenever the agency or center is open. The drop-in group program is characterized by various informal activities scattered throughout the room. Usually there are several group therapists, each of whom stays with a given activity and attempts to learn names of the youth, their interests, and eventually their concerns. Activities may consist of such programs as dancing, a set of computer games, an informal discussion session, a bike repair center, and reading, all occurring simultaneously in different areas of the room. Special events such as dances or sports demonstrations may be used to attract and maintain potential members.

The purpose of such an informal group is to bring in those adolescents who need help but who find it difficult to approach someone or an agency for individual or group counseling. The drop-in center provides a first step for the adolescent to meet with adults who have demonstrated they accept and understand the problems of young people. Gradually, discussion groups and problem-solving, sex education, study skill improvement, dating, and job-finding groups can evolve out of the informal activities. These will occur publicly so that new members can observe or sit in whenever they choose. As the group develops, adolescents may choose to become more focused to further their own learning.

In the shift from a drop-in to a therapy group, a number of difficulties have been noted. Transitions that are too rapid, highly deviant group leadership among the members, and inadequate resources may combine to prevent the participation of the adolescents in the program. Nevertheless, the transition from drop-in to therapy or training groups has been achieved in numerous ways. Interest groups can be set up around the special problems unique to this group that were outlined earlier, such as dating, sexual information, job hunting, and school survival skills. The interested volunteers can be involved in publicizing and organizing these time-limited groups.

As common problems are noted, long-term therapy can be organized to which those adolescents with identifiable problems can be invited. Even during the transition phase and following it, large group activities are maintained to keep adolescents coming to the center or agency.

The community center is not the only agency in which drop-in programs have been organized. Both schools, through their social work or educational psychology programs, and family service agencies have organized variations of the drop-in program with some success. Although there is some clinical experience with such groups, there are no data-based experiments or even data-based case studies. However, the need of something dramatic to attract the resistant adolescent recommends this alternative, especially when other, more direct methods have failed.

Once a successful recruitment program has been established, it needs to be screened and evaluated for its appropriateness and effectiveness in obtaining members. If the machinery is kept in place and modified to meet the changing needs of the community, it will serve the group therapist well for a long time, as long as the programs meet the expectations of the youth and their parents.

Once the potential members begin to refer themselves or be referred, a new set of decisions has to be made. Should the applicants be placed in a group, and if the answer is yes, what kind of group?

Placement in a Group?

Before therapy, the group therapist usually interviews the applicant and, depending on the resources of the agency and on the referral source, the parent, teacher, supervisor, parole officer, or other significant persons in the applicant's life. The purpose of these interviews is to make four basic decisions: Is therapy necessary? Is group therapy appropriate? What kind of group would work best for the potential member? How should the group be composed? (These interviews also play a major role in orientation and assessment.) The orientation function is discussed in Chapter 3, and the assessment function is discussed further in Chapters 3 and 4.) In this section, the focus is on the interview's function in putting the group together. These three functions, however, often overlap. The group therapist attempts to ferret out from each individual involved with the applicant at least some of his or her behavioral attributes and to focus on specific incidents in which these are manifested. Interviews are usually brief, focused on the applicant's view of precipitating events for his or her problems, and geared toward the interactive pattern of the applicant and the adult and the interactive pattern of the applicant with other youth.

To determine whether an individual should be treated at all, it is usually necessary to consider what the ultimate consequences of his or her present pattern of behavior will be if that pattern continues. For several boys involved in physically aggressive behavior against their peers in a given ninth-grade class, for example, the ultimate consequence is likely to be suspension from or failure in school. One also should not overlook exploring the concerns of the teacher and parent during their interviews. Finally, there are certain practical considerations in a recommendation for therapy. In the case of a teacher referral, do the parents agree that a referral should be made? Are adequate alternate resources available? Is there a danger that therapy will create only an additional handicap if the applicant, as a result, is labeled a "troublemaker" or "sick"? Is there an appropriate group available to which the applicant can be assigned, or must the applicant be wait-listed? Is wait-listing possible, or would individual therapy be better? Only with knowledge of community agency resources can these questions be fully answered.

A general guideline to consider in deciding whether to place an applicant in a group is "the absence of behavior so bizarre as to frighten others, and no wide differences that are personally or culturally beyond acceptance" (Klein, 1972, p. 60). Although it may be possible to have an entire group of youth who occasionally hallucinate, one member who hallucinates may be far too threatening to the other youth. Similarly, a group of passive youth with a limited repertoire of assertive skills may be startled and frightened by a highly aggressive member, who might be better placed in another group. These are issues of group composition. In the next section, we deal with the other issues involved in appropriate composition of groups.

Group Composition

Once each potential group member's problems have been described in a preliminary statement based on data from interviews and any pregroup testing (see Chapter 5) and a decision has been made that group therapy is appropriate, the group therapist must decide how the group should be composed. Though only limited research exists in this area, several models of composition extrapolated from this research, theory, and clinical experience can be proposed.

Presenting Problem

Most of the institutional and community groups addressed in this book are broad-based treatment groups; that is, they focus on whatever behavioral, affective, or cognitive problems youth bring to the group. Some groups are organized around narrow themes or specific problems. Among the major themes of groups reported on in this book are social skill training for youth who are either excessively shy or aggressive in many situations or for entire classrooms, anger control, stress management for anxious youth, classroom self-management skill training, adolescent weight loss, quitting smoking, alcohol and drug abuse, anorexia and bulemia, depression, agoraphobia, teenage pregnancy, job interviewing and preparation, and recent radical change in one's family through death, divorce, or incarceration of a parent.

Age and Socioemotional Development

In most groups, similarity of age and/or socioemotional development is preferred because a few youth who are much older than the rest tend to dominate the younger members in decision making and other group processes and because younger adolescents find it difficult to participate at all if the group is predominantly older. Occasionally, a highly aggressive child is placed in a group of older or at least bigger youth to protect the other members. Once in a while, where there are not enough youth of a given physical or developmental age, youth with somewhat diverse problems are placed together. Though this is difficult, it is possible as long as the group therapist is sensitive to the potential disruptive effect, the disparate participation, and the differences in concerns. Usually such a group requires more time. A slightly older and somewhat more adaptive individual is at times added as a model for the other youth. Models are an essential component of any group for reasons discussed in the following section.

Including a Model

Although the group therapist may serve as model, group members, because of their similarity to each other, are usually far more likely to be imitated (for better or worse). Often in heterogeneous groups, youth with major problems in one behavioral area may serve as models for youth with other problems. In groups with members having similar problems, models without major target problems may have to be placed in the group primarily for modeling effect rather than for their own treatment. The therapist can draw on former clients who have been through similar groups to serve as models. The models would do the same things as the other youth but would be encouraged to do them more effectively because of their earlier experience. This arrangement is not only helpful for the group but is an excellent generalization strategy for the model (see Chapter 9). The ideal model is slightly older, slightly more intelligent, and slightly more competent in the target area, but not necessarily in all areas (Bandura, 1973).

Some practitioners have expressed concern that the models or their parents may object to the model's being placed in the group out of the fear that he or she may learn undesirable behaviors from the target youth. No examples of this have been observed by my colleagues or myself. The models and their parents have for the most part been pleased to hear that they seem to be getting along well socially and could be helpful to other youth. Moreover, as parents have often pointed out, there are a few situations that even the best adapted models find difficult and could continue to work on in the group. A discussion of how models are explicitly used in the group is presented in Chapter 9.

Gender Composition

In most cases, we have attempted to put together, wherever possible, adolescent groups consisting of both genders. As Hansen, Warner, and Smith (1980) noted, those situations in which mixed groups are productive far outweigh those situations in which they are not. Certainly, with adolescents, many of the problems are concerned with the relationships of one sex to the other. Such problems can be best dealt with in an environment with both genders.

One problem we constantly have faced with mixed groups is that for latency-age youth the group often divides into boy-girl subgroups immediately. Communication tends to be among the boys and among the girls. Sometimes, the norms of the genders are so opposed to each other that youth of one gender group will not go into a group in which the other is present. Another problem is that certain issues of central concern are not readily opened up in mixed groups. Most of these problems can be addressed in the group and represent a valuable learning experience, although the cohesion of the group as a whole may not be very high.

Of course, some themes in CBIGT groups tend to be relevant for persons of one gender only, such as premenstrual syndrome or assertiveness training for the second phase of consciousness raising for young women. Moreover, practitioners are often dependent on referrals from others who see certain problems as uniquely male or female problems. It would appear that where the goal in a group is awareness of cultural inequities and instilling of female pride, all-women groups with all women leaders are advisable. Most CBIGT groups do not have this focus. Groups with a cognitive-behavioral focus can more readily be dealt with as mixed-gender groups because it is possible to examine values, assumptions, and other cognitions of male and female group members in these situations. Replacing self-defeating thoughts with coping self-statements and actions may be an appropriate way of strengthening female members' position in the group and of sensitizing young people of both genders to the inequities and the solutions.

In institutions, groups usually are of one gender because the therapy group usually overlaps with the living group. However, where the institution is coeducational, occasional sessions of mixed-gender groups may be organized to deal with issues of heterosexual relationships.

Racial and Socioeconomic Composition

Wherever possible, groups are mixed racially. In schools in which racial tensions are high or in which the problems are peculiar to a given racial group, the group therapist might consider the possibility of racially homogeneous community groups, especially if only one referral is from a racially different group. However, racial diversity is the nature of the world and represents the conditions under which youth must learn to live.

Because socioeconomic factors are often closely related to racial differences, it is useful to have socioeconomic diversity for the same reasons as having racial diversity. The problems of socioeconomically mixed groups are similar to those of racially mixed groups.

In ethnically or racially mixed groups, the problem of interethnic and racial bias and conflict may represent a formal or covert agenda for the group. Although most nonbehavioral groups working with minorities spend a lot of time on this issue, it may appear less obvious in cognitive-behavioral groups. If it is ignored, an important opportunity is lost to correct cognitive distortions about other ethnicities and races. It is possible to handle prejudicial values in groups in the same way that one handles any other cognitive distortion. Usually a list of common prejudices is distributed to the members. They are asked to indicate the degree to which they agree with each statement. Then a number of cognitive procedures, such as providing corrective information, training in alternative cognitions, or self-instruction (see Chapter 10), can be used to change the distorted racial or ethnic cognitions. Evaluation of the change is carried out by a post-treatment test.

Modifying Existing Groups

Even when a community group is carefully put together, problems arise that can be attributed to an unfortunate composition. Also, as

mentioned earlier, members may drop out for various reasons. Sometimes, as a means of resolving the problem, it is possible to add new
members to community groups. In one anger management group of
originally eight adolescents, three of whom were African American, two
of the African American members attended only the first session. To
attain a reasonable racial balance, two additional African American
members were recruited for the group. In a second anger management
group, all the members but two were highly aggressive. The two were
discovered to be extremely withdrawn. After the initial two sessions, in
which neither said a word, the therapist added two members who were
somewhat assertive but not nearly as aggressive as others in the group as
a means of achieving greater balance. In both groups, the addition of the
new members was first discussed with the others, and preparation was
made for the original members to provide the information missed to the
new members. In open institutional groups, as beds become available,
new members are constantly added. The same procedures for helping
new members to "catch up" are carried out.

In summary, homogeneity with respect to presenting problem is
desirable (but not necessary), provided that effective models are present
in the group. Some degree of heterogeneity with respect to behavioral
attributes is possible for youth therapy groups, provided that each person
is at least somewhat similar to at least one other person in the group. To
facilitate communication, homogeneity of developmental age is recommended. Diversity in areas such as race, gender, and socioeconomic status
has not resulted in serious problems and has in fact proven advantageous
in many instances insofar as issues of differences can be dealt with in the
group. At least one person in the group should be able to serve as a model
in the target area for each member. Last, it should be noted that a given
group composition is never final. Adjustments can be made by adding
new members, by splitting the group into several subgroups, or both.

Groups are always organized under some agency or private auspices
that provide the general purpose, organizational structure, and resources
for treatment. These are discussed in the following section.

Agency Auspices for Group Therapy

Though not all social agencies provide therapy facilities for youth, the
examples in this book are drawn from the experiences of group therapists
in various social and private agencies: residential treatment, day care

treatment, schools, health maintenance organizations and other health clinics, community social agencies, correctional institutions, and private practice. Schools have sponsored assertiveness training, anger management, pregnancy prevention, alcohol and drug abuse prevention, and family change groups, often from a cognitive-behavioral perspective. CBIGT and similar programs have also been sponsored by community centers and settlement houses in areas similar to those found in the schools. One community center used the groups as the basis of a first offenders project (see Rose, Sundel, DeLange, Corwin, & Palumbo, 1971), with the back of a station wagon or a storefront as the meeting room. Also, the typical psychiatric outpatient services, such as mental health and child guidance clinics, have been experimenting with CBIGT and similar programs. This approach has also been used in correctional institutions (Brierton, Rose, & Flanagan, 1975). A day treatment program for adjudicated delinquents that included anger management, problem solving, and assertiveness training was described by Rose et al. (1996). Hospitals and health clinics have sponsored pain management, stress management, weight loss and other eating disorders, smoking cessation, and alcohol and drug abuse groups for both adolescent outpatients and inpatients. All of the above-mentioned groups have also been offered by private practitioners.

Session Settings

In most cases, the setting for a given group is within the walls of the sponsoring agency. In institutions, special rooms are usually set aside for group therapy. There are, however, many creative exceptions to this pattern. Groups have met not only in the schools and agencies mentioned above but also in stores, members' homes, homemade clubhouses, station wagons, restaurants, and so forth. The principles involved in the use of these natural settings are twofold: Simulate as nearly as possible the setting in which the problems occur (see Chapter 15 for the rationale for this principle), and find as attractive a setting as possible to increase the attractiveness of the group. In the beginning, if the setting is too informal, it is sometimes difficult to hold the attention of the youth. Group therapists will usually begin in a formal setting and then on occasion move to more attractive locations. Sometimes, the group therapists contract with the group members that a certain degree of work will be required if they want to continue meeting in special places. Although some institutional groups do not have many of these options for security reasons, creative options may exist on the campus itself.

Although it is desirable to have adequate space, recreational equipment, audiovisual aids, chairs that move, opportunities for sports and crafts, and other facilities, most group therapy is carried out with only a few of these amenities. In our opinion, such facilities enhance but are not necessary for successful outcomes. In most cases, group therapists are able to take advantage of the facilities made available to them (or struggled for). It is indeed helpful to have a regular place to meet, at least for the first few meetings, and some protection from external disruption. The most important principle in the use of physical facilities is that the youth do not merely sit around a table and talk about problems and their solutions for an hour. There should be frequent opportunities and adequate space for movement, subgrouping, role playing, and occasional recreational activities.

Summary

In this chapter, the preparation and decisions required for both community and institutional therapy groups were examined. These included looking at factors to be considered in determining size, duration, and frequency of sessions; number of therapists; recruitment of group members; members' selection into the group; and the principles of composition in terms of personal and problem characteristics of the members. Also examined were issues related to the agency sponsorship and physical conditions of the meeting room. In the next chapter, the way in which therapy groups are started (giving orientation, building cohesion, and enhancing motivation) is presented.

CHAPTER 3

Starting the Group

Orientation, Cohesion Building, and Motivation Enhancement

As the group begins, it is first necessary to build a working relationship among the therapist and the group members. To build this relationship, a number of overlapping activities should occur. First, the members must become acquainted with each other, the group therapist(s), and the work of the group. At the same time, the members (and also parents or guardians) are oriented to what they can expect from the group and the therapist and what is expected of them in group therapy to dispel any fears or myths they may have about the group. As the group progresses, more specific orientation to new procedures is provided. Third, in starting the group, one must initially build the cohesion of the group so that the members can establish satisfying relationships with each other and the therapist. Fourth, because in both open and closed groups, members rarely come prepared to identify, much less work on, problems and/or work toward change, their motivation for change should be encouraged. All four topics are interrelated. Let us begin with a discussion of getting acquainted, which is also one way of building cohesion.

Getting Acquainted

In closed community groups, most members come as strangers to the group. No norms or special relationships have yet been established. In residential groups, members are introduced to the others one or a few at a time. The other members already have a history of working together. Norms and special relationships are established. In both instances, the new members are usually anxious about who these new people are and what will be expected of them.

Meeting new people is an uncomfortable and sometimes frightening experience for many. This is especially true when the others also have "problems" or when one is concerned about looking foolish. The first step in helping members to become comfortable in the group is for them to become familiar with each other and to find similarities or connections among themselves. Finding people with similar attributes rapidly reduces the threatening aspect of a new group. Yet the very act of meeting new people can be quite threatening in its own right. To make the task of meeting others as nonthreatening as possible, each person can be required to become acquainted with only one other person at a time. Thus, the initial discussion can take place in pairs. In pairs, everyone has the opportunity to talk about him- or herself immediately and begins to become well acquainted with one other person. Then having each person describe a partner to the larger group removes the pressure one would experience if required to describe oneself to the larger group.

Another advantage of becoming comfortably acquainted with others in the group is the discovery, early in treatment, that one is not the only person with the problem around which the group is organized. As Yalom (1985, p. 7) pointed out, most people enter therapy with the assumption that they are unique in having frightening or unacceptable problems. In this exercise, one rapidly begins to discover that one is not alone. Yalom (1985, pp. 7-9) labeled this "universality" and described it as one of the unique curative factors in group therapy.

A third advantage is that persons who are reluctant to self-disclose find the paired interviews a safe way to begin. In general, they are able to disclose as much as they feel comfortable to disclose. The structure and time limit prevent them from revealing more than they are ready for. In closed groups, the major procedure used is Exercise 3.1.

Exercise 3.1. Getting Acquainted

Purposes: By the end of this exercise, each participant

1. Will have stated the names of all the other participants in the group and described at least two important characteristics of each person in the group

2. Will have talked about him- or herself in a pair

3. Will be able to describe characteristics and expectations of at least one other person in the group in some detail

4. Will have identified concerns or problems shared with other members of the group

5. Will have increased his or her comfort level among the members of the group

Group Task 1: Each participant should interview one person unknown to him or her for 3 minutes. Each participant should find out the other person's hobbies, interests, family arrangement, proudest accomplishment, most frightening situation experienced, place of origin, favorite food, favorite color, the kind of concerns that brought him or her to the group, and the kind of concerns that he or she has about the group. (Depending on the nature of the group, other questions can be added.) So that each interview will be completed in 3 minutes, the group therapist will serve as timekeeper. Interviewers should take notes so that they can remember what to say to the group.

Group Task 2: After everyone has been interviewed, all persons will introduce a partner to the group. (Everyone has 1½ minutes for each introduction.) At the end of the introductions, the members will discuss similarities among them.

In institutional groups, a new member is sometimes interviewed by another member before the session. He or she is also oriented to the group (see below) by that member. Then the member introduces the new person to the group and each old member to the new member. Before the attendance by the new member, the group members discuss how they felt when they entered the group, and if they say they were anxious, the therapist asks how they as a group might make the new person comfortable. In some institutional groups, the introductory exercise as described above for community groups is used every time a new person becomes a part of the group. The sophistication of the interviews usually grows with practice.

Getting acquainted also involves self-disclosure. Exercise 3.1 is the first step in that process. The information, however, is factual and public and does not reveal very much about what the individual is struggling with. In CBIGT, especially in closed groups, the principle of gradual self-disclosure prevails. In that way, no individual is driven away by his or her embarrassment of having revealed too much or having heard too frightening accounts of the experience of others. A second step in this gradual process of self-disclosure is found in Exercise 3.2. In this exercise, rather than talk about themselves, the group members compare themselves to a fictional case. The case shown in Exercise 3.2 was developed specifically for a residential treatment group for adjudicated delinquents. Each therapist would need to design a case similar to but not the same as that of any of the members in his or her group.

Exercise 3.2. A Case Study

Purposes: At the end of this exercise, each participant will have

1. Described how he or she is similar and dissimilar to the case example described below in terms of patterns of responding to stressors and of perceiving which situations appear to lead to stress and anger

2. Revealed some personal concerns and characteristics of his or her behavior, attitudes, or cognitions to the rest of the group

3. Noted how he or she is similar to other members of the group

Individual Tasks: Each person should read the following case and write down how he or she is different from Mike.

Mike is a 16-year-old youth who was sent to the institution because he was found guilty of assault on several different occasions. He has difficulty controlling his anger with family members, peers, and even strangers. When he first gets angry, he feels throbbing in his head, his face tenses, and his fists clench. He begins to sweat. He is even tempered as long as people don't tell him what to do, criticize him, or bump into him. He likes to bowl, play computer games and basketball, and watch TV. He does fair work in school and seems to be improving. He admits that he doesn't work very hard and cuts class whenever he thinks he can get away with it. He hates getting up in the morning but likes to stay up late (when not at the residence) drinking beer and watching TV and just hanging out. He has frequent verbal fights with his mother, whom he hit once. His dad deserted the family 10 years earlier. When Mike is at home, his older cousin, Eddie, a bricklayer, looks in on him from time, and they go bowling together, which Mike says he likes a lot. He never gets mad at Eddie.

Group Task: In subgroups of 4 to 5 members each (assuming the group has 8-12 members), participants should compare their differences from Mike and from each other. They should also note any similarities among themselves.

If the group has some experience together, members may also discuss what characteristics of Mike they think he should work on and why. The subgroups then share their observations with other subgroups.

Orientation

Also at the first session, and usually following the introductory exercises, the members are oriented to the group. In the following sections, we examine orientation of the members and then orientation of their parents. Much of the same content can be included in both orientations.

Orientation of the Members

What?

In orientation, the members are presented with the purpose of the group, the methods used in the group, the rights and responsibilities of the group members, and the responsibilities of the group therapist. In addition, the members are presented with the details of the group program, including the kind the socio-recreational activities available to them. Stressed, too, in orientation is the importance of confidentiality— how they should not speak to others outside the group about the problems discussed by other group members and how this principle applies equally to the therapist.

Why?

There is evidence to support the contention that clear knowledge about therapy and agreement to participate are prerequisites for success in therapy (Hoehn-Saric et al., 1964). Ausubel (1963) provided evidence to link success in learning with advanced knowledge about what one is to learn. It also appears that knowledge about the parameters of a situation reduces one's anxiety about that situation.

Where?

In community as well as institutional groups, the pregroup interviews are an ideal place to initiate orientation. In some institutions, where the intake of new referrals is high, special orientation groups are set up, and the members complete the "course" before they enter regular CBIGT. Usually, in closed groups, orientation occurs in the first session of group therapy. In open groups, orientation is reviewed periodically.

How?

A number of tools are used to orient the members. A treatment contract gives them an overview of what they are expected to do and what help they can receive. Videotapes of a typical group session may be presented in the pregroup meeting or first group session. Former members may describe their experiences in similar groups. On a weekly basis, the group session agenda provides an orientation to the specific activities for the given session. Finally, as each new intervention procedure is introduced, a specific description of assumptions of that procedure is provided, and the specific activities involved in each procedure are briefly reviewed. Each of these procedures is examined below.

Therapy Contracts. The following is a contract for a group of young adolescents (aged 13-14) in a community group whose members were referred for disruptive behavior in the classroom. It is a closed group.

> I, as a member of the Players, agree to discuss the problems I am having at home and at school and to try to help myself and others to find better ways of dealing with problems. I understand that we'll do lots of role playing, too. I agree to attend all meetings and to come on time. I understand that the therapist will not talk about the group to anyone except her supervisor, and I agree not to talk about other individuals in the group to others outside the group. In return, Ms. Johnson and the clinic will give us a room to meet in, refreshments, games, and trips, and she'll lead the group every week. I will talk about concerns and role playing and will do fun things for 10 minutes at the end of the meetings. I understand that there will be eight meetings and that each meeting will last 60 minutes.

The therapy contract involves a statement, usually in writing, of the general responsibilities of the members and of the group therapist and the agency over an extended period of time. The contract usually specifies general goals and commonly used procedures as well as mutual expectations. One important condition of a group therapy contract is that the members agree to help one another. The therapy contract differs from a contingency contract (see Chapter 8) in that the latter specifies a more narrow relationship between an expected member behavior and the reinforcement that follows. The therapy contract is broader in scope and covers a longer time period than the contingency contract, which is usually from week to week.

The contract, however, is not a static set of statements or agreements. As the relationships of the members to each other are established, as negotiation skills are enhanced, and as early expectations are clarified, the contracts begin to receive greater input from the members. The conditions reflect increasingly the members' ideas as to what they can learn from the group and what they want from the group. Moreover, detail and structure are increasingly added to the contract. One cannot clarify every detail at a first meeting. The group therapist must successively structure the contract in a step-by-step process as the members experience growing success and satisfaction with the approach. In the initial example, after the members had interacted with each other for several meetings, the revised contract had developed as follows:

> I, as a member of the Players, agree to bring to each meeting a problem situation that I encountered during the week for which I will seek the help of the group. These problem situations are usually events that occur with other people in which I am dissatisfied with what I did or said. We will then help each other, through demonstrations and role playing, to try out new ways of dealing with the problems.
>
> I agree to do homework between sessions, which will usually be to try out what I learned in the group. I understand that at the end of each session I will evaluate the session and my own behavior in the session. If group problems arise, I will discuss them with the other members of the group. I will continue to have refreshments and games at each session and, if the group earns it, a field trip at the end of next month. The group also gets to meet in the music room from now on and to play the piano if the guys don't mess around with it. Ms. Johnson will also coach us to be the discussion leaders of the group ourselves, but only if we volunteer. Ms. Johnson and the guys and I agree not to talk about what any of the guys say in the group or what kind of trouble they are in.

Another example of a residential therapy contract is the following. It should be noted that there are more required elements in this contract.

> I understand that attendance and participation in the group sessions are an important part of my therapy. I agree to attend all sessions from which I am not formally excused, to come on time, and to participate to the best of my ability. I agree to develop extragroup tasks in the group and, once having agreed to them, to complete them in the time specified. I agree to the rules of the group. If I am dissatisfied with this agreement or the specific rules, I will bring this up for discussion in the group.

Early in the therapy of highly resistive members, the contract may be informal and extremely general, in contrast to the examples above. The expectations from the members may be minimal. The adolescents may be asked only to observe and to participate when they are willing. The only expectation is that they not be disruptive. They are made aware of the group therapist's long-term expectations, but initially they are asked to do nothing to advance those therapeutic goals. Vinter (1985a) referred to this as a *preliminary therapy contract*. The following is an example of the formation of a preliminary contract.

The eight group members were all early juvenile offenders referred to the agency by their parole officers. At the first session, they were reluctant to discuss problems or the reasons that had brought them into contact with the police. Because it was winter and they had no place to go, they agreed to meet with the group therapist twice a week and use the school gym afterwards for 30 minutes and eat the food provided by the group therapist. They agreed in exchange to spend 30 minutes talking about the school and their families. They also said they understood that they had to follow the school rules or that they would be kicked out of the session and reported to their parole officer. There was no formal written contract initially.

It was clear that the group therapist could not initially expect these youth to take much responsibility for the group activities or their contribution to those activities. The above minimal contract was informal, but it provided a foot in the door for developing a later, more demanding contract.

For most groups initially and for the above group in a later phase of development, the therapy contract is more specific and more demanding of the members. Just as the group therapy contract orients the members and significant others to the overall group approach, the use of weekly session agendas developed with the members orients members to the expectations and structure of each session.

Videotapes and Models. To give the members, other youth, and concerned adults a vivid picture of what happens in a group, some group therapists have used videotapes of a session. Because of the confidentiality of a given session, a number of youth were hired to role-play a part of a session in which members brought up areas of concern that were dealt with by the group. The tape included a game played at the end of the session. The tape was designed and produced by members of another group to be of help to others, in a task that was an excellent cohesion builder in its own right.

Where no such facility was available, older youth from a previous group shared their experiences with a new group of youth. They shared the difficulties as well as the usefulness of the experience. The models, too, found the orientation presentation a useful activity. They were enthusiastically reinforced by the new members. Moreover, such an activity served as a vehicle for enhancing generalization of change (see Chapter 15).

Session Agendas. Most group therapists use the session agenda to plan their weekly sessions. The agendas are either put on the chalkboard or duplicated and distributed to the members. Most adolescents seem impressed with having a typed agenda. Initially, the agenda is planned by the group therapist. In institutions, the treatment team may also suggest items to be included in the agenda. Soon the youth are also involved in the planning of the agenda as a way of extending their involvement. To prevent arbitrary items from being added to the agenda, one criterion is that each item must clearly be linked to the purpose of treatment or must be a reward for effective treatment behavior. At the end of a given session, the group therapist may describe his or her tentative plan for the next session to the group for their comments. Some group therapists offer special planning sessions between sessions with representatives of the group. Thus, the agenda is an excellent planning document and provides one more opportunity for adolescents to be involved in the planning process. Furthermore, the agenda makes it possible to set limits in a nonpersonalized way on off-task behavior, as we see in the following example.

Group Therapist: How many people would like to tell us what they did last week on their extragroup tasks?

Larry: Last night I watched the baseball game on TV. The Blue Hens won it with a home run in the ninth. Boy, was that great. Anybody else see it?

Group Therapist: Hey! Larry! Let's talk about that when we get to the break. Right now we're talking about "homework"; that's Item #2. Look on your agenda.

One example of an agenda—the one to which the above group therapist is referring—is the following for a third session.

   1. Gordie will introduce new member, Charlie.
  *2. Review home tasks.
  *3. Review postsession evaluations from the previous week and home task
      completion rates for the last five sessions.
   4. Discuss problem of irregular attendance in group; then problem-solve
      what we can do about it.
   5. Plan for next week's session with guests from school.
   6. Role-play Harry's and Annette's situation in trying to talk to the
      teacher about getting back into school.
   7. Discuss everyone else's success in talking with teachers in general.
  *8. Design home tasks for next week in pairs.
   9. Play board game for 10 minutes.
 *10. Fill in postsession questionnaire.
  11. Eat treats brought by therapist.

The items starred (*) are standard items in most agendas. Some of the
others, such as having some recreational activity and treats, may also be
standard in some groups.

Orientation to New Change Procedures. Before a change procedure is
implemented, the youth are presented with the assumptions of the procedures and steps to be followed. They usually practice the procedure under
simulated conditions by either discussing a case study or role-playing a
simulation. In this way, they are in a position to choose whether they will
use the given procedure in their own treatment plan. As each of the
procedures is explained in the following chapters, the orientation for the
youth is also described.

Orientation of the Parents

   Wherever possible, one contacts parents before the first youth group
session to inform them of what will occur in their child's group and how
they might assist in the therapeutic process. Where closed community
groups for the youth are organized, often the parents are oriented as a
group. Occasionally, the parents have asked for an additional group
session for themselves to learn the skills being used by the group
therapist. Such orientation sessions, either individually or in groups, are
sometimes a requirement for parents before their child is admitted to the
group.

In an ongoing program, parents can be used to orient other parents. Before the parents of a newly institutionalized client or client in a community group are finally admitted, they are contacted by another parent who tells them about his or her experience as a parent of a young person in trouble. Providing that the message is for the most part positive, the parent's message is much more palatable than the message of the professional staff member. Family therapists may orient the youth and parents at the same time. This communicates the message that the role of the parent is expected to be active.

Just as with the youth, the content of individual or group orientation sessions for parents includes an explanation of the purpose of the group, some of the basic assumptions of therapy, the activities of the group, the type of behaviors and situations to be worked on, the role of home tasks and the ways in which the parents might help in that area, and a brief explanation of the major intervention strategies. Brief testimonials by parents of youth in previous groups are often included in the parents' orientation session if carried out in groups.

Because orientation often reduces the anxiety associated with a new group, it contributes to building the cohesion of the group. Other contributors to building cohesion are discussed in the following section.

Strategies for Building Cohesion

As mentioned in Chapter 2, most group therapists have argued that cohesion is an essential dimension of group interaction (see, e.g., Flowers & Schwartz, 1985; Yalom, 1985) and is likely to stimulate further self-disclosure. Yalom, who referred to cohesion as a curative factor in itself, pointed out that cohesion in groups is akin to relationship in individual therapy. Thus, it is crucial to attend to this dimension. In most of the research identified in Chapter 1, it was noted that little description was given of how the group or cohesion was used in therapy. It is the major contention of this book that an important set of interventions is eliminated if therapists fail to build cohesion or deal with other group attributes. In the early phases of treatment, therefore, a set of therapist strategies is required for encouraging cohesion. High levels of cohesion seem to result in enhancing the members' motivation to change, their appreciation of the opinions and suggestions of other group members and the group therapist, and the challenge and enjoyment of the group experience. Some of the strategies for building cohesion have already been suggested earlier and will be elaborated on here. Most important among these strategies are finding similarities among the participants; developing interesting and challenging group tasks; creating opportunities for broad participation by all members; providing socio-recreational activities as reinforcers; enhancing members' careful listening to each other; providing protection from excessive punishment or confrontation; keeping the tempo fast, especially in the early sessions; and creating and taking advantage of opportunities for choice and decision making by the members. Let us look at each of these strategies.

Finding Similarities

As clients note that others have similar problems and similar characteristics, it appears that cohesion increases. To make the youth aware of such similarities, wherever possible, group therapists are encouraged to comment on resemblances among the members. In Exercises 3.1 and 3.2, the youth are asked to note similarities among them in the group discussion. Of equal importance is helping the youth to maintain their individuality. Thus, a balance of perceived uniqueness and similarities is emphasized. The message is frequently relayed that although the youth have many similarities, each is a unique human being with unique qualities and concerns.

Developing Interesting and Challenging Group Tasks

There are two types of group tasks: internal tasks and extragroup tasks. Both are essential to the model described here. Internal group tasks are therapeutic activities that occur during a group session. They may be designed by the therapist or members or both. They involve training in specific therapeutic skills or real-world skills necessary to complete extragroup tasks. They often are taught in the form of group exercises.

Extragroup tasks are descriptions of activities or behaviors that the youth agree to perform in the real world outside the group. They are usually designed by each member for him- or herself in the group with the help of other members and the therapist, and they are monitored at subsequent sessions. Occasionally, shared group tasks are negotiated. The more interesting and the more challenging both types of tasks are, the greater the cohesion in the group. Techniques for developing useful, interesting, and challenging tasks are discussed throughout this book, and extragroup tasks in particular are discussed in Chapter 11. Most, but not all, tasks are directly related to learning new ways of handling difficult situations. Some tasks are primarily related to increasing the cohesion of the group, such as the use of socio-recreational activities.

Socio-Recreational Activities as Reinforcers for Participation

At the end of most sessions, the youth have the opportunity of participating in 10 minutes of socio-recreational activities, provided that the work of the session is completed. Such activities include board games, small crafts, shooting basketballs, playing Hangman and other paper-and-pencil games, or whatever the members themselves choose the week before. Details of these activities, how they are planned, and how they are integrated into treatment are discussed in Chapter 13. A number of brief informal activities are also introduced to the group as cohesion builders. For example, one therapist used magic tricks at the beginning of a session. The trick was demonstrated but not explained until the end of the session as a reinforcement for getting the work done.

Projects more closely related to the treatment goals are also organized and carried out by the members. One group made a videotape of "guys like them." Many groups plan for and carry out service activities in the community. Several experienced groups prepare to and become models for new groups. Cross-age tutoring has also been used. The therapy group becomes momentarily a teacher education group that focuses on strengths. The preparation for such projects not only increases the attractiveness of the group but creates opportunity for diverse roles and broad participation by all the members.

Creating Opportunities for Broad Participation

To achieve broad participation, all the members must develop adequate discussion skills. These are useful not only in the group but in school and in other social organizations outside the group. Early in treatment, the youth must be able to share information with others, to participate actively, to self-disclose, to ask questions of each other, to listen effectively to each other, to provide constructive feedback for each other, and to receive positive and critical feedback from each other. The members are taught these skills as a part of therapy, usually in group exercises. The exercises themselves are structured in such a way as to achieve broad participation. First, the exercises (as opposed to the therapist) demand individual preparation, first usually in writing, either in the group or as an extragroup task. The results of this preparation are discussed in pairs or larger subgroups to ensure broad participation, and then the subgroups are expected to report back to the complete group. During role playing, the therapist makes sure that everyone has a role, including the observer, and the roles are frequently shifted. When information is disseminated, the members are asked to teach what they have learned to a partner, who in turns teaches it to the group. If the opportunity exists, they are asked to teach it to others outside the group. With these structures, it is difficult to avoid participating.

To evaluate the breadth of participation, one of the questions on the postsession questionnaire is "How much did you participate in today's session?" The precoded answers are "more than others," "somewhat more than others," "about the same as others," "somewhat less than others," and "much less than others." In addition, the therapist observes the distribution of participation as much as possible. In later chapters, other exercises that demand increasingly more self-disclosure and eventually commitment to change will be presented.

It should be noted that participation need not be always in a circle discussing given issues. The opportunity for physical movement also increases the attraction of the group. For this reason, physical movement is incorporated into role playing and the recreational activities. When no program opportunities present themselves, the therapist may arbitrarily shuffle the seating positions or do relaxation or stretching exercises to keep members from getting bored "just talking."

Gradual Self-Disclosure

Cognitive-behavioral and other treatment procedures cannot be applied unless the youth are willing to disclose or identify problematic behavior in specific situations. The youth cannot decide whether they are willing to work on a behavior unless it is first disclosed to the group. Self-disclosure at any one time should occur at about the same level for most of the youth in the group. Too much or too intimate self-disclosure in the first session will often drive away other members. A concern of many youth in approaching therapy groups is that they might reveal too much about themselves and appear strange or "weird" to other members of the group. To deal with this concern in the early phase of therapy, the sessions are structured so that the youth need only disclose their concerns and problems gradually. In fact, if one member begins to disclose his or her concerns in too intimate detail, the therapist may encourage him or her to postpone the details of the revelation. To ensure gradual self-disclosure and broad participation, a number of intragroup tasks are proposed. Exercise 3.1, the introductory exercise described above, provides each group member with objective information for the most part about every other member. Exercise 3.2 goes a little further and provides a picture of how each group member views him- or herself. Exercise 4.5, described in the next chapter, facilitates the sharing of situations that seem to induce stress, anger, or other strong emotions. All these exercises not only enhance gradually increasing self-disclosure but structure increasingly broad and relevant participation in the early sessions. In so doing, they increase the cohesion of the group.

Protection From Excessive Punishment or Premature Confrontation

Because ridicule by others is one of the major stimuli to eliciting anxiety and anger in youth, its occurrence in group interaction must be dealt with immediately as a group problem. Moreover, if it is used frequently by any individuals, its use can become a target of change. Ridicule and other forms of verbal punishment reduce the attractiveness of the group and the motivation to change.

Confrontation of a group member without his or her permission may be a form of punishment. It is well within acceptable limits for the therapist or for group members to point out that certain behaviors may have undesired consequences or that some individuals seem to respond to stress- or anger-inducing situations in certain stereotypic ways. But this is done only after members are trained in giving feedback constructively in a nonsarcastic and matter-of-fact tone of voice, in the form of a hypothesis ("One possibility is that . . .") and with the use of an "I" statement ("In my opinion, . . ." or "I think that . . .").

In CBIGT groups during the orientation phase, the members' protection from ridicule, inappropriate criticism, premature and inadequately supported confrontation, name calling, and other strong verbal punishment is explicitly stated. Should these occur anyway, they are identified, if not by the recipient, then by the group therapist. The reaction of those who receive punishing communications is discussed, and alternate ways of communicating negative or disagreeable messages are examined. Scrutinized, too, are the conditions outside the group under which each of the members receives heavy confrontation, ridicule, or other punishment, his or her response to it, and strategies for dealing with it. Not only does the reduction of such negative statements increase the cohesion of the group, but members are trained in the skills of delivering and receiving criticism constructively. Unique applications of feedback training in groups are discussed in detail in Chapter 8.

Encouraging Careful Listening Among Members

One factor that clearly reduces the attraction to the group experience is the impression that one is not being listened to. Many youth are notoriously poor listeners, although they would like to be listened to. To resolve this problem and increase the cohesion of the group, the youth are taught the skills of effective listening. They are taught how to use appropriate eye contact when someone is speaking, to paraphrase what others are saying, and to ask for clarification when they are uncertain what the speaker means. Exercises can be developed early in treatment to enhance these skills, should they be undeveloped, and the youth are reinforced by the group therapist when such skills are actually applied. In institutions, the residential staff also reinforce this behavior when they observe it in the residence. Not only does the general group climate change when the youth learn to listen effectively to each other, but these skills are essential to functioning in school and elsewhere in the extra-group world.

Another discussion skill related to effective listening is that of waiting one's turn before speaking. The opposite of this is constant interruption. In his or her enthusiasm, at times, one member may interrupt another. Occasional interruptions are not a problem. But when interruptions are a pattern, an exercise can be used in which each group member is required to say what the previous speaker has said before he or she tells his or her own ideas. This exercise is carried out for only 5 minutes at a time, but it may be repeated at frequent intervals. This exercise slows the interaction somewhat and in our experience seems to limit the number of interruptions dramatically. The brief duration is required so as to avoid boredom and annoyance with the slow pace.

Keeping the Tempo Fast in the Early Sessions

The attention span of many troubled youth is often limited. A few seem to suffer from attention deficit disorder. Others are just poorly motivated. To hold their interest, a wide range of rapidly changing activities that afford greater opportunity for frequent reinforcement are used. Specifically, role plays are short, feedback is brief, recreational activities last 10 minutes, and physical activity is interspersed with talking. To keep activities brief, the therapist puts time limits on each item of the agenda and, in keeping with the principle of maximum involvement (see below), uses a rotating member of the group as "time-keeper." Later, as the members become more interested in and enthusiastic about the group, activities can last longer and be more complex.

Teaching a Skill or Solving a Problem Early in Treatment

To demonstrate as well as explain what the group is all about, it is valuable as early as the second session to deal with some shared problem or teach some important skill that will be used throughout the rest of therapy. Examples of skills taught in community groups are how to give and receive constructive feedback and how to listen effectively because both these skills are used throughout all sessions of therapy.

Problems that often arise and can be dealt in the first or second session have been determining what and how to tell significant others (parents, friends, relatives) about the group and how to maintain confidentiality of what people share in the group. In community groups, in particular, practical problems such as transportation, parking, or caring for younger siblings are also dealt with. Solving problems and learning new skills early in therapy make most youth view the approach as eminently practical.

The steps for building group cohesion also contribute to building motivation to change, especially the opportunity to make choices for one's own life. In the following section, other principles for building motivation and hence cohesion of the group are scrutinized.

Building Motivation

Without motivation to change, none of the procedures discussed in this book will be effective in bringing about change. Motivation is defined as a state of readiness or eagerness to change that can fluctuate over time (Miller & Rollnick, 1991, p. 14). This state, according to Miller and Rollnick, can be influenced by the therapist and, I would add, also by the group. Motivation can also be regarded as a group phenomenon. When the vast majority of youth are committed to working toward change, they will often swing the minority to their point of view. The opposite seems to be true as well. In both cases, a "norm" is established. Thus, an early task of the group therapist is to help build that motivation or readiness to change as a shared norm.

When youth first come to group therapy, low motivation can usually be expected. After all, most youth are required or even coerced by others to enter therapy. Most come to the group with the intention of remaining silent, often out of embarrassment and fear of sounding stupid, as a way of showing how tough they are, or as a way of demonstrating that they do not need help. The youth often fear that decisions about their future are being taken out of their hands and that their freedom will be severely restricted. Part of building motivation occurs in the orientation, especially when the therapist presents models of how the group has helped others.

A number of overlapping principles can be applied to the task of building motivation. All these principles involve the actions of the therapist in facilitating the motivation of the group members and preventing reduction in the level of motivation. Building motivation takes longer with some groups than with others. Nevertheless, the following principles should guide group therapists' actions in the early phase of group therapy. The application of these principles does not precede the more structured elements of the program but runs parallel to them. One of the foremost principles is encouraging choice wherever possible and in increasing measure on the part of the youth.

Delegating Responsibility and Encouraging Choice

Initially, group members are asked to follow simple instructions during the session. But wherever possible, they are asked to help make decisions for the group and for themselves. Even in the first session, the members decide on the content of the introductory interviews, and the use of subgroups that cannot all be simultaneously monitored by the therapist allows members to function at times without the therapist present but within specified guidelines. The use of "brainstorming" whenever suggestions or advice is requested or advisable involves all the members in generating suggestions or advice, but the ultimate decision as to what the target person (or set of persons with a common issue or problem) will do is his or her own decision. However, the target person making a decision is always asked to evaluate the advice in terms of short- and long-term consequences and his or her resources and skills for carrying out the selected option. In designing extragroup tasks, each person uses either the group or a "buddy" as a consultant. But each must determine for him- or herself the content of that task. Though the therapist provides structure in the form of options, choice by the target person is essential to stimulate and maintain motivation. Later, youth are afforded the opportunity to select their own goals, although they are coached and evaluated in the process of selection with all the group members. Throughout this book, wherever choice is an option, it will be pointed out. In some group approaches, deviant youth are pressured to make certain choices. In this approach, the conditions are created in which youth can choose or not choose one of many options.

Self-efficacy refers to the client's belief that he or she can succeed with a specific task. According to Bandura (1977a), it is an important element in building motivation for change and a good predictor of favorable treatment outcomes. The more youth choose targets and change actions for themselves, the more likely they are to view their actions as something they have done for themselves and can do for themselves in the future.

Expressing Empathy

Problem behavior, conflict, aggression, stealing, argumentative behavior, and hyperactive behavior for many troubled youth represent a way of life. Most behavior is maintained by the environmental response to that behavior, and, for the most part, responses from peers and even family members (in the form of attention and control) have tended to sustain the undesired behavior. The group therapist and the group members are encouraged to listen to each person as he or she enters the group and to note how these behaviors are maintained and what these behaviors do for the person. A behavior may bring youth recognition in their peer group. It may help them adapt to an unchallenging and even boring school setting. It may give them control over their parents. If the group fails to listen and acknowledge the importance of this behavior, motivation will be dramatically reduced. Empathic listening permits members of the group to tell their story before they are asked to change. The role of the group therapist, in addition to listening, is to note that others in the group have had similar experiences and similar rewards for their maladaptive behavior and to encourage others to note those experiences.

In community groups, the opportunity for long discourse on each member's perception of his or her problems is usually limited. As noted earlier, everyone must have the opportunity to speak in a given group session. The dilemma is how we can listen empathetically and at the same time restrict extensive presentations. As group members compare themselves in predetermined and limited ways, they are free to describe themselves and a piece of their problem as they experience it. Even in frequent and brief responses, each person can experience the empathy of the group therapist and eventually that of the other group members. Participation in the exercises provides the work of a session but does not demand commitment to change. The work itself may eventually contribute to that motivation as the group members make small achievements and become involved in the interaction.

Contrasting Advantages and
Disadvantages of Group Membership

As problems are presented, not only are the functions or positive effects of those behaviors looked at, but also the consequences, both long and short term. The youth are helped to weigh both advantages and disadvantages of whatever their behavior may be. This process of weighing both the advantages and disadvantages of problem behavior is supplemented by the observations of the other members. Some members are more aware of consequences than others. This process of weighing the pros and cons of a given behavior and permitting each group member to choose whether a given behavior or even lifestyle is an important target gives greater control to the client and increases the likelihood of his or her decision to work toward change.

Rolling With Resistance

Miller and Rollnick (1991, pp. 59-60) stressed that in working with alcohol- and drug-addicted patients, ambivalence about changing is normal and should be expected. The same is true with troubled youth. By rolling with resistance, the group therapist notes the ambivalence and states directly that it is a common and perfectly acceptable phenomenon because every behavior has both advantages and disadvantages. In this way, the therapist avoids arguing with the group members about whether they should or should not change. To operationalize this principle, once a target behavior has been identified, youth are asked to list both the advantages and disadvantages of that behavior. If one member is stuck, the others in the group will suggest both possible advantages and disadvantages of performing the problem behavior.

Eliciting Motivational Statements

Miller and Rollnick (1991, pp. 55-63) identified at least four types of motivational statements: problem recognition, expression of concern, intention to change, and optimism about change. An example of problem recognition is the statement "This is really getting serious. I'll get kicked out of school." An example of an expression of concern is "I'm really getting worried about this." An example of intention to change is "I guess I'm going to have do something about my horsing around in school." And an example of optimism about change might be "I really think I can do something about this problem." Statements such as these can be elicited in the group by the group's looking at the consequences of present behavior. The therapist asks the group members (rather than telling them) what the consequences of their present behavior might be. The therapist may use a case study first and have the group look at the consequences for the person in the case. When a member describes consequences of present patterns of behavior that are negative, the therapist might state, "I can see how that might concern you," or might ask the others, "To what degree would that concern the rest of you?" Once a group member commits to a motivational statement, the therapist reinforces the statement with "That's an important step you've just taken" or I can imagine that that's really difficult for you to say, good for you. What do the rest of you think?" As motivational statements begin to increase in frequency, the therapist can summarize the statements he or she has heard and reinforce the group for their growing commitment to change. Of course, verbal commitment to change is not enough.

Summary

In starting a therapy group, four initial sets of overlapping strategies must be considered: helping members get acquainted, orienting the members to what they will be doing in the group, building the cohesion of the group, and increasing the motivation of the group members. Although all these activities are performed in the early sessions, they continue throughout therapy.

Getting acquainted involves the use of introductory exercises. Orientation involves brief descriptions and presentations by former members of what happens in the group. Cohesion building involves eliciting broad involvement of the members, protecting them from excessive confrontation, providing them with challenging tasks, and providing occasional recreational activities. All of these actions, if successful, increase the motivation of the members. Other strategies for motivation enhancement include giving maximum opportunity for choice to clients, supporting their self-efficacy, expressing empathy, normalizing and accepting ambivalence to change, helping members to weigh the advantages and disadvantages of the problematic behavior, and eliciting and reinforcing motivational statements. These principles are overlapping in that orientation contributes to both the building of cohesion and the enhancement of motivation and in that motivation and cohesion building contribute to each other. These principles will be demonstrated throughout this text as the specific components of the technology are presented. In the next chapter, assessment procedures as they are used in the group are presented because they too are initiated early in treatment.

PART II

Assessment and Goal Setting in Groups

CHAPTER 4

Assessment in Groups

Interviewing and Observation Strategies

Before intervention can take place, it is necessary to determine the nature of the presenting problems and the client's resources for dealing with the problems. In a cognitive-behavioral approach, individual problems are assessed in terms of specific situations that are perceived as problematic; the behavioral, emotional, and cognitive responses to these situations; and the consequences for the individual of these responses. Determining the resources for and impediments to the achieving of therapy goals is also a function of assessment. (For a more detailed discussion of assessment from an individual, broad-based cognitive-behavioral perspective, see Cormier & Cormier, 1991, pp. 171-213.) Special emphasis in this chapter is placed on group strategies and exercises that facilitate the assessment process. The functions of diagnosis and more general descriptions in the assessment process are also considered. But first, the purposes of assessment in the group are discussed.

One set of purposes of assessment of individuals in CBIGT involves the types of data that the assessment process is designed to collect. A second set of purposes is concerned with the types of decisions that must be made following the collection of data. Each set will be examined separately.

The data collection purposes are:

1. To determine what the individual and the parents or other significant persons in the individual's life perceive to be his or her "problems" and to help the individual formulate the problems in such a way as to make them responsive to therapy
2. To identify the situations that evoke anger or violence, stress, other strong emotional responses, and/or maladaptive behaviors that trouble the individual or the world about him or her
3. To discover the range and intensity of the maladaptive and adaptive (but deficient) responses and the consequences of these responses for the individual
4. To determine the individual's physical, material, and psychological resources for therapy and impediments to sucessful therapy
5. To ascertain the individual's initial and later motivation for change

The above data are collected:

1. To provide information for ascertaining the most relevant therapy goals
2. To develop a plan for ascertaining the most effective intervention strategies
3. To determine whether the small therapy group is the best place to deal with the problem(s) and, if so, the kind of group in which the individual can best be served
4. To ascertain whether the immediate family or other more distant relatives and persons in the community can be involved in the treatment process
5. To take the first step in evaluating whether ongoing therapy is effective or whether the completed treatment was effective by providing a baseline to which later achievements can be compared

To achieve these purposes, two methods of collecting information are used: mutual interviewing by the group members and therapist and systematic measurement. In this chapter, the emphasis will be for the most part on the uses of group interviewing to obtain an effective assessment and training youth in the needed interviewing skills and concepts. Measurement strategies will primarily be discussed in the next chapter, although they will be referred to in this chapter.

Three preconditions of effective group interviewing exist: the comfort of the individual with the therapist and other group members, the motivation of the individual to self-disclose, and the skill of the group members in interviewing each other. In the first phase of treatment, the group therapist must work simultaneously to enhance the relationships among members and with the therapist and to encourage and reinforce gradually increasing self-disclosure and motivation (see Chapter 3). At the same time, the group must begin the process of defining problem situations so that a work norm is established and members are trained in the necessary interviewing skills. Throughout this chapter, the group process issues of interviewing will be described along with the content issues.

Although assessment is the predominant theme during the pregroup interview and the early group sessions, assessment continues throughout treatment. As members learn to trust each other, the nature of the material that they share becomes more relevant and richer in content. Initially, determining the appropriate group for each individual and then establishing his or her target problems are the foci. As therapy goals and interventions occur, new data are collected that refine the content of assessment. Later, continuing assessment is used to facilitate decision making and finally evaluation of outcome. Determining whether someone should be in a group and the characteristics of that group has already been discussed in Chapter 2. In this chapter, situational and resource analysis aspects of assessment will be examined.

Situational Analysis

This section describes the ways in which situational analysis contributes to treatment planning, information is accumulated to make a situational analysis, and the group is used and trained in the process of collecting individual information and carrying out situational and resource analysis. Attention is also paid to the ways in which the family and significant others may facilitate the information-gathering process.

Cognitive-behavioral approaches to assessment are quite different from traditional approaches that emphasize diagnosis of personality traits. In CBIGT assessment, "The focus shifts from describing situation-free people with broad trait adjectives to analyzing the specific interactions between conditions and the cognitions and behaviors of interest" (Mischel, 1973, p. 265). However, as is pointed out at the end of this chapter, diagnostic categories suggested by referring sources may suggest areas of situational concern for the group therapist. Moreover, general patterns of responses and situations are identified through examination of recurring situations and responses.

In the following subsections, we will describe how each of the components of the situation-response-consequence pattern is formulated and how youth are trained in the group to describe these phenomena. Each of the components is described separately for purposes of analysis.

Situations

The problem situation is the set of stimulus events, both internal and external, that trigger or set the conditions for a response with which either the individual or society is extremely dissatisfied. In the following examples, the group members are telling about situations that they experience as problems for them. In most cases, these situations are related to a more general problem. Although the emphasis in this section is on the situation, in the excerpts below, the general problem, the responses, and the consequences are also exemplified.

Art: I have a lot of trouble trying to stop using drugs (general problem). I thought I had it licked. Then, just last week after school, this dude came along and offered me some free stuff, really good stuff. He really pressured me (situation), and I gave in but only took three drags (a behavioral response). The next thing I knew, I was higher than a rocket (immediate consequence). It was a great feeling. The next day, I was depressed and worried my parole officer might find out (long-term consequences).

Gwen: I guess I worry a lot (general problem). For example, yesterday, when my mom was gone and I was alone in my bedroom for a while (situation), I worried that she might die and then I'd be alone forever (cognitive response). Once I started worrying, I couldn't sleep (consequence).

Billy: I have a quick temper, and it gets me into trouble (general problem). Just this morning, some older guys were giving me a hard time at school. They called me some names (situation). No, they didn't hit me or anything like that. I don't let anybody mess with me (cognitive response). I started yelling names at them, and I pulled out my pocketknife and opened it up (behavioral response). They ran off (immediate consequence). That's when the principal caught me (intermediate consequence). That was the third time something like that happened this week. I'm going to get suspended (long-term consequence), but it wasn't my fault. They shouldn't have threatened me (cognition or belief).

Sue Jane: I don't let anyone push me around, no matter what happens (problem). Last night, my mom told me to do the dishes. She didn't ask. And when I didn't come right away, she dragged me away from the couch and put me in front of the dishes (situation). So I broke a few of them (behavioral response). I showed her (cognitive response), and she grounded me for a month (consequence).

In the above examples, group members identify recurring situations to which they responded with dysfunctional behaviors or cognitions. All of the situations involve interaction with others. Each of the situations is further characterized by being problematic or stress or anger inducing to the person who describes it. Most had immediate or long-term negative consequences. The goal of treatment would be to help clients either to modify their overt responses to the situation, change their evaluation of the situation, or avoid the situation. None of these strategies can occur without a careful definition of the components of the situation and the client's responses to it.

Interactive Situations

In the above examples, the description of the situation or problematic event was complete insofar as the following questions could be answered: Who was involved? When did the situation occur? What was happening in the situation? Where did the situation take place? What were the characteristics of that location? Was this a recurring event? Two additional questions are asked later in the assessment process: What were you thinking during the situation, and what were you feeling? Usually, answers to each of these questions will eventually reveal the appropriate target and eventually the method of intervention. If asked to describe a problem they recently encountered, youth rarely in the initial phases of treatment do so in terms of specific components. The situations tend to be presented in vague or highly complex terms. When a situation is introduced, the above questions are asked first by the group therapist and eventually by the members of each other.

Noninteractive Situations

Most but not all situations are interactive. For example, a youth may have the urge to have a drink without any obvious external personal stimulus. He may see an ad on TV, see a bottle lying around the house, or even just remember how he felt the last time he had a drink. Or a youth may begin to think about the death of his brother for no apparent reason and then become sad or depressed. In most cases, the stimuli are private or cognitive. Obviously, the question of who was involved is answered by the target person as him- or herself.

Shared Situations

Whether a situation is interactive or not, in most groups some situations are discovered to be held in common by several or most of the members. Although the responses to shared situations are usually quite varied, the discovery of common situations serves to make the intervention process in groups more efficient because of both mutual modeling of self-disclosure and a wealth of potential alternative responses made available to each of the group members. The group therapist can also devote more time to helping the group deal with a shared situation because it is relevant to almost all the members of the group. All of the examples in the preceding section involved shared situations with some or all of the group members. One example of a shared situation commonly discussed by many troubled youth is the situation in which they are criticized or "put down" by another youth, a sibling, or an adult. In most cases, anger, violence, threats, defensiveness, dysfunctional thoughts, and/or escape are common responses. Another frequent situation involves friends or family members pressuring the youth to perform an illegal behavior (e.g., taking drugs, breaking and entering a house, or participating in nonconsensual sexual activity).

Training Youth in Formulating the Situation

To orient group members to situational analysis, the therapist explains very briefly the concepts of the general problem, the situation, the response, and the consequence and then provides examples. He or she notes the link of the general problem to the specific situation. If the group is an open group, the therapist asks older members of the group to explain the concepts to the new members and provide the newcomers with examples from their own experience. It is also possible in closed groups to use former members for this purpose. This strategy, used throughout therapy, is based on the assumption that youth learn better from other youth. Moreover, it provides additional practice for experienced youth, which increases the likelihood of generalization for them.

After orientation and the presentation of many examples by the group therapist and/or experienced group members, group members are asked to describe the kinds of situations they have encountered in which they (or other people) have been unhappy or dissatisfied with their responses. Usually, they are first asked to describe the situation briefly in writing that may occur either in the group or as homework. Then they are asked to present it aloud to the group one at a time or to a partner, who shares their situation with the full group.

Sometimes, to prepare the group for the above task, the following exercise can be used. The therapist distributes one or two cards to each of the participants. On one of the cards is written "Describe a problem situation." The other cards contain one of the following questions: Who was involved? When did the situation occur? What was happening in the situation? Where did the situation take place? What were the characteristics of that location? Was this a recurring event? What were you thinking during and following the situation? What were you feeling during and following the event?

Usually the group therapist will describe the first problematic situation from his or her own experience and then prompt the group members in the use of their cards. Afterwards, he or she redistributes the cards. (The therapist may take one him- or herself depending on the number of people in the group.) In the following excerpt, the group therapist has just provided her own situation, and the group members have asked the questions on their cards. After answering their questions or acknowledging their corrections, she has redistributed the cards.

Group Therapist: (Like a circus barker) Okay, everyone pick a card. Be sure you get a good one! Now think for a moment how you will ask the question that is on your card. Feel free to ask it in your own way. Okay, who has the "problem situation" card, that's a hard one. Aaaah, Maya?

Maya: My situation is when anybody tries to boss me around.

Group Therapist: Hey, that fits you to a T. Now who is the big winner? Who has the card with "Describe a recent experience" on it?

Toni: (Excited) Hey, I got that one. (In serious voice) Tell us about a recent (looks at group therapist) . . . uh?

Group Therapist: Experience?

Toni: Yeah, that's it . . . a recent experience. Tell us about a recent experience.

Maya: Let me think. Oh yeah. Last week when I was hanging out with Betty in the rec room, Danielle came over and bossed us around. She said we should stop talking so loud, they couldn't hear the music.

Group Therapist: Okay, do we have another winner? Who's got another card?

Claire: My card says, "Who was involved?" Okay, Maya, who were you hanging out with?

Maya: I already said it was Danielle who bossed us around. And I was with Betty.

Group Therapist: What lucky person has the "when card"?

Celia: I do. (to Maya) When did it happen?

Maya: I said last week. Oh, I know what you mean. It was before school, about 8:00 a.m.

Note the use of humor in dealing the cards. The use of patter makes the activity more interesting. There is danger, though, that in some groups the members will find it patronizing. The therapist could have used tokens or points to reward people for each time they asked a useful question. The distribution of cards limits the talking by the therapist and trains the group members in asking questions themselves for which the cards serve as prompts. It also ensures broad participation. Eventually the cards will be faded.

Responses

Of course, the relevance of situations depends on the target person's response to those situations. Three types of responses can be identified: behavioral, cognitive, and affective. These often occur at the same time but are separated out below for purposes of analysis.

Behavioral Responses

Just as in the description of the problem situation, most adolescents have to be taught to be equally specific in their description of their own behavioral responses to that situation. The criteria used to evaluate whether the behavior is sufficiently specific are the following: As it is described, is it observable? Is it a response to the preceding situation? Does the response have a definable beginning and end? Is it formulated as an action someone performs rather than as one he or she does not perform? An affirmative answer to each of these questions results in a description of a behavior that is readily amenable to later intervention and hopefully change. An appropriate description of a behavioral response is found in Sue Jane's statement, above, "I broke a couple of them [dishes]" as a response to her mother's pushing her in front of the sink. When Billy said, "I pulled out my pocketknife," the group therapist or members, to obtain a complete picture of the behavioral response, should have asked whether he pointed it at the others or threatened them physically or verbally. When Art said, "I gave in," it was imperative that he be asked what he actually said when he gave in. It should be noted that all these responses were formulated in terms of what was done or said rather than what was not done or not said.

There are many ways in which youth can be trained to identify specific behavioral responses to situations. In groups, Exercise 4.1 has been demonstrated to capture the interest of the members and to be effective in teaching them the basic concepts.

Exercise 4.1. Defining a Behavioral Response

Purpose: By the end of this exercise, each participant will be able to describe a behavioral response to a situation meeting the following criteria.

1. Is it highly specific—that is, observable or hearable?

2. Is it a response to the preceding situation?

3. Does the response have a definable beginning and end?

4. Is the response formulated as something a person does rather than as something he or she does not do?

Individual Task: Each participant is given the following situations to which he or she is to describe his or her responses in writing. The responses should fit the criteria described above, but they do not have to be "right" or "good" answers.

1. (You have been pushed around a lot by the big guy at the locker next to yours.) When he demands that you give him your only dollar because he wants a Coke, describe what you would say or do, and role-play how you would say it.

2. (Your roommate is always getting into trouble. He sometimes tries to involve you.) When he asks you to cover for him when he sneaks out one night, describe what you would say or do, and role-play how you would say it.

3. (You like to stay out as late as possible and are only 3 minutes away from your house. It's 5 minutes to curfew, and you are on your way home.) When the police officer suddenly drives up and tells you, angrily, to "Get your butt over here," describe what you would say or do, and role-play how you would say it.

4. (You feel your mother bosses you around a lot more than your younger brother.) When she tells you that you have to do the dishes and your brother is in the other room watching TV and you have a date in 5 minutes, describe what you would say or do, and role-play how you would say it.

5. (You feel you are often blamed for things you don't do.) When the residential worker yells at you for leaving the sink dirty and you know that Fred did it, describe what you would say or do, and role-play how you would say it.

Group Task: The participants present to the group their answers to each question, one at a time. They provide the presenter with feedback on how well the response meets the above criteria. They should also comment on the effectiveness of the tone of voice in which the response was delivered.

Continuing with the example in the previous section, the therapist can use the same training procedures. He hands out cards with the new questions on them.

Group Therapist: Okay, Maya did a great job in describing the situation. Let's see if we can do as well in describing her behavioral response. Okay, who has the "response" card? Okay, Sylvi, ask away.

Sylvi: Maya, what did you do and/or what did you say?

Maya: Nothing much, I just didn't agree with her.

Group Therapist: Okay, read your questions aloud to all of us, and then you answer them yourself.

Claire: I got the card "Is it highly specific?" I don't think so. What words did you use? What did you actually say or do and in what tone? I guess that means "How did you say it?" Act it out for us.

Maya: Okay, I said (angrily) she could just stuff her ears with whatever. I wasn't going to play it one bit softer. And then I turned it louder.

Claire: Wow, that was a great description. It sure is specific now, but I don't think you should say that, though.

Group Therapist: Hold it, we are only interested in what she did say and how she said it. Next week, we will talk about what else she could say and how she might say it differently.

Celia: I got the dead man card ("Could a dead man have this response?"—i.e., is the response formulated in terms of what someone does not do rather than what he or she does?). No dead man could say what she said. Not many live men either.

Everyone: (laughs)

Toni: It sure is a response to the preceding situation.

Group Therapist: And it certainly answers my question, it has a beginning and an end. Well, she sure described the situation in a way that we knew what was said and done and how she said it. I know that some of you disagreed with the appropriateness, but we can talk about that later when we deal with alternatives next session.

In later sessions, whenever a person brings in a situation with a behavioral response, the group therapist makes sure that the criteria are met by asking the other members to recall what was on the cards and then say whether the criteria are met.

Cognitive Responses

A cognition, as the term is used throughout this book, is an identifiable thought, a belief, an expectation, a value, an evaluation, an attribution, or a self-instruction. Many of these concepts overlap. Cognitions may be vague or extremely clear to the individual. Although often spoken aloud, a cognition is usually a private or covert event. One can usually identify it by asking the person with the cognition to describe it in writing or aloud or by deducing it from other behaviors or statements. Of particular concern here are cognitive responses to situations or recurring thoughts across situations. However, cognitions may also occur immediately before the situation or continuously during the situation. In an earlier example in this chapter, one client had the recurring thought (or, in Beck's [1976] terms, an "automatic thought") that her mother might die. In another example, a youth responded to an insult with the thought, "I don't let anyone mess with me." Because of their private quality, cognitions are often difficult to ascertain. Nevertheless, because they often appear to impinge on the definition and resolution of many problematic situations, it is important to explore their presence as a response to problematic situations and as part of the situation that elicits other responses. Cognitions are also often associated with behavioral and emotional responses.

Training in the Identification of Cognitive Responses. Most youth are not readily able to identify their thinking in response to or as a part of a given situation. For them, training in cognition perception and expression is an important prerequisite for cognitive assessment and treatment. To train them to examine their cognitions, the group therapist provides the list of cognitions in Exercise 4.2 to choose from or to use as a point of departure.

Exercise 4.2. Looking at Cognitions

Purpose: By the end of this exercise, each participant will be able to describe a cognitive response to a situation meeting predetermined criteria.

Individual Task 1: Each participant is given the following situations and possible cognitive responses and asked to write down, for each situation, another cognitive response that is different from (not necessarily better than) the original one.

1. (On seeing a massive guy pushing the other guys around, he thinks), "Hey, that guy's big, I'd better get out of here."

2. (On being blamed for something she didn't do, she thinks), "Why is it always my fault?"

3. (On seeing a policeman when driving over the speed limit, he thinks), "I'd better slow down or I'll get a ticket."

4. (On being pushed by another kid at school, he thinks), "Nobody pushes me around. I'll get even."

5. (On being criticized harshly by his mother, he thinks), "She can't talk that way to me."

6. (On being assigned a difficult task by his teacher, he thinks), "Wow, am I dumb. I'll never be able to do that."

7. (On hearing that almost everyone in the class did better than she did on the quiz, she says to herself), "Boy, does that make me depressed."

Group Task 1: The participants tell each other what the cognitive response was. They give each other feedback on whether a given response is indeed cognitive and why. Each participant discusses whether he or she has similar cognitions.

Individual Task 2: Each participant reads the following situations and describes in writing what he or she might be thinking, saying to him- or herself, or believing in the following situations.

1. Imagine that I kicked you out of the group because I thought you were disrupting the group meeting. Actually it was someone else doing the disrupting. What would you say to yourself?

2. Imagine that you give a store clerk a ten and he gives you change for a five and begins to walk away. What would you think or say to yourself?

3. Imagine that you are 1 minute late for class, and your teacher asks you why you are so late. What would you think?

4. Imagine that the teacher is asking you a question, and you haven't the slightest idea as to the answer. What would you think?

Group Task 2: Same as Group Task 1, using the four statements above.

Meichenbaum (1977) suggested a range of other tasks that may be used in assessing an adolescent's cognitions: (a) imagery exercises, (b) tasks during which internal dialogues are verbalized, and (c) projective techniques using pictures of people interacting. Meichenbaum suggested that the use of imagery focus on having the adolescent recall a critical incident and run it through his or her mind "like a movie." During the recalling of an incident, the adolescent reports his or her cognitions as the event occurred. In the same manner, the adolescent's cognitive strengths may be assessed by "running through" situations in which he or she succeeded in some way. Although usually carried out individually, these exercises can be used in the group to provide repeated practice and mutual modeling.

Similarly, Meichenbaum suggested the use of behavioral tasks for assessing cognitive responses. Much as in the role-play tests (see Chapter 5), the youth is asked to engage in a problematic target behavior. This can be done in a real-life setting or in a role-play simulation. The difference here is that the adolescent is asked either during the event or immediately following it what he or she was saying to him- or herself during the event as well as what physiological events (e.g., faster heartbeat, tight stomach, sweaty palms, headache, fast breathing) were experienced.

Another procedure suggested by Meichenbaum is the use of a set of pictures depicting youth with problems similar to those of the person being assessed. As in the case study method described earlier, each person or group is asked to report on what is happening in the picture. Youth are also asked to describe what the person in the picture is thinking or feeling during the interaction pictured. The use of a series of such pictures might yield a wealth of information on how each person in the group would think and feel (physiologically) in a similar situation.

Occasionally, youth will identify a given cognition as occurring continuously or across so many situations that its specific relationship to situational cues is unclear. For example, one client stated that "in all situations in which I find it difficult to do what is asked of me, I think to myself that I'll never get it done." Such a situation is usually dealt with by asking the client to discuss the most recent occurrence of the response and the situational attributes at that time. Repetition of this analysis for a number of such situations often yields identifiable situational components that precede or covary with the undesirable response. Nevertheless, patterns of self-defeating cognitions may be discovered that interfere with the client's functioning in many diverse situations and thus deserve early attention in the treatment process.

Another technique for assessing cognitions occurring in stressful situations is the three-column technique described by Beck and Emery (1985, p. 202). In the first column, the individual describes an anxiety- or anger-producing situation; in the second, his or her automatic thoughts; and in the third, types of errors found in these thoughts (see Chapter 10, Table 10.1, for an example). Another strategy used to teach youth to recognize their automatic or self-defeating thoughts and to link them both to situations in which they occur and to intense feelings is the thought chart (Wilkes et al., 1994, p. 146). The first column is used to describe the situation, the second column is used to describe the feelings on a scale of intensity from 1 to 10, and the third column is used to describe thoughts that occurred immediately following or during the situation (see Chapter 10, Table 10.2, for an example).

Affective Responses

Exercise 4.3 can help group members to describe their affective responses to situations more specifically.

Exercise 4.3. Defining Feeling Words

Purpose: By the end of this exercise, each participant will have used at least different five feeling words experienced in various situations and described the experience to the group members.

Individual Tasks:

1. The group therapist should describe to the group members a recent example of a situation of his or her own in which he or she experienced a strong emotional reaction. A written description may be handed out to members of the group. The members should describe how they would feel in the same situation.

2. The participants should describe in writing one situation inducing strong feeling that each experienced, preferably a recent event. They may draw on situations they used in the previous exercises, but the emphasis in this exercise is on how they *felt* in the situation.

3. The therapist and each participant choose five emotions from the list below that they have experienced in the past or are experiencing right at the moment.

bored	embarrassed	lonely	grieving
angry	anxious	apathetic	frightened
shy	proud	unhappy	delighted
elated	confused	silly	joyful
funny	worried	peaceful	ashamed
annoyed	stimulated	glad	irritated
weary	depressed	in love	content
hurt	despairing	down	tense
jealous	nervous	frustrated	cheerful
worthless	uneasy	calm	uptight

4. When a person describes his or her feelings in a given situation, he or she also should rate the intensity of each feeling on the following scale (1 to 9):

Almost nothing		Slight		Moderate		Strong		Very strong
1	2	3	4	5	6	7	8	9

Group Task 1: Beginning with the therapist, each person describes a situation in which he or she experienced one or more emotions and rates the intensity of each emotion from 1 to 9. To get diverse emotions, no one can use a given feeling word more than once. The participants should be encouraged to recall situations in which they felt strongly at school, at work, in treatment, with family members, on the playground, at the movies, and so on.

Group Task 2: In subgroups of four to five persons, the participants should discuss their reactions to expressing emotions in the group. They should discuss the advantages and disadvantages of expressing feelings in the family, the residential group, and the treatment group.

Another exercise can be carried out as well if the members still have difficulty in linking feeling words to situations. Exercise 4.4 is similar to Exercise 4.2 except that it taps emotions or feelings rather than cognitions. Both exercises can be combined to ask for cognitions and emotions in each of the situations.

Exercise 4.4. Looking at Feelings in Situations

Purpose: By the end of this exercise, each participant will be able to describe his or her emotional responses to a wide variety of problematic situations.

Individual Task 1: Each participant is given the following situations and asked first to write down what the emotional response in each situation might be and then to write down another emotional response that is different (not necessarily better) than the original one. Participants should also compare their potential physical responses.

1. On being blamed for something he didn't do, he feels irritated, annoyed, and upset. (He also notes that his fists are tightening and his head is beginning to ache.)

2. On being pushed down on purpose by another kid at school, he feels extremely angry. (He notes that he is breathing hard and grinding his teeth and that his hands are sweaty.)

3. On being criticized harshly by his mother for something his brother often does without criticism, he feels jealous and worthless. (He notes that tears come to his eyes.)

4. On hearing that almost everyone in the class did better than she did on the quiz, she feels disappointed and depressed. (She notes that she is holding her breath and tearful and that her head hurts.)

Group Task 1: The participants tell each other what their emotional responses might have been in the same situations. Each participant discusses whether he or she would experience similar or different emotions. Participants should also compare their physiological responses.

Individual Task 2: Each participant reads the following situations and describes in writing what feelings each might experience in the following situations and any physiological reaction each might have in such circumstances.

1. Imagine that I kicked you out of the group because I thought you were disrupting the group meeting. Actually, it was someone else doing the disrupting. You had nothing to do with it.

2. Imagine that you give a store clerk a ten and he gives you change for a five and begins to walk away. When you complain, he says, "Who are you kidding, punk?"

3. Imagine that you are walking in the woods when a big snake suddenly appears in front of you.

4. Imagine that you have just heard that you have been diagnosed with a very serious disease.

5. Imagine that you have just been rejected by your best friend, who says that he or she likes someone better and would rather not see so much of you anymore.

6. Imagine that you are with a person whom you like who says he or she would really like to get you know you better.

Group Task 2: The participants tell each other what their emotional responses to each of the situations might be. Each participant discusses whether he or she would experience similar or different emotions compared with the others. Participants should also compare their physiological responses.

Some youth who learn to express emotions may still have difficulty in determining their physiological reactions in the situations. Although such reactions provide a cue for alternative responses, it is the experience of many CBIGT therapists that their recognition is a useful but not a necessary skill. The group therapist can let this awareness of physiological responses evolve over time if the exercise does not immediately teach it.

The Critical Moment

The interface between the situation and the response is the critical moment. It is that point in the situation at which one determines that a response is called for. Arnold describes a recent encounter as follows: "At the moment that Jerry brushed up against me in the hall, I hit him." The critical moment is that instant in time in which Arnold (from his perspective) had just experienced being brushed by Jerry but before Arnold hit Jerry.

The purpose of establishing a critical moment is to determine that point in time when the client could do (think and/or feel) something other than what he or she actually did (thought and/or felt). With younger adolescents, the words *tough point* have often been used instead of the more technical-sounding term *critical moment*.

In any complicated event or set of ongoing interactions, there are often multiple critical moments. For example, as Penny was rushing to get out of the house on time for school, she tripped over her brother's lunchbox (the first critical moment) and yelled at her brother, who ran screaming to their mother. Mother in turn told her to leave Pierre alone (the second critical moment), so Penny screamed that it was his fault, angrily slammed the door, and ran out of the house. Her mother called her back and began to admonish her once again (the third critical moment), to which Penny responded, "I'll be late forever." In the group, Penny would have been asked to identify the critical moment that was of most concern to her. The group would then help her to find alternative responses to that situation at the given critical moment.

If the group therapist and/or members do not agree that a given moment is the most critical, the members will discuss it. But the client whose situation is being discussed is the final arbiter of his or her own critical moment. In the evaluation of various alternative responses, youth will often shift implicitly from one critical moment to another if, in a given event, the critical moment of concern is not at least momentarily pinned down. The implication of the critical moment for treatment will be discussed further throughout the intervention chapters.

Training in Identification
of the Critical Moment

In training youth to use the concept of critical moment, one first presents them with a definition and a number of examples. Afterwards, one gives them a list of situations and responses from which they are asked to identify the critical moment. First, a set of examples is presented, and then a series of situations from which the group members are to determine the critical moment, as in Exercise 4.5.

Exercise 4.5. Identifying
the Critical Moment

Purpose: By the end of this exercise, each participant will accurately identify at least one critical moment in five different situations and identify at least one critical moment in a situation of his or her own.

Individual Task 1: Each participant should read the following examples of critical moments.

1. When Jerry's brother, Tom, called Jerry a fat pig (critical moment here), Jerry ignored him.

2. When Susan was being hassled at school by Sara and EmmyLou (critical moment here), she ran crying to the teacher.

3. Just as Alexander came into the house, 2 hours after curfew, his mother said that if he wanted to live at home, he'd better get home at the agreed-on time (critical moment here). Alexander yelled at

her not to nag him all the time. His mother slapped him (second critical moment here), and he slapped her back.

4. When Beatrice was in library last week looking at all her assignments (critical moment here), she began to think, "I'll never get all my homework done. I'll fail for sure. I'm just an idiot."

Now each participant should read the following situations and determine the critical moment.

1. Raoul was shooting baskets when Jerry came along and grabbed the basketball, then ran off with it. Raoul swore at Jerry and started chasing him. (From the point of view of Raoul, what was the critical moment?)

2. GiGi was putting on her favorite jeans when Dianne said, "You're too fat for those jeans. You need two sizes bigger." GiGi grabbed Dianne's hair and pulled, while screaming at her. (From the point of view of GiGi, what was the critical moment?)

3. Marty and Goren were playing checkers. Art came along and asked to play the winner. Marty said, "Take off, punk, we're going to play all day." Art knocked the board on the ground and ran off. (From the point of view of Art, what was the critical moment?)

4. Lex was sleeping when Mike pulled the covers off him. Lex chased Mike into the kitchen and squirted him with water. Mike threw an orange at him. (From the point of view of Lex, what were two critical moments? From the point of view of Mike, what was one critical moment?)

Group Task 1: In subgroups of three, participants will share their ideas as to what are critical moments. If they do not agree, they will ask the other subgroups.

Individual Task 2: Each participant will describe one situation he or she has recently experienced and his or her response to it. He or she will then indicate where the critical moment was.

Group Task 2: Each participant will read his or her situation and describe the critical moment to the group, who will provide feedback as to the accuracy of the formulation.

Identifying Immediate and
Long-Term Consequences

The situation-response-consequence set obtains its significance and its priority as a target of change on the basis of the immediate and long-term consequences to the client if the presenting pattern of responses continues. Heloise's violent responses to losing games (swearing, blaming others for their mistakes, shoving those whom she blames) has the immediate consequence of giving her control of the game and the long-term result of her being ostracized by her peers and getting into fights with some of them. Immediate consequences may appear, as in the above case, to be reinforcing. Similarly, Anatole's worrying aloud to his peers about the slightest low grade he obtains results immediately in getting their attention, but the long-term result is avoidance. Such situation-response-consequence sets can then be identified as legitimate objects of change.

Training in Identifying Consequences

Having identified a series of problematic situations and the possible responses to those situations, another group exercise similar to those described above can be introduced to the group. First, the youth are presented with examples of situations and responses in which the consequences are given. Then, having been presented with lists of situations described in earlier sections, they are asked to identify and evaluate the short- and long-term consequences of using the given response described in the situation. Finally, they are asked to identify in their own situations and responses the consequences of those responses. (See Exercise 4.6.)

Exercise 4.6. Identifying the Consequences

Purpose: By the end of this exercise, the members will have correctly determined the immediate and long-term consequences of responses to at least five different situations and ascertained whether the immediate consequences might be reinforcing to the target person.

Individual Task 1: The group members should read the following situations and note what the consequences, both long-term and immediate, are. They should assess whether the short-term or immediate consequences are reinforcing.

1. When Jerry's brother, Tom, called Jerry a fat pig (critical moment here), Jerry ignored him. The response is that Jerry ignored him. The immediate consequence for Jerry might be that Tom would increase the volume of his name calling. What might be the long-term consequences if Jerry continued to ignore Tom's name calling?

2. When Susan was being teased at school by Sara and EmmyLou (critical moment here), she ran crying to the teacher. The immediate consequence of this response would probably be Susan's escape from the teasing. What might be the long-term consequences for Susan?

3. Just as Alexander came into the house, 2 hours after curfew, his mother said that if he wanted to live at home, he'd better get home at the agreed-on time (critical moment here). Alexander yelled at her not to nag him all the time. What might be the immediate consequence of the response and the long-term consequences? To what degree might the immediate consequence be reinforcing?

4. When Beatrice was in the library last week looking at all her assignments (critical moment here), she began to think, "I'll never get all my homework done. I'll fail for sure. I'm just an idiot." She continued to just sit and worry. What might be the immediate consequence of the response and the long-term consequences? To what degree might the immediate consequence be reinforcing?

Group Task 1: The members will share with each other their analysis of consequences and the reinforcement potential of each of the short-term consequences.

Individual Task 2: Each participant will describe in writing a situation and the responses at the critical moment that he or she described in an earlier exercise. The participants will also describe the consequences of the responses.

Group Task 2: The members will share with each other their new situations and responses and analyze the short- and long-term consequences of the responses. Each should also report on the reinforcement potential of each of the short-term consequences.

Sources of Relevant Problem Situations

In almost every session, each group member is encouraged to bring a new situation to the group for consideration or one on which he or she is working. In situational analysis, the situations are defined primarily by the youth themselves on the basis of their perception and their willingness to share their experiences. Other sources are possible: (a) The group itself can be a source of situations; (b) to facilitate the members' keeping track of these events, keeping a diary may be helpful; (c) assessment role plays provide detail on situations that go beyond the verbal contribution of the target person; and (d) to get other perspectives, often parents and teachers are interviewed and the target person in residential treatment is observed, and relevant situations are noted in the daily logs. Let us look at each of these sources of situations in more detail.

The Group as a Source of Situations

Sometimes, when someone has difficulty finding a situation to discuss in the group, it is possible for the group therapist to propose one that occurred in the group. One of the advantages of the group is that problematic and stressful situations arise within the normal interaction of the group. Because such situations are directly observed by all the members and the group therapist, they can be validated. Most other situations rely solely on the self-report of the target person. The in-group situations provide a natural laboratory for reanalyzing and redoing them and ultimately finding more effective responses to them. For example, one member was giving feedback to another member about his speaking too loudly. The person receiving the feedback interpreted it as a "put-down" and reached across the room to grab the offender. The other members and the therapists stopped him, and later, when both parties had cooled off, the group therapist asked them to analyze the situation following the above criteria and then to determine why such a response is problematic or dysfunctional. Later, the group used this assessment to determine how such a situation might be handled differently without losing face.

Diaries

To sensitize the group members to looking at situations within the situation-response-consequence framework, the therapist often asks them to keep a diary of situations that are stress or anger inducing and that were encountered between sessions. In the beginning, they are asked to record one situation in which they are dissatisfied with their response and one in which they are satisfied. This makes it possible in group meetings to reinforce youth for satisfactorily handling stressful situations effectively and at the same time to target situations in which they are dissatisfied with their response.

Role-Playing Assessment Procedures

Diaries and interviews either in the group with all the members or individually with each member may not be sufficient to discover what the target person actually says or how he or she physically and affectively reacts. Less costly than observations and less intrusive, role-playing problem situations as if the target person were in that situation provides a great deal of information about his or her responses to a wide range of predetermined problem situations. In this technique, the target person presents to the group a description of a situation that he or she has found problematic in the course of the week and recorded in his or her diary. He or she is asked to role-play the actual response that he or she made while in the situation. An example of one situation and how it is presented to the group is as follows:

Gary: I was standing in line at McDonald's, waiting to order a hamburger, when an older guy with his girl pushed in front of me. The man behind the counter asked me if I wasn't next. I said it didn't matter, but I was really mad.

Group Therapist: Listen, why don't we role-play this situation like we did with Ernie? Remember, he said exactly what he said to his mother and in the same tone of voice. Don't improve on it—we'll do that later. I'll be the guy behind the counter, and Larry will push in front of you. Here's the counter.

(Larry pushes ahead of Gary)

Group Therapist (as counter person):   Hey, kid, aren't you next?

Gary: (almost in tears) Oh, I guess it's okay. I'm only in a little hurry.

Group Therapist: Okay, no skin off my nose.

Gary: (Looks away, very disappointed, and mutters underneath his breath) Shit, I'll never get home on time.

In this situation, the group therapist gets a better picture of the target person's affect than when he told about the situation. Moreover, the group therapist can go on to question the target person about his cognitive emotional responses as well. A more systematic role-play procedure is a behavior role-play test. This test may be given before treatment and uses from 6 to 12 standard situations (see Magen & Rose, 1994). Examples of other role-play tests, how they are used, how they might be developed, and how they are coded are presented in Chapter 5.

Behavioral Checklists

These tests may also be used to determine responses to problem situations. Easier to code than role-play tests, they are often preferred by practitioners. Unfortunately, most of them focus primarily on general responses rather than on a response to a situation. These too are presented in detail in Chapter 5.

Interviewing Parents and Teachers

Up to now, we have relied almost completely on the perceptions of the target person and his or her peers and the in-group observations of the group therapist for the development of situations to be analyzed and dealt with. Other vital sources of situations are parents, teachers, residential workers, and other significant persons in the lives of the adolescent. If we rely solely on the adolescent for his or her picture of situations, we may end up with an incomplete or even false picture of the kind of situations the adolescent must deal with. Moreover, the adolescent may ignore or not even be aware of a large number of problems not defined as problematic. To obtain the perceptions of parents and other significant adults, one gives them examples and trains them briefly in what is a relevant situation. In an individual or group session, they are asked for examples from their own experience and then asked to keep a diary of events that occur.

In summary, the group therapist, together with the target person and significant others, develops and keeps track of all situations (a) that are obtained in interviews and observed in various situations, (b) that evolve out of the group discussion, (c) that are recorded in the diaries, and (d) that have been extrapolated from role play, observations, situational checklists, and other tests. The situations listed are grouped into common themes for purposes of session planning. The group therapist searches for serially related situations. These situations, the responses of the clients at critical moments, and the short- and long-term consequences of those responses form the foundation for further assessment, goal setting, and eventual treatment strategies.

The task of determining in greater detail the nature of persistent unsatisfactory responses to situations that the client finds difficult can also be determined by means of more exact psychometric or measurement procedures. These are discussed in the next chapter. Once these typical inappropriate responses are discovered, the task of finding alternative responses for coping with the situations is discussed in Chapter 6.

Training Youth in Complete Situational Analysis

In the following exercise, all elements of the interactional situation-response-consequence sequence are considered. A set of criteria have been summarized, and group members will first practice describing whether the criteria have been met on a case example. Then they will apply the same criteria to situations of their own. If there is an insufficient number of sessions, Exercise 4.7 may replace Exercises 4.1 to 4.6.

Exercise 4.7. Situational Analysis

Purpose: By the end of this exercise, each group member will have demonstrated his or her skill in formulating at least two situations, the critical moment within the situations, his or her responses at the critical moment to these situations, and the consequences of his or her responses.

Individual Task 1: Each person should read either of the examples below.

1. Anita, age 14, wanted to be friends with Eileen. When Anita saw Eileen yesterday in the hall running to class, she tried to approach her by telling her she was late to class. Eileen just got angry. Anita reported to the group that she was very unsatisfied with her own response because it had made Eileen angry and that now she was upset and depressed. Anita said to herself, "I do everything wrong."

2. Caleb, age 16, needed some help with his homework. He was uncomfortable about asking Sam for help, but Sam was the best in math. So when Caleb saw Sam at lunch, Caleb demanded that Sam help him because it was so easy for him. Sam told Caleb to take off, he didn't have to do anything that Caleb demanded. Caleb was dissatisfied with his response because it had annoyed Sam and turned him off. The situation was important because he would like to get help from Sam or even be friends. It was interactive because it involved Caleb talking to Sam. (Caleb tended to make demands rather than requests from everyone.)

The person should then identify each of the following criteria for defining a problematic interactive situation:

1. What is the evidence that the situation is recent?

2. What is the evidence that it is a relatively uncomplicated event (only in the beginning phase)?

3. What is the evidence that the situation is interactive (unless the group is working on noninteractive situations)?

4. What is the evidence that the situation has a specific beginning and end and a time and a place?

5. Describe the critical moment for each response.

6. What is the verbal response?

7. What is the physical response?

8. Identify the emotions and physiological response of the target person.

9. Identify any cognitive statements of the target person.

10. What is the evidence that the target person was significantly dissatisfied with or anxious about the response?

11. What is the evidence that the situation was important to the target person?

Group Task 1: Members, in pairs, should compare their analyses of the above situations and provide each other with feedback as to how well criteria have been identified. Then each person will describe his or her partner's problematic situation in terms of the criteria that were met.

Individual Task 2: (This is usually carried out at a subsequent session.) Each person should describe in writing a problematic interactive situation that each experienced that meets the above criteria. Be sure the critical moment is clearly identified.

Group Task 2: Everyone should present a situation to a neighbor. Partners will interview each other to help each to remember any relevant information. Then the partner will make sure that the criteria are met. Both members will present their partner's situation to the larger group for evaluation of how well it met the above criteria.

Resources and Impediments

In assessment, it is essential to determine both resources for and impediments to therapy that are part of the client's personal characteristics and environment. These include personal skills, motivation, health and physical attributes, potential support persons in the client's environment, material resources, and other personal attributes. One determines these characteristics in pregroup interviews with the client and significant others and, once the group begins, through observing, informal conversations, and group interviewing in the sessions. Such resources can be used directly to enhance treatment if they are incorporated into the treatment plan. Impediments must often be resolved before intervention on the major problems can take place.

Every client comes to therapy with a number of skills and interests. They include social, problem-solving, academic, job, and recreational skills. Other personal attributes that may serve to enhance or interfere with the achievement of treatment goals include knowledge or information relevant to the presenting problems, a certain level of motivation, health, and physical characteristics.

Social Skills

Social skills are those that relate an individual to other people. Although there are a wide range of social skills, they are important ingredients in building relationships and carrying out social interactions effectively. Important social skills in which youth are deficient may become direct targets of change. But the ones in which they are already competent may serve as treatment tools for the target person or for others in the group. For example, on entering the group, Wilbur is already skilled at role playing. Henrietta makes extremely good suggestions when asked. Annalee listens attentively to the other youth when they are despondent. Jolanda has well-developed leadership skills (summarizing and tying diverse points together) and demonstrates these often in the group. These skills may serve to facilitate the group interaction as well as to enhance her own social status in the group. Those skilled in a given area may serve as teachers and models for the less skilled in that area. The therapist searches for social skill competencies for everyone in the group so that all have the potential of teaching as well as learning. Social skills also may function as a source of recognition and reinforcement, even though such skills are not, in these cases, the targets of intervention. Early in therapy, the members assess each other and themselves in terms of the social skills they already have in their repertoire. To ascertain these skills, a guided interview in pairs or a social skill checklist is most often used.

Problem-Solving Skills

A set of cognitive skills that mediates the achievement of treatment goals is problem-solving skills. These involve skill in systematically bringing information to bear on a situation, evaluating that information, and making an informed decision. They also include alternative thinking, consequential thinking, and means-end thinking. Many troubled youth solve problems impetuously. To enhance these skills, systematic problem solving is taught to them directly (see Chapter 7 for details). Throughout therapy, problem solving is used to identify and resolve individual problems. The group works together to solve group problems as they arise. Thus, these skills are an important target of change in their own right. They make it possible to solve other problems as well. In open-ended groups in particular, the more experienced members can serve as models for these skills. The problem-solving skill level of members can be assessed by observation and by an adolescent problem-solving measure for conflict (Lochman & Lampron, 1986).

Recreational Skills and Interests

Skills in games, computers, board games, crafts, storytelling, and drama can all serve as important resources for therapy. If youth are permitted to demonstrate some of these skills in the limited group time available for recreation or are encouraged to demonstrate their skills at a given school activity, their status can be enhanced. Where skills are limited, the therapist may help the client to find training outside the group in a given area to supplement the therapeutic activities. Occasionally, the group as a whole learns a recreational skill together outside the therapeutic session. In one anger management group, the therapist was able to engage the group in bowling—an area in which she was expert. Not only did this enhance the cohesion of the group, but their newly learned skill served as a source of positive recognition for them among other students in the high school they attended. These activities are so important in therapy that Chapter 13 is devoted entirely to the subject. These skills are assessed in the initial interview in pairs (Exercise 3.1), in group interviews, and by means of a hobbies and interests checklist.

Relevant Information

The possession of certain information relevant to the presenting problem or its absence is a particularly important resource that in most cases is missing from the client's repertoire. For this reason, many group therapists spend a lot of time providing or helping youth to obtain information about the nature and consequences of the target problems and their resolution in such areas as drug abuse, sexually transmitted diseases and their prevention, stress and anger management, attention deficit disorder, depression and its control, and physiological functioning. Absence of essential information related to the central problem may be a major barrier to change. Experienced members, who often have this information, can provide it to the new members with coaching by the therapist. Group members may assume tasks to obtain the information and provide it to others. The group therapist may invite expert guests to fill the gaps. Before information is provided, deficiencies must be assessed. The informational gaps are often determined by a simple informational quiz or by informal discussion about relevant topics. The quiz can be in the form of a quiz show to make it interesting.

Motivation

Moderate to high motivation to change is an important personal resource that serves as an important precursor to the change process.

Similarly, low motivation is a major barrier to participation or goal achievement. Motivation changes over time. For this reason, it is necessary to assess continuously the level of motivation.

To determine an individual's level of motivation, an examination of what he or she perceives to be the long-term consequences of behavior is conducted. If the individual acknowledges long-term negative consequences and is concerned about them, that can be considered one index of motivation. A second indicator of motivation is willingness to take a risk. As we discussed above, each individual examines the risk involved in any set of alternative responses. If the individual persistently chooses the lowest-risk strategies, one may also infer low motivation. A third indicator of low motivation is the persistent blaming of others for one's problems. Although initially most youth fail to assume responsibility for their part in interactive problems, the poorly motivated client continues to blame others over time. A fourth indicator is the rate of extragroup task completion. Consistent success at completing tasks or at least attempting them indicates high motivation.

Fortunately, the level of motivation is not static. With most youth, it tends to increase over time. As others in the group identify clearly problematic situations, as the program becomes attractive, as the reinforcers become of greater interest, and as the relationships to peers and the group therapist are enhanced, motivation, as evidenced by the client's ability to identify problematic situations and later to work on them, dramatically increases in most cases. However, in those instances in which motivation remains low, each of the above indexes can be worked on separately. For example, a poorly motivated adolescent, Arnie, in one group rarely admitted to dissatisfaction with his responses, was unwilling to risk any new strategy for dealing with what he perceived to be the central problem, and blamed others for all his problems. He was paired in the group for many activities with a high-status member of the group who was better motivated along the same dimensions. On occasion (during the 10-minute recreation period), the group therapist also encouraged the group to play soccer, a game in which Arnie excelled and received positive recognition. Gradually, Arnie was willing to disclose an event he found difficult to manage. On these rare occasions, Arnie received praise from his partner and the group therapist. As a result, the behaviors associated with apparent motivation clearly increased over time. In summary, motivation is continually included in the assessment of each client so that, if necessary, it can be dealt with as part of the treatment package.

Health and Physical Attributes

The client may come to the group with major physical health impairments or assets, low energy levels, unique physical attributes, required medications, or limits on particular activities, all of which may facilitate relationships, separate him or her from others, focus attention on him or her, or in other ways affect the progress of treatment. The group therapist usually inquires about such attributes from the person referring the adolescent. Group members are also asked their perception of their own characteristics. Physical limitations in particular may be closely linked to self-defeating cognitions. Such characteristics often become embedded in the problem situations and the kinds of response that might be made. It is helpful to have a medical clearance and knowledge of physical restrictions on activities if any exist. If a client is receiving any medication, the group therapist should be aware of it. Some medications may interact with even such innocent-appearing activities as relaxation training to create surprising side effects (see Everly & Rosenfeld, 1981, pp. 112-113, for more detail).

Supportive Persons as Resources

In addition, the client's environment may possess certain persons who may affect the achievement of treatment goals. For example, cooperative parents, a concerned grandparent, interested teachers, a good friend, an interested coach, or a helpful club leader is in a position to enhance treatment. The same persons may also interfere with treatment. Some parents may punish the same behavior being rewarded in the group or may nag the client excessively. Some siblings will attempt to retrain the client in the very behaviors the group has been working to eliminate. Some significant others merely remain passive and leave everything up to the group. In assessment, such family situations must at least be ascertained, and, where possible, the significant others should be included in goal setting and the treatment process. In our experience, the greater the involvement of family members in the treatment process, the greater the likelihood of success. These data are collected by means of social support network inventories (see, e.g., Exercise 12.1, this volume, and Barth, 1986, pp. 106-135).

Material Resources

A job or a steady source of financial support from parents, health insurance, necessary clothing, one's own place to sleep, regular meals, and a home are resources that not every group member has. If deficient in these basic needs, behavioral change may have low priority in the mind of the client. Even small practical resources may be important. In a group of teenage mothers, attendance and motivation were enhanced dramatically by the provision of both transportation and baby-sitters at the session. Usually this information is collected in pregroup interviews, and steps to ameliorate the most imposing of these deficiencies may be taken before or while therapy is occurring. This may involve referral to social agencies or direct actions by the therapist.

Other Personal Attributes

A number of other personal proclivities may also affect outcome. Some examples are energy or creativity, thoughtfulness or slowness, being quick to act and damning the consequences, and intelligence. In many cases, these general characteristics may be subject to change through cognitive strategies. In other cases in which these characteristics are persistent across numerous situations, it may be necessary to consider them as part of the material the therapist has to work with. Often, situations closely linked to these attributes need to be targeted despite the possible advantages of the attributes. For example, a youth who was not very energetic and was of less than average intelligence dealt with problematic situations that reflected these attributes. It was difficult for him to assimilate new information. But he dealt with problem situations with a great deal of slowly thought-through creativity and persistence, which enhanced the quality of new solutions and the consistency with which he carried them out.

Occasionally, personal characteristics can be encountered in situations and targeted as objects of change. For example, one youth had been disorganized in schoolwork and in his home environment since early childhood and later was disorganized in the part-time jobs he held. Because the stress he experienced in most situations was consistently related to this characteristic, he was taught in very small steps a simple strategy of personal organization required to deal with very narrow-range situations that resulted in the removal of a great deal of stress. However, the new organization was modest and did not readily generalize to other situations because of the persistence of the characteristic, so he began to organize himself to live, whenever possible, in situations demanding limited personal organization.

Resource or Impediment?

No one skill or characteristic is always an advantage or disadvantage in facilitating behavioral or cognitive change. For example, a high level of intelligence may result in greater ease in understanding the concepts that youth must learn to analyze situations or to make use of sophisticated cognitive strategies. But this same level of intelligence may cause youth to become excessively critical and rejecting of the therapy process. Social skills may be used to enhance the quality of one's relationships but may also be used as a tool in manipulating others. Each attribute must be considered within the context of specific situations as to its contribution to the achievement of treatment goals and as to whether it should be encouraged or ignored. However, the therapist needs to explore these attributes and weigh them in terms of their potential as resources or impediments to treatment in order to have the most informed basis for treatment planning.

Training in Identifying Resources and Impediments

To train group members to look at resources and impediments to effective treatment, Exercise 4.8 is carried out.

Exercise 4.8. Identifying Resources and Barriers

Purpose: By the end of this exercise, each participant will have identified the resources for and barriers to treatment for at least one case illustration, for him- or herself, and for at least four other group members.

Individual Task 1: The participants should read the following vignettes of individuals and write down their positive attributes and resources for therapy.

1. Lucky, age 15, was on parole after being adjudicated for breaking and entering. Although he was failing school now, he pointed out that he could do passing work in school, especially in the manual arts class. He said he hated to study and would rather hang out with the guys. He was a fair basketball player but liked to play. He could make pizza from scratch that everyone said was delicious. He protected his kid brother on the streets and told him to stay out of trouble even if he himself didn't. He worked out regularly and was healthy. Even if he had trouble with his mom, he got along well with his grandparents, and when things got too hot at his house, he went there. Sometimes he would do what his mom asked him. He made friends easily. He noted that girls liked him. He admitted that he got angry easily and that sometimes he teased his sister until she cried.

2. Clara, age 13, complained of persistent anxiety, a sense of isolation, and occasional depression. She stayed home most of the time. She related to the group that she was interested in music and played the guitar moderately well; in fact, she often played guitar when she was feeling bored or anxious. She studied moderately hard in school. Her grades were always okay, though she thought she could do better. She had one good friend whom she could call any time when she was at home, and she had a good relationship with her older brother, who lived in another state but who called her from time to time. She fought a lot with her parents, but on occasion she could control her temper. Later, she added to her list, after she heard others, that she was willing to do something about her problem, as evidenced by the fact that she tried to speak up in group. But usually she is a good listener. She also noted that she ate a healthy diet with lots of fruit and vegetables. If she was healthy, she was less tired and therefore could participate better in the group and family counseling.

Group Task 1: In subgroups of four to five persons, the participants should share their perception of resources and barriers for both (or either) Lucky and/or Clara. Participants should justify why each characteristic should be considered a resource for, or impediment to, helping in therapy.

Individual Task 2: In pairs, each member should interview the other to draw up a similar vignette of resources for his or her partner. This vignette should include positive interests, skills, relationships, concrete resources (e.g., the possibility of a job, mechanic's tools), and personal qualities, as well as barriers to treatment in the same categories. The interviewer should also ask the partner what he or she or others have done for him or her that might be of help to him or her in resolving his or her problems. What has the participant done that others have complimented her or him on? No matter how small the achievement, it should be noted.

Group Task 2: Everyone should read the partner's vignette aloud to the group. Then each person should add one more characteristic that he or she discovered from the vignettes of others to his or her own vignette and share it with the group. Members are asked to keep track of any other attributes that might facilitate or hinder the progress of therapy.

After this exercise has been completed, it is possible, whenever a new situation is brought to the group by a member, to ask the others to analyze the member's potential resources and barriers in dealing with the problem situation, as well as analyzing the situation in terms of the content of the event, the critical moment, the responses, and the consequences of those responses.

General or Diagnostic Statements

Thus far, when general descriptive or diagnostic statements are made by the client, parents, or other referring persons, the client has been helped by the group therapist and/or the group to formulate these in as specific terms as possible. But the general description of the problem is not eschewed. In addition to becoming a point of departure for describing concrete situation-response-consequence statements, these general descriptions of problems suggest covarying phenomena that the group therapist should also consider. General statements tend to refer to general categories of situations and responses. For example, Malcolm was referred because of his constant fighting, arguing, and defying adults. These are general patterns of responses. He tends to demonstrate these behaviors in school and at home, but not in church. These are the situational contexts in which the behaviors occur. Such general statements suggest specific events that can be worked on. Diagnosis, a more systematic form of general statements, if suggested by referring persons, is used in the same way. For example, if the group therapist receives a diagnosis of childhood depression for a client, he or she is advised to look for inappropriate mood manifestation, involved negative self-talk, and sleeping and eating dysfunctions. Above all, the diagnosis of depression should warn the therapist of the possibility of suicide. Occasionally, certain behavioral patterns are seen across many different kinds of situations; such a phenomenon suggests that a situational focus may not be the appropriate method. An example of such a ubiquitous problem would be a youth who is hyperactive in virtually every situation in which he is observed. In our experience, such generalized responses are the exception rather than the rule but can occur. General descriptive statements or diagnoses at the very least suggest avenues of assessment. For example, Gloria was referred because her parents perceived her as suffering from depression. When it became clear that Gloria, 17, indeed suffered from intense sadness at times but showed no other manifestations of depression, her therapy focused on making friends, developing conversation and other interactive skills, and becoming involved in a range of social activities. At the end of the group, the therapist could still point to success in the general goal of reducing the frequency of sadness as well as the more specific changes in prosocial behavior. Moreover, in the process, the diagnosis of depression was not confirmed.

In the above example, the thematic and abstract complaint of depression was of central concern to significant adults. Often, as the problem is defined in terms of situations and the client's response to those situations, the diagnosis loses most of the relevance of its original formulation. In such cases, the original thematic determination serves at least to point to possible covariates of the problem behavior or cognitions—not a trivial function. If these situations and responses are indeed linked together by some diagnosis or other general pattern, it may be possible to ascertain, when a certain proportion of these goals are achieved, that the original diagnosis must be revised. Of course, in some cases, serious diagnoses may be supported or new ones determined by observations in the group. In such cases, referral to other, more intense psychiatric services that specialize in the treatment of persons with the given diagnostic category may be called for.

Summary

In this chapter, the purposes and essential components of a situational analysis were defined and exemplified. Emphasis was placed on how group members are trained in the concepts and the carrying out of the analysis itself. For the most part, the training takes place by means of models and group exercises. The major components of situational analysis are the problem situation, the critical moment, the responses (behavioral, cognitive, and affective), the consequences of the responses, and the resources and barriers to treatment. Also examined was the relationship of assessment to diagnosis. But assessment is not complete with only interviewing strategies. In this chapter, several measurement strategies were briefly discussed. In the next chapter, the use of measurement instruments in assessment and evaluation is considered in detail, along with the relationship of these instruments and the entire assessment process to goal setting, treatment planning, and evaluation.

CHAPTER 5

Measurement Procedures in Assessment and Evaluation

Measurement is used to supplement interviewing strategies in assessment and to facilitate the formulation of problem situations. It also serves to make evaluation possible and to make data available both for ongoing treatment planning and, in some cases, for contributing to knowledge. In CBIGT, two sets of measures are used: instruments that measure the client's individual behavior, cognitions, and emotions and instruments that measure group phenomena. Some of these measures are overlapping. In this chapter, measurement strategies for both sets will be discussed, with emphasis on those that have been or could be used in CBIGT.

Measurement Procedures for Individuals

Because, even in group therapy, changes in individual behavior, self-evaluation, beliefs, and feeling responses to situations are ultimately the focus of treatment, individual measures are essential both in focusing the assessment and establishing goals and in evaluating outcomes. Group therapists can use a number of measurement procedures to achieve these ends. The most common ones are checklists and rating scales by parents and teachers, self-rating checklists and inventories by the client, extra-group observations by others, self-monitoring, role-play tests, sociometric tests, social impact measures, knowledge tests, and goal attainment scaling. Most of these measures can be used equally well to evaluate the outcome of individual treatment, family treatment, and parent training and are not specific to group conditions, although specific uses in groups will be pointed out in this chapter. Each of these will be described briefly as it has been used in evaluation of outcomes as the result of group interventions with youth and parents. How each can be used in assessment will also be discussed.

Parent/Teacher Ratings of Youth Behavior

At times, significant others, such as parents, teachers, or residential staff, may fill out standardized rating scales or practitioner-designed scales to assess or determine progress of group members. The advantages of ratings of youth by teachers and parents include the following (Piacentini, 1993):

1. Rating scales establish a standardized format for the collection of data. This reduces the subjectivity inherent in judgments by observers.
2. Rating scales and checklists draw on the informants' past experience with the client. This minimizes the day-to-day variability noted in direct observations.
3. Rating scales are efficient and economical to use in terms of time and cost.
4. Rating scales are sensitive to revealing situations that are relatively rare, such as fire setting.
5. Rating scales permit a broad analysis of problems or an in-depth analysis of specific areas, such as depression, conduct disorders, or hyperactivity.
6. Rating scales provide quantifiable information regarding the severity and frequency of both positive and negative behaviors and other attributes.

For these reasons, most research evaluating group outcomes employs, in addition to other measures, some form of rating scales of youth by parents or teachers or other significant people in the life of the client.

One of the most commonly used broad-band scales is the Children Behavioral Rating Checklist (CBCL) (Achenbach, 1991; Achenbach & Edelbrock, 1983). The CBCL is designed to assess, in a standardized format, the social competencies and behavior problems of children aged 4 through 16 as reported by their parents or others who know them well

(Achenbach, 1991). Social competence is assessed by up to 40 questions measuring the amount and/or quality of the child's involvement in sports, nonsport activities, organizations, chores or jobs, friendships, family, and school. The behavior problems section lists many childhood problems, the frequency of which parents are asked to rate. Space is also provided for parents to list and rate items that are not specifically included in the checklist. Test-retest reliability for nonreferred samples that Achenbach (1991) reported is generally very high. Achenbach (1991) also presented "stability" data comparing checklists completed before treatment began with those obtained 6 and 17 months later. Overall, the behavior problem scores appear to be reasonably stable, yet almost all show post-treatment decreases in problem behaviors, thus indicating sensitivity for clinical use.

According to Mooney (1984),

> While many checklists have been developed, none has been done so in as careful and well-constructed a manner and is as potentially useful across a wide variety of settings as the Child Behavior Checklist. It is easy to administer, well normed, has outstanding psychometric properties, and is appropriate for a large clinic-referred child population. (p. 181)

The CBCL helps the therapist evaluate a wide range of phenomena as perceived by a parent or teacher. Unfortunately, when using the CBCL, the group therapist should be aware that the test is long and that the person being tested requires a high school level of competence to respond adequately to all items.

In addition, scales to be rated by parents or teachers are available for more specific or narrow-band behavioral problems. The Conners' Parent and Teacher Rating Scales (Conners, 1990; Rosenberg & Beck, 1986) are used with parents or teachers when hyperactivity is being evaluated. The Eyberg Child Behavior Inventory (Eyberg, 1980; Eyberg & Robinson, 1983) is used when the presenting problem is in the area of conduct disorders for children ages 2 to 17. Thirty-six items are rated on two dimensions: a 7-point frequency scale and a yes-no scale indicating whether the behavior is a problem. Because there is a high correlation between the two, only one is usually necessary. Other psychometric properties are moderately acceptable.

In the treatment of depression, the most frequently used rating scale is the Children's Depression Inventory (Kovacs, 1981). A version is available for children and parents to complete. Both versions consist of

27 items that assess behavioral, cognitive, and affective manifestations of depression. Though parental agreement is high, child-parent agreement is quite low. Test-retest reliability is moderate.

The Matson Evaluation of Social Skills with Youngsters (MESSY) (Matson, Rotatori, & Helsel, 1983) is a 64-item scale designed to identify strengths and weaknesses in children's social functioning and to evaluate treatment outcome of social skill training. Although forms are available for both parents and teachers, norms are available only for teachers. A parallel form for children is available. For a more detailed description of these and other parent/teacher rating scales and their sociometric properties, see Piacentini (1993) or the original references.

On the above and other rating scales and checklists, changes in perceived behavior of children have been used by researchers to evaluate the results of parent training. For example, Magen and Rose (1994) evaluated outcomes of the parent training program by analyzing perceived changes of child behavior on the Revised Behavior Problem Checklist (Quay & Peterson, 1987), which is also a broad-band measure of child behavior. This test has excellent psychometric properties, including construct validity.

Self-Report Strategies

Self-report is a method that requires the subject to give his or her responses to a set of statements or questions (Reynolds, 1993). The statements or questions may concern the subject's mental state, the degree of agreement with a given belief, or a choice between two or more personal performance possibilities in a given situation. Self-report has a number of advantages. Foremost is that, for internal phenomena such as cognitions or mental states, the best observer is the client. His or her unique perspective is an important part of any assessment. These instruments enable the client to report systematically on behaviors, beliefs, expectations, or internal emotional states related to a specific target or to a general problem area. The specific checklist or rating scale used depends on the theme of the group or on the specific target problem that the client has identified. For most groups with similar presenting problems, the same checklist is used for each member to provide intragroup comparison and comparison with the membership of similar groups. Often, each group member in heterogeneous therapy groups will be given a checklist specific only to his or her target problem; this permits comparison only with others who have used the same checklist in other conditions.

According to Reynolds (1993), a number of issues influence the effective use of self-report measures. One of these is developmental issues. Obviously, the same questions or statements cannot be presented to 7-year-old children as to middle-school youth. Self-monitoring skill level, reading apprehension, physical and cognitive development, and other factors are quite different from one stage of development to the next. A second issue of concern is the willingness of a client to self-disclose. In working with delinquents, I found that, early in group therapy, some will merely check the same point on a scale, regardless of the content because of their unwillingness to self-disclose and their lack of relationship to the tester. Furthermore, there is no way of monitoring the accuracy of their checks. Many children and adolescents answer the questions so as to place themselves in the best light (Kazdin, 1992, p. 238). This has been referred to as a "social desirability" error. A third issue is the strength of such psychometric properties as reliability, validity, and normative information. All too often, in the use of nonstandardized self-reports, these psychometric properties are overlooked.

Some examples of self-rating inventories for children and adolescents commonly used in groups with specific themes are the Children's Inventory of Anger (Nelson & Finch, 1978), the Revised Children's Manifest Anxiety Scale (Reynolds, 1985), the Children's Depression Inventory (Kovacs, 1981), and the Locus of Control for Children (Nowicki & Strickland, 1973). Many researchers (e.g., LeCroy & Rose, 1986) have also used rating scales to measure consumer satisfaction as part of a package of instruments evaluating the outcomes of children's social skills groups. A large selection of such self-report measures are available to the practitioner. The criteria for selection are relevancy to the presenting problem of the group members, intrusiveness of the instrument, ease of administration, and such psychometric properties as acceptable levels of reliability, validity, and sensitivity and the existence of norms for the given population. (See Reynolds, 1993, as a resource for the selection of such tests and a description of the above attributes.)

Observations Outside the Group

The major problem of rating scales and checklists is their failure to take into account the situational variability of most behavior. A great deal of variation of responses by diverse raters on checklists and rating scales can be attributed to the absence or the vagueness of anchor points and the range of time frames during which the behavior occurred. Most checklists and rating scales also suffer from response sets, the effects of client fatigue, mood aberrations, and perceptual distortions. One way to minimize these particular problems is through the use of direct observation of the client in extragroup situations. Unfortunately, such procedures are quite costly and difficult to implement. Furthermore, they do not capture low-frequency behaviors. Simple observation systems, however, have generally been used in institutional settings, where the clients are readily monitored by others. Occasionally, parents have indicated a willingness to monitor ongoing behavior. In these cases, staff, family, or school personnel have been trained to look for highly specific target behaviors and the situations in which they occur, such as cooperation with others, approach responses to others, put-downs, disruptive group behavior, reinforcing statements, overt indications of mood swings, or anger responses. Usually, these are low- to moderate-frequency behaviors. In the youth groups, the behaviors to be observed are usually discussed with the members, who may coach their parents in the monitoring process. One group of parents agreed to have the children monitor one parental behavior, which in most cases was "yelling," in exchange for their monitoring one behavior of the child. Not only did this yield an excellent monitoring result, but it was highly therapeutic for the family interactive process.

With younger children, it is possible to monitor in-group behavior. (Older children have sometimes objected to the presence of an observer taking notes in the group.) In unstructured group events for young children, the behavior tends to replicate behaviors in other unstructured situations and thus tends to provide a meaningful sample of behavior from the real world. However, as soon as any control or structure is placed on the children, the behavior may no longer be typical of behavior found outside the group, so that subsequently the researcher must reconsider whether the observations are worth the extensive effort.

An example of a structured extragroup treatment environment for evaluation was demonstrated by Hepler (1994), who, in a study of the effectiveness of social skill training, placed children in the study in informal play groups. Well-trained observers rated each child in the group on the following behaviors, which were carefully defined and illustrated: (a) engaged in positive conversation; (b) engaged in cooperative play; (c) engaged in negative behaviors; (d) received a negative behavior; (e) onlooking, ignored by peers; (f) solitary play; and (g) no interaction. The observations included those behaviors that had been identified as contributing to children's positive and negative interactions with peers and that were related to social status.

The children were placed in groups of 10 in free-time situations with games and other leisure-time activities available to them. The coding system consisted of observing each child (identified by a number on a T-shirt) in the group over a 30-second period, alternating between 5 seconds of observing and 5 seconds of recording the previous observation. At the end of the 30-second interval, the observer moved to the next child (T-shirt number) on his or her recording sheet and repeated the same procedure (each recording sheet had a random list of students to observe). Reliability of the observations seemed reasonable on the basis of an 85% rate of agreement. Such observational situations are probably more difficult to create with adolescents than with younger children.

Self-Monitoring

Self-monitoring, a method of observing one's own overt behavior or one's own thoughts or feelings, requires the individual to record his or her own behavior or thoughts or feelings at specified intervals or under specific conditions in a systematic manner. Self-monitoring may involve the client in either tallying his or her behavior as it occurs or rating his or her overt or covert behavior (such as the degree of anxiety) periodically (e.g., every 4 hours or once a day at noon). Of all the measurement procedures, self-monitoring is the most "reactive" (having a potential independent effect of the measurement on outcome), although reviews of studies of the reactivity of self-monitoring procedures are inconsistent (Shapiro & Coles, 1993). In fact, self-monitoring is sufficiently reactive to be considered a self-control intervention strategy. For the practitioner, this is less of a problem than for the researcher, for whom the interpretation of the results might be confounded by the measurement process. If self-monitoring is carried out systematically, results may contribute to, as well as measure, the ongoing and final outcome of group therapy.

Overt behaviors may also be self-monitored, especially when the frequency of a given behavior indicates the severity of the problem. It has been observed that children and adolescents more reliably record positive behaviors than negative behaviors. For example, in a group of conduct-disordered children, members agreed to tally each time they ignored or walked away from a "challenge" by other children. In social skill groups, children were asked to count the number of people they asked to play with them in a week. In an anger control group, adolescents recorded the frequency with which they used calming procedures such as counting to 10 or using deep breathing (instead of episodes of verbally and physically abusing others). Examples of overt behaviors monitored by group members in self-control groups have been the number of low-calorie foods eaten, the number of occasions they refused to have a drink offered by others, and the number of minutes spent in prosocial recreational activities.

In groups, self-monitoring is especially useful when external observational methods do not provide the private data necessary to assess cognitive behavior. For example, clients in eating disorder groups will often count, in addition to their actual caloric intake, their urges to eat high-calorie foods. They may also record their responses to those urges. In anger management groups, some youth will record the frequency and intensity of anger that they experience either periodically or during stressful situations. Others have kept track of self-put-downs, often together with the number of self-praise statements. Table 5.1 shows a filled-out card on which a client recorded the level of anger that he experienced four times a day for a week (morning, noon, late afternoon, and evening). This self-monitoring card was given to all of the members of an anger management group. They were instructed to fill in the card every 4 hours, indicating their most intense feeling of anger in the previous 4 hours on a scale of 1 to 9. Each group member carried the card with him and pulled it out at the designated times. Each asked his "buddy" to check his card each day and to remind him at the agreed-on times. The youth were asked to comment on the situation when the rating was 5 or higher.

Self-monitoring is a measurement as well as a self-control change strategy. It may be used as a measurement strategy in other types of groups with a different theoretical perspective. Because most youth and parents have had limited experience with self-monitoring, it must usually be shaped like any other behavior or learned strategy. Failure to carry out self-monitoring is often due to inadequate definition of the monitored behavior, excessively high expectations of the therapist or the client in the early phase of therapy, or inadequate training in monitoring or counting the behavior. Lack of motivation can also play a role. For those

TABLE 5.1 A Self-Monitoring Card: Ratings of Anger Every 4 Hours

	Sunday	Monday	Tuesday	Wednesday	Thursday	Friday	Saturday
8:00	2	3	3	2	1	4	5
12:00	5	4	6	6	7	6	7
4:00	9	3	6	4	6	8	7
8:00	9	3	4	2	3	4	6

NOTE: In this example, the high scores the youth noted were usually following arguments with or criticism from peers or staff. He said he was usually too tired in the morning to pay any attention to them and that, except for Sunday, he was too tired at night.

reasons, self-monitoring tasks are negotiated rather than assigned. They are peer monitored rather than therapist monitored, and they are peer reinforced when completed. No punishment or criticism is attached to failure to complete. Because of its unique structure, the group lends itself to efficient training of clients in recording common self-observed behavior. The group therapist can readily model the process of self-observation. For example, one therapist informed the group that he was monitoring his own sarcastic statements that he occasionally employed when he did not agree with someone. In a group exercise, the members were encouraged in pairs to provide each other with diverse examples and to describe these to the group as a whole. The others then commented on the appropriateness of the behavior selected to be monitored. (Was it important? Was it doable? Could someone check on it? Was it clearly defined?) In addition, the group provided an opportunity for practicing self-observation with ample feedback from the client's peers as to the accuracy of his or her self-monitoring activity. Ample peer reinforcement exists for those who appear to monitor carefully. The group also lends itself to monitoring of the self-observations. Because each member must report publicly to the group the results of his or her observations, group pressure usually exists to carry out the assignment and to be as accurate as possible in the recording. Some group therapists provide incentives for monitoring by reserving an extra portion of group time for recreation if all of the members have successfully completed their ongoing monitoring assignments.

Role-Play Tests

Although observation of complex interactive behavior in the real world would be an ideal way of obtaining information about the client's success in manifesting goal behavior in situations where it counts, because of the limitations cited above, observations are rarely used in group treatment as the major source of information. Often, important events such as fights or serious arguments do not occur in the presence of the observer. One possible substitute for observation of problem events as they occur in the real world is the standardized role-play test. Role-play tests simulate clients' real-life problem situations, but the events are controlled by the researcher. The tester presents the client with descriptions of a number of situations one at a time, generally 6 to 24 in total. The tester asks the client to imagine being in a given situation and to respond just as if the client were in that situation. The role-played responses are recorded, often on video- or audiotape, to facilitate evaluation of the client's responses. The client's responses are evaluated according to some criteria; for example, the social appropriateness, the probable effectiveness of the response, and the long-term consequences of the response. Using the results of the role-play test, the group therapist can determine which types of situations are difficult for the client. In addition, the group therapist can compare the results of a pregroup role-play test with the results of a later one to evaluate the client's progress.

Role-play tests are most effectively used when the target response is (at least in part) a response to an interactive situation. Most targets of change in groups fall into this category. Some examples for which the role-play test is suitable are the following: dealing with persons in authority, with persons who impose on one, or with persons one would like to know better; asking someone for help; requesting one's rights; informally socializing with others; interviewing or being interviewed; dealing with racist or sexist remarks; expressing feelings appropriately; and receiving and giving feedback.

The following are two examples of items on role-play tests that have been used with juvenile offenders.

- You got a job at McDonald's. A coworker complains to you that you are not doing your fair share of work. You believe he has no grounds for these complaints. He gets really angry and starts yelling. What are you likely to do or say?
- You come home a little later than usual. You've had just one beer. Your mother greets you with "Goddamn it, you've been drinking again. That's all you ever do is drink." What are you likely to do or say?

Group therapists may draw situations from a number of existing standardized role-play tests for different populations. Role-play tests used in groups included a test designed by Freedman (1974) to evaluate social skills of the delinquent male adolescent and a test designed by Rosenthal (1978) to evaluate social skills of the delinquent female adolescent. The authors of these tests reported acceptable levels of reliability and validity. We (Edleson & Rose, 1981; Hepler & Rose, 1988) have used our own shorter versions of the Freedman role-play test modified for younger children. Most of these particular tests have precoded scoring systems and have been developed following the methodological steps recommended by Goldfried and D'Zurilla (1969).

Role-play tests also have major limitations. Role-play skill can be confounded with the behavioral skills the test is designed to measure. The extent to which improvement on skills in a role-play test really reflects changes in real-life performance is unclear and has not been empirically established. If role playing is used as part of intervention, the tests are reactive. For these reasons, other tests should also be used to evaluate outcome in addition to role-play tests. (See Bellack, Hersen, & Turner, 1976, for further criticism of the role-play tests.)

Sociometric Strategies

A number of sociometric measures exist to determine the level of interpersonal liking in groups. The most commonly used is the Roster and Rating Scale Sociometric Measure (Gottman, Gonso, & Schuler, 1976), in which all children rate each class member on a 5-point Likert-type scale on such questions as "How much do you like to play with this person in school?" In several studies, sociometric tests have been used to evaluate outcomes because the goal was to increase social skills well enough to influence the relationship of the child to his or her peers. In one study, Edleson and Rose (1981), we found that the children in the group undergoing social skill training did significantly better in raising their social status than children in the control group, as assessed by the roster and rating scale method. Hepler and Rose (1988), using a peer nominations method in which the participants "nominated" those with whom they would like most to go camping, demonstrated that students in the treatment group showed significant improvement on a sociometric rating. Low-status children in the treatment group ($n = 5$) showed significant improvement on negative peer nominations at follow-up. It should be noted that in both studies the authors were not interested in the pattern of interpersonal attraction in the therapy group but rather in the classroom because a therapy group is only a temporary social phenomenon. Though useful, the sociometric procedures are time-consuming and require cooperation of the school and the teachers involved. Some teachers have objected to use of sociometric devices because they have assumed, that by asking children to rate each other in a classroom, one fixes a permanent social status for each child. However, no evidence of this phenomenon has been observed. Although the method has been used with young children, we have not found it useful with older adolescents. For further information on sociometric tests, see Hops and Lewin (1984).

Social Impact Measures

Social impact measures assess phenomena outside the clinical setting that are of importance to the community at large (Kazdin, 1992, p. 361). Examples include whether delinquents are working or in school, arrest records, pregnancy, health problems, and passing grades in school. The initial intent in organizing groups is to address or change social behaviors, but often social impact measures are ignored. These data are obtained directly through observation, in-depth interviews with significant others, and examination of public records.

Knowledge Tests

Whenever information is presented to group members about such topics as drug and alcohol abuse and how it affects the body, it is useful to develop a knowledge test to determine whether the information presented was actually learned. Though not sufficient in itself for determining the major outcomes of therapy, the information test is a valuable adjunct for evaluating one's teaching methods. In the studies below, several authors used knowledge tests. Schinke, Blythe, and Gilchrist (1981), in a psychoeducational group to prevent teenage pregnancy, used a sexual facts test. Gwynn and Brantley (1987) used a knowledge test about divorce and how it affects children in the treatment of children whose parents had divorced.

Goal Attainment Scaling

Goal attainment scaling (GAS) (Kiresuk, Smith, & Cardillo, 1994) is another procedure commonly used in group therapy both for defining and for determining the level of attainment of individual and group goals. This method of goal definition and goal measurement permits individualization within a standardized format. Goals of group therapy for each individual are selected before treatment or during the first two group sessions. These goals are stated in observable and highly specific terms, in terms of realistic levels of achievement, in commonsense language, and on a 5-point scale of graded equal-appearing intervals ranging from "much less than expected outcome" to "much better than expected outcome."

For example, one youth in an anger management group was highly aggressive in his communication with his parents. "It wasn't my fault," he claimed. "They pushed my button." His overall "aggression response" was expressed in terms of the following 5-point scale:

- *Much less than expected outcome* (–2). When his parents made (what he perceived to be) unfair demands on him, he would respond most of the time (51% or more) in an angry tone of voice.
- *Less than expected outcome* (–1). When his parents made (what he perceived to be) unfair demands on him, he would frequently respond in an angry tone of voice and would only rarely ask them to clarify and then ask them to reconsider their demands.
- *Expected outcome* (0). When his parents made (what he perceived to be) unfair demands on him, he would respond most of the time (51% or more, but less than 90%) in a matter-of-fact tone of voice by asking them to clarify and then asking them to reconsider their demands. Only occasionally would he respond in an angry tone of voice.
- *Better than expected outcome* (+1). When his parents made (what he perceived to be) unfair demands on him, he would respond almost all of the time (90% or more) in a matter-of-fact tone of voice by asking them to clarify and then asking them to reconsider their demands.
- *Much better than expected outcome* (+2). Whenever his parents made (what he perceived to be) unfair demands on him, he would respond in a matter-of-fact tone of voice by asking them to clarify and then asking them to reconsider their demands.

Once goal attainment scales have been determined, it is possible to rate each scale for each individual (or group) in terms of its relevance,

TABLE 5.2 Monitoring Individual Treatment Goals in Group

Client _____ Group _____ Date of _____

General goals of group _____

1. *Relevance* of each treatment *goal* to the client's general problems

	No Relevance	Slight Relevance	Moderate Relevance	Substantial Relevance	Total
Goal 1	1	2	3	4	5
Goal 2	1	2	3	4	5
Goal 3	1	2	3	4	5
Goal 4	1	2	3	4	5

Comments: _____

2. *Realism* of the *expected level of outcome* for each goal for *this* time, in *this* group

	Much Too Difficult	Too Difficult	Realistic	Too Easy	Much Too Easy
Goal 1	1	2	3	4	5
Goal 2	1	2	3	4	5
Goal 3	1	2	3	4	5
Goal 4	1	2	3	4	5
Comments: _____					

the availability of services necessary to attain the goal, and the realism of the expected level of outcome (Kiresuk et al., 1994, p. 53).

Not all goals are equally important. To compare their relative importance, a form has been used that has been modified from a form reported by Cardillo (1994, p. 53) (see Table 5.2).

GAS has a number of limitations as a research instrument (see, e.g., Seaberg & Gillespie, 1977, for details). Validity and reliability data have not been particularly impressive. Conceptual clarity and consistency across studies can often be questioned. Major scaling problems have not been resolved. In using GAS, one must indeed proceed with caution in interpreting one's results. Despite these limitations, GAS remains a useful clinical tool in establishing individualized and group goals and in evaluating their achievement. It is a method for involving youth and their parents in determining their own goals. The goals consequently tend to be relevant. And it is an excellent means of clarifying the specific purposes of treatment. Moreover, few alternatives appear to be available that permit both individualization and standardization for purposes of comparison across groups and across members.

Group Measurement Instruments

The purpose of group data collection is to identify dimensions of the group structure, group processes, group performance, and group problems. Insofar as these attributes interfere with or enhance the achievement of individual treatment goals, they are formulated in such a way that the group therapist can eventually act on the information. It should be noted that many of these group data collection procedures provide information as to how individuals respond to the group. Thus, the group data also facilitate individual assessment.

Many different procedures are used in collecting data in small groups. To describe most structures and processes, data can be collected on a regular basis throughout the history of the group. Because these data collection procedures are used by group therapists as part of the ongoing assessment process, only those procedures are presented that are minimally intrusive in the treatment process and relatively inexpensive to administer. The major means of collecting data about groups are in-group observations, postsession questionnaires, group GAS, rates of extragroup task completion, attendance and promptness rates and, and rates of dropouts.

In-Group Observational Tools

To get a picture of group phenomena, data can be collected through direct observation of members' interaction with each other. There are many types of observational systems, ranging from simple to highly complex. Because the simple systems have proven to be quite useful and require minimum observer training, they seem to be the most useful to investigate group process. The observers are often colleagues who wish to learn the group method, and observing gives them a function in the group. Students who wish to learn about the treatment method may also be employed as observers. Occasionally, when some of the simpler techniques described below are being used, members of the group have served on a rotating basis as observers.

Of the simpler observation systems, the most commonly used is a fixed-interval system of recording who is talking. This system provides the frequency of participation of each of the members and the therapists, from which one can calculate the distribution of participation among the members and the ratio of member-to-therapist participation. I found that these data correlate highly with outcome in assertiveness training groups (Rose, 1981). In this method, data are recorded every 30 seconds on who is speaking. Shorter time periods may be used, depending on the skill of the observers.

Noting who speaks every time the speaker changes is another simple method of recording participation. This is usually recorded on a pie circle with a segment for each person in the order in which members are seated. The observer merely places a tally in the segment of the pie assigned to the person who is speaking. Consideration is usually not given to the length of time, although some group therapists instruct observers to give an additional check every 20 seconds that a given person is still speaking.

The first method gives one an estimate of the length of time that each person in the group is speaking but often ignores brief interjections. The second provides the group therapist with a better estimate of the frequency with which the low-frequency or short-response speakers speak and tends to exaggerate somewhat the importance of the brief interjection.

If the observer is also asked to indicate, in the first method discussed above, the person to whom the statement is being addressed (with the group being the default category), a whole new dimension in terms of who speaks to whom is added. It should be noted, however, that even this simple addition requires considerably more training before reliable observations can be made.

The major use of observers by group therapists has been individualized categories rather than general observations on everyone. For example, data have been collected by observers on participation in role playing, off-task behavior, positive reinforcement or praise, and criticism or other negative categories. The specific category to be observed depends on the therapist's preassessment of frequently appearing behaviors in the group and the specific research question. If, for example, the group therapist has noted informally that there is too much off-task behavior, it may be useful to observe systematically on-task and off-task behavior for several meetings. In this case, the observers can be trained to identify off-task behavior and then record on a stopwatch all behavior that is off task. As soon as all off-task behavior stops, the stopwatch is stopped. With this method, a group indicator of off-task behavior has been created, but not an indication of who is being off task.

Another commonly observed behavior has been interruptions of others, especially in groups in which aggressive and shy clients are mixed. If one person is speaking and another begins, the act of the second is regarded as an interruption. The initials of the interrupter or a code letter is recorded for every interruption. A group therapist used this method before and after social skill training in an adolescent girls' group to determine whether interruptions would diminish.

In a residential treatment group in which one of the purposes was to increase the positive reinforcing behavior in the group, all responses to others in the group discussion were classified by the observer as positive reinforcement ($+$), punishment ($-$), or neither (0). Although it was found that after 2 hours of training the rate of observer agreement was low (.35), the general trend indicating increase in reinforcement was the same for both observers. It was clear that even with a simple category system more training was required. In this brief study with a time-series design in one group, positive reinforcement in the group did appear to increase, and a self-reported use of positive reinforcement increased in the family. All the above observations can be readily programmed to carry out on laptop computers, providing immediate totals, averages, and standard deviations to the group therapist, who can then inform the group members.

Other, more sophisticated (and hence more costly) observational methods in which multiple categories are observed may be also used to classify the content of the interaction. One of the most commonly used is the Hill (1977) interaction matrix analysis system. Piper, Montvila, and McGihon (1979) described the use of a modified version of the Hill interaction matrix in research on group therapy with adults. There is no reason that the same observation systems could not be used with children or adolescents. However, the problem of cost and the fact that the systems are not narrowly focused on potential target behaviors suggest that such observation systems are best used for a study of general group process in youth groups rather than for relating specific processes to outcome.

Like all assessment and evaluative measures, observational techniques have limitations. Reasonable reliability of observations is always of concern. As in the above example, observations can be quite complex and expensive to administer and provide adequate training for.

All of the above observational methods lend themselves to time-series analysis. Unfortunately, few studies using such designs are actually published. Most of the above examples came from clinical practice. Changes in group attributes have rarely been used in studies on outcomes in groups.

Postsession Questionnaires

One type of self-rating scale is the postsession questionnaire, in which participants rate their own responses to various aspects of each group session. These are in the form of 6 to 12 questions administered to all the members and the therapist at the end of every session. They have two major purposes. The first is to gain information as to how members evaluate the various components of each session and general "consumer" satisfaction with the program. The second is to provide the practitioner with an estimate of how well various group factors are perceived by the members and how the therapist's perception is at variance with that of the members. No one questionnaire is appropriate for every group. The postsession questionnaire below was developed for a general therapy group of adolescents in a day treatment program for adjudicated adolescents. In this group, the staff had very specific hypotheses as to what they thought were curative factors and wanted to see whether these were present in the perception of the clients. They were also interested in expanding the number of comments as to what should be done differently in the group as a basis for correcting the program to fit the needs of its members more closely. This questionnaire is sufficiently general as to provide a point of departure for therapists of other types of groups.

Specifically, this questionnaire was designed to get some estimates of perception of youth concerning the following attributes: usefulness of the experience (Question 1), involvement in group discussion (Question 2), degree of mutual helping (Question 3), degree of self-disclosure (Question 4), degree of autonomy (Question 5), closeness or cohesion (Question 6), emotionality of the group members (Question 7), degree to which the group kept on task (Question 8), autonomy of the group from the leader (Question 9), degree of conflict in the group (Question 10), and intensity of anxiety experienced (Question 11). The amount of agreement among members provides a rough estimate of interjudge reliability. The data can be used in time-series studies on any of the above group attributes.

Group Goal Attainment Scaling

Group GAS can also be used in group therapy as a way of determining whether group goals are achieved. Group goals usually refer to a change in process, such as broader participation, greater cohesion, increased on-task behavior, greater decision making by members, or reduced in-group conflict. Group goals cannot be determined immediately. They are best determined when a problem is identified, usually by postsession questionnaires, observations, or group discussion. The best judges for rating the group are a combination of the members and the leader, who, after presenting their individual judgments, attempt to come to a consensus. In my therapy practice, I commonly use this method to clarify the nature of group problems and to involve the members in evaluating whether the group problem in their minds is resolved. A commonly used example of a group GAS in CBIGT is the following:

- *Much less than expected* (–2). Members talk almost exclusively to group therapist (91% or more of the time).
- *Moderately less than expected* (–1). Members talk primarily to group therapist (65%-90% of the time).
- *Expected level* (0). Members talk about equally to other members and to group therapist (35%-64% of the time).
- *Moderately more than expected* (+1). Members talk primarily to other members (10%-34% of the time).
- *Much more than expected* (+2). Members talk almost exclusively to each other (9% or less of the time).

Although having most of the same difficulties as individual GAS, group GAS appears to be easier for group leaders to formulate. Group GAS is as much a group measurement procedure as it is an intervention strategy.

Rate of Task Completion

The rate of task completion is the percentage of extragroup tasks negotiated with all the members at one session and completed and reported on at a later session. Because each client negotiates a separate set of tasks, the group rate is estimated as the average individual rate of completion. This rate has been shown to correlate highly and significantly with behavioral change, as indicated by the findings on a role-play test with adults in assertiveness training groups (Rose, 1978). The rate of task completion has been used as an index of ongoing session-by-session productivity (Rose & Edleson, 1987) because an extragroup task is a product of the preparation to carry out that task at the previous meeting. Only if that assignment is actually carried out can one consider it an indicator of positive productivity. A low weekly rate of extragroup task completion is a major group problem and usually requires group consideration as soon as it is detected.

One way to determine the rate is to ask members at the beginning of each session what they assigned themselves and which of the tasks they were able to complete partially or fully. The group therapist must determine the percentage to be given to partial completion. Usually, the rate of completion is calculated as if all assignments were of the same importance or relevance to outcome. One problem with this index is that all tasks are not in fact equal in terms of level of difficulty or time required to perform them. An assertive task such as "talking to a new person on 4 different days" might be far more important, time-consuming, and difficult than "writing down a stressful situation that you recently experienced." Some group therapists give more weight to behavioral tasks because of their greater relevance to behavioral change in ascertaining weekly productivity. Despite its limitations, one should probably consider the completion of all tasks alike in ascertaining productivity because of the arbitrariness often involved in weighing tasks.

Attendance and Promptness Rates

One can assume that the more time spent in the CBIGT situation (considering the fact that the average number of sessions is less than 14), the greater the opportunity for learning. To estimate the group rate of attendance, one uses the percentage of members attending a given meeting or the percentage of minutes attended out of total meeting time: For example, if a meeting of a four-person group is 60 minutes long and one person is 10 minutes late, another leaves 5 minutes early, and a third is absent, the ratio would be $(240 - 5 - 10 - 60)/240 = 0.69$. The general formula is $R = (MT - t - AT)/MT$, where R is the percentage of minutes all members are present in the group, M is the number of members in the group, T is time or length in minutes of a meeting, t is the total number of minutes late or leaving early for all members, and A is the number of persons absent.

This measure is useful primarily if attendance is voluntary, although even in groups with involuntary clients, such as adjudicated delinquents on parole, irregularity of attendance is a strong indicator of low cohesion or lack of interest. Resistance may also be indicated by high level of lateness. However, important reasons such as illness of the client or a family member or extreme weather conditions may influence the interpretation of the data.

Dropout Rate

The dropout rate, also for voluntary clients only, is the percentage of members who leave the group against the advice of the therapist. The reasons that youth drop out of therapy prematurely are also worthy of study to determine what the therapists might do differently to maintain their attendance. At the very least, dropouts should be contacted to determine the reasons they are willing to share for their not returning. It is also useful in a given agency to compare dropout rates of staff with comparable groups and with different type of groups.

The collection of group data has primarily been for clinical purposes. The potential for including the findings of group data in evaluation of outcomes is promising. Theoretically, many of these processes, such as cohesion, establishment of protherapeutic norms, broad participation, dropping out of treatment, rates of attendance, and rates of homework completion, have been found to be related to outcome in adult groups (see, e.g., Rose, 1981).

Summary

In this chapter, it was noted that measurement plays an important role, not only to supplement assessment in the determination of problem areas, responses to situations, and clients' resources, but to facilitate the evaluation of outcome and to enhance treatment. Two sets of measures were described: those that measure the client's individual behavior, cognitions, and emotions and those that measure group phenomena. The most common ones are checklists and rating scales by parents and teachers, self-rating checklists and inventories by the client, self-monitoring, extragroup observations by others, role-play tests, sociometric tests, goal attainment scaling, knowledge tests, and social impact measures. The major means of collecting data about groups are in-group observations, postsession questionnaires, group goal attainment scaling, rates of extragroup task completion, attendance rates, and dropout rates. Emphasis was placed on measures that had been or could be used in CBIGT, particularly in youth groups, and that could enhance situational analysis.

CHAPTER 6

Goal Setting and Intervention Planning

With growing frequency, scholars of group therapy are advocating the use of clearly formulated goals (see, e.g., Bednar & Moeschl, 1981; Yalom, 1985) as a vehicle for intervention planning and as a strategy for improving the quality of practice. Yet as one peruses the literature, one finds many different types of goals that are used interchangeably. The purpose of this chapter is to define goals in such a way as to differentiate the types of goals used in goal setting and to relate each type to intervention planning. These definitions have evolved out of our practice, and other authors have used other terminology. In general, the distinctions proposed here seem most effective in achieving the purposes, stated below, of having goals in the first place. To begin with, it is necessary to identify two distinct categories of goals in group therapy, individual and group. Each has a different purpose, and each is discussed separately.

Individual Goal Setting in Groups

The careful articulation of individual goals in group therapy has a number of advantages. First, goals provide a structure around which to organize the group session. In the goal-directed sessions, the foci are on orienting the members to a goal approach, getting information from them (assessment) so that goals can be formulated, training them in goal determination, formulating appropriate goals, examining the potential consequences of goal achievement, selecting interventions appropriate to attaining individualized goals, and evaluating whether goals have been realized. As a result, the structure provided by goals gives both members and the group therapist a sense of direction.

Second, the process of establishing goals can help youth to clarify their expectations for the type of assistance they require and to evaluate their resources and competencies for accomplishing ascertained goals.

Third, the process of goal setting provides a basis for the group therapist to determine whether he or she has the necessary skills or whether the agency has sufficient resources to assist the group members. If not, referral to a social resource more suitable for goal achievement may be the appropriate plan of action.

Fourth, once goals are formulated, they establish the criteria for evaluating the effectiveness of the intervention, the therapist, the group, and the agency. As youth observe their attainment of situational or narrow-range goals, they can be reinforced for their ongoing modest achievements. Failure to achieve or partial achievement of goals suggests reconsideration of strategies for achieving goals and perhaps revision of the goals themselves.

Fifth, careful goal setting increases the likelihood of successful treatment. At least in one study in which goals were determined with one set of adolescents and not with another set, the goal-oriented practice was found to be the more effective of the two (Maher, 1987). Goal setting has had some cross-cultural validation. Taussig (1987) found that Mexican Americans responded as positively to goal setting as did the Anglo-Americans in a group work project.

The group therapist must also be aware of some crucial limitations of goal setting. Without adequate assessment, premature goal setting may result in massive efforts on behalf of something of little significance to the client. Not all youth in the same group are ready at the same time to venture into goal setting. Goals tend to be threatening to the poorly motivated client, although sometimes the process of goal determination may increase that motivation. Goal setting requires considerable attention to detail and awareness of what the client is saying. The attempt to establish goals can easily become a control issue if the therapist-client relationship has not been clearly established. A preliminary goal might in this case be the establishment of goals to which the client is committed.

Types of Individual Goals in Group Therapy

Let us briefly distinguish and illustrate the following types of individual goals used in CBIGT: treatment goals (or long-term goals), mediating goals, situational goals (or short-term goals), shared goals, service goals, and mandated goals.

Treatment Goals

Treatment goals are derived from the general presenting problem determined in assessment. In particular, two types of treatment goals can be identified. The first are those that involve a change in behavioral, attitudinal, cognitive, and/or affective responses or emotional and physical states under implied or specified conditions. The second are those that involve the obtaining of deficient resources or some product. Examples of treatment goals in which the situation is explicit and the response (cognitive or behavioral) follows the situation are the following:

- By the end of treatment, I will respond to stressful situations by relaxing and correcting any self-defeating or anxiety-inducing thoughts.
- By the end of treatment, I will respond to criticism with which I do not agree with a request for greater clarification.
- By the end of treatment, when people make requests that impose on me, I will refuse politely but firmly.
- By the end of therapy, when adults tell me to do things that I don't think are fair, I will explain to them in a matter-of-fact tone of voice the reasons for my concern.

In the formulation of treatment goals, the steps for achieving them are not stated.

Examples of treatment goals in which the situation is implicit or nonexistent and the achievement is a product are the following:

- By the end of treatment, I will have received my GED.
- Within 2 months, I will have gotten a job in the post office.
- Within 2 to 3 months, I will have made at least two new friends.

■ By next month, I will have increased the number and amount of time spent in socio-recreational activities.

Usually both types of treatment goals are designed to be achieved by the end of therapy or at some specified time after treatment has been completed. For this reason, they are also called *long-term goals*. They are more specific than a general statement of the problem but not as specific as the situational goals described below. Achievement of the treatment goal should contribute to the resolution of the presenting problem. An example of a general problem that Garth presents is excessive anger when he does not get what he wants or when he is criticized. With the help of the group, Garth defined the following treatment goal: "By the end of treatment, when I am presented with criticism, anger of others, or other (what I perceive to be) stressful events, I will take a deep breath, relax, and remind myself of the consequences of anger or violent behavior."

To operationalize treatment goals, at least two types of subgoals can be defined: mediating goals and situational goals. Each of these is described separately below.

Mediating Goals

Mediating goals are the acquisition of or improvement in the behavioral or cognitive coping skills that a client requires to achieve the more general treatment goal. For example, if the treatment goal is to be more relaxed and to experience less discomfort in stressful situations, some of the skills needed to be learned may be managing one's time more effectively, using relaxation to deal with arousal, and applying systematic problem solving to a problem. Many of these skills are also important end goals in their own right in that they are helpful in day-to-day functioning. Another set of mediating goals is intermediate goals that must be achieved before the long-term goal can be achieved. For example, when the long-term goal is getting a job, the mediating goals might be reading the want ads daily, learning effective interviewing skills, and learning to dress appropriately for the interview.

Situational Goals

These involve the application of behavioral, cognitive, and/or affective coping responses to specified or implied conditions within a specified but short time period. The time period in which situational goals are to be achieved is usually shorter than the end of treatment, and the performance that indicates goal achievement is more specifically formulated. Most commonly, situational goals are to be completed the next time a given event occurs or by the next session or within a month or less. They are also restricted to a highly specific set of conditions or situations. They are usually formulated positively. That is, rather than stopping being angry when criticized, the person performs a behavior or expresses a self-thought that is an alternative to being angry. The achievement of situational goals usually contributes to the achievement of the more general treatment goals and points directly to home tasks that can be performed by the youth. Continuing with the above example, a situational goal that might be formulated would be "In the course of the following 2 weeks, whenever anyone criticizes me (what I perceive to be) unfairly, I will tell the person in a matter-of-fact tone of voice what he does that upsets me." The treatment goal to which this situational goal is related would be "By the end of .treatment, I will manage unfair criticism with stress-reducing strategies." In this case, the treatment goal covers a wider range of circumstances and a longer period of time with a more general category of responses.

In summary, mediating goals and situational goals are subsets of treatment goals. They usually involve a shorter duration and/or a narrower range of behaviors or cognitions that need to be changed. It should be noted that the distinctions between treatment goals and subgoals are not always as sharp as in the examples above and that each treatment goal is usually associated with several situational goals.

Table 6.1 clarifies further the relationship of general treatment goals to subgoals.

Shared Goals

What is particularly important in group therapy is that some treatment goals, many mediating goals, and occasionally situational goals for individuals are shared by some or all of the members of the group. For example, in a group for adolescent victims of incest, a shared treatment goal was that by the end of therapy all clients would discuss their victimization with relatives and others who had been aware of their victimization as a child but who had done nothing about it. The shared mediating goal might be "By the next session, all members of the group

TABLE 6.1 General Problems, Treatment Goals, Mediating Goals, and Situational Goals

General Problem	Treatment Goal	Mediating Goal	Situational Goal
Terence is extremely bossy with his peers. If people don't do what he wants, he gets angry.	By the end of treatment, when I want something from others, I will request it and give my reasons rather than demand it.	By next session, I will identify situations in which I make demands and put them in my diary.	The next time I would like someone to do something, I will ask him in a matter-of-fact tone of voice, and if he refuses, I will say, "That's okay."
Billy is a socially isolated youth with few friends and few interests. He says he is lonely.	By the end of treatment, I will participate, weekly, in several new socio-recreational activities.	Before next group session, I will explore the available social activities at the local Y.	By next month, I will go bowling with Peter at least once and go to the movies with someone else at least once.
Shelly is in constant arguments with her parents and teachers. If she disagrees, she argues, and it ends up with her getting in trouble at school and punished at home.	By the end of treatment, when I disagree with my parents or teachers about a specific issue, I will attempt to resolve the differences calmly and systematically.	By the end of the month, I will demonstrate how to use systematic problem solving and negotiation in the group.	The next time a problem occurs between my parents and me, I will ask to problem-solve it systematically with them and negotiate any differences.
Laura, who dropped out of school last year, is having difficulty in finding a good job. She can't afford to quit her minimum-wage job to go back to school.	By the end of treatment, I will obtain my GED.	By next month, I will work with my tutor in math for a total of 10 hours and learn how to study more effectively on my own.	Next week, when I go to my tutor, I will make a plan as to how much I will study each week.

will write a statement in which they tell the significant other about their victimization." A shared treatment goal would be one in which all the members, by the end of treatment, would improve their skills in meeting new people and making new friends. A shared situational goal related to the above would be that during the course of the following week each member of the group would inform the person who was aware of the victimization, when that person was present, about what the experience had done to him or her and would ask the person for an explanation of why he or she had ignored what was going on. Such goals held in common by two or more members of the group usually increase the attraction of the group and the likelihood that the goal will be achieved. Moreover, as we pointed out earlier, shared goals are efficient to work toward because practice by one represents modeling to the others in the area of concern. The most common shared goals are mediating goals because learning concrete skills is an important part of CBIGT.

Service Goals

In working with delinquents or low-income group members, a special category of either treatment or situational goals needs to be considered: that is, goals involving situations in which the client requires concrete information or financial or physical supports and resources in some given time period. These are referred to as *service goals*—for example, "By next week, Jim and his family will have received food stamps from the local welfare office." (He may have first had to achieve the mediating goal of calling the agency and filling out the forms necessary to get those food stamps.) To expect that juvenile offenders will make psychological changes when their living conditions are abominable and they are hungry is usually expecting too much. Working toward the achievement of service goals may or may not be appropriate in most types of group therapy. When major real-world problems are found, such as hunger or a lack of adequate clothing or housing, and these cannot be dealt with directly in the group, at the very least, referral to other services is required.

Mandated Goals

All of the goals above are to a large extent selected by the client, though they may be suggested by or modified with the help of other group members or the group therapist. But some treatment goals are mandated by the referring agency or the referring persons. For example, the client who is on parole may be referred to the agency by the courts as an alternative to going to jail. The goal of finding less damaging ways to handle anger-inducing situations is implied in the referral. The likelihood of attaining mandated goals is limited until the client accepts the mandated goal as something he or she would like to strive for. As the more reluctant members observe the process of goal definition by the more accepting members, they often begin to participate more actively in the process. If all of the group members are reluctant, models from previous groups may be brought in.

In conclusion, all of the above types of goals appear to be interrelated. In many cases, it is necessary to sequence goals in terms of their degree of abstraction, from more concrete and simple to more complex, and from shorter duration to longer duration. This permits the therapist and client to determine the order in which goals need to be worked on.

How to Formulate Useful Goals

A number of principles can help guide the group therapist in assisting youth to formulate and select useful goals for themselves. These principles are related to level of specificity, the target of change, the time frame, the situation in which the goal is to occur, the relationship to the presenting problem, the positive formulation, the level of difficulty, and the degree of importance. Each of these is described in more detail below.

Relate the Treatment Goal to the Presenting Problem

Good assessment leads to the establishment of one or more presenting problems. Usually, the presenting problems are quite abstract. Informed goal setting makes use of the information acquired during the assessment process as defined in Chapter 5. It is formulated in such a way as to reflect the nature of at least one aspect of the presenting problem. For example, if the presenting problem is that the client is rarely involved in any physical activity other than fighting, the treatment goal might be that by the end of treatment the client will be participating in intramural sports after school. For other examples of the relationship of the general problem to treatment, mediating, and situational goals, see Table 6.1.

Formulate Specifically

The presenting problem is often quite general. Goals are formulated at several levels of abstraction, all of which are less abstract than the general problem. The most general are the treatment goals. But even these should describe observable conditions or observable behaviors or should refer to more concrete phenomena. The general problem is Hank does not get along with his mother. The goal "By the end of therapy, I will get along better with my mother" is too general. It would be more in keeping with the principle of specificity to add to the goal, "as evidenced by fewer arguments, more requests of each other and fewer demands, and more time spent in normal conversation."

Situational and mediating goals should be formulated with verbs such as *do, describe, demonstrate,* and *increase,* and not *understand, be able, feel,* or *want to.* Adjectives such as *appropriate* should be defined in terms of the specific behavior. Thus, it is better to state a mediational goal as "By next week, I will describe the conditions under which I become angry" rather than as "I will understand the relationship of my anger to the conditions that elicit it." It is also better to state a treatment goal as "The next time someone puts pressure on me to do something I don't want to do, I will tell him or her in a matter-of-fact tone of voice that I'd rather not do it, but thanks for asking" than as "The next time someone puts pressure on me to do something I don't want to do, I will behave appropriately." If the goal is described in the more specific way, it can be more readily monitored, and one knows more clearly when and if it is achieved.

When the treatment goal involves prerequisite skill situations, multiple goals should be formulated for each of the skills in the appropriate order. For example, if Billy's treatment goal is to improve his relationships with his friends, the mediating skill goals might be, first, to describe how his present behavior affects other people. Then, on the basis of this information, he might set as subsequent goals to demonstrate what to say when approaching others, to show minimal conversational skills or "small talk," and to express feelings appropriately. Similarly, if the treatment goal involves multiple situations, a number of situational goals should be established. Joy's treatment goal is to improve her relationships with others. Two of her situational goals are "Whenever people tease me, I will ask them what they mean" and "Whenever I feel overwhelmed by someone, I will state how I feel."

The process of goal definition involves continuously becoming more specific. When goals are too general, the therapist and other group members will assist the client in defining terms. When Jerry stated that his treatment goal was to reduce his sense of isolation, the therapist asked the group what each of them understood by *isolation.* Then Jerry was asked to define the concept in terms of the concrete phenomena he experienced. In Jerry's case, it meant no friends with whom he could talk about his problems and accomplishments and no one to call up at the last minute "to hang out with." Therefore, the situational goal became "By next week I will call Damien and plan to do something with him."

Identify the Situation

In the formulation of situational goals, the conditions under which the goal behavior or goal cognitions should be performed should be described. In all of the situational goals in Table 6.1, the situation is described. Usually the situation is external and, as in situational analysis, involves a place, a certain time, certain people, and certain actions or interactions. Sometimes the situation is internal; thus, in Jerry's example, it is whenever he feels sad and lonely.

Identify the Target Person

First, every individual goal posits a target person whose condition, behavior, attitudes, cognitions, beliefs, emotional state, or available resources will change (or be maintained) under a given set of conditions. The target person is that client who brings her or his problem to the group during the assessment phase. Often, a client will request or even insist that change in another person such as the parent or residential worker or change in the environment must be his or her goal.

Of course, some youth do indeed find themselves in devastating circumstances over which they have little or no direct control. But while environmental change strategies are being considered, attitudinal or cognitive change goals may also be contemplated. An example of two inappropriate goals set for others are the proposed goals of one youth that his dad will be more understanding when the youth comes home exhausted from a bad day at school and that his residential worker will become more flexible about interpreting the rules. In most cases, these very attempts to change others represent a major source of the client's present unhappiness or sense of failure. When a client insists that a significant other should be the target person, the other group members are encouraged to discuss the difficulties involved in changing others. Usually, examples are employed to enhance the group discussion. This is not an easy step for many youth to take, but it may be a major step required before they can achieve significant change. This does not mean that the therapist may not attempt to bring about changes in the significant other by referral or by family counseling. But these do not occur in the context of the group.

Formulate a Time Frame

Inherent in the formulation of goals is the estimated time frame within which the goal is expected to be achieved. "Within 3 months," "by the end of therapy," "within 2 to 4 days," and "by next session" are examples of such qualifications. Without an appraisal of the time element required, little pressure is generated for achieving progress toward the given goal. Instead of a fixed time frame, one may also use a range, such as "within 2 to 4 days." Most, but not all, treatment goals are limited to those that can be achieved during the time within which treatment is occurring. As the group approaches termination, goals are set within a longer time frame beyond termination from the group; for example, "Within 3 months of leaving the group, Dora will reenter school and complete the last year of her high school program." Chapter 15 discusses the issues of formulating goals for time periods following treatment (generalization) and plans and strategies for increasing the likelihood that they will be achieved.

Formulate Positively

Often problems are stated in terms of the nonperformance of certain behaviors, such as "not fighting when someone pushes my button." The better formulation is in terms of performing an alternative behavior to fighting, such as "When a guy on the street tries to start a fight with me, I will walk away as quickly as I can." Most intervention strategies seem to be more effective in achieving positively as opposed to negatively formulated goals. There are some exceptions to this rule. Mandated goals such as avoiding persons with a criminal history, stopping abuse of siblings or of parents, or stopping any other behavior that is considered an illegal act or violence toward another may be stated in their negative form. At the most concrete situational goal level, however, it is particularly important that positive alternatives be stated. Thus, the mandated treatment goal stated for Jamala may be that she will stop her physical abuse of her brother. But the situational goal will be that when her brother teases or otherwise annoys her (the conditions under which she currently abuses her brother), she will report this to her mother or leave the room without comment. Similarly, although 14-year-old Joey's treatment goal is to stop drinking alcoholic beverages, he will have as one of his situational goals that when he is with his friends and they insist that he have something alcoholic to drink, he will explain that it will get him into deep trouble, firmly refuse an alcoholic beverage, and ask for a soft drink.

Training the Group Members in the Use of the Above Criteria

To train youth in using the above criteria in the formulation of goals, the criteria are shared with them, with many examples given by the therapist. Then the group is presented with Exercise 6.1.

Exercise 6.1. Goal Formulation

Purpose: By the end of this exercise, each participant will formulate a goal for him- or herself meeting the criteria for effective formulation.

Individual Task 1: Read the following goals and correct them, using the principles of goal formulation. Determine which goals are or are not correctly formulated, and explain the principles that each example demonstrates.

1. Jeff's situational goal is to get his dad to give him more money.

2. Andrea's situational goal is that whenever she gets the urge to eat, she will exercise.

3. Madeline's treatment goal is to get along better with her sister.

4. Delmar's treatment goal is that whenever anyone "gets in his face," he won't hit them.

5. Richter's goal is that by the end of the group sessions, when the teacher or any other adult criticizes him and he doesn't understand why, he will ask for an explanation for the criticism in a matter-of-fact tone of voice.

6. Gifford's goal is that if the counselor gives him a task he really doesn't want to do, he won't complain.

Group Task 1: Each participant will share his or her results with a partner and then with the group as a whole.

Individual Task 2: Each participant will formulate a goal for him- or herself and show it to a partner.

Group Task 2: The partners helps each other to edit their goals, and they present each one's goal to the group for further evaluation. Then the therapist once again reviews the principles and the examples that the participants have provided.

The Process of Goal Structuring

The following principles are related to the process of developing goals: Involve the client and significant others, make sure the goal is important to the client, determine an appropriate level of difficulty, determine if adequate resources are available, ascertain the risks involved in goal achievement, and describe the restraints on goal achievement.

Involve the Client and Significant Others in Goal Formulation

Through involvement in goal formulation, goals become relevant to the client and motivation to achieve them increases. The group therapist occasionally checks whether a given goal continues to be important to the client. The group therapist may encourage other group members to suggest possible goals, and he or she may present models of goals, but each person is expected to determine his or her own goals. The other group members are expected to provide each member with feedback on how well each goal meets the criteria.

The more the group as a whole is involved in goal formulation, the wider the range of goals selected and the greater the likelihood that the goal will be achieved. The group has more ideas than any one individual, so each individual has more goals to choose from. In addition, the group is committed to helping those people who have selected goals from ideas generated by the group. The more experienced members can model for the less experienced ones, especially in open-ended groups. Individual and Group Tasks 2 in the above exercise are also good ways to involve the members in the formulation of their own goals.

Parents and teachers, if possible, and relevant others should also be involved in goal setting. If they are involved at this early phase of treatment, they are more likely to cooperate in facilitating the intervention process. Many of the important goals are for changes of behaviors that are a nuisance to, or painful for, significant others. Their input is essential for relevant selection and formulation. The client may be forced to negotiate with the significant others as to the eventual specific content of the goals. To involve parents, the client is often given the home task of asking parents, teachers, or other significant others what goals they see as appropriate for him or her. The client may have to present the significant others with the criteria for goal formulation. If communication with significant others is not well enough established, the group therapist may act as intermediary.

Make Sure the Goal Is Important

All too often, in the pressure to formulate something, the client proposes trivial goals. Of course, the group therapist does not always know what is trivial and what is important. At the very least, the client should be asked whether a given goal is important and why. Important goals are those that have long-term consequences that are better than the present state of affairs. Important goals are those with which parents and significant others are also concerned. Importance is also closely linked to the level of difficulty.

Determine an Appropriate Level of Difficulty

Although the level of difficulty of a given goal should be such that achieving it will be a challenge, a goal should not be so difficult that even with training it is not achievable in the stated period of time. In the beginning of treatment, it is more effective to take very small steps in setting situational or mediating goals and to help the client accrue a history of success than to set more demanding goals, many of which will fall by the wayside. It is often not possible to determine how difficult a goal will turn out to be. At the very least, the level of difficulty should be considered by the client for each goal formulated.

Determine Available Resources

How realistic a given goal might be depends at least in part on an appraisal of the personal and environmental resources available to the client for those goals, the barriers to achieving them, and the potential long- and short-term consequences of the proposed responses. Whether stated in the goal or as part of a general statement associated with the goal, the client's skills and resources for achieving the goal should be taken into consideration. Such information makes it possible to determine how realistic the goal is. As Gambrill (1983, p. 117) pointed out, goals should be built on the client's assets, not only on deficits or problems.

Pay Attention to Risks

Each person should be aware of the potential risks involved if his or her goal is achieved. The client must decide whether the level of risk is something she or he is willing to accept. In discussing risks, the client should be asked to compare the risks of continuing the present pattern of responses with those that might be encountered in carrying out the new goal responses. In a group of young women having difficulties with their parents, one decided that her goal was to tell her parents face to face that she did not want any more restrictions and would not tolerate them. That turned out to be the trigger for the parents' grounding her for a month. If she had better evaluated the risk and noted the potential consequences, perhaps she would have experienced less devastating results.

It should be noted that some risk taking is essential to change and that unwillingness to take any risks is as likely to result in failure as excessive risk taking. Some youth are disinclined to do anything that is new or challenging because their central problem is not taking risks and being fearful of all new situations. Such adolescents should be encouraged with the help of the group to aim their sights a little higher and to gradually formulate more challenging goals.

Identify Restraints on Goal Formulation

The content of a goal is delimited by agency purpose, except in private practice, and by the skill of the therapist. If an agency has as its avowed purpose to serve the needs of recovering alcoholics, then goals should be related to that purpose or the client should be referred elsewhere. However, agencies tend to interpret their own purposes broadly or narrowly in terms of the pressure on their staff and the availability of resources. In groups, to a large degree, the individual treatment goals are restricted in their definition by the general group purpose or theme to which the members agreed when they joined the group. This may have been a greater specification of the agency purpose. For example, in a group organized for the purpose of helping pregnant teenagers to be better parents, one member set up goals to improve her relationship with her boyfriend. Unless the members could find a clear relationship between group purpose and the goal, the goal would have to be modified or a different goal pursued.

The content of goals is also delimited by ethical constraints. A client who wants to set a goal that results in harm to another would not gain the cooperation of the group therapist or the group. Lyon's goal was to get his younger brother to give up a small part of his allowance to Lyon. The therapist discussed the goal with the group as a whole, who found it to be dishonest and manipulative; however, the proposal of the goal turned out to be an opportunity to raise questions about moral responsibility in goal setting.

Common Problems in Goal Setting

One problem that often arises in goal setting is that youth select goals that they do not have the resources or competencies to realize. The problem may lie in such conditions as an economic downturn, the total unavailability of inexpensive housing, or extreme criticism by the person on whom the client is dependent to keep his or her job. It is often helpful to determine with the client which aspects of the problem are immutable and over which aspects he or she has some influence. Often, what is defined as unchangeable will reveal new possibilities under close examination. While environmental change strategies are being considered, attitudinal or cognitive change goals related to what is in the control of the client may also be contemplated. One adolescent was the major caretaker of her father, who had Alzheimer's disease. Although she could not rid the father of his Alzheimer's disease or immediately find a high-paying job because of her own lack of skills and the economic situation, she did set as her goal maximizing the use of the welfare system for which she was eligible and getting respite care. She also set the (cognitive) goal for herself of recognizing that she was doing all that her own resources permitted.

A common error is to confuse the goal with the intervention. For example, the group therapist or client states that the goal is to provide the client with emotional support. Here, the activity of providing support is what the group therapist does and thus is an intervention. A goal should usually be defined in terms of the client's attribute to be changed or the resource to be received by the client. In the above example, the goal could be that the client, who evaluates almost all social situations negatively, will evaluate an increasing number of his or her life experiences as positive. The intervention is emotional support provided by the group therapist or self-reinforcement provided by the client.

Group Goals

Group goals are interactive patterns among groups that the group as a whole agrees to modify or maintain or are products of group interactions to be achieved within a given time period. Examples of group goals involving a change in group process are the following:

- If the norms in the group (an agreement among members) are for members to blame their parents for their own patterns of violence, a group goal might be to replace the above norm with the norm that each person take responsibility for his or her own violent behavior. (Some might prefer to call this a group value.)
- If the pattern of interaction in the group is primarily directed from member to therapist and not from member to member, the group goal might be to increase member-to-member interaction by next month.
- If the cohesion of the group is low (as evidenced by infrequent attendance and poor participation), the group goal might be to increase the attraction of the members to each other and to the program as a whole within 2 weeks.
- If the distribution of participation among members is too high (the group problem), the group goal might be to lower that distribution (lessen the differences among them) within two sessions.

Examples of a modified product of group interaction would be the following:

- If the extragroup task completion rate is generally low (about 60%), the group goal might be that by the end of the next week the rate of task completion would be 80%.

■ If the group is not finishing its agenda items, the goal might be to finish at least all but one of the items by the end of the given session.

It should be noted that many group goals tend to aim at resolving group problems associated with a particular phase of group development. Attention in the early phase needs to be paid to increasing group cohesion and establishing protherapeutic norms. Also in this phase, a shift from predominantly therapist-to-member interaction to youth-to-youth interaction patterns becomes an important goal. Later, as it is determined that extragroup tasks are not being completed, an increase in completion rates and the selection of more relevant tasks become the goals. With the advent of increasing interpersonal conflict among the members in the revision phase, the group goal would be to increase cooperative activity. Lowering the cohesion of the group relative to other social or family groups represents a late-phase goal. Other types of group goals are those that aim at the attainment of those attributes required to relate to and work with the group therapist and other group members.

Group goals may be suggested by the members or the therapist on the basis of his or her observations or the weekly data that are collected on the postsession questionnaires. Members may be annoyed by a given norm, and the majority may wish to change it. How a group therapist involves the group in strategies for bringing about such changes is discussed in Chapter 14. Two possible strategies may be systematic group problem solving and the formulation of group goal attainment scales (see Chapter 5).

Like treatment goals, group goals can be defined at different levels of abstraction. The achievement of the more general group goal is facilitated by first aiming at a more specific goal. For example, increasing the frequency of mutual positive feedback is a group goal that, if achieved, facilitates the achievement of the more general group goal of improving interpersonal relationships in the group.

The achievement of each group goal should also enhance the achievement of individual treatment goals. For example, if the members achieve the group goal of effectively giving more constructive critical feedback to each other, this improves the likelihood that each member separately will give effective feedback to significant others at school or at work. One could basically ignore the group and work with each individual to determine the most efficacious goals. One could probably get more goals and perhaps even better quality goals than if one involved the group. But the group therapist would be unlikely to generate much enthusiasm for pursuit of the goals, and the members would be relatively uncommitted.

Shared Goals Versus Group Goals

Shared goals are individual goals held in common by several or all of the group members. Though often referred to as *group goals,* shared goals do not focus on group interaction. Group goals, moreover, are usually not treatment goals; rather, they are focused on conditions that optimize the achievement of treatment goals. There are some exceptions. For example, in residential treatment, when the group lives together for many months, the group goal of increasing cohesion or creating cooperative norms may very well be considered a treatment goal as well as a group goal.

Principles of Planning for Interventions

Once the group members have carefully formulated their desired goals, an intervention plan can be developed. An intervention plan is a statement of a set of strategies designed to facilitate the achievement of designated goals. Goals most likely to be achieved are those for which some strategy is advocated to achieve them. Although it is true that sometimes careful formulation of a goal will result in goal attainment, if the goal is not readily attained following its statement, intervention planning and subsequent implementation of interventions are required. Principles of planning for those interventions are discussed in the following sections.

One can distinguish between treatment, service, and relationship/cohesion-building interventions. Treatment interventions consist of such methods as facilitating insight, modeling and rehearsal, feedback, problem solving, providing information, coping skill training, relaxation training, moral reasoning, social networking, self-reinforcement, group member reinforcement, and budgeting training. Service interventions consist of ways of helping youth to identify, obtain, and use social and physical resources available to them. Examples of relationship-building interventions are therapist self-disclosure as a means of promoting youth self-disclosure, a description by the therapist of the group members' right to confidentiality, empathic statements, and general supportive statements.

The following principles have evolved in practice for selecting the best possible intervention plan: Select strategies with the best empirical foundation, encourage the client's responsibility in developing the plan, permit a flexible intervention plan, evolve a multiple intervention plan, and monitor and evaluate the effects of intervention.

Select Strategies With the Best Empirical Foundation

Intervention strategies are preferred that have the best empirical foundation. Because only a few goals suggest interventions that demonstrate a strong empirical relationship, this principle is often overlooked. In the treatment of phobias, depression, and anger control and stress management, cognitive-behavioral strategies have achieved a modicum of success as compared with control conditions and other methods and should be given serious attention when selecting a strategy. Often, these strategies have been combined with insight strategies or medication so that there is a blurring of what is causing successful outcomes. There are some data to demonstrate that the goal of solving concrete problems is often achievable using systematic problem solving (see, e.g., Locke, Frederick, Buckner, & Bobko, 1984; Locke, Shaw, Saari, & Latham, 1981). In the absence of empirical evidence to support an intervention approach with a given goal, clinical support is usually drawn on.

Increase Members' Responsibility in Planning

In the initial phases of intervention planning, the group therapist in community groups usually guides the planning process. In residential groups, there are usually some experienced youth who can help guide the process at all times. It is often the group therapist who is best informed about the range of potential strategies that might be employed. However, just as in goal setting, youth may provide a rich source of ideas as to what they might do to achieve a goal. Furthermore, youth have had previous problems that they have solved successfully or other therapeutic experiences in which useful interventions were employed. As the relationship progresses, youth accrue greater experience and new therapeutic skills and are in a continually better position to contribute to the planning process. Thus, involvement in goal formulation is a function of group development.

Permit a Flexible Structure

Plans developed early in the relationship for strategies to be employed or specific actions to be taken are only tentative. As information accrues and as such plans are tried out and found to be inadequate to achieve the client's purposes, the plans are usually revised, sometimes eliminated, and occasionally replaced with new plans. An initial plan may be regarded as a point of departure to guide future planning. Adequate time must be allowed to give the interventions a realistic test.

Employ Multiple Intervention Strategies

It appears that one single procedure is rarely if ever sufficient to achieve the complex goals to which most youth aspire. For this reason, consideration is given in intervention planning to multiple strategies, each of which aims at the achievement of a given set of goals. In achieving the goal of obtaining better health services, one youth visited several free clinics and found out whether he was qualified, looked at the insurance plans of several potential jobs, and contacted the ombudsman for health care in his city. To carry out these discussions, he was trained by the other group members through modeling and rehearsal procedures on how to interview, and, together with the group therapist, he gave himself successively more difficult extragroup tasks.

Monitor the Effects of Intervention

Goals are relevant only insofar as progress is made toward their achievement. Interventions are useful only if they facilitate that progress. To determine the level of progress toward goals, a number of monitoring strategies are available to the group therapist.

The least intrusive way to monitor the effects of intervention is to ask youth at the beginning of every session where they are with respect to each of the goals established in the counseling process. First, the goals are reviewed, and then the work related to each is discussed. The evidence for achievements or failures is anecdotal, but it can be explored in some depth in the group discussion. Some practitioners also use a self-rating scale on which youth rate themselves at each session or periodically on each goal from 1 (little achievement) to 5 (complete achievement). The group therapist then discusses the reasons for the given rating with the client. On the basis of this discussion, the group therapist usually fills in the same scales. Increasing use is presently being made of rapid-assessment instruments (see, e.g., Hudson, 1982). These are brief sets of rating scales (10-25 items), each of which is related to a given goal area.

In monitoring the client's achievement of goals, teachers or parents may be asked to comment periodically on goal attainment. In the case of institutionalized youth, residential and treatment staff can be asked to observe the achievement of goals as well. This serves to coordinate the efforts of staff or parents and the group therapist in the clinical process. Rating scales and nondirective accounts of performance are also particularly helpful (see Chapter 5 for details).

Treatment Planning Is an Ongoing Process

Treatment plans do not remain static. As new information accrues and as new skills in self-treatment are acquired by the client, more sophisticated plans can be developed. The client, too, runs into new problems and has new concerns. Treatment planning must take these experiences into account. As a result, one can plan more concretely for nearest sessions and somewhat more generally for the future.

Treatment Planning Must Consider the Group

When developing a plan of treatment, the group therapist must consider the impact on all the members. If the members were being treated individually, this would obviously not be a concern. Helping one member to learn the skills that he or she needs to achieve his or her goals should either help the other members of the group to achieve their treatment goals or put them in the position of assisting the one member with his or her problems. For example, if one group member needed to be assertive with friends who wanted him to join them in illegal activities, the other members either would serve to give him ideas about what he could say or, if they had similar problems, would profit from his role plays. They would also act as significant others in a role play. One of the reasons that groups should be somewhat homogeneous as to presenting problems is that most goals can then be shared goals and require the same or a shared intervention plan. Even when the intervention in the group is similar, the extragroup tasks can be highly individualized.

Summary

In this chapter, different type of goals have been defined. A major distinction has been made between goals for individuals and goals for the group. Individual goals have been classified as treatment goals, mediating goals, and situational goals. The latter categories are the more concrete. Also, service goals, mandated goals, and shared goals have been identified, and a distinction has been made between shared individual goals and group goals, which refer to group interaction.

Goal setting and intervention planning appear to be powerful clinical tools in directing the group therapy process. Goals should be viewed primarily as part of a larger problem-solving process. Goal setting is usually preceded by orientation and assessment and followed by intervention planning, implementation of the intervention, and preparation for generalization. One must recognize that goal setting and intervention planning are complex processes and demand care at each step of the way. Training and practice in appropriate goal setting and planning are essential prerequisites to their use. Adherence to the various principles discussed above for maximizing goal attainment and planning effective treatment should further enhance the usefulness of the CBIGT approach.

The content of intervention planning is twofold: developing a plan for solving problems determined in assessment and developing a plan for learning skills necessary to solve those problems. This occurs simultaneously with planning for building and maintaining the cohesion of the group. In the next set of chapters, a wide range of interventions will be examined that facilitate problem solving and the learning of skills. Although examined separately for purposes of analysis, in practice the intervention strategies are often combined, as will be illustrated in the following chapters.

PART III

Interventions In and
Beyond the Group

CHAPTER 7

Solving Problems and Negotiating Differences

Solving Problems

Social problem solving has been defined as a cognitive-affective-behavioral process through which an individual or group identifies or discovers effective means of coping with problems in everyday living (D'Zurilla, 1986, p. 11). It is at the same time a social learning process, a self-management technique, and a general coping strategy. Most youth in trouble are characterized by impetuous problem solving (Lochman, 1985; Lochman et al., 1981). Most seem to have dedicated and rigid strategies of dealing with problems and are disinclined to look at other possibilities. Hops, Tildesley, Lichtenstein, and Ary (1990) examined social problem-solving interactions of adolescents in 128 single-parent families on substance and non-substance-related issues. They discovered that families of substance abusers may not be very skilled at resolving issues, whether or not these are drug related. The purpose of social problem solving in group therapy is threefold: first, to solve the immediate problems with which youth are being confronted in their everyday lives; second, to help them learn the behavioral and cognitive techniques and knowledge of material and social resources necessary to solve these problems; and third, to help them learn the particular skills of social problem solving so that they can, on their own, solve problems methodically when these occur following therapy.

D'Zurilla (1986) has developed problem solving as a complete therapy in itself (problem-solving therapy). In groups, it is used as one major element of a cognitive-behavioral program (similar to the usage proposed by Lochman & Curry, 1986). Because of the presence of multiple sources of ideas, problem solving especially lends itself to a group context. Although drawing heavily on the works of D'Zurilla (1986), this chapter presents problem solving as one of many interventions that can be used in groups. Nevertheless, it is an extremely important intervention because it lends itself, for reasons explained later, to the unique characteristics of the group.

Social problem solving assumes a set of skills to be applied differentially to difficult situations. Most amenable are those situations for which no apparent solution is available to meet the client's needs or resolve the client's concerns or discomfort. The specific skills taught by problem-solving training are (a) alternative thinking, or the ability to generate multiple alternative solutions to interpersonal problem situations; (b) consequential thinking, or the ability to anticipate short- and long-term consequences of a particular alternative and then to use this in decision making; and (c) means-end thinking, or the ability to plan a series of specific means or actions necessary to carry out the solution to an interpersonal problem (Spivack & Shure, 1974).

Steps in Problem Solving in Groups

The problem-solving process discussed in this book is carried out by and in the group in a series of more or less sequential phases and in relation to given problematic situations. Generally, variations of these phases have been outlined previously by D'Zurilla (1986), who proposed the following steps:

1. Problem orientation
2. Problem definition and formulation
3. Generation of alternatives
4. Decision making
5. Solution implementation and verification

Although drawing for the most part on the above steps, we have found it useful to formulate them somewhat differently for use within the context of the group by breaking down some of them into their components:

1. Orienting youth to problems as part of everyday life
2. Defining the problem
3. Determining client goal(s) in the situation
4. Generating tasks and strategies to facilitate achievement of the goal
5. Evaluating, selecting, and preparing for tasks most likely to facilitate achievement of the goal
6. Training and preparing youth to implement the tasks
7. Implementing the selected tasks in the real world
8. Evaluating the effect of implementation

Social problem solving is viewed as a general organizing framework within which many other group therapeutic activities take place. For example, in Step 6 (training and preparing youth to implement the tasks), modeling, reinforcement, and cognitive restructuring may be used. When a problem is brought in by a group member, it is dealt with in the order proposed by the above steps of problem solving to reach some type of new solution for the member to try out. A solution may involve performing differently in the problem situation or evaluating the situation differently. Let us look at each of the eight steps above as they are applied in groups.

Orienting Youth to Problems as Part of Everyday Life

Because the group as a whole is oriented to the problem-solving process, orientation occurs intermittently. It is presented before trying the problem-solving process for the first time. Members review the basic assumptions of problem solving periodically, and the frequency of orientation is gradually eliminated. The basic orientation involves pointing out to the group that everyone has problems, that problems can be solved, and that social problem solving is usually more effective than impulsive problem solving. Furthermore, because most troubled youth tend to be impulsive problem solvers, problem solving includes developing a habit of "stopping and thinking" and then acting to solve problems. In addition, all the steps in the process are presented, explained briefly, and illustrated with examples. Insofar as some of the group members themselves have had experience with systematic problem solving, they are asked to explain the basic assumptions and steps of the approach and to provide examples. The group therapist may rehearse this orientation activity with the senior members before the meeting. Where many of the youth have had previous experience, as in open-ended groups, orientation may occur in pairs as well as in the entire group.

To "rub in" the assumption that everyone has problems, the group therapist asks the group to describe someone they know who has no problems. After the brief silence that usually follows, the therapist points out that having problems does not make the group members unique and provides examples of staff and other adult problems.

To demonstrate that problems can be resolved, the therapist asks the youth for examples of people who have had problems and done something about them. The youth may also use themselves as examples. In the discussion that follows, the therapist distinguishes between impulsive and systematic problem solving. He or she notes that at first systematic problem solving may seem like a slow and calculating process but that as they develop skills in it they will be able to speed it up.

Defining the Problem

In general, the youth have difficulty in defining problems. Initially, they tend to be vague and indefinite. Several kinds of problems (which often overlap) can be identified. The first are those in which the problem is manifested in specific situations. The second are those in which the client needs to obtain important skills or resources in which he or she is deficient. The third are group problems. For a problem to be worked on, the client must clearly have a question as to what he or she can do, and the other group members and/or the therapist must have the expertise to deal with that problem. The client must be able to define the problem in concrete terms. He or she should also commit (be motivated) to work on the problem.

Situational Problems. Most problems can be defined situationally. Examples are getting in trouble at school, not finding anything interesting or fun to do, and not getting along with parents. The youth are asked to define their general problems in much the same way as in situational analysis (see

Chapter 4 for more details). When someone presents a general problem, such as not being able to get along with his or her parents, the following questions are asked: "Tell us about a recent situation in which you did not get along with your parents." "What happened?" "Where did it happen?" "Who else was involved?" "What was your response to the situation at the critical moments?" "How did you think and feel at various critical moments during and after the occurrence of the situation?" The client must be frustrated or otherwise upset by the conditions of the situation. When presenting a problem, he or she should, as suggested by D'Zurilla (1986, p. 79), describe all his or her emotions when and immediately after the problem occurred. He or she should also be asked to provide his or her cognitive evaluations and expectations of what happened. One group member, Melissa, came up with the following problem, which could be readily defined into situations:

Melissa constantly fights with her parents, especially if they try to hold her to any rules or limits. They have recently threatened to throw her out of the house. She wants to remain at home. She thinks that her parents are to blame for the arguments and that their demands are unfair. In answer to questioning, she describes a number of situations in which her parents ask her to do things she thinks are unreasonable. Her response is usually angry, and she screams at them.

Problems Related to Obtaining Skills and Resources. Examples of problems related to skills and resources to which problem solving can be applied are (a) Jack's problem of getting D's in all his classes, (b) Vinnie's problem of not getting into a trade school, (c) Lisa's problem of not getting a job, and (d) Art's problem of not being able to handle his money efficiently. Often, such problems are interrelated with other more situational problems, such as Lisa's inability to carry out a job interview or Jack's habit of always arguing with his teachers about homework he is assigned. In most cases, clients need to define what they think they are missing, what resources they already have for obtaining what they are missing, and whether these are resources or skills that the group realistically can help them to obtain. Clients' attempts at dealing with the problem are also included, as well as their feelings and cognitions related to the problem. The following is Jack's formulation of his problem:

> My grades are dropping. I don't study very often, and when I do, I am all over the place. Also, my late nights watching TV and late morning rising reduce the time I have available for studying. I've tried to go to bed earlier, but the programs I really like are on late at night. Besides, others in the family watch programs I don't like earlier in the evening. I try to get up earlier, but I'm just too tired. Sometimes I think I will study, but then I get anxious and say to myself "I don't feel like it and I'll do it later." I feel awful about it because I know I have to pass all my classes to graduate and get a decent job. I think about it a lot. I guess I would rate my emotional distress as a 7 on a 9-point scale.

This is a relatively simple situation, but it is clearly defined and important to the client. It contains his cognitions as well as his feelings about the problem. The client has included what he has tried to do to solve the problem.

Group Problems. Group problems are interactions in the group that are unproductive or that interfere with the therapy process. Examples are groups that are relatively unattractive to their members, groups in which the members talk primarily to the therapist and rarely to each other, and groups in which the norm is to self-disclose as little as possible. These problems are determined either by the members themselves or by the therapist, who proposes the problem to the group members. It can be dealt with if they agree it is a problem. Group problem solving will be dealt with more in Chapter 14.

Enhancing Problem Definition. To help youth develop meaningful situations, many group therapists provide a number of "canned" situations that are predetermined and ask the group members to modify one of them to fit their own particular conditions. Melissa's and Jack's problems are good examples of such canned situations that those working with similar youth might include. These may also be used when discussing the later phases of problem solving. Other techniques commonly used are examples from the experience of more experienced members and problems dealt with by the therapist.

Determining Goals

Goal setting is defined much as it was in Chapter 6. For Melissa's problem, formulated in the "Situational Problems" section above, the treatment goal was to talk to her parents on a regular basis without arguments or fights. For Jack's problem, formulated in the "Problems Related to Obtaining Skills and Resources" section, the treatment goal was to get and maintain a C average by the end of the semester. Note that the treatment goal meets a number of criteria. It is clear, achievement depends on the actions of the client, and the client is responsible for deciding what his or her own goals will be to solve the problem or achieve the goal. Both the group and the group therapist are used as consultants. Goals are to be realistic. If Jack aspired to an A average, considering his history and intellectual level, he would probably be further frustrated. (Sometimes, though, we have been surprised!) Achievement of the goal should be able to monitored; in Jack's case, it can be shown by a report card. If the goal is not sufficiently clear to the other youth in the group, they may ask questions so that it can be clarified.

In some cases, such as Jack's, the goal is obvious. In other instances, it is helpful to have the group and, if necessary, the therapist suggest possible goals. One can even use brainstorming (see below) to generate potential goals. Usually the goals are treatment goals. More specific situational goals are often defined later in the process.

Generating Tasks and Strategies

After review of what each client has already tried in dealing with the problem, new strategies must be explored. The resolution of the problem is defined in terms of tasks and subtasks that need to be performed to achieve the goal. To establish a range of tasks, brainstorming is used. The group therapist reviews with the group members, or they review with each other, the principles of brainstorming.

1. Defer judgment of the quality of each suggestion until all ideas have been given. This is particularly difficult in groups. The first time that brainstorming is actually used, the group therapist has the members monitor each other. If anyone makes an evaluative statement, the others are instructed to "boo." Then the therapist makes a series of evaluative statements, which the group members inevitably "boo" with great delight.

2. Generate quantity first, on the assumption that it will breed quality. Troubled youth tend to fall back on a very few strategies or tactics for dealing with problems. The peer group is a rich resource of ideas. The more problem solving is used, the larger the repertoire of ideas for the group. However, sometimes a series of case studies have to be discussed first to

enrich the repertoire before the group works on actual problems. The youth are encouraged to be as creative as possible. Sometimes creativity gets out of hand, and the discussion breaks down completely in a fit of out-of-control laughter. The criteria are temporarily suspended.

3. Select strategies (general directions one might take) before tactics (specific tasks for implementing the strategies). In working with a group rather than with one client at a time, it is sometimes difficult to differentiate strategies from tactics early in treatment. Moreover, there is a dearth of suggestions for strategies. For this reason, we have put them all together in brainstorming in the initial examples and then singled out the more general strategies. Finding appropriate goals, too, may lead directly to brainstorming about tasks.

After reviewing the rules, the group therapist instructs all the members, including him- or herself and the client with the problem, to write down all possible tasks and strategies. When everyone is finished, the group therapist reminds them to defer evaluative statements ("Good," "Great idea," "I like that," "No way, man," "That's not possible," "Are you crazy or something?" etc.) and to read their suggestions aloud one at time until everyone in the group has made all the suggestions. When the list is complete, any new suggestions that come to mind may be added or old ideas modified or combined. The following tasks were suggested for Jack, which he wrote, without comment, on the chalkboard as they were offered.

- Ask your residential worker to sit with you while you do your homework.
- If you don't do your homework, no food.
- Set a regular time each day for studying.
- Watch TV only after you have completed your homework.
- Ask your friend in the morning to review with you what you did the night before.
- Do your homework after school before you come home.
- Make sure you understand the homework before you leave the classroom.
- Keep a diary of all homework assignments and whether you completed them or not.
- Quit school and get a job.
- Examine your thinking when you are faced with having to do your homework.

The group therapist identified for the group some general strategies that could be ascertained from the tasks (tactics) that had been proposed:

- Make it worth your while to study.
- Structure your time, and find ways of keeping to your structure.
- Have a friend or someone monitor whether you are studying or not.
- Make sure you are studying the right thing.
- When your thinking keeps you from studying, find ways of changing your thinking.

These general principles or strategies are helpful in encouraging other group members to come up with meaningful strategies when working on their problems. After problem solving has been used a number of times and the repertoire of strategies has improved, discussing or brainstorming strategies can be done first. (Incidentally, the group therapist can use this example as a model for his or her group.)

Evaluating and Selecting Tasks for Achieving the Goals

Once a list of tasks has been established for resolving the problem, they are evaluated and prioritized. Tasks are evaluated in terms of their potential outcomes, including relative risks, potential benefits, available time to carry them out, skills and knowledge required to complete them, and resources available to carry out the task. Which tasks should be performed first should also be established. On the basis of the above criteria, Jack chose the following tasks:

- I will set a regular time each day for studying, from 3:30 to 6:00 or from 7:00 to 9:30.
- I will watch TV only after I have completed my homework. Benny will have to see it before I am allowed in the TV room.
- I will explain to Henry after class my understanding of the homework to be performed.
- I will examine my thinking when I don't feel like doing my homework. If I am giving myself excuses for not doing it, I will remind myself of the consequences of not doing the homework and ask my residential worker for help.

In the above list, most tasks are behavioral. Some of these involve self-monitoring or external monitoring. One is a cognitive task. If most of the tasks are performed on a regular basis, it is likely that the goal will be achieved. However, one reason for not completing one or more tasks is the lack of adequate skills.

Training and Preparation
to Implement the Tasks

It is at this step that most of the cognitive-behavioral and social network enhancement interventions are integrated into the model. Some tasks need only be described and then be carried out without further attention by the group or therapist. Often, however, a client must be prepared to carry out the tasks or even trained in their performance. The training may involve any or several of the following interventions: provision of information, modeling and rehearsal of the desired tasks, cognitive restructuring of thoughts that interfere with the performance of the task, reinforcement of completion of the task, monitoring or self-monitoring of the performance of the task, and extension of the social support network so that the individual may be supported in achieving the task. The therapist normally asks the group what the target person needs to know or have as support to be able to carry out each task. If there are any gaps, the client is trained in the skills he or she needs or is prepared in an appropriate way. As part of Jack's preparation, he was asked by the group the details of being monitored, such as when it would take place each day, where, and in what form. In most groups, ongoing skill training is used primarily for preparation to perform interactive tasks. For example, in Jack's group, the members role-played asking the teacher for help, asking a friend to monitor, and approaching someone who had treated them unfairly. (Interactive skill training is elaborated on in Chapter 9.) The youth in Jack's group all were trained in monitoring their thoughts and replacing self-defeating ones with self-enhancing ones. In this way, Jack could monitor his "resistive" thoughts to doing homework and replace them with "goal" thoughts that encouraged him (see Chapter 10 for cognitive training procedures).

One additional part of preparation is the design of an extragroup task to perform in the real world (see Chapter 11). The extragroup task is central to this model as a means of extending learning to the real world and, except in dealing with group problems, is a step that is rarely omitted. One principle of increasing the likelihood that a task will be understood and completed is the act of writing down the task and showing to a partner or the whole group what one has written.

Implementing the Selected Tasks

This step refers to the actual performance of the tasks in the real world, in the home, at school, in the residence, on the streets, or with a friend outside the group. We refer to this as the *extragroup task* or *homework,* and Chapter 11 describes the strategies used to maximize the likelihood of completing it. The performance may be monitored by family members, residential staff, friends, or no one but the client. Initially, the likelihood of task completion is increased if a monitor is used. Eventually, all tasks should be carried out independently. Tasks may not necessarily be carried out all at once. They may be carried out in some rational order—for example, from easy to more difficult or from preparation and monitoring to performance of new behavior or cognitions. They may be carried out between sessions or over an extended period of time. In fact, in the step involving evaluation of new ideas, attention should be given to the sequencing of tasks.

Jack completed all the above tasks the first week except the cognitive one, for which he did not feel adequately trained, and he planned to continue the tasks for a month. He would begin the cognitive task in 2 weeks when the skill training in the group for cognitive restructuring was finished.

Evaluating the Effect of Implementation

When the task is or was to have been completed, the client reports on the results of his or her experience. If effort has been made but very little success in carrying out the task is reported, additional training and/or preparation may be called for. In some cases, negative cognitions in relation to the task may have been overlooked and can be examined at this time. In some cases, expectations were too high and may have to be reduced. In other cases, the client was inadequately prepared for exigencies or surprises in the environment, so a plan is directed toward dealing with the new conditions. If no effort was made ("I forgot," " I changed my mind," "It didn't seem important anymore"), the individual is passed over quickly ("That can happen"), and the group therapist goes on to the next person. The most powerful reinforcer in the group is the attention of the therapist and one's peers. All too often, attention is given those who have made no effort in an attempt to convince them to do better next time. Extinction is usually a better strategy than critically evaluating failure to attempt to do the task. Attention is reserved for those who have made the effort.

When home tasks are for the most part completed, the therapist and later the group members respond enthusiastically to each other's achievements. With preadolescents, tokens or other tangible reinforcers may be used also. When everyone has completed his or her extragroup tasks, the therapist asks the members to "give themselves a big hand."

At the end of the first week, Jack evaluated how well he had carried out his tasks and how well he was meeting his goals. He noted that he had gotten a B and a C on two assignments and that he had not forgotten any of them. He had not done one of them because he had not known what to do, but he had asked the teacher for help. He was having trouble meeting with his monitor, but it did not seem to be necessary, and he said he would rather do the work on his own. The other group members enthusiastically praised Jack and encouraged him to keep up the good work. He continued to report back to the group until grade reports came out 4 weeks later and he showed them to the group. He had gotten slightly above a C average.

Some Miscellaneous Comments on Problem Solving

Many adolescents are not accustomed to solving problems in such a social way. It may be necessary early in treatment for the group therapist and/or experienced members to be quite didactic. Gradually, responsibility is shifted to the group members completely, with the group therapist acting as consultant.

Sometimes it is possible to go back and forth among the various phases. Sometimes the generation and completion of good tasks lead to new and more useful goals. At times, when a client reports his or her inability to carry out a task, it becomes clear that he or she is working on the wrong problem. On occasion, it becomes apparent that the wrong general strategies are being used and that several of the group members need training in these strategies. The training and preparation phase is the longest in the initial problem-solving attempts if the adolescents have a limited repertoire of tasks at their disposal and a limited number of coping skills to use in carrying out the tasks.

The problem-solving method proposed here appears to be somewhat static. In a more dynamic problem-solving approach, evaluation is carried out in each phase of the problem-solving process. As a result, new goals may be developed for subsequent phases (Kanfer & Busemeyer, 1982).

Empirical Support

Although there is some research to support the efficacy of problem-solving therapy as the solitary method with adults and with children, little research is available with adolescents. However, a number of researchers have investigated treatment packages in which social problem solving was incorporated into their group programs for adolescents or preadolescents as a major component and have demonstrated success in achieving the treatment goals, which in most cases included the reduction of aggressive behavior (see Etscheidt, 1991; Guerra & Slaby, 1990; Lochman & Curry, 1986; Schinke et al., 1981; Tisdelle & St. Lawrence, 1988). Unfortunately, problem-solving interventions have been confounded with group and other interventions such as social skill training, self-instructional training, and cognitive restructuring, and the relative contribution of each intervention strategy is unclear.

Limitations of the Problem-Solving Process

As we mentioned earlier, problem solving appears to be an extremely calculating approach to dealing with everyday problems. Haaga and Davison (1991) recommended that the therapist point out that "life is replete with problems, but only a subset of them merit cranking up full blown PST apparatus to arrive at a solution" (pp. 279-280). The authors also suggested that the highly structured approach be gradually faded so that it can be applied naturally in everyday life. Solutions may require skills that are well beyond those of the client and may not be teachable in the time available. In this case, either someone will have to resolve the problem for the client, or different solutions will have to be sought. Sometimes, in the formulation of the solution to a given problem, no matter what the client does, the environmental conditions contributing to the problem are unchangeable. It may be necessary to help the client recognize this and help him or her to change his or her evaluation or beliefs about what his or her expectations can be.

A big problem is premature problem solving. This is an attempt to find a solution before it is clear what the problem is. The question is often posed to the group, "Do we have enough information about the problem to be able to recommend possible tasks that might remediate the problem?" Of course, one can make the opposite error of spending too much time on assessment.

Training Youth to Use
Systematic Problem Solving

The use of problem solving in the group occurs after the members are given an orientation to problem solving, including the basic assumption and the specific phases of problem solving. As in all procedures, the therapist provides a case study or other examples of problem solving in action and draws on the experience of the group members. At this time, the following small group exercise is introduced.

Exercise 7.1. Systematic Problem Solving

Purposes: By the end of this exercise, each participant will have

1. Demonstrated the skills involved in social problem solving in general and response generation (brainstorming) in particular

2. Described the major principles of response generation

3. Identified the major steps in the problem-solving sequence

Individual Task: Each participant selects one of the following problems. He or she can change it to fit his or her own situation. It is permissible for participants to make up any additional facts necessary to answer the questions until the situation is real for them. The participants may select personal situations if the information is relatively succinct and the parameters of the problem are as clearly outlined as those in the following examples (5 minutes or homework).

1. You are usually late for class, appointments, and most social occasions. A number of friends are really angry with you, and your teacher is threatening to lower your grade if you are late again. You have difficulty getting up in the morning, and that starts the day being behind for everything. You tend to wait until the last minute, and then something happens, like the bus is late, or you get a call from your mother just as you are going out the door.

2. You are trying to stop smoking. You have tried "cold turkey, " but it didn't work. Some of your friends smoke. You usually smoke while studying, after meals, while drinking beer, and while watching TV. Your parents don't smoke, and your boyfriend/girlfriend hates the smell on your breath, clothes, and hair. If you are willing to try to stop, they would be willing to help. You really like smoking, but you are convinced that it is indeed a dangerous activity.

3. Your boyfriend/girlfriend has been unusually cool lately. You have asked him/her what the problem might be, but he/she says "nothing" in a way that leads you to believe that something is the problem. You are getting more upset every day. Finally, you decide you must do something, but you are uncomfortable about being too insistent.

4. You have just gotten a reasonable job with a reasonable income. You should be able to live on it and save a little bit. You live at home and give a little money to your mom for rent and food. Somehow, each month you seem to go a little more in debt. You have maximum amounts on each of your credit cards. You like to eat out a lot, and clothes are important to you. You also just bought a car, and the payments, though small, are more than you can afford. You may find it difficult to meet your payments next month if you don't do something about the financial situation.

5. Your parents are getting a divorce. You somehow feel guilty and feel that your behavior and the trouble that you are in have driven them apart, even though neither blames you. Each has explained what happened in the divorce, and both want your approval and want you to live with them. You have no brothers or sisters. You get along better with your dad than your mom, but you hate to hurt either of them.

6. In 6 weeks, you will be leaving the institution. You want to finish your GED and to work to make enough money to go to technical school. You don't want to be dependent on your parents, but you are willing to live at home so that you can save money. Unfortunately, you think that if you do, you are likely to be constantly fighting with your parents about hours, friends, drinking, etc., and that this may result in your leaving home. Your long-term goal is getting into the area technical college. There are several subgoals, such as getting your GED, finding a job, and getting along with your parents.

Group Task 1: The group will be divided into subgroups of four to five members. One person assigned as leader will guide the problem-solving process while making maximum use of all the members (1 hour). It is possible to shorten this exercise by assigning only one problem to each subgroup. In each situation, take the following steps:

1. Interview the person with the problem.

2. Determine the conditions under which the problem occurs, the emotional state or feelings of the person, his or her thoughts about the situation, and his or her current ways of approaching the problem.

3. Determine a concrete treatment or situational goal or set of situational goals.

4. Have each member write down tasks that are necessary to achieve each of the goals.

5. One at time, have each person describe one task aloud until all possible tasks are recorded (with no evaluation during the process).

6. When the list is complete, encourage adding any new suggestions or combinations that come to mind.

7. Have the group evaluate the suggestions in terms of potential usefulness, available resources, significant barriers, possible risks, other potential consequences, and likelihood of completion.

8. Have the group select a set of tasks that are most likely to achieve the goal and that meet the criteria discussed in the rationale.

9. Have the group decide how the tasks will be monitored.

Group Task 2: The larger group will reconvene, and the members will share with each other any problems or noteworthy observations on the process that they discovered (10 minutes).

Task of Group Therapist: Before splitting into subgroups, the first problem could be led by the group therapist in front of the entire therapy group so as to demonstrate each of the steps in the process. As the group therapist moves among the various subgroups, he or she should make sure that no one is evaluating the suggestions made before all ideas are on the table. Even such statements as "That's a good idea" are considered evaluation. A better statement would be "That's one possibility." The group therapist should feel free to draw on any problems that the group members would like to deal with, but he or she should check it first to make sure that it is not too complicated. The group therapist should conduct the final group discussion of strengths and weaknesses of the process and then provide feedback about what he or she observed.

Only when the orientation and exercise are complete are the members encouraged to bring in their own specific problems.

Negotiating Differences

Sometimes members have disagreements with their families about goals, rules in the household, rewards, distribution of family resources, and family activities. Sometimes in school there are differences among members about topics of group projects, games they should play, and classroom rules. Such disagreements require negotiation rather than problem solving. Negotiating is an important skill. Though only occasionally used in the group itself, it is taught to the members for use outside of the group. It differs from problem solving in that two or more parties to the conflict already have what they perceive to be the best solution. In negotiation, it becomes necessary to find a solution that meets the interest of all parties as well as possible with as little cost as seems reasonable to each of the parties involved. Aggressive youth usually want to win at all costs in every situation. If a youth who is grounded wants to leave the house despite his parent's adamant refusal, only one can win. Unfortunately, aggressive and other troubled youth often have limited strategies for obtaining what they want. This may be equally true for the parent(s). Both parties demand rather than negotiate. If they fail, they either argue and fight for what they want or withdraw. The notion of compromise is absent from their behavioral repertoire. For this reason, one of the major skills taught in groups is negotiation, first with each other in the group and then, once they have mastered the skills, with their families, peers outside the group, and even teachers.

Of course, if the major persons with whom youth must negotiate are parents, it is particularly helpful for them to learn these skills, either in family treatment or in parent training. Even if other family members do not receive this training, youth skilled in negotiation have enhanced flexibility and a greater likelihood of obtaining at least some of their goals.

Goldstein and Keller (1987) analyzed the process of negotiation in a way that particularly lends itself to the training of youth in groups. In this process, they articulated three sets of skills: preparation, the negotiation itself, and breaking deadlocks. I have added a fourth set of skills, generalization of negotiation skills.

Preparation

A set of preliminary skills is necessary before youth can use negotiation. First, they must be able to remain calm while under the stress of the conflict situation. It is almost impossible to be rational and angry at the same time. It is helpful also if they have learned to look at and, if necessary, to develop coping cognitions related to decision making. If such cognitions as "I have to get what I want at all costs" are not modified, negotiation is virtually impossible. If the parents believe that any form of flexibility is a weakness, that, too, limits the possibility of negotiation. Negotiation also requires a realistic appraisal of one's own power and the power of others. In the above example, if the youth understands that leaving without his parents' permission will result in their calling the probation officer and sending him back to the correctional institution, then he recognizes in that situation the power of his parents. If the parents realize that some limits are impossible for the youth to submit to without his "losing it," then they are acknowledging the youth's power. In this phase of preparation, the therapist prepares negotiating parties by training them in how to stay calm, look at their cognitions, and identify the real consequences of their actions. Situational analysis of situations amenable to negotiations can be carried out as well.

To orient the members on how to negotiate, the therapist can introduce a case study such as the following to point out the major principles of negotiation.

The group members of a residential treatment group were arguing in the session about what their booth would be at the agency carnival. Several members wanted to tell fortunes, but others wanted to throw balls at a target for prizes. The members were quite angry with one another, and no one seemed willing to budge.

Remain Calm

The group therapist pointed out that this was a great opportunity to learn new skills in negotiation. The first principle is to remain calm. To do this, the group therapist suggested that they stop at that moment and practice their relaxation and breathing skills. He led them in a brief version of the exercise. Then he stated, "It looks to me like everyone is calm. I think we are ready to begin."

Ascertaining the Consequences of Not Negotiating

At first, the members were still reluctant to give up anything. Then the group therapist asked the members what would happen if they did not negotiate. They realized that they would have no booth and would remain angry with one another for a long time. One added that there would be no money coming in. The therapist commented that if they wanted to avoid these results, clearly everyone would have to give up something. Perhaps they could even find an activity that everyone liked.

Choose Negotiation Goals

The group therapist stated that the next principle of preparation was to determine the goals of negotiation. He suggested that they consider what they wanted to achieve by the end of the negotiation session. All agreed that they wanted to decide on what they could do. They thought that the activity should not be too costly to develop and that it should be sufficiently attractive so that people would use it. "Then it doesn't have to be one of the activities that has been proposed so far as long as we meet these goals?" asked the group therapist. The members agreed.

Determine Where and When to Negotiate

The members agreed that they would meet in the classroom rather than on the basketball court to discuss the issue because outsiders were "butting in." They also agreed to come back after lunch when they had cooled down a little and thought about it a little more. But it was important to them that no one would talk about it until they got to the meeting room. Even preparation required some preliminary negotiation.

The Negotiation Process

The following negotiation skills have been proposed by Goldstein and Keller (1987): Each party should state its own position, each should then state the position of the other, each should be asked if it agrees with the understanding of the other, each should be requested to listen openly to the other's position, and eventually each should be requested to propose a compromise. The group therapist reviewed with the members listening skills such as effective listening, paraphrasing, and asking for clarification.

Each Party Should State Its Own Position

In the above example, the group therapist asked each of the subgroups to design a statement of what they wanted to do and explain why they wanted to do it. Then a representative of each subgroup presented the position to the group. He asked the others to take notes on what they heard from the others. (It would also have been possible, as the group sat in a circle, to ask each person to state his or her recommendation and give reasons for it.)

Each Should Then State the Position of the Other

Continuing with the same example, the group therapist asked the members in their original subgroups to write a statement that reflected the position of the other party. The therapist requested that they listen openly and carefully to the proposal of the other party and take notes on similarities and differences in the proposals. First the similarities and then the differences are read aloud by one person in each subgroup to the group as a whole.

Ask If Agreement Exists

Each party was asked the degree to which the other party understood its proposals. Similarities and differences were noted. Differences in understanding were ironed out. The group therapist stressed the similarities.

Propose a Compromise

After the members had reached a general perception that the other party at least understood their position, they went back to the subgroups, where they developed a proposal for a compromise. They needed some help in understanding the nature of compromise and received it from the therapist, who floated between the two subgroups. Early attempts were often merely the rewording of the original proposal. To provide an example, the group therapist had posed two possible compromises to the group as a whole in the earlier stages of negotiation training, and the subgroups now considered these.

Breaking Deadlocks

The group asked the therapist what might be done if, despite the therapist's best efforts, no agreement was reached. He pointed out that several strategies to break these deadlocks were available, such as increasing bargaining room, helping the other person or party save face, taking a break, and bringing in a mediator (Goldstein & Keller, 1987). To implement the strategy of increasing bargaining room, the therapist could go to each party and encourage them to lower their goals a little, concede a bit, lessen demands somewhat, or increase their willingness to take risks.

To help one party save face, the group therapist would try to make it clear what the other party was giving up and how they stood to lose something too. "If this goes through, what does each group face losing?" "What in the other person's position do we respect, even though we disagree with it?"

If all else failed, the group therapist would advise the parties to take a break before they became further entrenched in their positions. The parties would be advised to consider once again what they would gain by compromise and what they might be willing to give up to get that compromise. This is especially important if anger is beginning to escalate. During the break, they might consult with an outside person to get his or her opinion. But the outside person would have to be initially neutral with respect to the issue; otherwise, he or she might reinforce the tenaciously held position of one of the parties.

In addition to these strategies, it may be helpful to examine the cognitions associated with the positions held by the antagonists. Sometimes these cognitions are clearly unreasonable, and their change becomes the basis for compromise. One additional technique is what Beck and Emery (1985) referred to as *point-counterpoint*. The group therapist has the antagonist take the position of the other person and debate it. Although this is usually done with much laughter, it takes the venom out of the arguments.

Generalizing Negotiation Skills

To facilitate the generalization of negotiation skills to interactions with the family, peers, and even teachers, a number of strategies can be employed. Summarization of the negotiation process in the case example can be presented to the group, or the therapist can ask the group to give a summary. Then the members should be specifically asked how this might occur in other settings. A home task can be suggested in which the youth are requested to describe in their diaries any situations in which negotiation was used or could have been used. The results of these are discussed in subsequent sessions. Because negotiation cannot be carried out in the family unless the other family members are willing to participate, the major way to increase the likelihood of generalization is to train the parents or the family as a whole in negotiation skills. Some situations that can be negotiated in the family are

- The use of the family car
- Sharing of rooms among siblings
- The bathroom schedule in the morning
- Distribution of chores among family members
- Time of curfew during the week and on weekends
- The amount of allowances
- The content and times of meals

If the other family members agree to negotiate, the therapist or a family worker can serve as mediator. The steps are the same as in the group example above.

Summary

In this chapter, the importance of systematic social problem solving in CBIGT was emphasized. The steps of systematic problem solving as used in CBIGT were then outlined and described. These were orienting youth to problems as part of everyday life, defining the problem situation, determining the client's goals in the situation, generating tasks and strategies to facilitate achievement of the goals, selecting and preparing for the tasks most likely to facilitate achievement of goals, training and preparing the client in the group for implementing the tasks, implementing the selected tasks in the real world, and evaluating the effect of implementation.

Negotiation differs from problem solving in that two or more parties to the conflict have what they perceive are the best solutions already. In negotiation, it becomes necessary to find a solution that meets the interest of all parties as well as possible with as little cost as seems reasonable to each of the parties involved. Although negotiation is occasionally used in groups, it represents a skill that youth can use in their families as a way of dealing with conflict. To negotiate, four phases are proposed: (a) preparation, which consists of teaching the negotiating parties to remain calm, ascertaining the consequences of not negotiating, choosing negotiation goals, and determining where and when to negotiate; (b) the negotiation process, which consists of each party stating its own position, each then stating the position of the other, the therapist ascertaining whether agreement exists, and, if not, a compromise being proposed; (c) breaking deadlocks: and (d) generalizing negotiation skills to family situations. The youth are trained in the group in the skills they need to use in the family. The families, however, must be involved in or at least advised of the process if negotiation is to be effective.

CHAPTER 8

Reinforcement and Stimulus Control in Groups

During the meeting, every time one of the adolescents assisted another person with her project, the group therapist gave her a token and praised her warmly. At the end of the meeting, each person added up her tokens and put the number on the group thermometer. When the thermometer overflowed, the group would get tickets to a performance by the Exalted Hot Stuff Singers and would get to meet the singers after the performance.

During the group session, the youth one a time were discussing some of the events in which they got in trouble in school. The timer was set at random. Whoever was talking when the timer rang received five points. When a person received 100 points, she could become the camera operator for a session for the videotape that the group was making.

As each of the young women finished presenting her homework, the therapist and the other group members applauded, and each young woman received a ticket for the group lottery. The winner would get a free pair of movie tickets after the drawing in 2 weeks.

At the beginning of the first two sessions, pretzels were served to the women as they arrived. When they asked for the reason, the group therapist said, "It's just for coming."

Reinforcement and stimulus control are essential tools for the group therapist in the CBIGT. In this chapter, those aspects of operant theory that are readily applied in groups are discussed. For a more thorough discussion of operant theory as it is applied to clinical work in general, the reader is referred to Nemeroff and Karoly (1991) and Kazdin (1989). In each of the above examples, the group therapist responded to a given set of behaviors with positive feedback, praise, tokens, material goods, and/or food. In each example (except the last one), the positive reinforcement was delivered on the basis of some prior agreement. As was pointed out in Chapter 1, a positive reinforcer is defined by its effects on the behavior. If the response frequency of a given behavior increases when followed by the event, the event is a positive reinforcer. This is not quite as circular as it appears in that a reinforcer effective in altering one response in one situation may be effective in altering other behaviors in other situations as well (Kazdin, 1989, p. 105). In groups, youth receive many kinds of rewards that seem to function as positive reinforcers for the performance of prosocial group behavior and the completion of extragroup tasks. These potential positive reinforcers may take the form of praise, tokens, points, goods, small objects, activities, and whatever is small, manipulable, and valued by and appropriate to the given age and developmental category of the recipient. In all cases, these reinforcers are delivered according to a systematic plan called a *schedule of reinforcement*. Reinforcers such as attention or tokens can be withheld in response to undesirable behaviors (although in groups, the attention of other youth is difficult to control). This is referred to as *extinction* and is a common response in groups. Occasionally, reinforcement is removed (usually in the form of tokens) following undesirable behaviors, a process known as *response cost*. Occasionally, aversive stimuli are presented to the youth in a process similar to that of punishment. Response cost and punishment are designed to reduce the frequency of the behavior that precedes them. Because CBIGT focuses on strengths whenever possible, positive reinforcement is the method of choice. Strategies involving the alteration of consequences (positive or negative) of a behavior are referred to as *operant procedures*.

Circumstances that precede or set the conditions for the given behavior are often referred to as *antecedent* or *stimulus conditions*. Treatment strategies are frequently employed in which stimulus conditions are also altered as a means of modifying the future probability of a given behavior.

This is referred to as *stimulus control*. In this chapter, the focus is on strategies for the modification of both antecedent conditions and consequences that are commonly used in CBIGT.

Reinforcement

Various types of reinforcement (some of which overlap) are commonly used in CBIGT, any of which may be directed at individuals or at the group as a whole. Positive reinforcement includes the presentation of social reinforcers, material reinforcers, and token reinforcement (for material goods or activities). Punishment includes time-out from reinforcement, response cost, and other aversive stimuli. Because most troubled youth have problems in the area of control, some form of control in the sessions is necessary if the work is to be carried out. Positive controls are preferred to negative ones because the former increases the cohesion of the group and the latter increases the likelihood of negative side effects. Sometimes, however, positive reinforcement is not sufficient to control negative behaviors; in that case, some form of punishment procedures, such as response cost or time-out, or stimulus control, such as firm limit setting or coaching, may be required. In the following section, we will elaborate on both reinforcement and punishment, how they are delivered in group settings, and how the group itself plays a role in their determination and delivery.

Positive Reinforcement

Social Reinforcement

Many troubled youth have only limited experience with positive social reinforcement. Of the available types of reinforcement, the social response seems to be a powerful reinforcer of social behavior (Kazdin, 1992, p. 114). The use of praise, a nod of approval, a touch, a wink, a smile, and criticism are major influences on human behavior. Even the use of material reinforcement is enhanced when paired with social reinforcement from a person valued by the client being reinforced. Although most social approval is given noncontingently in most traditional therapies, the client must earn social reinforcement in CBIGT, at least in the early phases of treatment, by the production of desired behavior. The group therapist praises or in some nonverbal way indicates approval of a client for concrete accomplishments. Thus, the members receive a high frequency of reinforcement for individual accomplishments and for their part in group accomplishments. So as not to satiate group members with praise, the group therapist must use a variety of statements and gestures of approval. One group dubbed their therapist the "good job king" because of his overuse of that expression. But more often than not, the error is one of too little rather than too much or too unvaried reinforcement.

Training Youth to Provide Social Reinforcement to Others. Because most troubled youth rely primarily on negative contingencies, such as yelling, anger, and avoidance, as ways of controlling others, their use of positive communications with others is a welcome option, at least to others in their environment. Usually, if appropriately delivered, it enhances the relationship to the person reinforcing. The act of reinforcing involves a set of social skills that are taught like other social skills to the group members through modeling, instruction, and sometimes social skill training exercises (see Chapter 9) in which members practice reinforcing each other. Such a climate of mutual reinforcement tends to create high cohesion of the group and a reinforcing milieu. To increase the skills of reinforcement, a number of exercises can be used. An example of a reinforcement exercise that is commonly used with children and adolescents is Exercise 8.1.

Exercise 8.1. Reinforcing Others

Purpose: By the end of the exercise, each participant will demonstrate his or her skill in praising others and giving others positive feedback.

Individual Task: In pairs, each will write down one behavior he or she has observed the partner doing well in the group; for example, "You give good eye contact when you give feedback to others in the group." The participants are instructed to be specific, praise a behavior each has observed, and praise only behavior that the partner could be proud of and not embarrassed by.

Group Task: After group members write down their praise statements, each person praises his or her partner aloud one at a time while others listen. The group members then evaluate each praise statement in terms of the above criteria. The partners are then exchanged and the exercise is repeated, but this time each participant describes a behavior that he or she has observed his or her partner performing outside the group. (This last variation assumes that group members have extragroup contact.)

An alternative to this exercise is having each group member look at the person on his or her left and writing down one thing that the person does well. Then everyone reads, one at a time, what he or she has written while looking at the person. Because reinforcing exercises are used several times in a series of sessions, the second exercise can replace the first when repeating the exercise to provide variation.

The exercise can also be modified to help youth receive as well as give positive feedback by preceding the exercise with a brief discussion as to what one should say or do when receiving praise or other forms of positive feedback. The purpose of this variation is not only to increase the mutually reinforcing statements made in the group but also to prepare youth to give feedback following role plays. The variations are usually followed by the suggestion of a home task to give honest compliments to one or more persons who are not members of the group before the next meeting and then to report back to the group the nature of their experience.

These exercises are usually punctuated by a great deal of giggling and laughter. Most youth are uncomfortable with the giving and certainly the receiving of praise. After several rounds, the members become more comfortable.

Problems in Social Reinforcement. Because many youth have had a bad experience with praise and other forms of social reinforcement, they may not initially trust the person who gives it. The gamelike way in which reinforcement is taught may make it more palatable. Nevertheless, some youth become sarcastic or quickly dismiss any praise they may receive. They often question the motives of those who praise them. If any of these problems happens, the group therapist describes what he or she perceives is happening, and the group, if they agree, discuss how this might impinge on the effectiveness of the procedure and the fun involved in using it. If the problem is not resolved, group problem solving is invoked to deal with it.

Material Reinforcement

For many of the troubled youth in our groups, because of their learning history, praise or other forms of verbal approval may not be adequate to modify or even maintain given levels of target behavior and therefore may not serve as reinforcement. For this reason, material goods such as trading cards, marbles, pieces of puzzles, crayons, paints and brushes, stamps, and small pieces of food may serve as effective reinforcers, especially for children and younger adolescents. To be most effective, reinforcers should be small, low cost, easily distributed, and highly valued by the potential recipient. With adolescents, group contingencies can usually be used more effectively. These are discussed later in the chapter.

Token Reinforcement

Another way to break a large reinforcer into small parts is to let group members earn points or tokens for performing behaviors that are specified in advance. Members can exchange their earned tokens at various intervals, either individually or as a group, for the desired item. This practice is commonly employed in children's groups and occasionally with younger and even older adolescents.

Tokens are symbolic units of exchange that, like money, may be used to purchase large items or activities. Tokens usually have a very small value. They may be paper script, poker chips, clicks on a counter, tally marks, stickers, points on a thermometer, or any other small indicator of achievement. Materials and activities are at a given time exchanged for a number of tokens that is specified in advance. Because reinforcement is most effective when given immediately following the performance of a given behavior, the tokens mediate the giving of the concrete reinforcer or activity. Tokens are usually paired with praise or other social reinforcement when they are distributed for a satisfactory performance.

In groups, one of the common ways of exchanging tokens for material reinforcement for youth is to set up a group store with predetermined prices. Members have access to the store at regular intervals—for example, at the end of each meeting or at the end of several meetings. Differing in value, the items in the store might include gum, model airplanes, a certificate to be first in line for class, assistance with one's homework from the group therapist for 10 minutes, tickets for a sports event, coupons for a beauty parlor, or credit for buying a hamburger or pizza at a local fast-food shop.

In any particular store, items should be designed for the unique population being served. Youth should be able to earn social as well as

TABLE 8.1 Price of Store Items for a Girls' Group

Items	Cost
Listening to CD or tape, per 5 minutes	5 tokens
Lessons in makeup, per 10-minute lesson	10 tokens
Sticks of gum	5 tokens
Used romance novel	15 tokens
Nail polish	20 tokens
Trip to the group therapist's house	20 tokens
Dance lessons, per 10 minutes	15 tokens
Use of agency telephone, per 3 minutes	25 tokens
Going shopping with group therapist	20 tokens

concrete reinforcement. Prices are usually determined by the group therapist in terms of supply and demand. Bubblegum might cost 10 tokens, whereas a box of raisins might cost only 2. Table 8.1 shows a menu developed for a group of 13- to 14-year-old girls who had been referred primarily for lack of appropriate social skills.

The major source of tokens for youth is the performance of extragroup tasks because the performance of these tasks is essential to the achievement of treatment goals. In some cases, the more difficult the assignment, the greater the number of tokens awarded. In other cases, the therapist, to avoid discussions, negotiates the same amount for all assignments. Also, instead of using a group store in which to make individual purchases, the therapist uses a thermometer that, when filled, provides a group reinforcer (see below), such as a trip, a special guest, or attendance at a sports event.

Tokens are also used to develop certain forms of member interaction. For example, in an anger control group for younger adolescents, members were unwilling to discuss general principles of handling their anger. Token reinforcement was used to shape their participation, as in the following example.

Therapist: What did we discuss last week about the anger cycle?

(Blank looks) (Therapist remains silent)

Tyrone: That's when I get mad at Eddie and dis him, it makes him madder at me and then he shoves me and I sock him and then I'm dead. He shot me.

Everyone: (Laughter)

Therapist: (Handing Tyrone 10 tokens): It usually doesn't go that far, but it could. You got it.

Eddie: We talked about reminders, too.

Therapist: And?

Eddie: Like when Tyrone starts to get mad at me and scream and swear, he reminds himself that it will end up in a fight and to cool it.

Therapist: (Hands him 10 tokens)

Alvin: What'd he get that for?

Eddie: For knowing this stuff and telling what he knows.

Most groups remain in the token economy only in the initial phase of treatment, which may be extended as long as eight sessions for younger children in outpatient groups and much longer for youth in institutions. As target behaviors become reinforced by peers and adults in extragroup situations or as the behaviors become self-reinforcing, tokens are gradually removed until activities occur noncontingently. The announcement that the award of tokens is being removed altogether usually provokes renewed discussion about being in the group. Some preparation is required before the tokens are eliminated, as in the following example.

Peter: What do you say if we don't give any tokens at all for cooperating with each other, for giving good feedback, completing the assignments, and all the other things you've been getting tokens for? You've probably been noticing that I've been giving fewer and fewer lately and that it doesn't seem to keep you guys from doing what you agreed you should be doing.

Tim: Ah, c'mon, Pete, why not? They're fun!

Peter: Anybody have any ideas why not?

Jerry: Well, maybe we really don't need 'em anymore. At least, I don't need 'em.

Eric: I don't need them either. They're just for kids, anyway.

Tony: Besides, the group's nearly over. We won't get tokens anywhere else for doing those things.

Peter: I'm really impressed with the things you guys are saying. Dropping the tokens has to do with the reasons you guys are here. And
I agree, you don't need them anymore. (Peter goes on to review
their recent achievements.)

In all groups, social reinforcement is used throughout the history of
the group. Concrete reinforcement and tokens that mediate concrete
reinforcement can be readily used in most groups, with the exception of
older adolescents (over 15 years).

Problems With Tokens.   "You can't get me to do anything with your goddamn
points!" Occasionally, such statements represent an attitude reflected by
some participants in the program. If this is the norm of the group, the
usefulness to members of the token system is discussed. If the attitude
persists, the token system is not initiated, or it is discontinued. The token
system is helpful but not essential to the success of the program. Even verbal
praise may be handled more gingerly in distrustful groups, but it should
not be eliminated. If the above quote represents the attitude of only one
person in the group, he or she is permitted to participate in the group
without receiving points and can get into the point system whenever he or
she chooses. Usually, the therapist responds with the comment, "We use
tokens or reinforcement to make the group more fun and to provide
incentives to try out new things. We don't expect anyone to change
dramatically because of a few tokens. It's up to each person whether he or
she finds it helpful or not."

Group Reinforcement

Although tangible individual reinforcers are often not acceptable to
adolescents, more often group reinforcers are. These are administered in
the form of group activities for group achievements. An example of
group achievement might be the accumulation of individual points or
tokens awarded for completion of extragroup tasks and placed on a
thermometer. When the thermometer overflows, the group receives an
agreed-on reward. Group pressure exists to comply with the expected
behavior to the degree that the opinions of the peers are important to
each individual, as they would be in a cohesive group. However, if the
individual has more important social alternatives, he or she may ignore
the pressure, find the negative attention reinforcing of his or her non-

conforming behavior, or even leave the group for more valued social relations.

For highly vulnerable and rejected youth in the group, the group reinforcer may be the cause of increased rejection, especially if they are relatively unskilled and have few successes. Under these conditions, the group may blame them for preventing the group from obtaining maximum rewards. It is not sufficient to be merely aware of the problem; it is important for the group therapist to create frequent opportunities for rejected members to be the cause of large amounts of reinforcement for the group through contingent arrangements especially designed for highly probable success. For example, LaToya, a rejected individual as demonstrated on a classroom sociometric test, was to receive 10 points for the entire group every time she participated in the group discussion. The group therapist permitted the members to address questions to LaToya or even to prompt her. This combination resulted not only in her increasing her participation but also in her gaining more attention, encouragement, acceptance, and cooperation from the other group members.

Types of Group Reinforcers. There are a wide variety of potential group reinforcers. They may be determined in part from the reinforcing survey that the members submitted as part of assessment, from the experience of other group leaders, and from brainstorming by the members. One particularly powerful group reinforcing event for both younger children and adolescents of both genders can be achieved through the use of a videotape recorder. Group behavior is taped, provided that certain behaviors are being performed (e.g., the members are cooperating with each other, they are playing a game and keeping to the rules, they are giving feedback to each other while meeting prescribed criteria, or they are discussing seriously a problem of one of the members). As soon as an undesirable or unacceptable behavior occurs, the tape recorder is turned off in a very noticeable way, the timer is set for 5 minutes, and the cameraperson (often a member) sits down. When the timer rings, the taping begins again. The group members can also earn time to watch the tape or, if facilities are available, to edit the film or tape. Often, such an activity leads to the group's requesting to design and carry out their own film. This can also be earned as a group reinforcer. (See Chapter 13 for more details.)

Of course, not every group therapist has such facilities available, nor does every group take to videotaping. For this reason, we have attempted to develop a menu of potential group reinforcers. For adolescents in particular, the purchase of a junkyard car and the right to work on it has been quite effective. This assumes that the group therapist, at least one of the members, or a volunteer has mechanical skills. Sometimes a volunteer can be recruited to guide the group in this activity. Riding around one's neighborhood in a car chauffeured by the group therapist has been highly valued by some groups. Driving lessons have had notable success as a group reinforcer. Provided that the youth have the necessary minimal skills and the resources can be made available, such activities as swimming, ice skating, cross-country skiing, bowling, horseback riding, and sailing have proven to reinforce youth of limited interests. (For other ideas, see Chapter 13.) The juvenile offender is not able to obtain many of these activities by means of delinquent acts. For delinquents, such recreational activities must serve as far more powerful reinforcers than the delinquent act itself.

Another set of group reinforcers that we have used primarily with adolescents has been visits by high-status guests. Group therapists have invited disc jockeys, local singing groups and other local entertainers, newspaper reporters, and sports heroes from the local university or professional teams. We have found that such persons have given of their time generously and at no cost when the purpose of the activity was explained. In some cases, the potency of the group reinforcer can be increased by requiring the members to earn not only the visit but also the right to lessons in the given sport or entertainment skill that the guest manifested. Other group reinforcers that we have used especially for young women include dancing lessons from the group therapist or from a dance instructor who volunteers her time, lessons in makeup and personal appearance, music, meals at a restaurant (although, in several cases, desirable restaurant behaviors had to be shaped before the reinforcer was offered a second time), and karate lessons. Success in obtaining potent group reinforcers requires extensive exploration of the community and the interests of the group members. We have been able to get many resources free or at a minimal cost when our purposes were explained. It must be recognized that organizing such reinforcers can often become a time-consuming activity.

Expanding Reinforcement Repertoires

Many youth who come into treatment have only limited interests or activities that might serve as reinforcers. Programming and reinforcement for these youth become extremely difficult to arrange. To offset this problem, a number of strategies can be employed. Where the majority of the group members have narrow interests, a high-status model with broad interests may be introduced into the group as a guest. It will be he or she who will enthusiastically introduce new activities, which may often become much more acceptable to the group members than those ideas presented by the group therapist. Later, the models will be invited contingently to the group sessions (i.e., the group will have earned, through their behavior, the opportunity to have the visitor at their meeting).

A somewhat similar procedure is used in which youth are noncontingently confronted with a broad range of potentially reinforcing activities. These are usually paired with already demonstrated reinforcing activities. For example, in a group of early juvenile offenders, the boys were provided with the opportunity to go on field trips to an employment agency, a museum, and an auto repair shop. None of these activities were initially reinforcing in their own right. Following the trips, they ate hamburgers at McDonald's. Later, as they found these new activities satisfying, they had to earn the right to go on field trips, which had become highly attractive activities. A group of African American girls talked to a series of successful African American women in various fields. The talks were often preceded by self-selected music on tapes and followed by ice cream. After a while, the girls began to choose the talks as valuable experiences in their own right, and these could be used as group reinforcement of other activities.

Shaping

Shaping involves the reinforcement of successive approximations of a desired end behavior. First, relatively easy-to-perform behaviors are reinforced, and, as these are mastered, more difficult behaviors are expected to be performed before reinforcement follows. To use shaping, clear identification of the end behavior and the successive steps to achieve that end behavior must be specified. Generally, the group therapist must determine in advance at what levels reinforcement for one behavior should cease and reinforcement for new behavior should begin. These levels are usually discussed and sometimes negotiated with the group members.

This particular training process involves a combination of instruction and reinforcement of successive approximations to the desired end behavior. By strict definition, shaping should involve only the reinforcement of successive approximations. In practice, many other procedures are combined with reinforcement in the shaping of youth's behavior. The target behavior in most situations is a set of different but related behaviors that must be performed, though not necessarily in a given sequence, rather than a complex behavior that must be learned one step at a time. For example, in teaching social skills to unassertive youth, the members may first learn approach responses, then how to carry out simple conversations, and then how to make a request for future contact. While learning these steps, they will also focus on various nonverbal behaviors. Reinforcement and modeling strategies are combined in the training process for each of the steps. A more appropriate term than *shaping* for teaching complex behaviors in groups might be "a small step combined with increased demand."

Schedules of Reinforcement

Thus far, reinforcement has been discussed as if it always follows every presentation of a given behavior. In groups, this regular arrangement of behavior and consequence in fact rarely occurs. Many other arrangements also exist, each presenting a unique contribution to the modification or stabilization of behavior. Ferster and Skinner (1957) provided an extensive description of the effects of various arrangements on the speed and acquisition of a response, the strength at which it is maintained, and the rate of decrease of an established response. Only those arrangements that can be administered with any frequency in groups will be reviewed here.

In establishing new behaviors in the repertoire of an individual, the group therapist attempts to reinforce as immediately as possible every occurrence of the desired behavior. This ideal, rarely achieved, is referred to as *continuous reinforcement.* Perfect continuity is not usually achieved in the group setting, for the group therapist and the members combined cannot help missing some of the occurrences of any one behavior when so much interaction is going on at any one time, and the group therapist may observe the behavior but be too busy with another group member to reinforce it. The only exceptions to this are highly visible behaviors with low frequency, such as a usually uncooperative member's act of assisting another group member. At best, then, the group therapist can only approximate perfect continuity of reinforcement.

Some behaviors that occur in the group can better be reinforced if they occur in a given period of time. This is referred to as a *fixed interval of reinforcement*. To implement this in the group, the group therapist sets a timer for a given period, usually 5 to 10 minutes. When the timer goes off, the group therapist can then reinforce each person in the group who has performed at least once a target behavior specified in advance. This is easiest to do if all the members have the same behavior to work on: for example, speaking in the group, praising another person in the group, or self-disclosing. The greater the diversity of target behavior among the members, the more difficult it is for the group therapist to keep track of it.

If the behavior is a high-frequency behavior, such as participating in the group discussion, the group therapist may reinforce the client only after a given number of occurrences. *This fixed-ratio schedule of reinforcement* is probably just as difficult to observe as continuous reinforcement and therefore is also seldom used in groups. More frequently used is a variable schedule of reinforcement in which the client is reinforced after varying frequency of the occurrence of the target behavior. For example, when Charlene requested something (in contrast to demanding) something from another group member or from the group therapist, she was praised by the group therapist and given a token. Ideally, the frequency of reinforcement should have been random. In practice, it occurred only when the group therapist noticed it. If she noticed it too frequently, she would occasionally omit giving reinforcement intentionally. She estimated that the frequency ranged from two to six performances before she gave reinforcement. The advantage of the *variable-ratio schedule* was that it was a procedure for thinning the schedule of the reinforcement received. Thinning serves to stabilize the behavior learned in the group.

Another schedule occasionally used in groups is the *variable-interval schedule*. In this schedule, the group therapist sets the timer at varying lengths of time. In one group, the girls were working on giving eye contact to each other. The group therapist had set the timer at 5, 7, 3, 10, 12, and 16 minutes. When the bell rang, he asked the observer to reinforce each girl who had given eye contact to at least one other girl during the given period between bells. To thin the reinforcement still further, the frequency of desired behavior would be increased, and intervals would continue to grow until the interval might be an entire meeting, and finally no reinforcement would be given at all.

Although behaviors tend to build up more quickly under rich reinforcement conditions such as continuous or small fixed or variable intervals or ratios, the same behaviors tend to disappear more quickly when reinforcement is suddenly terminated (Ferster & Skinner, 1957). For this reason, any treatment plan usually takes into consideration the process of gradually changing schedules of reinforcement from high frequency (rich) to low frequency (thin) and from regular frequencies and intervals to random frequencies and intervals before terminating the reinforcement completely.

The focus so far has been on strategies of increasing desirable or adaptive behaviors. Next, we will focus on strategies for decreasing undesirable or maladaptive ones.

Reducing the Frequency of Undesirable Behavior

Positively Reinforcing Behaviors
Incompatible With Undesirable Behavior

In one group, several members complained constantly at home, at school, and in the group meeting about the most insignificant events. This resulted in their rejection by classmates well as the other group members. The group therapist negotiated with the members that they would be reinforced with tokens every time they described an event in positive terms, stated something they liked, or otherwise indicated approval of an activity or a person while ignoring the negative aspects. The group therapist and other group members agreed that they would ignore any complaining or grumbling.

In the above example, the group therapist was differentially reinforcing behaviors other than the behavior she wanted to reduce in frequency. Because this response usually results in weakening a behavior without some of the side effects of other more aversive or intrusive procedures, it is commonly used in group treatment. It should be noted in the above example that the group therapist negotiated the plan with the members involved. Moreover, the other members were receiving high frequencies of reinforcement for other behaviors. One of the difficulties in using this procedure is trying to decide on behaviors that are incompatible with the target behavior. In this case, we have found it useful to ask the group members to brainstorm ideas as to what might be reinforced. They have often come up with creative possibilities.

In one anger management group, all of the members felt annoyed by criticism from peers and adults. The group therapist suggested that the members brainstorm all the things they could do when they were upset at someone's giving them unfair criticism instead of just getting angry or arguing with the critic. They came up with walking away, disagreeing in a matter-of-fact tone of voice, asking for examples, ignoring, taking a deep breath and letting it out slowly, and thanking the person for his or her concern. These were excellent examples of alternative behaviors that could be reinforced for not performing the anger behavior. In the treatment plan, members were to receive tokens every time they performed any one of these behaviors when they were criticized in the group.

Extinction

Extinction is the process of weakening a response by nonreinforcement. A group example of extinction is the following: The group therapist and the other youth ignored all manifestations of obscene gestures that Jerry made in the group. The application of extinction procedures in a group is complicated by the fact that not only the group therapist but also all the members must refrain from responding to a given behavior. If the members continue to attend to Jerry's obscene gestures, despite the nonresponse of the group therapist, the frequency of the behavior is likely to be maintained or even increased. Thus, whenever the group therapist includes extinction as a treatment strategy, he or she must include the group in the discussion of that application; if the members are unskilled in the use of extinction, the group therapist must train them through exercises, instructions, modeling, and rehearsal. Once trained, the group members can be asked to assist in this strategy on other occasions. Of even greater importance with aggressive youth is that the skill of planned ignoring may provide another alternative to fighting or arguing about some trivial thing. Usually the behavior by the members of successfully ignoring a maladaptive behavior of one of their peers throughout a designated portion of their meeting results in their receiving group reinforcement.

For groups whose members have contact with each other outside the group, group member extinction can have some important advantages. The foremost is that the members can agree to continue to refrain from responding to Jerry's gesticulating on the playground and in the classroom, where the behavior has been getting him into trouble. The disadvantage is that any one person can provide the necessary intermittent reinforcement of the undesired behavior with a giggle or a snort. Unless the group is committed to helping the target person, the procedure should probably not be used in the group. Another disadvantage of extinction is for the client who receives little reinforcement in the group except for his or her maladaptive behaviors. In this case, the behavior tends to persist longer than the ignoring behavior of the group. For this reason, if extinction is to be used in the group, care must be taken to see that the client is receiving high frequency of reinforcement for other prosocial behaviors.

Generally, extinction is used in the group for behaviors that are not too disruptive and that do not result in hurting another person. If extinction is not working or if the behavior is too disruptive or damaging to others, more intrusive actions may need to be taken. One such procedure is time-out from reinforcement.

Time-Out From Reinforcement

In working with preadolescents or younger children in families or in the classroom, one of the most common strategies to control disruptive behavior is time-out from reinforcement. The same procedure can be used primarily with latency-age and younger adolescents in the group. In this procedure, the client is removed from all reinforcing stimuli for a brief period of time in response to a disruptive or aggressive behavior (see Kazdin, 1989, pp. 149-154, for a more complete discussion). To be effective, time-out usually lasts from 30 seconds to 5 minutes in a quiet place where reinforcers are limited. The reason for the brief period of time is that the group therapist wants to keep every client in therapeutic interaction for as much of the treatment period as possible. Moreover, longer periods do not seem to be more effective than shorter periods. The time-out usually begins when the client has his or her behavior under control. For example, every time Harry destroys or damages even a small part of the work of another, the group therapist escorts him in a matter-of-fact way to a seat just outside the glass door. The group therapist states calmly, "The rule is, 'We do not destroy other people's work.' " At the end of the time period, the client is brought back to the activity. In groups, the procedure has some special difficulties. First, if there is only one group therapist, the client in the time-out is difficult to monitor. With two therapists, one can monitor while the other continues the group activities. Second, it is often difficult to find a suitable time-out place that has few if any reinforcers. The people who pass by in the hall or the coats of the other group members in the cloakroom can serve as delightful diversions. A chair in the room that does not face the group or the outside window may be the best arrangement. In general, time-out is a strategy of last resort in groups, although some group therapists report using it with great frequency in early sessions with acting-out groups of youth. If frequent time-outs are being used, the group therapist needs to examine whether the group is sufficiently reinforcing.

The advantage of time-out over more intrusive punishment proce-dures is that the group therapist does not model the very aggressive behavior he or she is trying to eliminate. To maximize its effectiveness, the group therapist will often train the members to take time-outs under simulated conditions. The group therapist will then reinforce the client for appropriate time-out behavior. Usually this is followed by a discussion of how one can avoid time-out in the group. Tyler and Brown (1967) described how time-out was used to control the behavior of adolescent residents of a training school cottage while in the recreation room. Whenever a resident broke the rules, he was put into his room for a short period of time. The study was divided into four phases. In the first and third phases, time-outs were used. In the second and fourth phases, reprimands were used. The time-out confinement was much more effec-tive in maintaining conformity to the rules.

In general, time-out works best in a highly cohesive group where there is a great deal of ongoing reinforcement. The client is much more concerned about leaving such a situation than about leaving a less attractive one. In contrast, time-out is often ineffective with the scape-goat in the group or the highly rejected client. One way that such a client can escape his or her tormentors is to behave in such a way as to receive a time-out.

Time-out in the above form is rarely used with older adolescents unless it is negotiated with them. Instead, when behavior is too disruptive, the therapist may stop all activities until the disruptive person stops the undesirable behavior. Usually this generates enough group pressure for the individual to stop the behavior. If not, the offender may be asked to leave and even escorted back to the living unit by the cotherapist or escorted out of the building if the group is a community group. However, such drastic actions are rarely used and, if used, are followed up with individual contact. Another strategy is to stop all activity and discuss what is happening in the group, how the group may be supporting the behavior, and what they as a group and the individual can do about it to terminate it so that group activities can go on. This is an effective device if not used too often.

Response Cost

Response cost is the removal of positively reinforcing stimuli from the client following an unacceptable behavioral response (see Kazdin, 1989, p. 153). In some groups, every time a client utters an obscenity, he or she is fined several tokens. The advantage of a fining system is that all undesirable behaviors can have certain specified fines attached to them that are administered on a continuous schedule. The disadvantage, and it is a serious one, is that the whole token system may degenerate into a punishment system. It seems that it is far easier for staff to fine than to reinforce. If data are kept on the frequency of fines and positive reinforcement, one can usually monitor the effectiveness of the group therapist on the basis of a ratio of four units of reinforcement to one unit of response cost. Our clinical observations suggest that this ratio is sufficient to maintain a basically positively reinforcing climate in the group.

Some group therapists have used a procedure similar to response cost in group treatment to reduce free time or some desired activity such as sports time in the gym in response to off-task behavior during the session. "If we get the work done, then we get the free time." This usually generates a lot of group pressure to cut out the off-task behavior. If this arrangement is used contractually, it may be an effective procedure unless the group continues to lose most of the activities that members value. In that case, the group loses its attraction for the members. If the procedure is used merely arbitrarily and too frequently, the reduction of cohesion is still more drastic. Frequent use of the removal of group activities has the added disadvantage of removing positive training opportunities for the members. Such activities should not be removed lightly.

Heavy response costs administered by the group therapist do not appear to be as effective as light response costs. In a study evaluating the effectiveness of a token system for predelinquent boys, Phillips (1968) discovered that large token penalties given to the entire group failed to reduce the members' maladaptive behaviors. On the other hand, the same behaviors were quickly eliminated when a group member, in his role as manager, levied lesser fines.

Stimulus Control

Whenever Ginny sat next to Nina in class, the two of them fought or argued and often got into trouble with the teacher. The group therapist arranged for Ginny and Nina to be placed on opposite sides of the room in all of their classes. As part of their contract, the girls eventually agreed to separate themselves for several weeks.

Ron told the group that to avoid his impulsive eating at home, he and his mother had removed from the house all foods that could be eaten without preparation, such as potato chips, crackers, and soft drinks. If the rest of the family wanted to eat these things, they were bought in small quantities, and leftovers were thrown away.

Allan, Mike, Bryan, and Juanita—the four members of the study skill group—all agreed to study at a clean desk with no music playing and with a set of presharpened pencils readily available. Furthermore, each would have a list of things that he or she agreed to do before he or she got up from his or her seat.

In the above examples, the client or the group therapist or the parent deliberately arranged the environment in such a way as to increase the probability that undesirable behaviors would decrease and desirable ones would increase. Although not included in the examples, success in completing the target behavior is usually followed by some form of reinforcement to maximize the effectiveness of the procedure. Research indicates that modification of the antecedent conditions alone rarely results in stable change (Gambrill, 1977, p. 47). To be most effective in changing behavior, consequences of the given desired behavior as well as the stimulus conditions should be modified. The prearrangement of the antecedent conditions or stimulus control procedures is especially useful when desirable behaviors occur but not with sufficient frequency or in appropriate situations (Gambrill, 1977, p. 47). For example, in a group of adjudicated delinquents, there was a low frequency of identifying personal cognitions or statements that were self-defeating. To increase the frequency, commonly occurring statements were placed around the room where everyone could see them, and the members were encouraged to use these if they fit. Anyone describing a self-defeating or distorted cognition of his or her own would also be reinforced.

Commonly Altered Stimulus Conditions

In self-management training, youth are most often trained to rearrange their own environment. The training may also involve instructions, modeling, and reinforcement. For example, in a group of adolescents, some of whom had sleeping disorders, youth were advised to get out of bed after 10 minutes of not being able to sleep, to perform some boring task until they felt tired, and to repeat this cycle until they fell asleep. In a group of smoke-enders, youth agreed to stop seeing friends who smoked, to avoid situations in which they previously had smoked a lot, and to go into situations where smoking was prohibited, such as the movies or the nonsmoking sections of restaurants. Success and failure were discussed in the subsequent meeting. In a group of adolescents with problems in studying, members were presented with a list of ideas that included the following: Sit in the front of class, take careful notes, organize your notes immediately after class, and ask yourself questions concerning the content of your readings and the lectures at some specified time following the reading and the lecture. The list was derived from the literature (Groveman, Richards, & Caple, 1975, pp. 28-29) and from an exchange of experiences by the group members. Each member chose and publicly stated what he or she intended to do and reported back to the group what had happened during the week.

Physical Proximity

One form of stimulus control often used to control the behavior of aggressive youth in the group is physical proximity: The group therapist sits next to the potentially disruptive group member. This is often sufficient to keep the behavior under control. However, as soon as the member shows signs of becoming disruptive, the group therapist prompts him or her to perform an alternative behavior. Such a procedure provides the aberrant member with somewhat greater attention than others, though often he or she considers it a form of protection. It usually cannot be used except in a small group or in a larger group with more than one therapist. Although more intrusive than extinction, physical proximity is not as intrusive as time-out from reinforcement, in which the client is withdrawn totally from the interaction in the group.

Commands

One additional procedure that involves verbal antecedent conditions is clear limit setting or commands. Used primarily in response to disruptive behavior, a clear command to terminate a behavior and begin a more appropriate one may be regarded both as a consequence of one behavior and as an antecedent to another. Although not effective as a long-term intervention strategy, telling a client in a stern tone of voice that the group therapist expects that he will get back in the window at once or that he is to immediately stop punching Jeffrey or that he must lower his voice may create the conditions that make it possible to use more effective long-term strategies. Often disruptive behaviors occur for which no treatment plan has been formulated. An occasional firmly stated command may be a useful holding action. On the other hand, excessive use of commands as opposed to other, more positive strategies mentioned in this chapter creates a highly aversive atmosphere and weakens the effectiveness of the occasional command. It has been our experience that beginning group therapists tend to rely far too heavily on instructions and commands or to avoid commands completely even when the situation demands it.

Summary

Reinforcement and stimulus control are powerful tools in the modification of behavior. In this chapter, we described the types of reinforcers commonly used in group treatment. These include material goods and activities, tokens for material goods and activities, and social reinforcers. Also discussed were the schedules by which these reinforcers could most effectively be delivered in groups. For youth who have a limited variety of reinforcers at their disposal, strategies for expanding their repertoire were recommended.

Most of the above procedures are used to increase the frequency of desired behaviors. Also described were group applications of consequences used to reduce the frequency and/or intensity of undesired behaviors. These included reinforcement of behaviors other than the one to be reduced, extinction, time-out from reinforcement, and response cost. The difficulties of using extinction and punishment procedures in groups were discussed. Finally, a number of group applications of stimulus control procedures were illustrated, such as direct modification of the conditions impinging on the behavior, physical proximity, and commands. It was noted that reinforcement procedures are used more loosely in groups than in individual therapy because the process is being observed and reacted to by other group members at the same time. Moreover, reinforcement is often combined with other procedures such as modeling and cognitive restructuring and has been separated out in this chapter for purposes of analysis.

CHAPTER 9

The Modeling Sequence

The modeling sequence is one of the major intervention strategies in CBIGT. Modeling procedures have been successfully used to teach youth to make friends and to carry on small talk in social situations, to ask for help from a parent or teacher, to apologize when one has made an error, and to help adolescent girls deal with the myriad oppressive statements they have had to endure because of their gender and at the same time to teach feminist values. Modeling has also been used to teach African American, Native American, Asian American, Hispanic, and European American youth strategies for handling racist or ethnic remarks or acts without getting into fights yet maintaining self-respect. Modeling techniques (often combined with other procedures) have also been used widely in teaching the unemployed job-finding and interviewing skills (Azrin & Besale, 1980; Kelly, Wildman, & Berler, 1980). In such programs, youth have been taught to locate job openings and to present themselves more effectively in the job interview. In some such programs, youth engage in extensive rehearsals of the job interview to increase their ability to convey information on job-related past experience, direct questions to the interviewer, and express enthusiasm and interest in the job. Through modeling techniques, youth have also been taught to deal with peer pressure to commit illegal acts.

The fundamental assumption of modeling theory (Bandura, 1977b) is that new behavior can be learned by observation, already learned but suppressed behavior can be unsuppressed, and infrequent but desired behaviors can be increased in frequency. For learning to occur, minimal levels of certain prerequisite conditions must exist (Bandura, 1977b).

The Simulated Modeling Sequence

As will be discussed in detail later in this chapter, not all modeling is role-played. The advantage of role-played or simulated modeling is that it can be focused and developed systematically. It can be applied in simple situations with one critical moment or in complex situations consisting of many critical moments. The group therapist can direct the action so that successful efforts can be reinforced and unsuccessful ones terminated and redeveloped. This sequence consists of more than modeling or demonstration by a model. The eight procedures of which the modeling sequence usually consists are

1. Orientation of the group members to the modeling sequence
2. Determination of a set of interactive behaviors in which one or several members of the group are deficient
3. Modeling (or demonstration) of a behavior or given sequence of behaviors
4. Behavioral rehearsal (or practice by the client of the modeled behaviors)
5. Coaching (the giving of hints or prompts to the target person while he or she is rehearsing)
6. Group feedback (after the rehearsal, the evaluation of what the target person did well and could consider doing differently)
7. Re-rehearsal (repeating the practice until the given client is comfortable and correcting for feedback)
8. The negotiation of an extragroup task (in which the client designs a task and tries out in the real world what he or she has learned in the group)

Each of these procedures is also used independently of the others or in combination with still other procedures not necessarily included in the modeling sequence (e.g., reinforcement for success). This sequence is most often used in its entirety to teach the overt verbal and motor components of highly specific interactive skills such as refusing a request when imposed on, approaching new people, handling or giving criticism, asking for help, telling friends about difficult problems, and expressing one's emotions. These same procedures may be used in more elaborate social interactions such as carrying out a job interview, negotiating a major family decision and plan, or carrying out a dating interaction over an extended period of time. I have referred to the above set of procedures as the modeling sequence because they draw their significance from modeling theory and occur more or less in the above order. Let us examine each of these steps in more detail.

Orientation of Group Members to the Modeling Sequence

As with all the procedures in this book, the assumptions of the modeling sequence and what the members can expect while using it are explained to the group. If the group is an open group, senior members explain the assumptions; if not, the group therapist may give the explanation. The particular assumptions that the group therapist or members stress are that people can learn both simple and complex behavior by observing it and practicing it in role plays. People can learn more efficiently if they get feedback on what they do and say from their peers. The youth are assured that the feedback will be "safe" in that it must follow certain rules (which are discussed later in this chapter). The group members are also told that modeling can be enjoyable, and if some members have had previous experience, they are asked to validate this. At this point, the therapist and a cotherapist or an experienced member role-play the entire modeling process, using a "canned" or predetermined situation (see below for further explanation).

Determination of a Set of Interactive Behaviors

Most of the interactive situations dealt with in modeling are obtained from the accounts of the group members. The members are instructed to record in their diaries both situations they handled well and situations in which they were dissatisfied with their response. The members are trained in defining situations in the exercises on situational analysis (see Chapter 4). The situations that lend themselves to modeling are those in which the target person interacts with one or more other persons. Once a series of problematic situations have been obtained, the group members share these situations with each other. Other sources of situations may be obtained by asking the group members to interview friends and relatives to get ideas from them as to what kind of interactive situations to work on. This also serves to facilitate their using their social network for help.

In addition, "canned" situations (those developed by the therapist) are distributed to the members as examples. These are situations that the group therapist has identified as commonly occurring problems for similar youth. Some examples of canned situations are the following:

- Jan, a recovering alcoholic, is trying to stay clean. He has to go to a class party where there will be alcohol, and he knows that some classmates will be pushing him to drink. The group has suggested and he has agreed that he should say clearly that he is a recovering alcoholic and that even one drink is one drink too much. If they pressure him, he is to say, "I don't think you understand how bad it is for me. I can't have even one drink." If they persist, Jan should repeat his position firmly and with eye contact but without further explanation.

- Jackie, who has just received her GED, has to tell her father that she is not going into the family business as was expected. She has decided to go to college and go into teaching. Her father has often stated that making a good living is very important to him. Jackie is afraid of her father and doesn't know what to say, but she is definite about going into teaching. She wants to relate to her father's disappointment, to say that she respects her father's choice, and to ask her father to respect her choice. She wants to be firm but understanding. She wants to use good eye contact as she speaks with a matter-of-fact, confident, and firm tone of voice.

- Ellen is looking forward to a quiet night at home. This is the first evening she has had free all week. She just wants to sit around and relax and watch TV. Her classmate comes excitedly to her. "I just got a call from Al, you know, the guy I've been trying to meet for ages. He wants to go out with me tonight, but I'm supposed to baby-sit for the Henks family. I know you're free this evening. I know you'll baby-sit for me just this once." Ellen really doesn't want to. A barrier to her refusing is her long-standing tendency to help others whenever they ask. As a result, her own needs often go unmet. Ellen decides, with the help of the group, that she wants to say that Alice will just have to find another person to cover for her, that she is not available. No matter what Alice says, she repeats that she is not available and will not explain what else she is doing, even when Alice asks.

In each of these situations, the target person is helped by the others to define what he or she wants to say or do in the situation but is insufficiently comfortable to do it without some demonstration and practice.

Role-Played Modeling

Modeling is a demonstration, by someone other than the target person, of what might be done and said in a specific problem situation. The event is role-played. Let us begin with an example and discussion of the technique of role-played modeling or the demonstration of target behaviors because this is the first step following assessment and goal setting. Many of the principles of modeling can be noted in the following example.

Group Therapist: Now that we have discussed ways that Cynthia can approach her principal to ask him if he will let her back into school, I wonder if we couldn't role-play for her exactly what she might say or do in that situation. Does that sound okay, Cynthia?

Cynthia: I guess I could give it a try.

Group Therapist: I think it should help a lot. JoEllen, since you seem to have ideas that came closest to what Cynthia wants to say, would it be okay if you play the role of Cynthia, and Vikki (the cotherapist), would you mind playing the role of the principal? I'll coach you, JoEllen, if you get into trouble. And Vikki might give you a couple of hints, too.

JoEllen: Okay with me.

Vikki: Me too.

Group Therapist: Great, let me just review what we agreed on. JoEllen, this is what you chose to do. First, apologize and tell him that the fighting won't happen again. Oh, you agreed to ask firmly whether you could get back into school, that's what this is all about. Oh, and you wanted to remind him that you are in this group getting help for your anger.

Vikki: I'll be careful not to be too hard on her the first time through. But I will be somewhat sarcastic, like Cynthia said the principal was.

Group Therapist: Cynthia and the rest of you are observers. Especially keep track of what they do well. Okay, let's start. Cynthia, why don't you remind them of the situation?

Cynthia: Okay, I would be in the waiting room. Mr. Harding's secretary would probably tell me to go in. I would open the door slowly. Then I would tell him what I want to say.

Group Therapist: Don't forget, knock at the door, enter the room, make it as real as possible. Before we start, let's have the observers sit over there. And Vikki, sit at that desk. Okay, the door will be there. Okay, we're ready. Let's begin.

JoEllen (as Cynthia): (Knocks at simulated door)

Vikki (as the principal): Come in. Oh, Cynthia, it's you. Sit down. (Waits while Cynthia sits down) Well, Cynthia, what do you want, as if I didn't know?

JoEllen (as Cynthia): First, I've come to say that I'm really sorry about the fight last week. I've thought about it a lot.

Vikki: (loudly) And what are you going to do about it?

JoEllen: (looking her right in the eye and speaking slowly and emphatically) I want to assure you it won't happen again. I really would like to get back into school. You know, I am in the group with Ms. R., and I am working at controlling my anger. I know I can control myself now if you give me another chance.

Vikki: Well, I don't know.

Group Therapist: Okay, let's stop there for the first time. That strikes me as a useful way of handling it. How about you, Cynthia?

Cynthia: Vikki was great as the principal, that's just the way he would be. I'm glad you stopped there, 'cause I wouldn't have known what to say next. And I loved the way JoEllen handled her. I'd like to do it that way

Others: (agree)

Let us examine some of the principles of modeling as they are demonstrated in the above example. First, the group therapist reviewed for the model what the situation was and what she might say. The therapist selected as a model a person who felt comfortable in playing the role and who made the best suggestion in "brainstorming" on how to handle the situation. Furthermore, the therapist attempted to make the situation as similar as possible to the original real-world situation.

In choosing a person to play the role of the principal, the therapist tried to find someone who would be perceived as an authority figure. Because there was a cotherapist who had some authority with the group, this was a particularly good choice. (We have also used other staff members for authority figures.) Because this was the first of many modeling trials, the cotherapist noted that she would take it easy the first time around. Any role player can make the model or the rehearser fail if he or she makes the situation particularly complex and difficult in the beginning.

The therapist kept control of the role playing. She would have prompted the significant other (the principal) if she had been at a loss for words. Because this was a first modeling session, the therapist kept the demonstration brief. She also reviewed carefully the major things the model might say (in one sense, this is an additional modeling session). When the model successfully responded to the matter-of-fact principal, the therapist stopped the modeling session. Finally, the group therapist was about to prepare JoEllen for the next, somewhat more difficult step as the principal would put on a little more pressure.

Had the model inadequately performed the desired behavior, the therapist would have stopped the modeling session at the point she noticed the modeling was not working and provided additional suggestions to the model. If it was clear that the client selected as model was completely inadequate, the group therapist might model the desired behavior herself, introducing it with a statement such as "Let me show you another alternative to choose from."

Characteristics of Effective Models

Although not as powerful as incentives, the extent to which a client imitates behavior is in part a function of certain characteristics of the model (Bandura, 1977b). Some attributes of models may increase the probability that their behaviors are imitated. These attributes include the high rewarding potential of the model, demonstration by the model of competence in areas highly regarded by the observer, and general prominence or relatively high social power with respect to the observer. If a good relationship has already been established, the group therapist may be regarded as having high rewarding potential for some youth. Some invited persons may be even more effective as models by virtue of their social role (e.g., a sports hero from a nearby university, a radio announcer) and may have a prominence usually not found in the group therapist.

Similarity of models to the group members also increases the likelihood of imitation. The group therapist may or may not be similar to the members in terms of socioeconomic, racial, ethnic, and educational background. If not, the therapist has a wide variety of sources whom he or she can use for models to increase the likelihood of imitation.

Sources of Models

Bandura (1977b) concluded on the basis of an extensive research program that the greater the number and variety of models available to youth, the greater the likelihood that they will find adequate models to observe and imitate. The group offers the possibility of both number and variety. Possible models include the group members, the group therapist, invited guests, the individual youth him- or herself (self-modeling), and admired persons outside the group. No one type of model possesses all of the above-mentioned desired characteristics. To compensate for deficiencies in one category of model, several are selected for any one set of behaviors from many of these categories. Let us look first at the group member as a model for others in the group.

Members as Models. As was pointed out above, the more effective models are those who show some of the observer's population characteristics (race, similar general problem area, age, sex, athletic prowess, interests). For this reason, the major source of models is usually the members themselves. Two other important advantages of using the group members as models are that the model obtains additional practice while demonstrating to others and that the group members report feeling more involved.

The major drawback of this source is that the members of many groups may have a repertoire of socially maladaptive behaviors and only a limited repertoire of adaptive or coping skills. This is especially true in groups of members characterized by extremely similar problems, such as depression or aggression, in a wide range of situations. But even in these groups, there are often dramatic differences among members in their coping skills and coping styles. Some members are excessively self-critical. Some can cope with some types of situations but not others. Some have only one coping style that they can teach others but that is clearly not adequate for all situations. As a result, almost everyone has some skill they can model for someone else, but no one person in the group will serve as a universal model. In institutional groups or open-ended community groups, there is usually a range of experience in role playing and modeling. The senior members have learned or practiced a wide range of behaviors in numerous situations and have learned many useful skills. As a result, the senior members are particularly suited to serving as models. It may also be valuable for the senior members to serve as models in that they get the opportunity to teach others, thereby increasing the probability of generalization.

Another drawback to consider in using members as models is that in role-played modeling the group members who are most competent in dealing with a given situation most often serve in role plays as models for the others. As a result, the more competent members may get much more practice time and reinforcement than others. To offset this tendency, the group therapist keeps track of the practice and modeling time of each member and makes sure that the total role-play time either in rehearsal or as a model is approximately equal over a set of two or three sessions for all the youth.

Group Therapists as Models. Although group members may be one of the most desirable sources of models, certain aspects of target behaviors may not be found in the repertoire of any of the members. Under these circumstances, the group therapist may also serve as model. The group therapist, though he or she sometimes differs radically in age, education, socioeconomic status, race, and other characteristics from the group members, can usually provide the members with demonstrations of a wider range of new coping behaviors than the members can. In addition, the group therapist often (but not always) has greater reinforcement power than any one member of the group, and the therapist as model usually can provide far more focus than the members can, with less risk that an undesirable behavior will be repeatedly modeled.

The group therapist, of course, serves as a general model in everything he or she does, whether he or she wants to or not. Unfortunately, youth often select unpredictable behavior and attitudes to emulate. It is in the role-played modeling that the greatest control can be brought to bear on the process. To obtain both focus and a wide range of desirable (i.e., imitation-inducing) characteristics of the models, not only therapists but also guests with desirable characteristics can be invited to the group and instructed in what behaviors are expected.

Guests as Models. Although it is difficult to alter the membership of a group in the middle sessions of a group, it is often desirable to invite as guests persons who have behavioral and cognitive skills that are undeveloped in the members of the given group but that are necessary to achieve treatment goals. For example, in a community group for paroled male youth, the level of self-disclosure was noticeably low, as it is in the first phase of most adolescent groups. The group therapist invited a member of an earlier group to attend for several sessions. (This guest was a person who had completed high school and had a job.) As a result of his presence and participation, the group members rapidly became more self-disclosing. In another example, a group of African American youth refused to use role playing despite modeling by the white therapist. The group therapist invited an African American colleague, who role-played with the group therapist a set of problem situations without asking the youth to participate. Following several of these role plays, the youth gradually became more willing to volunteer to play auxiliary roles and eventually to role-play (rehearse) their own problem situations. In a group of first-time female offenders, the therapist obtained the services of a well-known singing group who volunteered to tell them about their hard work in achieving some recognition and to teach them some of the latest songs. (The therapist also used their coming contingently; the condition of their coming was that all the members of the group had completed an average of two home tasks per person in a 3-week period.) The guests also served as models in demonstrating some of the skills that the members were working on. The therapist had practiced the demonstration of the skills with them before the session.

Behavioral Rehearsal

Having observed one or more modeled interactions under most of the conditions mentioned above, the probability that a client will duplicate the behaviors of these models in his or her own life increases (Bandura, 1977b). Practicing these behaviors in the real world or in the supportive environment of a group meeting will further increase the likelihood of performance of those behaviors in the real world (Bandura, 1977b). Having both observed and practiced a new set of behaviors, the client is better prepared to recognize the possible responses for dealing with a problem situation. Often the client is also less anxious about trying it out in the real world. Such practice in a group meeting usually involves the group therapist or members playing the role of significant others in the situation while the client plays his or her own role. This procedure is commonly referred to as *behavioral rehearsal* (Lazarus, 1966) or *behavioral enactment*. Although usually the rehearsal is first carried out in the group meeting, extragroup tasks are often suggested to rehearse or role-play a given behavior with a partner, a friend, or a family member in a setting outside the group to increase the number of practice trials. The importance of frequent and diverse trials offsets the possible damage of practicing the wrong behavior, which can be corrected at a subsequent meeting. Let us look now at the rehearsal that followed the modeling session in the previous example and then at the principles that affect both modeling and rehearsal.

Group Therapist: Now that you have seen one way of doing this, Cynthia, would you like to try it yourself?

Cynthia: It's a little scary, but I think I can do it. Could Vikki be the principal? She would be perfect. She sounds just like my principal at school.

Group Therapist: Is that all right, Vikki?

Vikki (Cotherapist):   Yeah, I don't mind. (Joking) Hey, that's what I get paid for.

Group Therapist: Great! Okay, Cynthia, why don't you review what you are going to do again?

Cynthia: (Reviews aloud what she is going to say)

Group Therapist: That sounds right on the target. Okay. The rest of you are observers. Watch whether she does all those things she says she will do. And make sure you would find it convincing. Oh, and remember eye contact and sufficient voice volume so that she can hear her. (Dramatically) Let the action begin, Vikki.

(Cynthia knocks at the door)

Vikki: (sternly) Come in, Cynthia.

Cynthia: (enters) Hello, Mr. B.

Vikki: (sternly) Hello, Cynthia. Sit down, please. What was it that you wanted? I don't have much time.

Cynthia: I just wanted to say that I'm really sorry about what happened last Wednesday, and I won't let it happen again. I really would like to get back into school.

Vikki: How can I be sure? This isn't the first time.

Cynthia: Well, I'm in the group where I'm working on controlling my anger. I'm doing better at home, with my sister, already. My mom says so too. And ask Ms. R., she's the group therapist. She says I'm doing better, too.

Vikki: Well, I'm glad to hear all that. But words aren't enough.

Cynthia: Yes, sir. I know I can control it.

Group Therapist: I think that's a good stopping point.

Group Members: "Great, Cynthia!" "Nice job, C." "Vikki wasn't bad either." (Light applause)

Principles in Effective Role-Played Modeling and Rehearsals

A number of principles have been demonstrated in the above example for effective role-played modeling and rehearsal. Because the same principles are applicable to both, they will be discussed together. The principles include maximally involving the group, reinforcing for success, structuring the situation for success, setting the stage realistically, repeating role plays, and preparing the role players. Let us examine these principles one at a time.

Maximum Involvement. In the above example, the group therapist involved the members in a number of different ways. In preparing Cynthia to role-play, the group therapist suggested that Cynthia review what she was going to say. In later sessions, such reviews are no longer necessary. Cynthia chose her own significant other on the basis of her realistic performance in the modeling session. Cynthia was also involved insofar as she was encouraged to depart from the model's verbal behavior and try out, within the agreed-on general guidelines, the specific words and physical behaviors she was most comfortable with.

The group therapist could involve the other members in Cynthia's rehearsal by using their recommendations before the role play in determining what they should look for and in providing feedback after the role play. The therapist could ask the group members to determine the characteristics of the significant other in the role play. The group could develop its own feedback system. Involving the client and the group whenever possible, whether in role plays or in planning, is a theme that runs throughout this book. It is often costly in terms of time but is effective in terms of the client's owning the procedure or the plan. In most cases, involvement of the client is gradually increased.

Reinforcement for Success. The group therapist stopped the role play when Cynthia had successfully dealt with the problem situation. It was then accurate to praise the effort. Often role plays are allowed to go on too long, so that they may ultimately result in failure. If role playing is to be reinforced, it should be stopped on a positive note. Not only did the group therapist end the role play when Cynthia was successful, but in earlier sessions she had encouraged the members to respond with applause and praise at the end of the role play in which the given player was successful. According to Bandura (1977b), reinforcement of the imitator increases the likelihood that he or she will duplicate the behavior in the real world. One cannot reinforce success unless the client is actually successful. For this reason, the group therapist must structure the situation in such a way that success in the modeling or rehearsal is highly probable.

Structuring for Success. In the early rehearsals, the group therapists or members may model one or two responses only, which the target person attempts to duplicate in the rehearsal. As the target person becomes competent in single responses, the significant other in the role play provides an increasing number of counterstatements to the responses of the person rehearsing. The object is first to provide the role player with an early success experience but eventually to work toward the more complicated and extended conditions of the real world.

The individual playing the significant other must also be instructed to keep the situation relatively easy in the beginning but difficult enough so that it is a challenge for the rehearser. When the significant other is an adult, it is more realistic to use an adult to play him or her, as in the first example with Vikki the cotherapist. If there is no cotherapist, the group therapist might play the role, or a coworker or guest might be invited to play it. The group therapist acts as a director, making sure that the level of difficulty created by significant others is only gradually increased. All too often in their flair for the dramatic or in a need to compete, the role players enacting the significant others create situations that are impossible to resolve. In such a case, the group therapist would stop the role play immediately, reinstruct the antagonist to "take it easy" on the client, and begin again. It is also possible to give some tips to the person rehearsing (see section on coaching below). Thus, to ensure early success, initial role plays should be brief and relatively easy for the client to perform. But gradually all this changes to approximate the conditions of the real world.

Incrementally Increasing the Level of Difficulty. In addition to gradually lengthening the rehearsals and making them more complicated as treatment progresses, it is possible to add new and more difficult situations related to the central problem of the target person. The number of critical moments increases. Also, time spent in preparation for the role play is reduced. Some therapists have arranged an entire curriculum of canned situations that move from less difficult to more difficult over a range of different problems (see, e.g., Goldstein, Carr, Davidson, & Wehr, 1981). CBIGT therapists have used all or selected situations developed by these authors in their youth groups. Goldstein et al. (1981) advised that the content of the vignettes should be varied and relevant to the lives of the trainees. It is helpful to let the members themselves readjust the vignettes in the group meetings to fit their interests and circumstances.

Eventually, in long-term groups, situations are rehearsed for which no preparation is carried out and no modeling is presented. It is assumed that youth at this point in the treatment process will have learned enough basic skills to be able to generalize to similar situations on which they trained earlier or even eventually to novel situations. Before members reach this phase, however, extensive training is required.

Repeated Rehearsals. Obviously, one rehearsal is not sufficient to teach a client a given set of behaviors. Replications by others with similar problems, replications as homework assignments, and replications in pairs in the group are all ways of maximizing the number of trials. When one has four to seven members in the group, arranging multiple trials to give every member a chance to role-play requires a great deal of creativity and effort. (See Chapter 14 for additional suggestions.)

Multiple trials take a lot of time. One way of using the group efficiently to carry out multiple trials is for the group therapist to provide the stimulus situation to each group member one at a time in rapid succession. A situation is chosen that most of the members have in common as a problem. The following is an example.

Group Therapist: Okay, we're going to do the round-robin exercise. Gavin (sitting on therapist's left) will trigger me, and I will respond to him. Then Ike (on Gavin's left) will trigger Gavin, and Gavin will respond. Then Ike will respond, and so on until we go around the group. Be as realistic as possible. Here we go.

Gavin: C'mon, Sheldon. No one will see you, grab the cigarettes from the counter.

Group Therapist: Not me, buddy, I got enough trouble. And don't you do it either. We'll both get caught. It's not worth it. So knock it off. (Pause) Now Ike, you trigger Gavin.

Ike: Hey, Gavin, look at those cigarettes. Nobody is looking. Grab a pack quick! Hurry up.

Gavin: Are you kidding? That's all I need. And don't you do it either, or we'll both be in trouble. Let's get out of here before you get tempted again.

Group Therapist: You're getting better each time. Okay, Ike, turn to Paul.

Paul: (to Ike) I'm out of cigarettes, grab a pack as we pass the counter. No one will see you.

Ike: No way, man. And if you do it, I'll break your arm. I'm not going back to Reed (correctional institution) again.

(Continues until everyone in the group has practiced)

Group Therapist: Okay, great job. They were all good, but who gets the award for the best expressions?

The therapist usually models the correct response first. Then everyone has a chance to model afterward. At the end, it should be noted that the group therapist has the group evaluate the expressions used. In this exercise, everyone has observed at least eight models and has practiced at least once. This repeated practice exercise also requires extensive experience in role playing by the members. Such a procedure can eventually be used with somewhat more complex behaviors. It is also possible with the round-robin to change the situation for every person. The therapist gives out different situations on cards, one to each of the eight members, and then the group goes around the circle, with each person responding to the card of the previous person.

Setting the Stage. In both modeling and rehearsal, the attempt is made to simulate in rehearsal the real world as nearly as possible. The group therapist acts like a director of a play. He or she has the actors stand where appropriate, knock at doors, enter rooms, use props, separate themselves from the audience, and, where possible, rehearse under the most realistic conditions. To make it realistic, the group therapist or the person rehearsing will also set the stage by reviewing briefly the events that led to the situation, the situation itself, and characteristics of the scene in which the event takes place. The person rehearsing may take a few seconds to imagine how she or he felt and thought in the situation at the critical moment. In this way, not only is the role play more enjoyable and lifelike, but it breaks the routine of sitting in a circle and talking.

Preparing Members to Role-Play. As was noted above, in early group sessions, some youth are very anxious about role playing in front of the group. A few may even initially refuse to participate in one. If one or more members refuse to role-play or even if they are initially anxious, role-playing behaviors are usually introduced incrementally. First, role playing is demonstrated by those youth who are more comfortable in role playing. Even then, only relatively nonthreatening situations are enacted in early meetings. Board games that have cards that instruct the participants to role-play a simple situation have also been found to be helpful in this regard for some youth groups. It seems to be easier for some youth to accept and follow through on instructions from a game than on requests of a group therapist. Games can be used only if the youth feel comfortable with one another and the group therapist. Otherwise, they may experience the games as patronizing.

After some preparatory rehearsals, the group therapist might ask reluctant group members simply to state what they would say aloud, without movement or affect. For example, Harry would be allowed to say, "I would say to him that I didn't like what he was doing and I wanted him to stop. If he didn't stop, I would then walk away." Another member might be more comfortable first in privately rehearsing the lines of the role play before actually rehearsing with appropriate movement, affect, and voice volume. At other times, the members of the group would be instructed to rehearse in pairs without audiences as a way of easing them into a more public display in the whole group. The more hesitant members might also be requested to role-play first a significant person in another member's situation, such as a parent or a friend of the person with the problem. The first role plays are usually one-sentence replies, as in the last example. Gradually, an increasing number of multiple responses to multiple responses of the significant other is required. This is another way to ease youth into role playing.

Another way of making someone's first attempts at role playing less difficult is to help him or her through difficult moments by a procedure commonly called *coaching*.

Coaching

Coaching may or may not be used as one of the eight steps of the modeling sequence. In coaching, the group therapist or a group member assists the given group member by whispering words or instructions to him or her during the rehearsal. Although used primarily with youth who are especially anxious or unsure of themselves, these youth, at least, find it extremely helpful the first time they try out a given role-played situation. After one or two coached rehearsals, the coaching is usually faded.

The coach usually sits immediately behind the role player and instructs him or her to speak a little louder, "be firmer," ask for help, look at the significant other more directly, or whatever the role player is working on. A variation of coaching is the use of cue cards or hand signals to remind someone of what he or she must attend to. For example, one client who spoke extremely softly was instructed with a finger to the mouth to speak more loudly. Another was reminded to give eye contact when the coach pointed to her own eye. Another coach used a soft clap for the same purpose because the client usually stared at the floor and could not see the hand signal.

To keep control of the level of difficulty of the role play, occasionally the group therapist will coach the significant other in addition to, or instead of, the target client. The significant other often has it in his or her power to make the role play so easy that the client learns very little or so difficult that the client is destined to fail. Although instructions to the significant other may help, coaching seems more effective. The coach makes sure that the role play is sufficiently demanding to be challenging but not so difficult as to ensure failure.

With open-ended groups in which many of the members are experienced, the coach may be a senior member. Former members may also be used as coaches. When using members as coaches, the group therapist should remind the actors of the conditions and content of coaching before the rehearsal begins. Often the mere presence of a coach is sufficient to provide support for the role players, and no actual coaching is necessary. In the following example, the group therapist serves as coach. Angelo is working on his communication skills with his mother—in particular, not swearing at her. Yesterday, he told the group that "he blew it" and that he wants to set things right with his mother. The rehearsal begins after an initial discussion of what he might say. Angelo expresses some uncertainty and indicates that he could use some help.

Group Therapist: Okay, Angelo, you have just lost your cool with your mom. You swore at her as if she were a street chum. She's really steamed. You realize that you went too far, and you want to say so. Could Leah be your mom? Is that okay, Leah? (Leah nods agreement) And I'll be the coach, since you said you were a little unsure. Okay, Leah, begin, and he just swore at you, you are really mad.

Leah: How dare you say that to me! I ought to kick you out of the house right now.

Group Therapist: (Whispers when Angelo doesn't respond) Okay, Angelo, apologize, tell her you lost it.

Angelo: Hey, Mom, I'm sorry. I didn't mean it. I lost it. I just got mad for a second. I shouldn't have sworn at you.

Group Therapist: (After a pause, whispers). I'll really try not to do it again, and don't forget to give her eye contact and sound sincere.

Angelo: I'll try not to do it again. I mean it.

Group Therapist: (Whispers to Leah) You just better not.

Leah: You just better not.

Angelo: Okay, Mom, and I am sorry.

Group Therapist: Nice touch. Okay, let's do it again, only this time you are both on your own. Observers, take your places.

In this example, the therapist coaches both the significant other and the person rehearsing. Note that the group therapist coaches both for nonverbal and for verbal behavior. Finally, he has the actors do it again without coaching.

Feedback

Feedback refers to the process of providing a given individual with information, observations, and impressions about the individual's performance or general attitudes in real life or in a behavioral rehearsal. These comments may be made by fellow group members, the group therapist, or significant others in the life of the client about his or her specific performance or general patterns. Under optimal conditions, these comments may be a highly effective teaching strategy. However, if delivered arbitrarily, vaguely, hastily, or in other inappropriate ways, feedback may be potentially damaging to the person receiving it. Constructive or therapeutic feedback from multiple sources is one of the major advantages of the group as a tool in treatment, provided that therapeutic criteria for the delivering of that feedback are adhered to. Through feedback, youth not only gain useful information on behaviors that they might improve but also learn the skills of giving and receiving both positive and critical feedback in real-life situations.

Behavioral rehearsal combined with feedback on performance has been found superior to practice alone when working with adult populations (McFall & Marston, 1970) in increasing effective assertive behaviors. The importance of feedback in the learning process has led Bandura (1977b) to conclude that everyday learning is usually achieved through modeling, performance, and self-corrective adjustments made on the basis of informative feedback on performance.

In this section, we will review the general guidelines used in providing feedback after rehearsals, the specific criteria used in evaluating the performance of peers, the techniques of giving feedback after a rehearsal or reviewing a tape, and the training for giving feedback. To illustrate many of the procedures, we will continue with the group that was presented at the beginning of this chapter. The group process described below begins just after Cynthia's behavioral rehearsal.

Group Therapist: Would everyone now write down as many things as you can think of that Cynthia did well in the role play? Cynthia, you can write too. Me too. (After a brief pause) Now, write down one thing that you might have done differently if you were in that situation. (After a moment) You all seem to be filled with ideas, the way you've been writing. First, what do you think she did well? What did you write?

Vikki: I really liked the fact that she referred to being in the group and gave proof that way that she was working on it.

Group Therapist: Good, I see others nodding in agreement. That's one thing Cynthia did very well. What else?

JoEllen: I didn't like . . .

Group Therapist: (Interrupting) Let's wait until we get all the ideas that you did like on the table. Then we can talk about the things (emphatically and slowly) you might have done differently.

JoEllen: Oh yeah, I forgot. I thought almost everything was good. In particular, I liked the way she referred to her doing good at home. Like if you do good at home, you can do good at school.

Glenda: She didn't let him scare her to death.

Cynthia: I'll be scared all right, don't worry about that.

Glenda: I know, but you sounded like you weren't scared.

Group Therapist: What did you think you did well, Cynthia?

Cynthia: I said what I wanted to say.

Group Therapist: I agree. There's quite a bit that Cynthia did well. Anything she might have done differently or you might have done differently if you were in that situation?

JoEllen: Now's my chance! (Laughing) I guess what I might have done differently was to look Vikki in the eye a little more. I thought you were looking at the floor a little too much.

Glenda: What you did wrong was . . .

Group Therapist: There I go again, interrupting, but perhaps it's better to formulate it as your own opinion or what you might have done differently.

Glenda: Yeah (laughs nervously), that's something I need to work on. What I thought you might do differently was to speak a bit more slowly and with greater emphasis on some of the key words, like

JoEllen did when she demonstrated it. But I agree the words themselves were great.

Melinda: I thought you might consider reminding him that that was the only fight you had had in 6 months and that was an improvement.

Cynthia: I could consider that. I especially need to work on eye contact and speaking more slowly, like some of you said. I better relax too so that I don't get too uptight. You know, deep-breathe and all that.

Group Therapist: Okay, Cynthia, why don't you summarize what was being said?

Cynthia: In general, you all seem to be saying thus far that the content was good, but I might add this was the only fight I've had in 6 months. Let's see, my eye contact and a slower rate of speech need to be worked on in the next rehearsal.

Group Therapist: Good summary. I have one last concern. Is there any risk involved in talking to the principal in this manner? You're the one, Cynthia, who has to face that risk.

Cynthia: It's a lot riskier for me to do nothing. He's the one whose support I need to get back into school. I guess it's only risky if I don't sound like I mean it.

After the feedback from the group was completed, Cynthia was asked to consider what she thought she might like to do differently. As often occurs, an additional role play was also performed in the group so that Cynthia could try to incorporate the new ideas she liked. She also gave herself an extragroup task of role-playing the situation with her "buddy" before she tried it out in the real world. Let us examine the guidelines for feedback and note which ones were used by the group therapist in the above example.

Writing Down the Feedback

As the group therapist above requested, all youth in the initial sessions are asked to put their feedback down in writing. This stimulates far greater involvement than merely asking for feedback verbally, which results in the more assertive members dominating the feedback presentation. Eventually the writing requirement is eliminated as the members are all able to come up with a wide range of ideas.

Positive Feedback First

A second guideline is that positive feedback is always asked for first so that the client can be reinforced as soon as possible following a rehearsal of new skills. The positive feedback also creates an atmosphere in which criticism is more likely to be accepted. If members attempt to give criticism first, as in the above example, the group therapist interrupts them and asks them to stop until the right time, as noted in the above example. The members are encouraged to express the feedback, whether positive or negative, as their opinion.

Criticism Formulated as Suggested Alternatives

The third guideline is that criticism of a performance is in the form of actions or statements the observer would do or say differently. "What I would do differently would be to speak a little louder and give a little more eye contact" is the desired form of a critical feedback statement. If a client fails to include such a suggestion when giving feedback, the therapist asks for one. In this way, the aversiveness of criticism is reduced dramatically. Although criticism is an essential part of feedback, it is possible to take some of its sting away and to reduce potential negative side effects by the way in which it is formulated.

Behavior Specificity

A fourth guideline is that, whether positive or critical, feedback is specific. When the feedback is too general, the group therapist (and later the members) will ask what the person meant by the general statement. In response to "You should be more careful in dealing with your friend," the group therapist might ask, "How would she be 'more careful' in that situation?"

Summarizing the Feedback

In the first session, following feedback by members of the group, including self-feedback by the client in the role play, and feedback from the therapist, the therapist summarizes it. In the summary, the critical feedback is usually sandwiched between the specific achievements and a positive summary. For example, the therapist might say, "In summary, then, Deanna noted that she appreciated the compliment, expressed her feeling about the sexist statement, and asked for a change of behavior. Some of you think she might give a little more eye contact and speak just a little more loudly. All in all, she is becoming quite accomplished in handling sexist statements where she's working." In a subsequent session, the therapist asks the role player to keep notes on the feedback he or she receives and to summarize it aloud for the group. If necessary, the member then tries out in a re-rehearsal those new ideas that he or she evaluates as helpful in the situation. After the feedback, if there is still disagreement, the member with the problem is the final arbiter of what he or she would like to do or say.

Training in Giving Feedback

As we pointed out earlier, feedback is a powerful but dangerous tool. Some youth are reluctant to be the recipients of it. Others use it far too critically. Still others do not know how to receive it appropriately. In teaching group members to give and receive both positive and corrective feedback, we initially provide a list of criteria.

A particularly useful exercise for training youth in the use of feedback has been the use of a role play in which the group therapist, in giving feedback, makes a number of mistakes. The group therapist then leads the group in a discussion of the group therapist's performance. In giving the therapist feedback, he or she encourages the members themselves to adhere to the feedback criteria. After the discussion, the group therapist or one of the members can model how feedback should be received. Finally, the group therapist evaluates with the group how well they adhered to the criteria and what still needs to be worked on.

It should be noted that group members are taught in exercises both to give and to receive positive feedback and constructive criticism for two reasons. First, it is a prerequisite skill needed to facilitate effective rehearsals and effective correction of errors in these rehearsals. It also provides group members with a set of essential interpersonal skills that facilitate effective and satisfying interaction outside the group. For these reasons, a significant amount of time is devoted, especially in early sessions, to developing and employing these skills.

Re-Rehearsal

One of the eight steps in the modeling sequence and one of the ways of increasing the likelihood that the rehearsed sequence of behavior will be tried out in the real world is the re-rehearsal. One-trial learning is possible but often unlikely. Each group member repeatedly tries out what he or she has practiced. Because of time constraints, multiple trials may not be possible. In that case, the client should practice at home or on the residential unit with a partner before trying out the interaction in the real world. The round-robin technique mentioned above can be used to develop opportunities for multiple rehearsing of commonly occurring situations.

Developing an Extragroup Task

The final step in the sequence is trying out the behavior in the real world. The client, having been taught the cues for the desired behavior, should try out and report back to the group his or her experience with the interactive response. If the interaction went differently than role-played at the previous session, a new modeling session can be organized. Chapter 11 spells out the way in which extragroup tasks should be designed so that they are most likely to be carried out.

General Versus Specific Modeling Strategies

Most of the examples we have used deal with a highly concrete set of observable behaviors. As Bandura (1969) has pointed out, "Modeled characteristics that are highly discernible can be more readily acquired than subtle attributes which must be abstracted from heterogeneous responses differing on numerous stimulus dimensions" (p. 136). The particular behaviors selected are often crucial subsets of a complex situation. In learning these a few at a time, the client may eventually be able to handle the entire complex situation. However, complex sets of interactions can be modeled in their entirety. Usually these more general role plays follow in hierarchical fashion a series of subsets, each with a more limited scope of required behaviors. In some groups, it is possible to move directly to the more general situation. Some youth, because of previous learning or innate capacity, are able to learn a general approach to dealing with problem situations without learning all of the detailed intermediate steps.

Some examples of global role-play themes commonly used in groups are job interviews, talking to an individual counselor, introducing oneself to a stepfather, confronting an uncle who abused the client when she was younger, and asking a principal to get back into school after being suspended. In general, the global modeling sequence takes much longer to carry out. The short situations can be expanded to more global ones by increasing the number of interactions.

Skill in Observation and Imitation

The set of eight steps may not be realized if the client does not carefully attend to the model's behavior. If the client is restless, if the cues are too vague, or if the perceptive abilities of the client are limited, attention to the model may be drastically reduced. One way of increasing a client's attention to a model is to give him or her a structured observational role. For example, in a group of adolescents who were substance abusers, the therapist modeled how one would ask for help when one was under pressure to take a drink or "hit." Before the modeling, the therapist handed out written instructions as to what the members should be looking for. These included such nonverbal behaviors as eye contact, voice volume, and body posture and such verbal behavior as how one got the attention of the other person. A second strategy for keeping the attention of the observers is to stop the modeling interaction intermittently and ask questions about what the members have seen. A third strategy for increasing attending behavior is to make the modeling session as interesting as possible by using props, keeping the initial modeling sessions short, frequently using reinforcement, and creating as much realism as the situation permits.

If youth are involved in the process of determining suitable criteria for observation, they are also more likely to attend to the observational cues. In the above-mentioned group of substance abusers, members were asked what they thought they should be looking for in a modeled demonstration of refusing when someone offered them a "hit." They suggested such criteria as firmness, brief answers, repeated simple refusal without explanation, and a calm facial expression. The group therapist recommended that they observe for these characteristics in the modeling demonstration that was to follow.

Frequently, however, training may be required to teach youth how to attend to models before giving them such observational roles. One way of training in observational skills is through the use of group exercises. In these exercises, relatively neutral and brief situations with clear-cut cues are presented on videotape or in role plays by cotherapists. The members are given a checklist of phenomena that occur on the tape. They are asked to indicate whether these did or did not occur. In the discussion that follows, the members compare results and give evidence for their position.

Before modeling (and rehearsal) role plays, youth who have limited attending skills or intellectual deficiencies are often given a cue sheet with instructions to observe a narrow range of behaviors. As is usually the case with cueing procedures, these are faded as soon as the members indicate they can operate without them.

Extragroup observation assignments are also useful. In one group, the therapist recommended that the members observe the things a TV comic did on the program that night that were funny. To make it interesting, the group therapist challenged the members to a contest as to who would have the longest list of specific observations.

Training in the Simulated Modeling Sequence

As in all other interventions, an exercise is used to train and orient the members to the modeling procedures. Exercise 9.1 also serves as a review of what has been discussed above.

Exercise 9.1. The Modeling Sequence

Purposes: By the end of this exercise, each participant will have

1. Demonstrated the use of the modeling sequence with and without the use of coaching in such a way as to maximize the probability of duplication of the target behavior by the target person in the extragroup world

2. Described the modeling-rehearsal procedures that will maximize the likelihood that learning will take place and the order in which they ideally occur

Individual Task: Each person in the group should read the following situations and choose one that he or she would like to learn to handle more effectively. (The group therapist may provide other situations that are more typical of the population being served.) He or she may also develop one of his or her own as long as it is not too complicated (5 minutes).

1. Elene, 18, is planning to interview for a job but is afraid to blow the interview. She wants to be a salesperson in a clothing store. She had 6 months of experience part-time while she was in high school. She has been unemployed for 6 months following graduation, except for some part-time work at a fast-food restaurant. She is particularly concerned about a formal interviewer. In particular, she wants to know how to begin the interview.

2. Jan, 16, a recovering alcoholic, is trying to stay clean. He has to go to a party that some of his drinking school friends are having at one of their houses, and he knows his friends will be pushing him to drink. He doesn't know what to say and how to say it when his friends push him to have a drink.

3. Jackie, 17, has to tell her mother and father that she is not going to live at home anymore. She and her parents seem to fight all the time. She has a job at Hardee's and can share a flat with her friend Julie and will finish high school before she leaves. Her father is extremely conservative and doesn't think a young woman should live on her own until she is married. Jackie is afraid of her father, but she is definite about going out on her own and wants to make that clear to her family.

4. Andy, 15, needs help from his teacher, who agreed to help him but at the last minute complained that she didn't have any time. He needs only about 5 minutes to clarify the assignment and the task that he must do. None of his friends can help him. He wants to be more persistent and make a definite appointment but not be rude.

Group Task: In the entire group, one person will be the director of the role play (usually the group therapist, although, if some of the members are experienced in modeling, one of them should be the director). One member will be the protagonist (the person with the problem) and the second will be the antagonist or another role in the interaction. One member will coach the protagonist the first time through if the protagonist wants. Another will coach the antagonist. The remaining persons and the director will be the observers. Their job is to give feedback following the rehearsal as to whether the verbal and nonverbal behaviors suggested by the instructions were performed. The director will assign roles (as indicated below) and instruct the participants where they should sit and stand and come in from. The director should separate the observers from the role players as if setting a stage and should give specific instructions as to what the observers should be looking for. The director should also instruct the role players to use such nonverbal behaviors as opening the window when called for or closing the door. No single role play should take longer than 15 minutes, including the preparation and the discussion.

Before the role play begins, the group therapist should review what is going to happen and explain some of the purposes of role playing and modeling. Then the action should follow the steps described below in the modeling process:

1. An interactive situation is selected from the above situations with which the protagonist is familiar but in which he or she does not know exactly what to do or say or how to say it.

2. The group suggests alternatives that the target person can employ. (To save time, this step may be skipped if the model knows what he or she should do.)

3. The target person selects a set of the suggestions that he or she finds useful.

4. One person who feels comfortable with the role of the client in the given situation is selected to model the client's role. It no one can be found, the director plays the role of model.

5. One or more persons are selected to play the roles of the antagonists or other people in the role play. The client instructs them as to their activities and attitudes.

6. The model, with the help of the antagonists, demonstrates what the client has selected as the best way to cope with the situation (modeling).

7. The director checks with the client as to whether he or she is satisfied with the role play or would like another model.

8. If the client is satisfied, then he or she role-plays the situation in his or her own role, using as much as possible of the model's behaviors (rehearsal).

9. Following the rehearsal, the client is given positive feedback first and then critical feedback in a constructive way.

10. On the basis of that feedback, the client re-rehearses the situation. (In this exercise, this step may be omitted, but not when the members are working with their own situations.)

At the end of the exercise, the group therapist will review the general principles, deal with any technical problems that occurred in the role play, and give examples, from situations already identified by the members, of how the members might use these procedures.

Training Members to Deal With Racial, Homophobic, Gender, and Ethnic Put-Downs

Regardless of the composition of the group and the theme of the group, a number of racist, homophobic, and sexist statements occur or are implied that can be efficaciously dealt with in the group if they are not allowed to slide. As preparation for sensitizing youth to these situations and helping them to deal with them, a number of canned situations have been developed that can be analyzed, modeled, and rehearsed. A number of these are found in Exercise 9.2.

Exercise 9.2. Dealing With Racial, Ethnic, Homophobic, and Gender Put-Downs

Purposes: By the end of the exercise, each participant will have

1. Described and carried out in a role play a variety of appropriate responses to racist, homophobic, and sexist remarks made in social situations

2. Evaluated his or her own perspective in relation to issues that the situations below raise

3. Described his or her cognitions when such situations arise

4. Increased his or her repertoire of strategies for coping with such situations

Individual Task: The participants should read the following situations and respond in writing to these questions:

1. What are the issues involved?

2. What values are reflected by the significant others in the situation?

3. To what degree do they reflect your values?

4. What might you be thinking if you were confronted with such a situation?

5. What would be an appropriate goal in such a situation?

6. What might one say or do or think to achieve that goal?

7. What are the risks and advantages of doing or saying that?

8. What are the risks and advantages of doing or saying nothing?

The situations are as follows:

1. You are in a group of three teenage friends. One of them says, "I'm not prejudiced, but I'm gonna push my mom to get out of the neighborhood as quickly as possible now that the blacks are moving in. You know what they do to a neighborhood, whatever the liberals think." The other two ignore him/her.

2. A male says to you (female), "I really love working on cars, but I guess you as a woman can't understand that."

3. You (female, single, and 17) are being interviewed as a dishwasher at McDonald's. The interviewer says, "I guess you're too young to be married. You'd just get pregnant and quit. But you might get pregnant anyway, that's the way you girls are nowadays."

4. Two of your male fellow students and a female fellow student are working on a report. One of the male students remarks that it's

great to have someone in the work group to make the coffee. You
see that the female student is embarrassed (and angry) but laughs
awkwardly with everyone else.

5. A new expensive Cadillac almost sideswipes your car filled with
   teenagers like yourself. Your companion says, "A black driver, I
   knew it! They all drive big cars. It's all that free money they get."
   All the others in the car seem to agree. You don't agree.

6. You (female) are being interviewed for a position as a volunteer in a
   shelter for abused women. You have been looking for 6 months, and
   this job is really important to you. The interviewer (a man) asks you
   if anything in your history leads you to look at this particular job.

7. An acquaintance introduces you to Reggie, who strikes you as being
   an interesting person. A little later, your friend takes you aside and
   says, "Reggie is gay, but in spite of that, he's an all-right guy, I guess."

8. (All females) You are in a pizza joint with several friends. One has
   told you she is a lesbian and is struggling with coming out. Another
   acquaintance comes to the table and says, "What's the matter, girls,
   can't you find a man, or maybe that's not your preference." The
   others at the table laugh, somewhat embarrassed.

Group Task 1: Discuss the values issues that each of the situations
implies. Discuss what your thinking might be in such a situation. Share
with each other what you think the goals should be in each situation.
Develop together what you feel are the most appropriate responses.
Then, in the same session, have everyone in the group role-play at least
one of the situations, and have the group provide feedback to the role
players on what they did well in dealing with the situation.
Group Task 2 (time permitting): In pairs, participants design another
situation that reflects some of the same values that the above situations
reflect. Then they ask the rest of the group to answer the same questions
as in the Individual Task.

Other situations can be developed that are more appropriate for the
population being served. Dealing with as few as four of these vignettes
carefully can take up a good part of a group session, so not all of these

situations need be used. Where an important focus of the group is on prejudice, several sessions can be devoted to this exercise.

This exercise is also useful as a means of providing additional modeling and rehearsal practice. The better the group members refine their skills in role playing in canned situations, the more effective they become in role-playing their own interactive situations.

Variations on the Modeling Sequence

A number of variations are possible in the use of rehearsal. Variations tend to add to the general interest of the members in the program and to increase the cohesion of the group. Also, different youth tend to learn better in different ways. These variations include role instruction, fixed-role therapy, videotape modeling, self-modeling, modeling through scripts, and real-world modeling.

Role Instruction

Role instruction requires the client to take a "model role" and act as if he or she were really such a person. This procedure can be used during ongoing group interaction: That is, a new role may be played while the group discusses other tasks. For example, one member of the group who tended to elaborate excessively on all issues assigned herself the role of being a person who made only succinct comments. She permitted herself no more than three sentences per comment. She asked her neighbor to let her know if she "ran over."

Another example of role instruction can be seen in the case of Doran, who rarely participated in discussions in the group or in other social events even though he was quite intelligent and, when pushed, demonstrated that he had a lot of interesting ideas. The group members designed a role for him in which he would act as if he were extremely assertive. He was required (and occasionally prompted) to interrupt and introduce his ideas. Because there was an observer, he was instructed to double the amount of his participation in the group. A few particularly difficult situations were rehearsed in the usual way first. The instructions were first reviewed by Doran at the beginning of the session. The group therapist sat next to him and encouraged him when he seemed to slow down. At the end of the 15-minute trial session, the group evaluated his performance and gave him enthusiastic approval, although members made some suggestions as to how he might have interrupted more effectively. Subsequent time periods were gradually increased in length to the point where an entire session was spent in the high participator's role.

To add even greater structure to a role instruction exercise, the group therapist prepared written role descriptions tailored to the specific difficulties that each group member was experiencing. In pairs, the members further developed their instructions for each other, and during the session each member attempted to play his or her new role as accurately as possible. At the end of the session, everyone attempted to guess the new roles of the others; they then evaluated the effectiveness of the new roles.

Fixed-Role Therapy

This procedure, developed by Kelly (1955), is a technique similar to rehearsal and role instruction. In this treatment modality, the initial assessment of a client is used to construct a fixed-role sketch for him or her. This sketch is carefully planned to include desirable behaviors, but the details are left to the "player." The selected behaviors are usually adaptive ones that are not being performed at the beginning of therapy and are frequently in marked contrast to the presenting behavioral patterns.

After an initial set of practice sessions, the client is urged to "try on" the behavior in the real world and to observe the types of reactions manifested by others in his or her life. The client is encouraged in the first phase of treatment to maintain, in his or her own mind, the fiction of playing a role. The assumption is that to play "as if" reduces the threat incurred by performing new behaviors in the real world. The role can be explored without irrevocable commitment, and because of the intentional lack of detail, the client is free to develop his or her new role in ways that are comfortable to him or her.

Videotape Modeling

When videotape resources are available, it is feasible to tape modeling sessions for the members and make VCR equipment available to review these tapes as extragroup tasks. These videotapes provide variety in the program and an opportunity for multiple observation of models. They extend treatment time beyond the boundaries of the group session.

Videotaped modeling does not, however, offer the flexibility of the tailor-made live demonstration. By using both live modeling and video-tape presentations, the advantages of flexibility and repeated trials can be combined. A unique use of videotaping is for self-modeling.

Self-Modeling

In addition to observing others in and outside the group sessions, adolescents can be encouraged to observe their own effective behavior in difficult situations. Even though a client may complain about social deficiencies in a given set of circumstances, there are usually some situations in which he or she has functioned in a highly adaptive manner. The most powerful means of self-modeling is having the client observe repeatedly his or her own adaptive or effective behavior in a given situation on videotape. Before taping, the client is well trained through the use of other models, extensive rehearsals, coaching, and feedback so that the taped performance is highly suitable for the problem situation. The tape is reviewed first by the group, and if it is considered appropriate, the client assumes the task of watching it several times a day. The same tape, if well done, may serve as a model for other youth before they develop their own tape. The process of developing such a tape is a unique opportunity for mutual aid and thus engenders a great deal of enthusiasm among the members. Because of the investment of the other members, the client is more likely to make use of the tape than if it were commer-cially made or developed by the group therapist. In one group, the members, in pairs, developed four videotapes for self-modeling. In addition, they decided to have a presentation of the tapes for their parents and built commercials into the tapes to advertise the benefits of the group.

Modeling Through Scripts

Sarason and Ganzer (1969) have used written scripts in both modeling and rehearsal with groups of institutionalized delinquents. Because it was recognized that most delinquents' models had been antisocial adults and older youths, the scripts were used to demonstrate the effectiveness of establishing new, socially acceptable, and, it is hoped, exciting social models for the delinquents. In working with juvenile offenders, my colleagues and I (Brierton et al., 1975) asked that the group members rewrite the Sarason and Ganzer scripts. The very process of script revision involved the group in formulating a realistic appraisal and definition of their situations and in developing effective interactions to resolve the difficulties they were confronting. Assignments to write an "ideal behavior" script can facilitate both observation of others and the generation of alternative ways of behaving. For many youth, a demand to write is an anxiety-producing event. Group members can share the responsibility, with several deciding on what to say and the others writing it down. On occasion, the therapist will act as the secretary. One group "hired" a secretary to whom the members dictated their scripts. In fact, she volunteered. They felt it increased their status, and the secretary was delighted to participate in the therapeutic task.

Thus far, most of the examples in this book have been simulation or role-played modeling. In the next subsection, an alternative to role-played modeling is reviewed.

Real-World Modeling

Systematic observation by the group members of persons outside the group meetings is a useful and accessible source of models. The group therapist can help members to identify persons in their natural environment who can serve as natural models. By giving an assignment to observe these models in particular situations, the group therapist can draw on a rich and varied source of demonstrated behaviors.

In one outpatient group of youth who were referred for their problems with uncontrollable anger, the members were requested to find one person whom each really admired and who was not aggressive. The group brainstormed all possible people they could choose from. Each selected one person from the list. Members agreed to observe the models in their roles on several occasions during the week. At the end of the week, six of the nine members described the specific behaviors and general characteristics of the model whom they observed. The six also discovered some model characteristics that they did not admire. Then each person, including the three who did not complete the task, chose a particular subset of behaviors as a target to work toward. Then, the group therapist and the members role-played these for each other.

Summary

The most commonly used modeling procedure in groups is the role-played modeling sequence, consisting of orientation, choosing a situation to be modeled, simulated modeling, rehearsal, coaching, feedback, re-rehearsal, and extragroup tasks. This sequence is derived from modeling theory and is one of the most commonly used sets of group treatment procedures incorporated into CBIGT. Any of the modeling procedures may be used alone or in combination with any other modeling procedure. A number of variations of modeling have been discussed in this chapter, including role instruction, fixed-role therapy, the use of scripts, videotaped modeling, self-modeling, and real-world modeling. In the next chapter, a similar sequence, covert modeling as one of the cognitive procedures, is used for dealing with private behaviors or thoughts that may be interfering with social functioning.

CHAPTER 10

Cognitive and Relaxation
Coping Strategies

Many negative emotional states, such as extreme anger, depression, and stress in response to life events, seem to be evoked by dysfunctional cognitions such as unrealistic expectations, distorted perceptions, faulty beliefs, illogical evaluations, and inappropriate attributions. These dysfunctional thoughts may also evoke maladaptive behavior or may prevent more appropriate behavior from occurring. Cognitive interventions aim at identifying and correcting this kind of thinking and related emotions and behaviors. Of course, these cognitive procedures cannot be successfully implemented until the client is committed to change (see Chapter 3) and there is a workable relationship with the therapist and the group members, who are beginning to be cohesive and motivated to change. Under these conditions, the group lends itself to the application of cognitive strategies because the group members support each other in the sharing of their perceptions of each other's dysfunctional thinking as it occurs in group interaction and are often willing to learn new methods. Peer group observations for adolescents are often more acceptable than those pointed out by the therapist. Furthermore, the group as a whole provides a wealth of alternative modes of thinking to members' distortions, as can be observed in the following example.

Marcus: I got kicked out of school just because the teacher said I talked back to her.

Group Therapist: Talked back?

Marcus: Yeah, I only said she should get off my back.

Rick: You should have heard him, the blood was dripping from his voice.

Group Therapist: What happened just before you talked back?

Marcus: Well, she asked me what the state capital was. We were supposed to memorize it for yesterday. I had forgotten to do it. No big deal. I looked away from her when she was about to ask, so she knew I didn't want to be called on. But she called on me anyway.

Group Therapist: What were you thinking when she called on you?

Marcus: I thought, "Why does this shit always happen to me?" Then, when she put me down for not knowing the answer, I realized she was out to get me. There are lots of other guys in the class who she could have called on. It's always me. So I told her.

Group Therapist: What do the rest of you think? Was she out to get him?

Ryan: Hey, no way, man. You aren't being picked on. She calls on everyone, especially when you don't look her in the eye. If you didn't do your homework, that's your problem.

Rick: You're my best friend, but I gotta tell you, you often think you're picked on. Like yesterday after school, when Mr. Kant asked you to help clean the blackboard. You yelled, "Why are you getting on my case?"

Marcus: Well, they do pick on me. Kant is always asking me to do things. He never asks anybody else.

Andre: Not true, any more than the rest of us. I got called on three times yesterday.

Ryan: Even if it were true, gettin' called on or wiping the blackboard ain't nuthin'. You get yourself in a lot of trouble, telling people off.

Group Therapist: It looks like a lot of people don't agree with you, Marcus. They all seem to think that you exaggerate when you get some little thing laid on you. And they seem to think you feel picked on when in fact you're not. And when you think that way, it seems to make you mad.

Marcus: (grumbles) Well, it's true, look, you're all doing it to me now. I got a right to be mad.

   In the example above, Marcus has shown that he believes he is singled out by teachers and residential staff and even his peer group most of the time. The group therapist encourages the group to identify other situations in which he believes he is picked on or given unfair treatment and to use evidence to dispute his interpretation of the events. Though in this instance it has no immediate effect, the pattern has been raised with him and will be continually noted by the group therapist and other members as it repeats itself in the group.

   Identifying dysfunctional thinking is a first step in cognitive intervention. Once patterns have been identified, at least four major goals of cognitive intervention can be identified:

1. To replace cognitive distortions or dysfunctional thinking (such as in the example above) with a more accurate evaluation and/or self-description
2. To increase positive coping statements in response to stressors or provocations by others
3. To reduce anxiety and anger previously associated with these cognitive distortions
4. To change maladaptive overt behavior by means of cognitive interventions but with the assistance of other behavioral procedures, such as modeling and reinforcement

To achieve these goals, a number of cognitive change procedures can be used. These procedures are derived from cognitive and cognitive-behavioral theory, which was given its early impetus by Ellis (1973) and was heavily contributed to by Beck (1976) and Meichenbaum (1977). Although other approaches to cognitive intervention have been used, CBIGT has drawn heavily on the assumptions and experiences of the above authors, and the following sections will discuss the unique applications of cognitive interventions in groups of troubled youth.

Rational-Emotive Therapy

One of the earliest approaches to the use of cognitive interventions in treatment was rational-emotive therapy (RET), developed by Ellis

(1973), who demonstrated to clients how their beliefs influenced their emotions and made them upset. He described an ABC(DE) model of emotional disturbance. An individual's beliefs (B) about an activating event (A) cause behavioral and emotional consequences (C). (This is in contrast with the more common explanation that events cause emotional upset.) Disputing (D) (questioning and challenging) these irrational beliefs will lead to more constructive and behavioral and emotional effects (E). Ellis assumed that all problems are the result of magical thinking or irrational ideas. Some of these ideas lead to self-condemnation, others to anger, and still others to a low tolerance for frustration.

The major intervention strategies in RET are disputation, verbal persuasion, and teaching. Disputation as used by Ellis is highly forceful in contrast to CBIGT. The RET therapist helps youth to identify the irrational ideas they hold, as evidenced by their statements to themselves in provoking or stressful situations, their emotional reactions, and their behavior. Occasionally the therapist will set up small experiments or demonstrations to help the clients prove to themselves that their assumptions are false or irrational.

Using RET in groups, the therapist employs the members as the major source of feedback, persuasion, and disputation of the irrational ideas, as was evidenced in the above example. As the members repeatedly examine the irrational ideas of each of their peers, many seem to see more clearly why some of their own thinking is irrational. Ultimately, they are taught to dispute those irrational beliefs for which there is no supporting evidence and to recognize the effects of holding such ideas.

Ellis (1973) identified a number of irrational ideas. Some of these have been identified more specifically for adolescents by Waters (1981) and edited by CBIGT therapists. These irrational ideas are presented in Exercise 10.1. Adolescents do not readily express their dysfunctional thinking in public. Exercise 10.1 has been effective for many adolescents in enhancing their self-disclosure in groups.

Exercise 10.1. Irrational Thoughts

Purpose: By the end of this exercise, each member will recognize 10 illogical thoughts and dispute them.

Individual Task: Each participant will read each of the following sentences and indicate on a 5-point scale how much he or she agrees with it.

1. It would be awful if peers didn't like me. It would be awful to be a social loser.

2. I shouldn't make mistakes, especially social mistakes.

3. It's my parents' fault I'm so miserable.

4. I can't help it; that's just the way I am, and I guess I'll always be this way.

5. The world should be fair and just, and it isn't for me.

6. It's awful when things do not go my way.

7. It's better to avoid challenges than to risk failure.

8. I must conform to my peers no matter what they do.

9. I can't stand to be criticized. I fall completely apart.

10. Others should always be responsible for what I feel.

11. If only my parents gave me what I want, I would be happy.

Group Task: The items to which the most youth agree are discussed in terms of their accuracy in clearly identified situations and the consequences of holding such beliefs. Then the group as a whole disputes the irrational beliefs one at a time until everyone's irrational belief has been disputed. The group therapist provides additional arguments and information for the discussion and coaches the members in their disputation.

At the end of the session, each member, with help from the others, summarizes the arguments against his or her belief. If several youth have the same belief, they can work in teams to develop a summarization of arguments that dispute the belief.

In subsequent sessions, as these beliefs appear in ongoing interaction, the member is asked once again to give the arguments against adhering to the given belief. Thus, it is possible in CBIGT to develop multiple occasions for disputing irrational beliefs as well as using multiple disputers. Another way of keeping the debate alive is by asking the group to summarize the disputation of the previous session. These same procedures can be used as a first step in cognitive restructuring. However, cognitive restructuring offers the group therapist a number of additional strategies that may encourage self-disclosure and eventually desired change.

Cognitive Restructuring

Beck (1976) posited the existence of stable, negative beliefs (or *schemas*) that create the conditions for people to become depressed or stressed. These schemas are activated by stressful events, which often result in negative automatic thoughts. These are automatic in the sense that people seem to have little control over them. The thoughts or beliefs give meaning to various situations that one encounters. Because they are often highly biased and repetitive and rarely objective, they tend to elicit inaction, repetitive behavior, and strong negative emotions, such as stress or anger, that interfere with effective behavior. Cognitive restructuring involves identifying these automatic thoughts and helping the client to find more constructive alternatives. The dysfunctional cognitions may be regarded as "self-defeating" (see Meichenbaum, 1977) because they stand in the way of attaining one's own goals, and this is the term most commonly used by CBIGT therapists. The constructive alternative thoughts are referred to as *coping statements* because they facilitate coping with stress- or anger-inducing situations.

The following steps (many of which are suggested by Meichenbaum, 1977) are often followed in cognitive restructuring as it is used by the CBIGT therapist. They include providing an orientation, identifying self-defeating cognitions and the situations in which they occur, identifying coping thoughts, identifying emotional cues, and changing self-defeating cognitions to coping thoughts.

Providing an Orientation

Cormier and Cormier (1991) pointed out the importance of providing an adequate rationale and overview, or orientation, as a means of reducing the ambiguity of the therapy and increasing the trust of the members. Orientation is a gradual process in which the assumptions and steps in the process are shared in advance with the group members, who are also provided with many examples of specific steps. The following rationale, adapted from Meichenbaum (1974), is one way to begin.

> One thing you will learn in this group is to take a look at how our thinking and how the way we talk to ourselves influences how we feel and how we act. We can make ourselves more angry by telling ourselves we are angry or we should be angry. We can make ourselves feel bad about ourselves by calling ourselves names or putting ourselves down in other ways. We can also get rid of the stress and/or anger we may be feeling by thinking about ourselves differently, by changing our expectations, by telling ourselves to take a deep breath and relax, by telling ourselves on a difficult task to go more slowly or to take one step at a time. Sometimes we tend to exaggerate, to make terrible tragedies out of one small failure. Then we allow ourselves to put ourselves down because of the tragedy that we created in our head. We can often make ourselves feel better if we reexamine stressful situations with the help of our friends here in the group and find new, more accurate ways of thinking about problem situations and our responses to them.

At this point, the group therapist asks if members have any examples of ways they think about situations that have made them feel angry or unhappy or kept them from doing anything about some situation. After a discussion of these examples, the group therapist goes on to provide an overview:

> In this group, one of the things we will be doing together is looking at day-to-day events that seem to make us unhappy, stress us out, or anger us. We will also be looking at the ways in which we think about those situations. If what you are doing or thinking isn't working for you, the group will try to help each individual find better ways of thinking and behaving in those situations. The process of learning can be fun as well as helpful. There is a board game called "Think Better," a game like Monopoly, that you will be playing, and the group will do lots of dramatics or role playing of situations in which we practice thinking more effectively.

As in the introduction of all new techniques, the group therapist will involve the members wherever possible in this orientation. In institutional or other open-ended groups, the more experienced members are invited to do the orientation with the preparatory help of the therapist.

If possible, more than one member is asked to share the responsibility of orientation.

Identification of Thinking Errors

Once orientation takes place, the concept of thinking errors or self-defeating statements is defined and illustrated. The following are examples of self-defeating cognitions commonly made by youth in their everyday interaction with others (see Belsher & Wilkes, 1994, for more detailed examples commonly used by youth). As part of training, the group members are presented with a handout of these definitions (Beck, 1976) and examples at one session; then, at a subsequent session, they discuss the concepts and, where possible, provide their own examples.

- *Exaggeration* is a common characteristic of most self-defeating statements. It is the practice of taking a relatively insignificant situation and giving it more importance than the facts of the situation call for. For example, Jane receives an average grade on a quiz. Although she did better on previous tests, she thinks to herself, "I'm doing terribly in this course. I'm so worried." Such an evaluation is an exaggeration and appears to increase her anxiety.
- *Catastrophization* is a form of gross exaggeration that makes a tragedy of some trivial event. In the above example, Jane's saying, "I'm failing the course, my life is ruined, I can't stand it" would be an example of catastrophization eliciting near panic.
- *Absolutizing* refers to statements that suggest that a given situation will continue unchanged regardless of changing conditions and that nothing can be done to alter that situation. Such statements are often identified by the presence of absolute terms such as *never, always, can't,* or *impossible.* Examples of absolutizing statements are Barry's statement that no one will ever like him and Marcus's statement, above, that "Kant is always asking me to do things. He never asks anybody else." Such statements ignore all exceptions and exclude the possibility that changing circumstances lead to different opportunities. Such statements often generate a feeling of hopelessness and anger that is clearly unrealistic and hence self-defeating.
- *Prophesizing* refers to self-statements that predict future unfortunate and unknowable outcomes. Many of the "absolute" statements and catastrophic statements also fall into this category. The danger of prophesizing negative outcomes is that such statements may serve as self-fulfilling

prophecies. "I'm going to fail, I know I will" and "I'm sure I won't be able to sleep tonight" are both examples of prophesizing that may result in undesired consequences.

■ *Selective perception* refers to the response in a situation of focusing on one small negative event and discounting the rest of the situation. The adolescent who made one mistake on his quiz and did well on the rest says to himself, "See, I made a mistake. I hardly know anything." This is an example of selective perception (as well as exaggeration).

■ *Excessive self-demands* are reflected in those statements in which an adolescent demands unrealistic achievement levels. Often the word *should* or *must* is included in the statement: "I must get that bike. It would be awful if I didn't." "I must get a hundred on all my tests." "I should always be good."

■ *Mind reading* is demonstrated by the youth who says that the prospective employer won't like him anyway, so why interview? (Note that this is also prophesizing.)

Another set of thinking errors has been identified by various authors (Beck, 1976; Ellis, 1973) as *fallacies:*

■ *The fallacy of changing others:* The belief that if only the other person would do something different, our lives would be better.
■ *The blaming fallacy:* The belief that one must find out whose fault something is and place blame where it belongs.
■ *The fallacy of fairness:* The belief that somehow life should be fair and situations are not fair to us.
■ *The "should" fallacy:* One is governed by what one believes one is obliged to do.
■ *The fallacy of always being right:* One is governed by the belief that one's ideas are always correct.
■ *Emotional reasoning fallacy:* The belief that what you feel must be true.
■ *Control fallacy:* The belief that one is controlled completely by others or that one is responsible completely for the behavior of others.
■ *Personalization fallacy:* The fallacious belief that whatever others do impinges on you.

To train youth in identifying these thinking errors and fallacies, the group therapist hands out Exercise 10.2 and the list of thinking errors described above.

Exercise 10.2. Identifying Thinking Errors

Purpose: By the end of this exercise, each participant will have identified at least 10 thinking errors made by 10 young people in fictional situations.

Individual Task: Each person in the group should read each of the following statements and indicate the kinds of thinking errors, if any, to be found in the statements—absolutizing, catastrophizing, predicting the future, mind reading, exaggeration, selective perception, and/or excessive self-demand—or the type of fallacy the sentence represents.

1. If only my teachers would stop picking on me, my life would be better.

2. Annette was criticized by her mother for getting dirty on the way home. Later that night, her dad said she wasn't working very hard on her homework. Annette said to herself, "Gosh, I sure am a dumb, terrible, awful person."

3. Putting up the basket and repairing the backboard was extremely complicated. Les thought, "I'll never get this thing done. I might as well quit now."

4. Listen. I'm right in this matter. I'm absolutely right. There is no room for any other opinion. It doesn't matter that some people disagree.

5. Mannie was picked on by the kids in class several times that day. When he got home, he discovered he had forgotten his lunch box. Mannie thought, "Everything awful happens to me. I can't do anything right."

6. Karla liked the pants but would not wear them anymore because all her friends kidded her about them.

7. Alissa's mother said that the new boy in class was on the phone. As Alissa approached the phone, she said to herself, "I won't be able to speak at all," and panicked.

8. I have to be on time to the party. I'm always on time. I don't want to change that.

9. Ken got bumped in the hall by another youth. He wasn't sure it was an accident. He thought, "I can't let him get away with that."

10. I know that those kids on the other side of the playground were making fun of me, even if I didn't hear them.

11. My teacher doesn't like me. It isn't anything she said, I just feel it.

12. It wasn't my fault. I'm going to find out who tore my best dress no matter what.

13. Sam wanted to ask out Alissa, but he said to himself, "I can't ask her out, she'll just refuse me."

14. It's not fair that my brother got all the brains in the family and the good looks too.

15. Tony's closest friend, Howie, didn't want to hang out with him today. Howie said he just wanted to stay home alone and listen to music. Tony thought, "Nobody likes me, not even my so-called friend."

Group Task: Participants share their responses with others in the group and compare their answers. The group therapist also shares his/her thinking with the members.

In the above exercise, the participants are advised that a given sentence may represent more than one kind of thinking error. In fact, multiple errors are the rule rather than the exception. Once the participants have successfully identified the thinking errors in the above statements, they are prepared to use self-monitoring procedures such as the three-column technique and the thought chart.

Three-Column Technique

The three-column technique was designed by Beck and Emery (1985, p. 202). In the first column, the client describes an anxiety-or anger-producing situation; in the second, his or her automatic thoughts or thinking errors; and in the third, types of errors found in these thoughts. These errors are identified in simulated cases and defined (see Table 10.1).

TABLE 10.1 Three-Column Technique

Situation	Interpretation	Type of Error
The teacher didn't call on me today in math, even though I had my hand up.	She doesn't like me. She thinks I'm dumb. She'll never call on me.	Personalizing Mind reading Prediction
When I tripped over my feet in phys ed today, the other guys laughed, and Chuck called me a nerd.	Everyone thinks I'm a clod. I can't do anything right. Nobody likes me.	Absolutizing Mind reading

Group members examine each other's charts and propose alternative interpretations to the errors in the given situations. They may also ask each other for help in identifying the errors when they cannot label the nature of specific cognitions themselves.

Dysfunctional Thought Record

Another strategy used to teach youth to recognize their automatic or self-defeating thoughts and to link them to both situations in which these occur and intense feelings is the thought chart (Wilkes et al., 1994, pp. 191-195). The first column is used to describe the situation, the second column to describe the feelings on a scale of intensity of 1 to 10, and the third column to describe thoughts that occurred immediately after or during the situation (see Table 10.2).

To train group members in the use of this chart, the same procedures are used as in the three-column technique. The therapist provides modeled examples and partially completes examples that the members fill in, solicits examples from the members, and negotiates an extragroup task to try using the chart for a week.

It is also possible to use both charts (Tables 10.1 and 10.2) together in a five-column chart or to add a sixth column for alternative ways of evaluating the situation, but this may demand too much from the group members, at least early in group therapy. In principle, cognitive tasks should be kept as simple as possible in the beginning.

Logical Disputation of Thinking Errors

The above self-monitoring strategies require youth to make a cognitive appraisal and to label certain thoughts or beliefs as automatic

TABLE 10.2 Thought Chart

Situation	Feeling (1-10)	Thoughts
I got my paper back in math with a C grade.	Upset (7)	It just proves I'm a failure. I'll never graduate.
I was sitting at the telephone trying to get up courage to call Libby	Anxious (8)	She won't go out with a guy like me. I'm sure she hates me.
Nobody called me today. I guess that's like most days. I sat around and sort of waited.	Depressed (7) Lonely (8)	It proves that no one likes me and that I'm unlikable.

thoughts or thinking errors. Once these are labeled, a number of strategies are identified for confronting youth with the inaccuracy and inconsistency of their beliefs and with how the beliefs interfere with their everyday functioning. The purpose of these strategies is to identify the dysfunctional thinking of the clients and in some cases to recommend alternative coping thinking. The group members use the concepts of exaggeration, prophesizing, mind reading, catastrophizing, and so forth (defined above) to label, as part of disputation, the errors that they perceive their fellow group members to be making and then to provide evidence that the specified errors are occurring.

Once a client identifies a thinking error statement that he or she is likely to make, the group therapist encourages the group to examine the statement and to explain why it is indeed self-defeating or distorted. In the following example, the group therapist leads the group in this step of the process.

Group Therapist: Tyrone seems to have a good example. Tell the rest of the group what happened to you and how you reacted to it, Tyrone.

Tyrone: Mine's sort of like that one on the list, you know, where Tony says that no one really likes him. That's the way I feel a lot of the time, especially since kids are always giving me a hard time.

Group Therapist: Why don't you give us a recent example of kids giving you a hard time.

Tyrone: Just yesterday in the cafeteria, I dropped my tray and had to clean it all up. And the guys from my class were making wise remarks and putting me down and laughing at me. I really felt they hated me and were trying to get at me. I was really upset. In fact, I was depressed the rest of the day.

Group Therapist: Anybody see any distortions in Tyrone's thinking?

Rudy: Hey, Tyrone my man, everybody in the school gets laughed at if they screw up. That don't mean they hate you. I would've laughed too and kidded you about it. And I sure don't hate you.

Shad: And you're, what do you call it, mind reading. No one said they don't like you. Where's your proof?

Tyrone: My gut tells me. You feel those things.

Rudy: Your gut lies, man, it tells you whatever you want it to tell you.

Tyrone: Well, maybe.

Group Therapist: I wonder if anyone else screwed up this week.

Abdul: I did, big time. I was sleeping in class, and Mrs. T. called on me. I gave some dumb answer, and you shoulda heard those guys laugh. They razzed me the rest of day. And I got a lecture about staying awake from Mrs. T.

Group Therapist: What did you think when they were razzing you?

Abdul: I knew that they didn't mean anything by it, that's just the way they are.

Group Therapist: Didn't it upset you?

Abdul: Nah! I just laughed with them and told them I was going to hit nothing but homers tomorrow like the rest of them.

Group Therapist: It looks like different people look differently at the teasing they get from other guys. Abdul shrugs it off and goes his merry way. Tyrone sees it as a personal attack and is depressed all day.

In the course of the discussion of thinking errors, the arguments of other members of the groups are sometimes sufficient to convince the client that his or her distorted cognitions are indeed interfering with his or her life and creating excessive anxiety and/or anger. But it is more likely that one trial will not be enough. The theme of the self-defeating statement returns repeatedly and is pointed out by the group therapist and group members each time it appears. There is a danger in repeated confrontation. It sometimes becomes a provocation to anger. It may be necessary to train the group in ways of giving confrontative feedback and in ways of receiving it before confrontation is used (see Chapter 9, p. 242-246). If, despite this training, certain members react angrily or with stress reactions to confrontation, the group therapist can deal with the underlying thinking errors that seem to underlie the intense emotional response. In some groups, youth are so sensitive to criticism and confrontation that the focus in the beginning is solely on developing and using coping statements in the face of stressful situations rather than pointing out the distortions.

Defining Coping Alternatives

Coping thoughts are realistic and accurate appraisals of situations. They may also include self-supportive statements and self-instructional statements that help solve a given situation one step at a time. Usually self-enhancing or coping statements do not stimulate strong negative emotions and may even reduce them because they suggest a way of dealing with the situations. By answering some of the following questions positively, one can identify coping or self-enhancing statements (not all the criteria need be met):

- *Is it realistic?* All coping statements are realistic appraisals of the situation. A coping statement is not overly optimistic or "pollyanna." It takes into consideration the real knowledge and skills of the individual as well as his or her limitations or the inherent difficulties in the situation. "I can get that job even if there are a hundred applicants if I put my mind to it" would not be realistic and hence would not be a coping statement. "If I do the best I can, I have at least some chance at getting the job; besides, it's good practice" is a realistic appraisal of the situation and hence a coping statement.
- *Is it self-instructive?* Some coping statements are self-instructive. They guide the behavior or set of behaviors in stress- or anger-inducing situations; for example, "If I take one step at a time, I can get through this difficult task," or Fred's strategy, when criticized by his teacher in a way he considered unfair, of thinking, "Wow, that doesn't seem fair to me; I'd better ask her what exactly I did."
- *Does it reduce expectation of threat?* Some coping statements define difficult situations as challenges rather than threats; for example, "The speech I am about to give will require the best of me." Usually this is paired with self-instruction or encouragement.

- *Does it provide self-encouragement?* Some coping statements involve encouraging oneself to carry out the task or deal with the situation as long as this is realistic: "It may be difficult, but I really can give it a good try."

- *Does it depersonalize?* Some coping statements correct for personalizing everything that others do as an attack or implicit criticism of the given individual: "It's not me in particular she's grouchy with, it seems to be almost everybody."

- *Does it give one relaxing or calming thoughts?* These statements are a special form of self-instruction that a person uses to calm him- or herself; for example, "When I feel tense or angry, I will take a deep breath, let it out slowly, and relax," "Stay cool!" or "Count slowly to 10."

- *Does it keep one focused on the task?* These are coping thoughts that bring the person back to what he or she is doing. For example, when Brandon's thoughts are wandering as he is trying to get his homework organized, he thinks, "Focus, focus on what I planned to do."

- *Does it minimize the importance of other persons' criticism?* This is used when the client is overwhelmed or excessively sensitive to the criticism of others. For example, Lucy, who fears that she may be criticized if she goes to the party, can think, "I'll do the best I can and wear what I can afford. It doesn't matter what people think. It's what I think that counts," and Abdul can merely dismiss his peers' criticism as good-natured teasing.

- *Does it draw on past successful experience?* Youth, in dwelling on failures and limitations, often forget about their many successes. Reminding oneself of these successes is an aid to coping; for example, "I've done this task before, and it was never as bad as I thought."

- *Does it make expectations appropriate?* Many youth have unrealistic expectations; thus, the failure to achieve results in stress or anger. In this case, stating one's realistic expectations is appropriate. For example, after making a dumb mistake, Cliff says to himself," I don't have to be perfect, I just have to do the best I can do at the moment."

- *Does it remind oneself of the consequences?* In anger management, the impetuous client forgets that his or her reactions have unfortunate consequences. A cognitive reminder is helpful to control the behavior. For example, Klaus reminds himself when he starts to be upset that "if I get angry now, she'll only get angry at me, and then the situation will get out of hand" or "Remember, if I hit him, I'll get kicked out of school."

- *Does it delay the anger or stress response?* For the impetuous client, taking a deep breath, counting to 10, and almost any one of the above statements will delay the automatic response.

Some statements definitely point to problems, but the thinking is an accurate description of a skill deficiency and is not distorted thinking. Such statements point to objective informational or behavioral deficits rather than different ways of evaluating situations and suggest other forms of intervention rather than cognitive restructuring. Some examples are as follows:

- *I don't prepare enough.* This is probably an accurate appraisal of what the client is not doing. Therefore, this would not be a self-defeating statement; rather, it would be an indication of a behavioral deficit that requires problem solving and/or operant strategies.
- *I get angry very easily.* This may be an accurate appraisal of a person's response to stressors. If it is accurate, then it is necessary to find new ways of restructuring the behavioral/emotional responses to stressors rather than merely changing the self-statement.
- *I don't know how to solve problems.* This may be an information or a skill deficit. As such, it may require training in problem solving, not in simply changing the evaluation of the situation.

Identifying Emotional Cues

At the critical moment following a stressful situation, a client will usually respond with both cognitions and emotions. Often, the cognitions are masked by the intensity of the emotions. The emotions become a cue to listen to one's cognitions or to use a coping statement. Most youth find it difficult to attend to these cues. They are not accustomed to it, nor do they have the vocabulary for it. Exercise 4.3 (in Chapter 4) is used to expand their vocabulary. In addition, the group therapist is constantly modeling expressing his or her emotions in difficult situations. Note that in the above example, Tyrone was "really upset," even "depressed," when he dropped his tray. Whenever a situation is analyzed, emotions as well as cognitions and behavior are examined and may suggest another set of interventions. Emotions often have physiological concomitants. Hands may sweat, the heart may beat fast, the stomach or head may hurt, breathing may be faster or slower. The group members are trained in identifying their unique physiological responses as clues to their being upset or angry and thus as prompts to use a coping statement.

Replacing Thinking Errors With Coping Thoughts

Coping statements may be used to replace thinking errors, but just as often youth may be trained in making a coping statement even if a thinking error cannot be identified in a given situation. In either case, the process is not simple. It requires considerable practice over time, cognitive modeling and rehearsal (see below), and continued analysis of one's cognitions throughout therapy. After all, most people have been practicing their thinking errors for a long time. Other strategies may be required as well, such as training the individual directly in the behaviors that are inconsistent with the self-defeating value. Often, substituting coping cognitions for self-defeating cognitions is merely part of a larger treatment package. Once the criteria for coping statements have been reviewed and exemplified in the group, the group members continue with Exercise 10.3.

Exercise 10.3. Replacing Thinking Errors With Coping Thoughts

Purpose: By the end of this exercise, each participant will have reformulated the statements in Exercise 10.2 as coping statements and pointed out the major criteria for determining that the statements are coping cognitions.

Individual Task: Reread the examples in Exercise 10.2. Following the discussion by the members, each person should change all the thinking errors into coping statements and explain why each is a coping statement according to the criteria (which are handed out to the members).

Group Task: The responses of the group members are compared and evaluated by the members and group therapist.

Corrective Strategies

By practicing with coping statements, youth are first taught the basic concepts in the simulations described above. For youth to change their own thinking errors, Beck and Emery (1985, pp. 190-209) suggested a large number of therapeutic strategies that can be readily administered in groups by the therapists and eventually by the group members with each other. These procedures are overlapping and include reframing, generating alternative explanations, decatastrophizing, providing information, decentering, enlarging perspective, reattribution, and point-counterpoint, all of which are defined below.

Reframing. Reframing involves the provision of a different context or frame of reference for viewing a situation or response. Nothing else in the situation changes (Wilkes et al., 1994, p. 197). For example, one youth described his situation in which his friends were teasing him as being completely unbearable. The therapist asked the others how he might reframe the description in such a way as to allow the possibility of dealing with it. The others came up with "I don't like being teased. It's really a tough thing to deal with" and "They're just kidding." Many of the strategies below also involve reframing.

Generating Alternative Explanations. Beck and Emery (1985, p. 203) recommended that the client search for alternative explanations once it is clear that the original thoughts are dysfunctional. In the group, the members plus the target person and the therapist can brainstorm alternative explanations. These are evaluated by the target person as to how realistic and accurate each statement is in comparison to the original explanation. In Table 10.2, the young woman thought, "I got my paper back in math with a C grade. It just proves I'm a failure. I'll never graduate." The brainstorming by the group members led to the following statements: "Lots of people get C's and don't fail." "A C means I have to work a little harder to get a B." "F's mean failure, not C's. I guess I'm exaggerating again."

Many of the extragroup tasks between sessions involve testing hypotheses. The therapist should encourage youth who catastrophize to write out their predictions of dire consequences for later evaluation so as to accumulate a recorded body of data disproving their catastrophic predictions. The group brainstorming serves as a "rub-in." For further practice, one could do cognitive modeling and rehearsal plus feedback.

Decatastrophizing. When youth describe a situation in which they catastrophize the consequences, the most common question is, "What is the worst that can happen?" In a group, the question is asked also of the other members for the target person, and if there are differences among them, the target person should explain why such differences exist. Similarly, the target person is asked what the evidence is for his or her interpretation, and the group is asked for evidence that the interpretation is incorrect.

When predicting dire consequences, the catastrophizing person does not use all of the information available to him or her and rarely takes into account his or her past dire predictions that failed to materialize. The therapist attempts to widen the range of information on which the person bases his or her forecasts by asking the group members as well as the target person what other catastrophes the target person has predicted that then failed to materialize.

Providing Information. Lack of information or erroneous information may exacerbate the client's anxiety. Where disinformation exists about such topics as the use of drugs, AIDS, other medical problems, masturbation, and sex, providing youth with information to correct their cognitive distortions can be regarded as an unintrusive technique. Delivering information to the group as a whole is efficient. The effectiveness can be tested with quizzes, sometimes carried out like a game show to add to the attraction. Also, the therapist, especially in institutional and other open-ended groups, can draw on the information of members who have already been through the informational program. Usually the therapist will review and rehearse the role of the disseminator of information before the session to ensure success of the delivery of the information.

Decentering. According to Beck and Emery (1985, p. 206), decentering is the process of having the target person and other group members challenge the basic belief that the target person is the focal point or center of all events happening in his or her vicinity. The other group members can point out to the target person occasions they have observed when he or she is (or is not) the center of all attention, and which behavior or attributes of his or hers are indeed being attended to by others.

Maria: There were a bunch of kids on the back of the school bus who were horsing around and laughing. I knew they were laughing at me, especially at what I was wearing.

Group Therapist: Way in the back of the bus? What do the rest of you think? I wonder if there could be any other explanations.

Lisa: I was there. They just seemed to be having fun.

Nettie: Kids are always horsing around in the back of the bus. It has nothing to do with you or anybody.

Carol: You look like everyone else, it wouldn't be worth making fun of your clothes. They be making fun of their own.

Group Therapist: It seems to most of us that you believe that almost everything people do in your vicinity is related to things you have done wrong. We saw a few other examples of that before. What do you think?

Enlarging Perspective. Anxious youth usually take a very narrow view of their situation, and one of the functions of therapy is to provide them with a broader perspective or long-range view of the situation (Beck & Emery, 1985, p. 206). In a group, one youth stated that he couldn't get a job because he was so ugly: "I know I'm ugly. My older brother always calls me ugly." The group suggested that he did indeed look different from others, but that being different was something to be proud of. The others agreed. Another youth suggested that employers were more interested in neatness and how one presented oneself than in how one looked in terms of beauty or handsomeness. The members suggested that he could make use of his unique features to make an interesting impression.

Reattribution. In reviewing an anxiety-prone client's automatic thoughts, the therapist often discovers that the client attributes to him- or herself an excessive amount of control for a potential negative outcome. In reattribution, the control is placed where it logically belongs.

Terrence: It's my fault that my mom and dad got divorced. If I hadn't been in trouble all the time and caused them so much pain and worry, they'd be together today.

Group Therapist: So you think that you have the power to control the major decisions of your parents by what you do. I wonder what the rest of you think.

Alan: Well, my parents were really upset with me when I was sent here, and they even argued a lot about what to do about me, but I guess they didn't make any major decisions like divorce or moving or something because of me. I can't imagine you can do that to your parents either. You're just a kid.

Phil: My mom gave me a lot more attention when I got caught. And she was embarrassed and all that she'd got a kid in the slammer. She didn't move or change her job because of me or anything like that. She was already divorced, twice. I guess we're not such big bosses.

Terrence: Well, I guess my parents had been thinking about divorce for a long time. I know I added to the burden, but I sure feel like I caused it.

Group Therapist: I certainly can understand that. We often feel like we cause things that in fact we have little control over. Sure, we might sometimes cause a lot of disappointment and pain, and of course joy too, but my guess is we don't have a heck of a lot of power to radically change their lives. Sometimes something like this is the straw that breaks the camel's back, but the load has been getting heavy for a long time.

Once again, the group therapist draws on the other members' perceptions of how much control the client actually has.

Point-Counterpoint. In this procedure, Beck and Emery (1985, pp. 208-209) suggested that the therapist tell the target person to give all the arguments why the feared event is not dire and highly unlikely to happen, while the rest of the members (who do not have this particular concern) will continue to give the reasons that the consequences are indeed dire and highly likely to occur. If the problem is shared by most of the members, the therapist plays the role of the antagonist.

Further Group Work With Corrective Strategies. Most youth are not convinced by any one of these strategies on any one occasion. Only after dysfunctional thinking is repeatedly brought to the group and discussed using multiple corrective strategies can change begin to take place. Often, in challenging the thinking of their peers, youth discover that they are making similar errors in thinking, and this adds to their motivation for change. As the first members succeed, they serve as models for the others. In open groups, the experienced members are actively engaged to model the self-disclosure of cognitions.

In many groups, the steps may stop at this point if the identification of the thinking errors leads by itself to a greater reliance on coping thoughts. Where the thinking errors persist, a more active replacement with coping thoughts may be advisable. It is possible to brainstorm with the group all possible alternatives to the self-defeating statements that meet the criteria of realistic appraisal and positive self-evaluation or self-instruction. Often, as in the preceding example, the alternative statements are sufficiently apparent that no brainstorming is required. Once the list is complete, the target person decides on the alternate cognitions he or she would like to use. To continue with the above example, the therapist has reviewed with the group all of the counterarguments to Tyrone's thinking distortion that he can tell that everyone hates him when they laugh at him.

To make sure that a client has readily available those arguments that attack the viability of the thinking errors, the group therapist may demonstrate the kinds of arguments that might be used. Many of these arguments are found above in the section "Logical Disputation of Thinking Errors." A case study may be used first so that youth can practice without anyone's feeling excessively criticized.

Cognitive Modeling Sequence

To train Tyrone in the use of the coping statements, the cognitive modeling sequence as described for individual therapy by Meichenbaum (1977) but adapted here for groups could be used. This sequence consists of setting the scene, cognitive modeling with thought stopping and cognitive rehearsal, group feedback, and fading. The cognitive modeling sequence is used in cognitive restructuring and self-instructional training. Let us first look at an example of the first part of the process.

Group Therapist: (Setting the scene) You've heard what the group members have said, Tyrone. Why don't you give us those same arguments in the most convincing terms you can. Remember how we do this. I'll set the scene. What would you usually say to yourself?

Tyrone: Well, I would usually say to myself, "They must really hate me to make fun of me like that. Otherwise they wouldn't hassle me like this."

Group Therapist: Okay, I'm going to show you what happens when we replay the scene. First I'll repeat your thinking, then I will stop it, then I will replace it with some alternative coping statements, the ones we brainstormed earlier. Then you get a chance to try it. Okay, let's start. Everyone pay careful attention. I imagine I'm at school in the cafeteria. I can smell the cafeteria food and hear the noise. Loud, isn't it? Guys screaming. Girls laughing. I put the spaghetti on my tray and pay for it, and then I suddenly trip over someone's chair and drop my tray and spaghetti all over the floor. Everyone is laughing, and I really feel embarrassed. I think, "Boy, they must really hate me. One small mistake and they're laughing at me as if I was crazy." Then I shout (loudly), "Stop it, Paul!" (Thought stopping) "That's just not true. They laugh at everybody. Just cool it, Paul, and laugh with them, and clean up the mess." (Looking at Tyrone) "So what if they laugh? I guess it's funny." (Shifts into therapist role) Would you feel comfortable in do something like that?

Tyrone: I'm not sure. Could I have another model?

Group Therapist: Any volunteers? I'll do the setting of the scene.

Abdul: I'll do it. (Goes through all the steps)

Group Therapist: That was great. Well, Tyrone, are you ready now? I'll help you if you get stuck.

Tyrone: Sure, but I won't be so convincing.

Group Therapist: It doesn't matter. Give it a try. As is my custom, I'll do the scene setting. Then you think your own thoughts. First the thinking errors and then the coping thoughts, with thought stopping in between. Okay, I want you to imagine you're at school in the cafeteria. Smell the cafeteria food, and hear the noise. Deafening, isn't it? Guys screaming. Girls giggling. You are putting the spaghetti on your tray, and now you pay for it, and then suddenly you trip over someone's chair and drop your tray and spaghetti all over the floor. It seems like everyone in the cafeteria is laughing at you. You get up and say to yourself (pause)?

Tyrone: (Cognitive rehearsal) "Oh my God, they're laughing. I can't stand it. Boy, they really hate me. Stop it, Tyrone, stop. (Therapist whispers, "Louder") Stop! (Screams it out) You know it's just not true. They are just teasing, having fun. They don't mean anything by it. It is funny, I have to admit.

Paul: Hey, that's a neat twist. Okay, everyone, including me and Tyrone, write down at least one thing Tyrone did well. (pause). Okay, guys, what did you write?

The group then proposed a number of things Tyrone did well in handling the situation. The therapist asked them to write down one thing Tyrone might consider doing differently in the same situation and then to tell Tyrone what they wrote. The therapist then asked Tyrone to do it again (re-rehearsal), incorporating any new ideas from the members that Tyrone liked. The second time, he had Tyrone set the scene for himself.

Setting the Scene. As part of training for shifting from thinking errors to coping statements, the therapist uses cognitive modeling and cognitive rehearsal. Before using these procedures, as can be seen in the above example, the therapist sets the scene in terms of the details of the physical environment, including the sounds and smells in the environment, to make the visualization and cognitive modeling and rehearsal as realistic as possible.

Cognitive Modeling. In cognitive modeling, the group therapist and/or an experienced group member, following the setting of the scene, models the various self-instructions while explaining aloud what is happening in the situation and what is happening to him- or herself internally. The group therapist asks the members to take notes on what is said so that after the demonstration they can point out the most and least useful self-statements. (With younger adolescents, tokens are often distributed for the identification of self-statements.) In the above example, the group therapist and Abdul, a group member, demonstrated setting the scene, the thinking distortions, the shift, and the coping statements—all the steps in cognitive modeling.

It should be noted that before modeling, the therapist reviewed the general self-defeating statements made by Tyrone. It is assumed that these had been discussed earlier and that Tyrone had acknowledged them. The therapist had brainstormed with the group earlier to elicit some alternative statements, and Tyrone had selected those with which he was most comfortable. The therapist set the scene, expressed his cognitions aloud, and expressed how he was feeling.

Thought Stopping. In the modeling, the therapist and later Abdul demonstrated a loud and intrusive transitional or thought-stopping statement, "Stop it!" Then the therapist stated aloud the alternative coping statements. For variation, the group members may call out the "Stop!"

Cognitive Rehearsal. Cognitive rehearsal is the role-played practice by the target person of the situation that was first simulated by the model. In the above example, after the therapist once again set the scene, Tyrone carried out a cognitive rehearsal, including thought stopping and shifting to the coping response. If the cognitive sequence is short (less than 2 minutes), each member of the group performs the rehearsal, as in the above example, to provide multiple models for the target person and opportunities for practice for the others, who often share the same cognitive distortions. The therapist uses the round-robin technique, shifting the "scene setter" and the "target person" each time.

It is also possible for youth to work in pairs, with one performing the cognitive task and the other setting the scene. If a significant other is present, it is best to work in triads, with the third person playing the role of the significant other. This arrangement provides additional practice in a short period of time.

Group Feedback. To let the target person know what he or she did well and what he or she might improve, the group therapist asks the members to write down at least one thing that the target person did well and one thing he or she might consider doing differently. Then, beginning with the positive feedback, one at time, the therapist asks the group to let the target person know how he or she did. If the group therapist does not indicate that the positive goes first, the members almost automatically will criticize the target person first. These are the same principles that guided feedback after the overt modeling sequence described in the previous chapter.

Fading. The previous step may be regarded as the "thinking out loud" phase of cognitive restructuring. In real life, youth usually keep their self-defeating statements or beliefs to themselves. After the target person has mastered the transition from self-defeating statements to self-enhancing statements, he or she is instructed to practice his or her covert response in a whisper. The overt components continue to be carried out in a normal voice. Because there is no feedback, these rehearsals can be carried out one at a time in pairs or triads to increase the number of trials for everyone in a short period of time.

Finally, the target person practices privately to him- or herself. This provides many additional rehearsals for each member. In this rehearsal, the target person sets the scene. If there is no overt component, it is possible for everyone in the group to practice his or her particular rehearsal at the same time. If there is an overt behavioral component, the people involved can speak the overt parts or do the overt actions while being silent or whispering the covert component. This must be done one at a time or in subgroups.

At the very end of the process, the group therapist summarizes the major steps and principles of what the group members have done or, if the group is experienced, asks them to summarize and note any problems involved in going through the steps.

Self-Instructional Training

Most people give themselves silent instructions, especially in difficult or complex situations. They tell themselves that they need a drink, they should avoid a certain person, or they should go home because they feel tired. They remind themselves, often subvocally, or are reminded by physiological cues to stop at the gas station, to buy some milk at the store, or to turn on a certain TV program. This habit of many to instruct themselves can be used in therapy—individual, family, or group—as a means of controlling one's own behavior, cognitions, and emotions in a step-by-step process. Self-instructional training (Meichenbaum, 1977) has recently gained wide support from both clinicians and researchers, especially in the treatment of children. However, its clinical applications have, thus far, outstripped its research support (Cormier & Cormier, 1991, p. 337). Most of the research applies to young children, although we have found the procedure useful with adolescents as well.

There is a great deal of similarity between self-instructional training and Meichenbaum's approach to cognitive restructuring. Rather than identifying isolated nonfunctional beliefs and trying to replace them with coping statements, self-instructional training involves preparing the individual to deal with a complex or extremely difficult situation by using a set of self-instructions to handle his or her anger or stress or anxiety differentially over time. The phases in time most commonly used are anticipating a stressful or anger-inducing event, immediately preceding the event, during the event, and immediately following the event. The specific things that a person might say to him- or herself are developed in the group through "task analysis," in which the members recommend to the target person what might be said to deal with the different phases.

Self-instructional training has generally been used with children and adolescents with a high frequency of hyperactive, aggressive, and impulsive behavior. It has been used directly to develop skills in such areas as resistance to temptation, delay of gratification, problem solving, reading, and creativity (Meichenbaum & Genest, 1980). CBIGT therapists have used self-instructional training in groups of adolescents to supplement an overt modeling-rehearsal strategy to help them practice dealing with provocations or other stressful situations. Therapists have found it particularly effective in helping adolescents to go step by step through stress- or anger-inducing situations with adults, such as the principal of the school to whom they must explain some misbehavior; a peer whom they would like to know better; a parent who is about to blame them for something they did not do; or a job interviewer for a job they really want. These simulations include self-instructions for both cognitions and overt verbal behavior.

A client can examine what needs to be done when he or she is faced with a difficult task by first developing, with the help of the group, a series of self-instructions. For example, if the client must study for an examination that he or she has previously failed, he or she becomes extremely anxious at the prospect. A group member in this situation might be advised by other members to say to herself, "I'm really exaggerating. I've done it before, I can do it again," "Take one step a time, that's all it takes," and "First get out my materials and organize them in a useful way, then read the material, and ask myself questions at the end of each chapter." She might be advised to reinforce herself periodically by saying, while the action is taking place, "There, that's going better, just take your time," "Hey, I'm not getting upset," and "Look, I can do it." Finally, if successful, she might be advised to say to herself, "I did a good job. Next time the situation occurs, I won't let myself get so upset. Clearly, I can handle these frustrations."

Self-instructional training as applied in groups consists of four major steps: providing a rationale, task analysis, cognitive modeling, and cognitive rehearsal. Because all of the phases lend themselves to a demonstration or to a performance by the entire group or subgroup, this is particularly efficient as a group method. Let us examine the process one step as a time.

Orientation to Self-Instructional Training

As in most procedures discussed in this book, the first step in self-instructional training is orientation, in which group members are provided with a rationale for its use and some examples. Usually the orientation is presented when the procedure is introduced for the first time and repeated only when a new member enters the group or as a review in a later phase of group treatment. The following explanation has been used with adolescents, and variations of the explanation have been used with younger children as well.

> Today we are going to learn a technique for helping ourselves get through difficult situations that take place over time. As you know, almost everyone talks to themselves. I certainly do. For example, last week I was supposed to give a speech to the staff at the agency. I was really nervous about it. So several days before I had to give the presentation, I reminded myself that I knew as much if not more about my subject than anyone else in the room and that I had time to prepare and that I had given reports in the past and they had been well received. As I went into the meeting room, I told myself to be calm and to relax myself using the exercise we learned in group (see below). I kept reminding myself to look at them and not at my notes, since I knew what I was going to say. When I made a little mistake, I reminded myself that everyone can make a mistake and I should just keep going. It really helped. What we are going to do is to learn special ways of talking to ourselves that might help us all to get through difficult situations. First, we are going to take a look at the steps that need to be performed in each situation. Then I'm going to have you demonstrate to each other what each of you could be saying to yourself to get through each of those steps. Then you will practice those same self-statements, first aloud and then to yourself. Are there any questions? (Group therapist answers questions)

Following the presentation of a rationale, the group therapist helps the members to analyze the problematic task by breaking it down into its components.

Task Analysis

In the task analysis phase, the group therapist attempts to examine the cognitions associated with the sequence of events of which the problem consists. Often, several must be dealt with and sometimes replaced. For example, in a group of adjudicated delinquent youth, the members and group therapist identified the following critical moments for a youth who wanted to do a term paper for his 10th-grade class. The group therapist had the youth describe the situation and then asked the group what cognitions might interfere with their doing the paper or an equally difficult task. The group arrived at a number of cognitions that the target youth agreed had been coming up for him:

- Before he started the task, it seemed overwhelming, and he didn't know if he would be able to do it.
- The task seemed to have so many steps, he felt he would never finish.
- At one point, he feared that he might make a small mistake and that this would make him terribly upset.
- He noticed as he was doing the task that his mind was wandering and he was having trouble concentrating.

The group therapist then asked the group members what they might say to themselves to cope more effectively with these stress-inducing cognitions or unpleasant emotions or both. Because the group's repertoire of ideas is sometimes limited in the early group sessions, many of the ideas for potential alternative cognitions may have to be suggested by the group therapist. In subsequent sessions, the members will usually increase the proportion of ideas that are their own. In this way, the group members can be maximally involved.

Cognitive Modeling and Rehearsal in Self-Instruction

Once the components of the task have been identified, cognitive modeling and rehearsal can take place. The same steps are used as in cognitive restructuring (Meichenbaum, 1977), except that there is no thought stopping. In the following example, many different self-instructions were suggested by the group members for the different phases of dealing with the stressful situation of having to meet with a father who had deserted the family several years earlier and now wanted to make amends. The therapist reviewed first the cognitions and then the steps that the target youth would be taking. Then the therapist modeled the following steps while pointing out the phase for each:

- *Preparing for a stressor or provocation:* I know it's going to be difficult when I see my dad again. But I have to remind myself that he is hurting too. I'll practice keeping my cool. I've done it before.
- *Just preceding the provocation or stressor:* There he is. Stay calm. Just go up and say, "Hi." No sarcasm. No jokes. Take a deep breath and relax. Talk

about sports. He likes sports. Ask him about himself. And listen! Remember, you don't have to be perfect.

■ *While experiencing the stressor or provocation:* You are doing okay. Continue to relax. Give him eye contact. Smile. Indicate that you're listening to him.

■ *Just after one has dealt with the stressor or provocation:* Good, I did it. It wasn't as bad as I expected. Next time, I have to remain just a little calmer.

After checking with the target youth, the therapist instructed him to rehearse the situation. This was followed by feedback from the group and fading strategies (discussed earlier). To create multiple modeling opportunities for the target youth and rehearsal opportunities for the other group members, everyone in the group went through the same process.

Teaching the Skills of Self-Instruction

To train youth in the use of self-instructional procedures, the following exercise can be used in groups after the members have been oriented to self-instructional training and given some examples.

Exercise 10.4: Self-Instructional Training

Purpose: By the end of this exercise, each person will have demonstrated the skills involved in self-instructional training.

Individual Task 1: Imagine that you have to go to the police station to testify about a burglary that you saw happening. You are afraid the police will blame it on you, even though they said they just want to hear what you saw.

Subgroup Task 1: Divide into four pairs. Pair 1, write down what you could tell yourself when you first hear about having to testify. Pair 2, write down what you could tell yourself when you are at the police station and just about to testify (note your emotions and the external smells and sounds in the station). Pair 3, write down what you could tell yourself when you are feeling anxious and you are in the middle of testifying. Pair 4, write down what you could tell yourself when you are finished testifying.

Group Task 1: In the whole group, the pairs tell all the ideas they came up with, beginning with Pair 1. Note any additional statements they could make. Evaluate the usefulness for you of each statement.

Group Task 2: The group therapist will set the scene for each of the phases, and each subgroup will role-play (cognitive rehearsal only) in front of the group, as carefully and seriously as they can, their cognitive responses for all four phases.

Variations

The group approach itself is a variation of Meichenbaum's self-instructional approach. In addition, one can invent a number of variations to keep the interest of the group high and the learning effective. For those youth to whom self-talk is a mystery, it may be first necessary to do training in conscious self-talk.

Group Therapist: (Writes a list of self-instructional statements on the board) Okay, everyone write down one self-instruction from the list I put on the board. Don't tell anyone. Okay, I'm going to act out my self-instruction. See if you can guess what it was. (Therapist looks totally relaxed, eyes closed, breathing slow) What did I instruct myself?

Charlie: You told yourself to relax.

Gavin: And to shut your eyes and to slow down your breathing.

Group Therapist: Right on. Now, one at a time, each of you follow your own self-instruction and see if we can guess what it was.

Another method involves the use of audiotaping. In this variation, the group therapist prepares several tapes with self-instructions followed by silence to permit compliance with the instructions. Each adolescent then puts on the earphones of a miniaudiotape recorder and listens to the instructions while performing the desired task. Later, the adolescent must repeat the task without the tape recorder while giving him- or herself the instructions covertly. Often, as an extragroup task, he or she will practice using the tape recorder at home.

Still another variation is to have the members rehearse in triads, with one person describing the situation, one person describing the internal stimuli he or she was experiencing, and one person describing his or her cognitive response. Gradually, the additional players are faded. A similar variation was used by a group that put on a play in which every character had a self-instructor whispering, loudly, in his or her ear. The adolescents liked the exercise so much that they decided to repeat it the following week, with both members of the pair dressing alike.

A number of authors have suggested supplementing self-instructional training with operant procedures (Kendall & Finch, 1976, 1978; Nelson & Birkimer, 1978), especially with younger children, who are reinforced for correctly stating a useful self-instruction and then following it. We have encouraged each member of the group to be a deliverer of tokens when a self-instruction was given by a person practicing a given task. This resulted in more careful observation as well as a more complete performance. The various procedures reviewed in this section appeared to increase the attraction of the group and the frequency with which self-instructional methods were used.

Problem Solving and Self-Instruction

Self-instructions may also be used in carrying out systematic problem solving because problem solving occurs in phases. There is considerable research supporting this method with young children (Kendall & Braswell, 1985), but no one has investigated the procedure with adolescents. In this procedure, the client is helped to memorize a number of potential responses to problem situations (suggested by Kendall & Braswell, 1985) that lend themselves to systematic problem solving:

- What makes this situation problematic?
- Let's see, what's the best way to handle this situation?
- I have to look at all the possibilities.
- What are the consequences of each possibility?
- I think the best is this one. . . .
- Hey, not bad. I really handled that situation well. (Or) I didn't do too well, but I'll do better next time.

To facilitate the group members' use of these self-instructions and positive self-judgments in problem solving, the group therapist provides all the members with the above list of self-instructions on a handout or puts them on the chalkboard. The therapist then presents the group with the following situations, and each person goes through the problem-solving process while incorporating covertly the above statements. This can also be done in pairs, with one person making the covert problem-solving statements and the other making the overt problem-solving statements.

- When Arnie is going out with his friends, he knows that some of them will want to go out drinking. If he gets caught drinking or using drugs again, he will violate parole and can be sent back to the correctional institution.
- Chuck knows that he has to explain to his teacher why he has missed so many classes and his intentions of not missing them anymore. He doesn't like his teacher, and he thinks she doesn't like him.
- Verna knows that the others in her peer group are going to put pressure on her to smoke, and she doesn't want to ruin her health. On the other hand, she doesn't want to lose their friendship.
- Gordon, Andy's best friend, is pressuring him to write bigger on the test so that Gordon can see Andy's paper and copy it better. Andy doesn't think it's right, first, and second, he is afraid of getting caught.

Note that each of these situations involves a highly specific event and poses a dilemma for the target person. After the group members have practiced with these "canned" situations, they are asked to bring a situation of their own to the group. The following week, they will practice in the larger groups and in pairs, using their own situations and giving their own self-instructions aloud.

Moral Reasoning

In the last example above, Andy was presented with a moral dilemma: Should he help his friend by making it possible for him to cheat? Problem solving is one way of dealing with the dilemma. One could also use moral reasoning. Delinquents, according to Arbuthnot and Gordon (1986), have consistently been shown to function at lower stages of moral reasoning than nondelinquents. The authors hypothesized that adolescents at risk for juvenile delinquency would benefit both cognitively and behaviorally from an intervention designed to accelerate moral reasoning development. Training in moral reasoning uses primarily cognitive and didactic strategies and group exercises as the major means of intervention.

In Arbuthnot and Gordon's (1986) study, discussion groups ranged in size from five to eight, and groups were led by one of two extensively trained male group leaders. The first two weeks were spent in building rapport, with the leaders paying particular attention to demonstrating warmth, humor, directness, and clarity. Several exercises were used to develop feelings of openness, group identity and cohesion, safety, acceptance, and respect for others' views. The treatment discussions focused primarily on moral reasoning and perspective taking. Two sessions were spent on active listening and communication ("I" messages) skills after the leaders discovered that the participants' general lack of these skills appeared to impede effective discussions.

The research design in this study was a randomized pretest-posttest control group design. Matched pairs of youth were assigned randomly to experimental and control groups. Before participation in a cognitively based moral reasoning development program (16-20 weekly 45-minute sessions), 48 adolescents were identified by teachers on the basis of histories of unruliness, aggressiveness, impulsivity, and disruptiveness, as well as of specific behavioral problems indicative of a high risk for delinquency, such as stealing, lying, vandalism, and setting fires. The participants were 35 male and 13 female Caucasian adolescents ranging in age from 13 to 17 years. The students were drawn in approximately equal numbers from each of the four school systems in one rural county.

The moral reasoning groups demonstrated (a) an advance in the moral reasoning stage and (b) improvement on several behavioral indexes, including behavior referrals, tardiness, academic performance, and police/court contacts. The results only approached significance for teacher ratings. For a subgroup, 1-year follow-up data showed significant effects for moral reasoning, behavior referrals, and academic performance, as well as for teacher ratings and absenteeism. The way this subgroup was selected was not explicated. Moral reasoning change scores were associated with all outcome change scores for pretest to posttest and with grades for posttest to follow-up. Arbuthnot and Gordon (1986), just like Lochman (1985), demonstrated that 18 sessions was a more effective length of time for treatment groups than 12 or fewer sessions. The authors attended to group process by looking at member participation. Despite their discovery of big differences in member participation, the researchers dismissed its importance. Nevertheless, this was one of the few studies that even considered a group attribute.

The findings of this study suggest that moral reasoning and perspective taking may be legitimate targets of intervention and that the specific discussion methods mentioned above should at least be considered in the treatment of delinquent and nondelinquent youth.

Behavioral Self-Management

One of the goals of therapy is to improve the ability of the adolescent to direct and change his or her own behavior. In psychoeducational groups, the therapist teaches and directs, and the clients are expected to learn. In CBIGT, clients are expected to learn the skills of changing or directing their own behavior. Thus, self-management is a major goal, and self-management procedures are used throughout therapy.

In a self-management paradigm, youth are trained to observe, assess, and evaluate their own behavior; define their own goals; rearrange their own environment; and reinforce themselves when they are successful in such a way as to increase the likelihood of goal attainment. Throughout this book, whenever any of these or other procedures are used, the group members are taught how to employ the procedure themselves. Self-management procedures are largely cognitive insofar as youth are taught to employ self-instruction to carry them out.

Self-observation and self-recording are of particular importance. Forman (1993) pointed out the following steps that training should involve:

1. Discussion of the use and importance of self-observation
2. Selection and definition of the target behavior, including a discussion of characteristics of the target behavior and role play of accurate and inaccurate instances of the target behavior
3. Selection of an appropriate and easily usable self-recording procedure
4. Modeling of the use of the self-recording procedure
5. Rehearsal of the use of the self-recording procedure
6. Reinforcement of appropriate instances of self-recording during training, with students rewarded when their records match those of an objective observer (pp. 133-134)

Forman advised that if the therapist can build in occasional checks by an objective observer, it will improve the accuracy of the observations. In the residential treatment situation, the youth can serve as occasional observers. (See Chapter 5 for more details and examples on the use of observers and other validity checks.)

Some of the other steps in self-management training are described elsewhere in this book. Goal setting for oneself is illustrated in Chapter 6, self-reinforcement is described in Chapter 8, self-management by means of self-instruction is described in the previous section, and self-modeling by means of taping one's own behavior is described in Chapter 9.

CBIGT in general lends itself to self-management training in that each client must design his or her own therapy plan while serving as a consultant to all the other group members. Group members point out to each other the situations in which self-management would be appropriate. They get practice not only by planning and managing their own treatment strategies but by providing advice and training for others in the group. This reduces the degree of dependence on the adult therapist and facilitates greater reliance on their own resources. Thus, self-management techniques are also vital skills for coping with the stress and anger induction of the real world.

Relaxation Training in Groups

In stressful situations, another extremely important coping strategy is relaxation. This procedure is maintained and practiced by means of self-instruction and self-reinforcement.

Relaxation procedures for the treatment of anxiety and stress disorders are widely used, and some modest research support exists for their use with adolescents. Reynolds and Coats (1986) investigated the effectiveness of cognitive-behavioral therapy and relaxation training for the treatment of depression in adolescents. The participants in their study met in small groups for ten 50-minute sessions over 5 weeks in a high school setting. The training emphasized the relationship between stress, muscle tension, and depression. Deep muscle relaxation training was taught, and subjects were taught to apply their relaxation skills in situations noted for producing tension or anger. Both the cognitive-behavioral and relaxation training groups were superior to a wait-list control group in the reduction of depressive symptoms at posttest and 5-week follow-up assessments.

Ewart, Harris, Iwata, and Coates (1987) used relaxation to reduce cardiovascular risk in students in the 9th and 10th grades. They screened 1,400 students and taught relaxation to all those above the 85th percentile in blood pressure. The relaxation training included training in four skills: (a) assuming a relaxed posture, (b) muscle relaxation, (c) slow diaphragmatic breathing (described below in the next section), and (d) hand warming. The trainers were quite flexible, urging the students to try out the various procedures and to select those that fit them best. About 15 to 20 minutes of relaxation training was provided 4 days a week for the 12-week semester. Compared with untrained controls, the experimental group members reduced their blood pressure significantly.

Deffenbacher, Lynch, and Oetting (1996) compared cognitive/relaxation coping skill training (CRCST) and social skill training (SST) in a group of sixth graders with a control group rated as high in anger. Both treatments were equally effective in lowering negative anger expression and personal situational anger, while increasing controlled anger expression. CRCST was more effective than SST in lowering depression, shyness, and general and school deviance. Although the term *relaxation training* in most of the above studies and program descriptions has referred to progressive relaxation, there has been extensive variability across procedures used. In this section, we explicate progressive relaxation training as it applies to the teaching of youth in groups. Also presented are a number of variations on this approach, specific uses of the group, and strategies for obtaining generalization of the procedures to the real world.

Because many of the youth with whom CBIGT therapists work suffer from excessive anxiety and stress, either in specific situations or chronically, the use of systematic relaxation has been increasingly incorporated into CBIGT. The skill of being able to relax on command creates a physiological set of responses that appear to be incompatible with anxiety and impulsive responses. Once an adolescent is well trained in the relaxation response, even his or her thinking the word *relax* at moments of high stress or the first signs of anger can provide that pause necessary to prevent out-of-control rage. Relaxation can be taught as a useful skill in its own right as a lifestyle skill or supplementary to cognitive procedures in the treatment of anger, stress, and such physical problems as headaches. In addition to being incompatible with strong negative emotions and impulsive behavior, skill in relaxation has often been observed to enhance an adolescent's self-esteem. The adolescent learns to take pride in the achievement as he or she demonstrates this esoteric skill to family and peers. In some groups, the relaxation activity becomes a highly valued group reinforcer. Finally, for many, just practicing relaxation on a regular basis seems to reduce chronic anxiety and stress across situations.

Teaching Relaxation

For older children and adolescents, the teaching of relaxation is done primarily through demonstration, instruction, and practice in and out of the groups. As training progresses, that instruction becomes self-instruction. One muscle group is tensed (initially for 5 seconds) and then relaxed (initially for 10 seconds) at a time. At the completion of the tensing of one muscle group, the group therapist checks each person to see whether it appears to be correct. Then the group therapist goes on to the relaxation phase of the same muscle group. When the relaxation of the given muscle group appears to be correctly carried out at least to some degree by most of the members, the group therapist goes on to the next muscle group. There are many patterns of giving instructions in the literature, although the pattern of alternate tension and relaxation prevails in most of them. The order and the sizes of the muscle groups are the major variants. The following description is the set of procedures that CBIGT therapists most commonly use with adolescents. It is also used, with some adjustment in language, for younger children. In the following example, the group therapist begins, as with all new procedures, by orienting the group members to the purposes of the procedure and the techniques to be used. Note also that self-monitoring of the degree of relaxation is called for. The following description begins with an orientation to relaxation and then follows with a step-by-step description of what one must do to carry it out.

> Last week, we talked about the different ways of using relaxation. This week, as we agreed, I will be teaching you a way in which you can use relaxation to help you to deal with those situations that you feel make you tense, nervous, and angry. The first few times we do this, you may find it difficult to follow the instructions, you may itch, or you may feel the urge to giggle or move. (Note that the group therapist gives the members permission to do what is highly likely to occur anyway.) Don't worry about it. You may even feel at times or in certain parts of the body some degree of relaxation or a whole lot. Sometimes, when it is a whole lot, it might even scare you a little bit. Do the best you can; if you get upset at how you feel or what comes into your mind, you can stop, but try not to disturb the others. But you may learn to really enjoy it. Any questions? (Answers questions) First, everyone rate themselves on the

10-point scale of relaxation, with 1 being complete relaxation and 10 being panic. Now lay it next to you, and I'll collect it. Okay, now listen to me carefully, and try to follow the instructions as best as you can. Okay, loosen any tight belts or other tight clothing. Take off your glasses, and remove your contacts if you forgot and brought them along. Lie on your back with your feet slightly separated. Place your arms alongside your body with your palms up and your hands open.

Focus completely on your right hand. Slowly make a tight fist. Feel the tension in your fingers and your hand. Remain this way for 5 seconds. Slowly release the tension in your fist. Now focus your attention on your right arm. Try to feel the muscles, and then concentrate on tensing the muscles in that arm. Increase the tension as much as you can from the hand to the top of the shoulder. Stretch the arm, but don't lift it, as you will then tense other muscles. Keep your focus on the tension in your arm, and try not to let any other thoughts come into your mind. Remain this way for 5 seconds. Slowly release the tension in your fist and then your arm. Your hand should be slightly opened once again with your palm up. Try to think about what is happening in the arm. Each of you may feel different things happening. Some of you may feel the arm becoming quite heavy and sinking into the mat. Now focus on your left arm. (The group therapist goes through the same steps with the left hand and then the left arm.)

Now concentrate on the right leg. Push the heel away and draw the toes toward you in order to avoid a foot cramp. (The group therapist examines each of the feet to make sure the position is correct.) Then slowly increase tension until the maximum has been achieved from the foot to the thigh. If it begins to cramp, relax immediately. Stretch the leg, but do not lift it. Wait 5 seconds in this tensed condition while focusing as much as possible on the leg. Now slowly release the tension in the leg. Some people feel the leg become heavy. Some feel it sinking into the floor. (Now the group therapist goes through the same steps with the left leg) Now relax the right arm as much as possible, now the left arm, now the right leg, and once again the left leg. Now both arms.

Now turn your attention to the pelvic girdle; that's the area around your waist. To tense this area, you tighten or contract the stomach (abdominal) muscles and draw them slightly upward. Then draw the buttocks toward one another. (With some youth the word *buttocks* will stimulate laughter. In this case, avoid this area the first few times.) Forget the rest of the body and concentrate on this one tensed area. Slowly release the stomach muscles and those of the buttocks, and let stomach and buttocks sink heavily into the floor.

Now direct your attention to the muscles of the chest. Gradually tense these muscles. Now move your shoulders toward each other from behind, tense the back and rib muscles. Now gradually relax the chest box, the shoulders, the back, and the rib cage. Let your lower and upper body sink into the floor. Relax once again your arms and legs.

Now focus on the neck. To tense it, pull back the neck toward the nape of the neck; hold it a few seconds, and slowly let it loose. You may note a difference between the tensed neck and the resting neck on the mat. Move your focus to the face. Clench your jaws together; tense the cheeks, mouth, and eyelids; wrinkle the forehead. One by one, release the tension in each of these—the jaws, the cheeks, mouth, the eyelids, and finally the forehead. Let these muscles feel the pull of gravity. Let your mouth fall open slightly.

Go slowly once more through the entire body, re-relaxing without tensing the feet, the legs, the pelvic area, the chest, the back, the arms, the shoulders, the neck, and the face. If possible, let your body sink still further into the mat. Now hold it for a minute (later 2 to 5 minutes).

Don't jump up and run off. Move your fingers slowly, now your toes, now your arms and legs just a little, now a little more, now your shoulders, move your head back and forth gently. If you feel like stretching, do so. Increase the depth of your breathing, sit up, stretch some more, hold each stretch momentarily; now, if you feel ready, stand up. Now everyone rate themselves on the 10-point scale of relaxation.

Before beginning such procedures, it is important to check out any history of injury or extensive muscle cramping with all the group members. Muscles that have been injured may be prone to knotting up when they are tensed. In these cases, avoid the tension phase of the previously injured and nearby muscle groups. Also, current medication being taken should be noted. If any member is on medication, the group therapist should have the parent or residential staff check with the physician whether the medicine might in any way interact unfavorably with the relaxation state.

Variations in Teaching Procedures

As we noted above, there are many variations of the relaxation procedures. Longer versions that consider, for example, the voice box and very minute muscle groups have been described by Jacobsen (1929) and Bernstein and Borkovec (1973). CBIGT therapists have found these to be especially useful when there is an impasse and the adolescent is unable to relax a particular large muscle group, or in situations in which a very minute muscle group seems to be the focus of the tension. In most cases, the above paradigm is sufficient to handle most problems. For most youth, the paradigm above is too long to be handled in one session. It is sometimes useful to do the arms and legs in one session and, after reviewing the first part, relaxing the trunk and head in another session. In a third session, the group practices relaxing the entire body in several additional sessions. In the remaining sessions, a highly abbreviated version is presented in which no tension is used at all. Both arms are relaxed at the same time, then both legs, the upper and lower torso, and the facial features. (Bernstein & Borkovec, 1973, go from 17 to 7 to 4 muscle groups in the course of a treatment that focuses primarily on relaxation as the major intervention.)

Although the above procedures seem to be suitable for most older children and adolescents, for many younger children (usually under the age of 12) seen in CBIGT or those who suffer from physical or emotional impairment, the paradigm described above may not be presented simply enough for them to follow it. For this reason, it has become necessary for the CBIGT therapist to have at his or her disposal several ways of modifying the commonly used paradigm to fit the unique requirements of young, extremely active, or emotionally or physically disabled youth (see Cautela & Groden, 1978, pp. 43-44, for a more detailed description of these variations).

Using the Group to Teach Relaxation

Almost all the procedures described can be taught in a group or in the classroom. Even in the small group, after the youth have learned the steps, they should monitor each other in pairs. One of the pair is the relaxor, and the other is the relaxee; then roles are switched. In open groups, the more experienced member will be the first relaxor in the pair. The group therapist should observe each adolescent separately to detect individual problems. This may occur within the group context while the others are observing each other in pairs.

Often, in the group, a relaxing atmosphere is created by dimming the lights, playing relaxing music, disconnecting the telephone and beepers, and putting up a Do-Not-Disturb sign on the outside door. This tends to cut down on disturbances, horseplay, and other silly behavior. In therapy groups, the relaxation procedure is usually not taught until a comfortable relationship has been established among members and between members and the therapist(s). This is often in closed groups the third or fourth week. In open-ended groups, relaxation is an ongoing part of the program, with the older members teaching the newcomers almost as soon as they enter the group. Thus, every adolescent goes through the relaxation procedure for the given session at least twice: once as relaxee and once as relaxor. Even when youth are giving the instructions to other youth, the group therapist is close by, circulating around the room and observing and prompting the relaxors.

On occasions when an adolescent has demonstrated unusual skills, he or she may be permitted to coach the entire group in carrying out the relaxation practice. The opportunity to coach becomes in this way a powerful reinforcer for mastery of both the relaxation skills and the teaching of them.

With most youth, frequent reinforcement should be given by the group therapist in the initial phase of learning. In addition to praise, tokens are often put into a paper cup lying next to the person as the group therapist inspects each person to note success in carrying out an instruction. Lack of compliance that is not disruptive is almost always ignored. Persistent lack of compliance by several persons or disruptive behavior is dealt with by firm limits as it occurs and may be discussed later as a group problem.

With adolescents, usually only social reinforcement is given for successful relaxation. One exception is rewarding those who do any of the steps especially well by allowing them to relax the entire group in the muscle groups in which they excel (if the cohesion of the group is high and the norms are essentially protherapeutic). In fact, adolescents can be reinforced by the other leadership responsibilities mentioned above, such as coach or assistant to the therapist. As a reward, certificates are sometimes issued to those with expertise sufficient to relax themselves, and teacher certificates are issued to those who demonstrate skills in teaching others.

Generalization of Relaxation Practice

To increase the likelihood of generalization, relaxation is practiced (following the suggestions of Cautela & Groden, 1978, pp. 77-78) in a number of different positions: sitting, standing, walking, and lying down. It is also taught in different settings, such as the classroom, the halls, community places, all the rooms of the house, and wherever the adolescent experiences tension or anger. Field trips can be taken to places where it is helpful to practice relaxation before and during the experience.

As has already been noted, a wide variety of persons are used to teach relaxation, including all the group members and the group therapist. If interested and willing to be trained, parents and teachers can be added to the list. In classrooms where the teacher practiced relaxation once or twice a week, it was noted that the use of relaxation was maintained. The same was true where parents used the procedure together with the client at home. For this reason, parents, teachers, and other significant persons are encouraged and on some occasions actually taught to do the relaxation procedures in a family group, a parent group, or even individual sessions. If there is a great deal of youth-parent conflict, the parents do not instruct the client in the various steps but merely go through the relaxation in the client's presence. If the parents are willing, they are encouraged to permit the client to teach relaxation to them.

Earlier in the chapter, it was noted that the group members are encouraged to review stressful and anger-provoking situations. To link the situations to relaxation, the members are then asked to imagine the situation and to go through the short steps of relaxation as soon as the critical moment in the stressful situation occurs. Thus, the initial onset of anger, stress, or anxiety becomes the cue to use relaxation in stressful or provocative situations outside the group. This exercise may be done in pairs, with one member of the pair acting as therapist and then with the roles reversed.

Of course, extragroup practice is an essential part of any generalization package. Of the research projects reviewed by Hillenberg and Collins (1982), 60% required homework practice, and most of the authors who did use homework claimed it was essential to teaching the procedure. Unfortunately, no one investigated the difference between training with and without homework, although some anecdotal evidence of the advantage of homework is cited above. Even in these studies with adults, compliance with carrying out relaxation at home was difficult to obtain. With adolescents, such home practice is still more difficult.

The use of tapes, which the group members borrow along with a tape recorder, seems to enhance compliance. So does the use of daily buddy contacts in which partners practice with each other. Some group therapists have special daily relaxation sessions that are carried out with the help of aides immediately after school for 10 minutes or on the unit in residential treatment. These daily sessions are gradually faded until the home practice seems to be carried out without such a structure. Finally, the use of reinforcement for relaxation is gradually faded. Concrete reinforcement is faded first, and social reinforcement becomes more intermittent. However, we have found that premature elimination of all social reinforcement runs the risk of losing all home practice.

There is often too little time in groups to give relaxation training the attention it deserves. In this case, it may be useful to enlist the families or the school to obtain additional training for the members. The occasional use of relaxation in the group may for most youth not be significant enough to warrant the use of in-group time. Of course, relaxation training is usually only one of many strategies of intervention used in the group to achieve common and individual group goals. The appropriateness of the relaxation strategy and the extent of its use will depend on the nature of the target behaviors. Certainly, when the client complains of chronic or acute anxiety or stress and impulsive anger, relaxation training should be a central feature of the program.

Imagery

Earlier in this chapter, visualization of various scenes was used to enhance the perception of problematic situations. It also possible to train youth in visualizing quiet scenes as a way of deepening the relaxed state. Many CBIGT therapists and other practitioners have found that imagery is particularly useful in enhancing relaxation. The following is an example that has been often used in CBIGT:

> Imagine you are lying under a tree on thick bed of grass on a warm day. Hear the birds singing in the trees. Feel the warm, gentle wind blowing across your face and body. See the rolling hills in the distance. A few white billowing clouds roll across the clear blue sky.

The use of imagery has to be negotiated with the group because often the adolescents will become silly and restless if they are not involved in the decision. They are more agreeable if the visualization is first tried out as an experiment one time to see whether they like it. Also, if any member has a relaxing quality in his or her reading voice, he or she can readily become the instructor, provided that he or she is not the lowest-status person in the group. Another way of involving the members is to permit and even encourage their writing a scene of their own. In our experience, youth are more likely to use imagery of their own creation.

Breathing Exercises

Diaphragmatic Breathing

An additional skill for improving the quality of relaxation is the use of diaphragmatic breathing (Everly & Rosenfeld, 1981). In diaphragmatic breathing, one first inhales slowly through the nose (to warm the air) for 2 to 3 seconds; during this period, the air causes first the abdomen and then the chest to expand slightly without discomfort. The client may be instructed to lift the chest slightly to permit the entry of the air. Without a pause, the client expels the air (first from the chest, then from the abdomen) through either the nose or the mouth (depending on personal preference) for 2 to 3 seconds. After a 1-second interval, the client may inhale again. The cycle can safely be repeated for several minutes without the danger of hyperventilation. The client is told to stop if light-headedness is experienced. In a variation of diaphragmatic breathing, the client is instructed to count the number of seconds in each phase. In the beginning, the group therapist does the counting; however, this works against individualizing the capacity of each person, so, after several demonstrations, the members count the seconds to themselves.

Stress Reduction Breathing

A short form of breathing has been also shown to induce a state of relaxation in 30 to 60 seconds (Vanderhoof, 1980). Because this short form is easier to teach than either diaphragmatic breathing or deep muscle relaxation, CBIGT therapists are beginning to make extensive use of the procedure, which Vanderhof (1980) called *stress reduction breathing*. Research has shown stress reduction breathing to be effective in reducing muscle tension and subjective reports of anxiety as well as heart rate (Vanderhoof, 1980).

The instructions of Everly and Rosenfeld (1981) seem most suitable for groups and are presented here. After orienting the group members to the procedure and explaining how it can help reduce stress, the therapist instructs them to assume a comfortable position and to place their left hand on their abdomen and the right hand on top of the left. They are then directed to relax and imagine an empty bottle or pouch lying directly under their hands. They are next told to begin to inhale so that the imaginary container fills with air and their hands rise gradually. The exercise, which will take about 2 seconds at the outset, will probably take 2½ or 3 seconds after further practice. (This first step can be eliminated after several weeks and replaced simply with the instruction to breathe in deeply.)

Group members are told to close their eyes and think, while holding their breath for about 2 seconds, "My body is calm." Then, as they slowly exhale, they should tell themselves, "My body is quiet." This last step takes about 4 seconds—that is, about as long as the first two steps combined.

The group members are warned to stop the practice if they experience any dizziness or light-headedness and to reduce the length of inhalation in subsequent sessions. As with all relaxation procedures, group members are advised that they may not immediately experience beneficial results but that persistent practice (10 to 12 times a day) will enable them to relax at will during stressful periods. It is helpful to have a model from a previous group tell of his or her experience with the procedure. The same steps are used to teach this relaxation procedure as the others mentioned above: modeling by the therapist, teaching the entire group, working in subgroups, and reinforcing for success. Usually the group therapist will have the group members organize a time and place for subsequent relaxation practices before the initial session ends.

Meditation

One can increase the attraction for adolescents of systematic relaxation by linking meditation to its yogic origins because of its counterculture implications. For the same reason, meditation has a particular allure for some youth. Because there is no consistent difference noted in the research literature between these two approaches for the treatment of anxiety and stress (Everly & Rosenfeld, 1981), it is possible to offer the group members their choice, provided that the skills of the group therapist are well developed in both areas.

Meditation is a "family of techniques which have in common a conscious attempt to focus attention in a nonanalytical way and an attempt not to dwell on discursive ruminating thought" (Shapiro, 1982, p. 268). Carrington (1978) developed a procedure called *clinically standardized meditation* (CSM), which is a Western version of more esoteric Eastern practices. He instructed the clients, while sitting in a relaxed position, to repeat a soothing sound such as the word *one* without a conscious effort or concentration.

CSM can, for the most part, be taught in ways similar to those used for relaxation training. It is more difficult to use ongoing group monitoring procedures in meditation training, and the buddy system does not appear to be useful. Meditation can be taught in the group because it is just as easy to demonstrate, explain, and teach it to many people as to one person; however, it does not take full advantage of the interactive nature of the treatment group because interaction disrupts the meditative process. Interaction can occur after the meditative process through discussion; however, discussion immediately after a meditative session is also disruptive.

Meditation is not suitable for all people. Shapiro (1982) warned that people with perfectionistic, self-critical, and goal-oriented approaches to problems, associated with the type A personality, might bring these attitudes to meditation. This is also true in my experience with deep muscle relaxation. These attitudes are likely to interfere with the meditative process and increase anxiety. Some youth experience adverse side effects when meditating, especially if it lasts too long. Effects noted by Shapiro (1982, p. 47) are increased anxiety, boredom, depression, restlessness, and decreased reality testing. Similar side effects have been found for neuromuscular relaxation. To reduce these potential side effects, Carrington (1978) recommended that youth initially meditate with and under the direct supervision of the therapist. After demonstrating the process, the group leader can monitor the members one at a time (as with the breathing exercises), while the others look on.

Summary

This chapter has described the place of cognitive and relaxation coping strategies in CBIGT. It has emphasized the group applications of such procedures as rational-emotive therapy, cognitive restructuring, self-instructional training, and self-management training. The use of group exercises is a major tool in educating the members in the basic concepts. It was noted that all of these procedures overlap. In addition, the use of the group in training youth in relaxation as an overt coping skill has been described. Similarly, breathing and meditation procedures are described as they can be used in groups of stressed and easily angered youth.

In the use of cognitive and relaxation coping skill training procedures, just as in the use of modeling and operant procedures, effectiveness is to a large degree dependent on the use of extragroup tasks. Although these tasks are discussed in every intervention chapter, their centrality in the approach warrants a separate chapter.

CHAPTER 11

Extragroup Tasks

Once cognitive, behavioral, and other strategies are taught in the group as ways of dealing with problems, the client must implement these strategies in the world outside the group. Almost no intervention is complete unless it is followed by an extragroup task, which is a set of behaviors the client agrees to perform under some given circumstances at some specified time in the future.

Many authors have noted the importance of homework assignments, or what are in this text called *tasks,* in treatment (e.g., Goldstein & Kanfer, 1979; Henggeler, Melton, & Smith, 1992; Reid, 1978), and several entire books on the subject have already been written (Maultsby, 1971; Shelton & Ackerman, 1974; Shelton & Levy, 1981) on the theory and principles of extratherapy tasks. The latter authors found the extratherapy component to be central to the therapeutic process and to be the component around which all other aspects of treatment are organized.

Purposes of Extragroup Tasks

One major purpose of the extragroup task in the therapeutic process is to encourage youth to try out in the real world what they have learned in the group. To a considerable extent, the performance of behavior
308

appears to be limited to the situation in which it is learned. It is therefore incumbent on the therapist and the client, with suggestions from the group, to create real-life situations in which new behaviors or cognitions may be practiced. Thus, the extragroup tasks are a major vehicle for the transfer of learning from a clinical to a real-world setting. (Additional methods of increasing the probability of generalization are discussed in Chapter 15.)

A second purpose is to provide the members with the occasion to try out new behaviors in the absence of the therapist and the pressure of the group's immediate feedback. It is also a method of helping youth to become the principal agents of their own change and to decrease their dependency on the group as the major source of help. However, the absence of any supervisor when the task is being performed reduces the control over the given client. Fortunately, strategies have been developed to increase the probability of compliance with tasks, even in the absence of the group therapist or adult monitor.

A third purpose is that cognitive extragroup tasks permit treatment access to private behaviors, such as sleeping disorders, sexual disturbances, or private thoughts, that would not be available in the group context.

A fourth purpose is that, in the absence of group and therapist support, youth are often pushed to develop self-control strategies to comply with the extragroup task requirements. A study by Bandura (1975) showed that self-control behaviors decreased when clients thought that treatment gains were due to support in the therapeutic setting rather than their own resources.

A fifth purpose of tasks is to take advantage of the unique characteristics of the small group in task design and group monitoring that the group members provide each other. Furthermore, because much monitoring is solely verbal report, it is our experience that group members are less likely to falsify the description of their experiences to a group of their peers than to an adult. They appear to display, at least in cohesive groups, some responsibility to their fellow members.

Finally, an important purpose of simulated extragroup tasks is to provide an opportunity for multiple trials beyond the limits of the group. Often, in the group, because of the limited time available in any one session, only a few role plays can be carried out for each person. Simulated extragroup tasks provide an opportunity for continued and repeated practice.

Types of Extragroup Tasks

There are several different kinds of extragroup tasks, each of which deserves separate examination: behavioral interactive tasks, cognitive tasks, behavioral noninteractive tasks, simulation tasks, and observational tasks. These categories may also be combined. The first three categories are related closely to the attainment of situational goals. The last two categories facilitate the eventual achievement of the first three categories of tasks and/or assessment to determine what appropriate tasks in the first three categories might be.

Behavioral Interactive Tasks

Behavioral interactive tasks are those in which youth interact with others outside the group in highly specific ways. In general, these tasks are observable social phenomena with limited boundaries in terms of situation, time, place, and action to be performed. An example of a behavioral interactive task is the following: "Next time I don't understand an assignment, I will ask my teacher for help in class or immediately after class."

Most tasks are either behavioral or a combination of behavioral and cognitive. Because there is a verbal component of the task, preparation for behavioral interactive extragroup tasks most often lends itself to group modeling and behavioral rehearsal procedures, described in detail in Chapter 9. If the target person does not know what he or she wants to say in the situation, "brainstorming" may be used to generate ideas (see Chapter 7). Often, reinforcement (social and/or material) is provided for successful completion of the task.

Cognitive Tasks

Cognitive tasks involve changing one's self-talk associated with stressful or anger-eliciting situations. A cognitive task was demonstrated by an adolescent just before having a job interview. She agreed to instruct herself covertly to relax, to tell herself to take one step at a time, and to remind herself that she really knew the job for which she was applying. Cognitive tasks may also involve shifting from self-put-downs or negative self-talk to more positive self-descriptions.

Louis constantly pointed out to family and friends that he was too dumb to do anything and that he was sure to fail if he tried. After training in recognizing when he made these statements and rehearsing alternative statements in the group, he decided that his extragroup task would be that whenever he was presented with a difficult task, he would state only that he thought it would be difficult but that he would certainly give it his best effort, and if he was well prepared, he would have a good chance of succeeding.

Finally, cognitive tasks may involve self-reinforcement after the completion of an interactive task or another cognitive task. After Louis described his success in carrying out the above extragroup task, he would praise himself subvocally for his success and aloud at the next group session. His extragroup task was not only to carry out the above assignment but to reinforce himself every time he succeeded in using an alternative statement to self-put-down statements. The cognitive procedures are explained in more detail in Chapter 10. Often cognitive and behavioral interactional tasks are combined. For example, in the job application situation described earlier, the adolescent, in addition to using self-enhancing statements, agreed to perform the actual behavioral task of carrying out the interview. In fact, most of the behavioral tasks described earlier could have been combined with a cognitive task as well. Because cognitive tasks are difficult to monitor, only self-report at subsequent meetings or contacts with buddies are used. With youth, we have found that concrete reinforcement of cognitive tasks or any other nonmonitorable task is not advisable. Because the material objects are often so highly valued, the therapist may end up reinforcing lying behavior. Praise alone, in our experience, does not seem to have this result as often, possibly because most youth know when the praise is not deserved.

Simulation Tasks

These are special cases of behavioral or cognitive interactive tasks. They differ only insofar as the behavior or cognition performed in the real world is a role-played interaction rather than an actual interaction with a significant other. Often there is not enough time during the sessions to permit repeated practice in the group. To provide this practice and to extend training time into the rest of the week, such simulated extragroup tasks are often given. Simulated extragroup tasks are only useful if situations to be role-played are clearly spelled out and if the time and place of the role play are stipulated, as in the example below. To ensure this, an abbreviated script is often developed and practiced in the group and given to the protagonist, who also acts as director of the role play and as provider of feedback. Usually this type of extragroup task is used in middle sessions and with individuals who have previously demonstrated role-play and feedback skills. It is a task especially useful for those adolescents who require a lot of preparation before trying out something new. It also provides practice in a self-help skill. An example of such an extragroup task is the following:

> After school on Wednesday at my house, I will role-play three times with Pete (a group member) the situation in which I continue to refuse to take a drink that is offered, even when the guys pressure me. I will explain once and use the "broken record" technique afterwards. No role play will be longer than 5 minutes, and Pete will be the "director" and provide me with feedback about what I do well and what I might consider doing differently. Pete and I will report back to the group what happened.

Behavioral Noninteractive Tasks

Behavioral noninteractive tasks are behaviors that do not directly involve the client in interaction with other persons, such as doing school homework, keeping a budget, writing down one's ideas for treatment goals, keeping an exercise program, learning a game to teach to the other group members, or reading an article. The major intervention procedures for preparing for this type of task are for the therapist or another group member to provide instruction on and examples of how to do the task and for the target person to practice carrying out the task in the group and to plan carefully when and how the task will be carried out.

These extragroup tasks often have concrete products. When shown to the group, these products may be praised by the group members or group worker. Examples of such products include budgets and data to support how each budget item was met, a written statement of treatment goals, a game being taught to other group members, and a report on a book or an article that was read. In addition to the report to the group, whenever possible, parents, teachers, and peers will also serve as monitors.

Often this task is combined with cognitive elements. For example, Sheila has the task of doing her homework once a day for 2 hours. When she is getting organized to do her homework, included in her task is that she will remind herself to take one step at a time and not rush. Among literate youth and adolescents, reading tasks have been frequently negotiated, especially readings from self-help books. These can be monitored by questions about the content at the next session.

Observational Tasks

In observational tasks, a special case of noninteractive tasks, the person observes his or her own behavior, cognitions, or emotions in specific situations and records them. In the early phase of therapy, observation is a frequent task to further the assessment process (see Chapter 4). Commonly used examples of such tasks are monitoring one's own level of anxiety in given situations on a scale of 1 to 10, counting the number of arguments with a sibling, keeping track of the amount of time spent in chore behavior, recording one's thoughts in stressful situations, and recording the frequency and intensity of anger responses, These are for the most part all emotional or cognitive responses. The person can also monitor his or her own behavior and keep track of behavior, cognitions, or emotions or specified stressful or anger-inducing events in an ongoing diary.

In the observation of others, the target person notes the behavior of potential models in the community when insufficient models exist in the group. A group of adolescent males who were extremely unassertive in their relationships with girls and were interested in improving their dating skills were assigned the task of identifying one person in their class who seemed to have these skills and to note those behaviors, both physical and verbal, to which the girls seemed to respond favorably. The group members were then to report their observations back to the group, who discussed the observations (see Chapter 9 for more details on this type of modeling).

The behavior of observing either oneself or others is not directly translated from a situational goal. Rather, it serves as assessment or mediates the achievement of such a goal. The person would count his or her anger responses as a means of eventually reducing their frequency.

Developing Extragroup Tasks

To integrate extragroup tasks into group therapy, the following steps must be taken: orienting the group members to what extragroup tasks are and their importance, helping the group members to design tasks in such a way that they are likely to be completed, and finally reducing the structure of these tasks as the group approaches termination.

Orienting the Group to Extragroup Tasks

All procedures used in CBIGT are preceded by an orientation by the therapist or by informed members or guests. To introduce the group to extragroup tasks, the therapist explains their purposes (see the above section "Purposes of Extragroup Tasks") to the group. The therapist should point out that extragroup tasks are not readily completed unless the guidelines and principles discussed in the next section are followed. Often, as part of that orientation, the procedure is demonstrated by the therapist or an experienced group member.

Increasing the Probability of Completion of Extragroup Tasks

The description of an extragroup task does not ensure clients' completion of that task in the real world. The following principles provide guidelines for defining a task in such a way that the likelihood of completion is increased (cf. those proposed by Shelton & Levy, 1981).

1. The task should include a description of the characteristics of the potential situations in which the desired behaviors should occur. The more detail the target person can bring to the description of the situation in which the task is to be performed, the more likely it is that he or she will complete the task because he or she knows when the task is to be done. (Some noninteractive tasks do not have a specific situational component, e.g., the task of exercising three times a week or practicing relaxation every day.)

2. The target person should describe the range of acceptable desired responses. There doesn't have to be (but there can be) just one response: "When I cannot understand my school homework, I will (a) ask my mom for help, (b) call Terry or Brad and ask him, or (c) ask the teacher." All of the responses should be described in moderately specific terms, as in the illustration above. Multiple possibilities increase the likelihood

of completion because they allow for situational flexibility. CBIGT therapists often will permit the target person to call their office, if all other options fail, as one more opportunity to succeed.

3. The target person should describe the time range in which the desired behavior should occur. Terms such as *next week, before the next session, either Wednesday or Thursday,* or *whenever the given stimulus event occurs* narrow the range somewhat. The target person should plan to complete the task with adequate time remaining before presenting his or her work to the group. In this way, the target person allows for last-minute exigencies.

4. The target person should select a task that is related to his or her treatment and situational goals. (It can be a preliminary step to achieving the goal.)

5. The target person should actively participate in the selection of the task; it should not merely be assigned.

6. The target person should formulate the task positively, that is, not (only) in terms of something that a person will not do. For example, rather than stating that "next week I will not hit anyone, even if they are trying to provoke me," he or she should formulate the task as "Next week, I will walk away from anybody who appears to try to hassle me."

7. The task should be of reasonable complexity and level of difficulty so that it can be achieved in the given time period. If the task is complex, it should be broken down into smaller subtasks over smaller units of time. The task should be sufficiently demanding that the target person must do something somewhat challenging to complete it, but not so difficult that it goes well beyond the range of his or her existing or trainable skills.

8. (optional) The target person should develop a tangible and reasonable reward for completing the task that is appropriate to the nature of the task. Natural reinforcers are preferable. Eventually, reinforcement should be faded. With some groups, contingency contracts may be negotiated. When the task involves cognitive activity, self-monitoring is the only form of monitoring that can be carried out. Only social reinforcement is provided for completion of the cognitive component because without verification, at least early in treatment, some youth might lie about what they had done.

9. The target person should write down the task and all its components and give the monitor or therapist a copy. Our experiences reveal that if a task is not written down, youth often forget or modify dramatically what they agreed to do.

10. The target person should select a task that is related to his or her treatment and situational goals. This principle is often forgotten in the name of getting a task quickly at the end of a given session. The group

therapist will review the goals with the target person before the actual task is designed.

11. The target person should be adequately prepared (or have the requisite skills) to perform the task. If he or she is not adequately prepared to carry out the task, he or she should be trained with such procedures as modeling, rehearsal, and self-instruction. Much of group therapy is invested in helping the members to prepare each other to carry out the tasks.

12. The target person should go public with the task as much as possible. At the very least, all the youth should describe their tasks to the other group members.

13. Where possible, the target person should develop some form of monitoring as to whether he or she is working on the task and whether he or she has completed it. If possible, the target person should initially work with a "buddy" from the group or the family. The buddy should be informed also as to what a successful performance is.

14. The target person should examine potential barriers to completing the tasks and make plans to deal with these.

The principles illustrated above are defined primarily for behavioral interactive tasks, but most of the principles apply to the other types of tasks as well.

Training Youth in Developing Extragroup Tasks

In training youth to develop extragroup tasks, the members are provided the principles mentioned above for increasing the probability that a homework assignment will be completed (see previous section). Then they are given Exercise 11.1.

Exercise 11.1. Increasing the Probability of Task Completion

Purpose: By the end of this exercise, each group member will demonstrate how to formulate an extragroup task in such a way as to optimize the probability of task completion.

Individual Task: Read the following cases. Using the principles discussed in the section "Increasing the Probability of Completion of Extragroup Tasks," point out what is wrong with the assignment, and suggest some alternative formulations and ways of approaching the development of an extragroup task that increase the likelihood that it will be completed. (You can make up information to fit your argument.)

1. Although the therapist hadn't discussed it earlier, last week he gave Charles, age 16, an assignment to keep track of the number of times he argued with his mom or dad. The family members rarely talked; they mostly yelled their orders, and Charles yelled back. His mom and dad had expressed a willingness to help in treatment. Both had admitted to being quick-tempered. The assignment was given after the second session, when the therapist believed he had a good relationship with Charles. The therapist had talked to the parents on the phone, with Charles's permission. (Criticize and correct.)

2. Alice, age 13, was always getting in trouble because she talked back to teachers. The principal had threatened her with suspension if she didn't stop talking back. She told the group that it was not her fault because the teachers picked on her. The worker pointed out that that didn't matter because she was going to be suspended and, if she was, would be unlikely to graduate because her grades were marginal already. The group therapist gave her the assignment of using self-control with her teachers. (Criticize and correct.)

Group Task: Compare your criticism of the assignments and corrections with that of a partner for 5 minutes, and then present to the entire group jointly agreed-on new assignments for Charles and Alice. The group will discuss how well each of the pairs has met the criteria for an effective homework assignment.

The next step in training is to ask a model—either a guest from a previous group or a more experienced member—to describe his or her homework assignment. In the following example, the therapist has requested that Gary, a longtime member, describe one of his extragroup tasks to the group. The group therapist has chosen as the first model someone who has experience with developing extragroup tasks.

Group Therapist: Gary has had a lot of experience doing extragroup tasks, so he is going to give you an example. Gary is going to be leaving soon, so we want to use his expertise before we lose him. Gary?

Gary: One of my goals was to get along better with my dad. In particular, I wanted to be able to talk to him in a calm manner about my plans for the future. My extragroup task that I designed together with my partner was to make an appointment with my dad to talk about my future and to talk to him for at least 10 minutes. We're usually in a fight after 2 minutes.

Group Therapist: Now look at this poster (with the principles of task formulation on it) and let me know which of the principles Gary adhered to and which ones he might have considered further. As usual, write your comments down on the handout right next to the principle. (The group therapist shows the group the above principles)

Art: Hey, man, it's specific, I think. All the things you say you would do are clear to me.

Roberto: It sounds like it's pretty important to you, Gary.

Gary: (nods) Yeah, it was.

Andy: I guess they didn't make you do it, then. It was your idea? You know what I mean?

Gary: Yeah, I know. It was my idea. I wanted to do it. And I did most of the work in formulating it.

Kareem: Hey, man, what were the barriers?

Gary: Yeah, the guys in the group talked about that. The big barrier was what would I do if my dad wouldn't talk. We seemed to agree that if I did my best, I would just tell him I really wanted him to hear me out, but that if he couldn't, I would just do it on my own.

Group Therapist: How were you prepared to carry out the task?

Gary: I role-played it in the group several times after watching someone else model it for me. I even practiced it on my own at home with my brother. I guess that was another extragroup task.

Noren: You went public with us. Who else did you go public with? And what about rewards?

Gary: I told my brother I was going to do it. The guys in the group and my brother thought it was a good idea. (pause) I guess the only reward I got was in the satisfaction I got from talking to my dad and the applause of the group when I told them I did it.

Once the youth have learned how to develop tasks, toward the end of every subsequent session pairs of youth work on developing an extragroup task with their partners. Each group member designs his or her own task; then the partners give each other feedback based on the criteria listed above. When all the pairs are finished, time permitting, each member describes his or her partner's task to the group for further feedback.

Tasks in the Later Phases of Group Therapy

To facilitate the further generalization of the behaviors and cognitions that are practiced in the tasks after the group has terminated, additional steps must be taken. Toward the end of treatment, planning for extragroup tasks becomes looser. Less preparation is required. Tasks become more complex and more general. Reinforcement, especially material reinforcement, is faded and eventually eliminated. The youth assign tasks to themselves for longer periods of time. Many extragroup tasks in the later phases of therapy are merely the continuation of tasks already started. In short-term groups, not all these principles can be adhered to because insufficient learning may have taken place. These and other principles of generalization are discussed in more detail in Chapter 15. The tasks are more clearly related to treatment goals than to situational goals.

The Place of Extragroup Tasks in the Treatment Process

It is possible to view the treatment process that leads to and follows the design of an extragroup task as consisting of the following steps: formulating the general area of concern, defining the treatment goals, generating the situational goals, designing a behavioral extragroup task, preparing to carry out the task, implementing the task, and monitoring the results of the task. Ideally, the process is continually repeated with increasingly difficult and complex tasks until the major goals are achieved. Thus, the task is central to the cognitive-behavioral approach.

Let us work through all these phases with an example. The *general area of concern* that Shad has described to the group is his poor relationship with his mother, a single parent. She wants to kick him out of the house because, as he admits, he rarely does anything she asks and frequently talks back to her. He is concerned because she bosses him around too much so that he can't help talking back. One *treatment goal* that the group has proposed and Shad has agreed to is that he will help his mom with household tasks when she asks as long as it is his fair share. This may contribute to improving his relationship with his mom.

One *situational goal* in particular that Shad has agreed with the group to propose to his mother is that next week, at least once a day, whether his mom asks or not, he will perform at least three home tasks: taking out the garbage, putting away the dishes after his mother has washed them, and making his bed in the morning. He thought that was fair, though he said he hated to have to do anything with dishes.

The *behavioral extragroup task* that he wrote down and shared with the group was "Next week, I will take out the garbage every day, make my bed, and put away the dishes after dinner. If I forget and my mom reminds me, I will do it without arguing. If I have plans, I will ask her for another time to do it or negotiate another task.

Preparation to carry out the task entails role-played modeling in the group with someone playing his mother reminding him to do one of the jobs and his rehearsing the same situations in the group. The *simulation extragroup task* is that before the next session he will role-play explaining what he is trying to do with Uriah, another group member, who will provide additional preparation.

Implementation of the behavioral task will take place during the following week at home when Shad responds to his mom by agreeing to do the chores she requests or initiating the chores himself.

Monitoring of the results of the task will be carried out by Shad's mother and by Shad. Shad's mother has agreed to send a note to the group about the results, and Shad will also report what happened to the group.

Summary

In this chapter, the place of extragroup tasks in the treatment process is spelled out. The types of extragroup tasks have been defined as behavioral interactive, cognitive, behavioral noninteractive, simulated, observational, and various combinations of most of these categories. The purposes of extragroup tasks are to encourage youth to try out in the real world what they have learned in the group, to provide the members with the occasion to try out new behaviors in the absence of the therapist and the pressure of the group's immediate feedback, and to provide an opportunity for multiple trials beyond the limits of the group. The principles of increasing the likelihood that a task will be completed have been listed and examples provided. The steps taken in developing extragroup tasks have been discussed. The steps in the task development process are formulating the general area of concern, defining the treatment goals, generating the situational goals, designing behavioral extragroup tasks, preparing to carry out the task, implementing the task, and monitoring the results of the task. Finally, the way in which the tasks are integrated into the treatment process has been presented and illustrated.

Some extragroup tasks are related to the clarification of strategies for assessing the client's social network, changing it, or using it differently. The following chapter is devoted to these issues.

CHAPTER 12

Assessing and
Enhancing Social Support

As Kamerman and Kahn (1982) pointed out, most interpersonal helping comes from informal networks of elements such as friends, family, and clergy. Group and other therapists typically refer to this extragroup interpersonal helping as a form of *social support,* a term given many definitions in the literature. Social support may be viewed as coping assistance (Thoits, 1986) that buffers the effect of stress. It can occur as an active process in which some party attempts to provide support for the other or as a passive process that flows out of a mutual relationship without any conscious plan.

Most youth in our groups have contact with persons, groups, or institutions who have the potential of enhancing their achievement of treatment goals or their sense of well-being. The same or other social groups or persons in a person's network may also support or encourage antisocial behaviors and create anxiety, depression, or intense anger in the individual. If youth learn the skills for evaluating their social network,

AUTHORS' NOTE: This chapter was coauthored by Sheldon D. Rose and Katherine P. Reardon.

they will formulate more realistic expectations of what a particular social network element can offer. They may also learn what social units to avoid and under what conditions. Feelings of rejection, abandonment, and anger in certain social environments can be diminished when youth become more realistic in their expectations and in their dealings with network elements that usually fail them. The social network existed before therapy and will exist long after therapy has ended. The client will have to learn to assess its potential, modify it if necessary, and develop a constructive mode for living with it.

Barth (1986) suggested that informal social networks, despite their therapeutic potential, are often ignored by professional helpers. Some of the reasons given by professionals for neglecting this important area are the difficulty in maintaining client confidentiality and in protecting the rights of the client to privacy. Nevertheless, if a vast therapeutic resource is ignored, the client's right to effective treatment may be compromised (Barth, 1986, p. 110).

Throughout this chapter, wherever possible, youth are trained to do what is necessary to assess and modify their own social network. Sometimes the group therapist or other therapy staff (e.g., a family therapist) may have to intervene directly. In the case of the client's being abused or neglected, it may be necessary to call this to the attention of the authorities. In the case of limited resources such as inadequate clothes, housing, or food, the therapist may have to act immediately. Sometimes the therapist will have to act directly with the school to get a client back into school or with an employer to get a client into a job when the client's actions are clearly inadequate.

Social Networks:
Social Support or Interference?

The existence of an extended social network does not always imply the ready availability of social support (Rook, 1992). Most social networks in all probability have the capacity both to enhance and to interfere with a client's progress toward the achievement of treatment goals and his or her sense of support. An example of a predominantly enhancing social network might include a cooperative brother, close family, a concerned grandparent, interested friends, a support group, a concerned teacher, a sports team, and an active church group, all of which could enhance treatment through affection and interest or provide the issues around which conflict takes place. A nagging friend, an oversolicitous mother, an antisocial peer group, and a highly competitive athletic team in a sport in which the youth does not excel could increase anxiety, anger, and resentment toward these central persons in the client's life. Where social resources are limited, absent, or predominantly detrimental, new elements may need to be added and developed before effective treatment can occur.

Social support is a complex process. It is clearly multidimensional, with different individuals and groups often providing different kinds of support. At least three major categories of support can be discerned: tangible, informational, and emotional. *Tangible support* refers to money, food, clothing, housing, recreational facilities, educational opportunities, and similar concrete sources of help. *Informational support* refers to the provision of information on such topics as health, job education, sex, and drugs. *Emotional support* refers to the support provided by a person who listens well, who is relatively nonjudgmental, and who shows interest in the client. The tangible and informational forms of support may be delivered in such a way as to enhance or work against emotional support. What is intended by the giver to be a gesture of support may be perceived by the receiver as nonsupportive (Antonucci & Israel, 1986; Barrera & Baca, 1990). Providing money to a teenager in such a way as to imply that he should be eternally grateful will in no way engender a feeling of emotional support. Giving a lecture on the side effects of alcohol to a friend who overindulges in alcohol consumption will only result in damage to the relationship rather than conveying a sense of emotional support.

In groups that focus on change, persons within the social network may actually sabotage the efforts of a given person to achieve certain types of change. Many friends and even family members established their relationships on the basis of the "old" client and how he or she behaved. Such friends may attempt to maintain the very behaviors the group has been helping the given participant to eliminate. Also problematic are persons or groups in the social network that remain passive and leave everything up to the treatment process. Various persons in the support network may be in conflict with each other. When support is offered by network members with demands for change, the client often perceives this demand as pressure or as detrimental to his or her best interests. The intention of this kind of support may be viewed by the client as interference or nagging. These are examples of failed support attempts in which the giver of help intends to be supportive but the recipient may perceive the attempt as harmful or upsetting (Schradle & Dougher, 1985).

One can experience conflicts in social ties that may complicate the helping process. Recipients of support in such relationships may experience feelings of resentment, indebtedness, or relative lack of capability (Barrera, 1981). Wortman and Lehman (1985) suggested that misguided helpers may lead the recipient to feel rejected or guilty. In discussing the use of social supports in the group, the negative potential as well as the helping potential of each social unit should also be examined.

The group setting is particularly suited to facilitating the assessment and use of social network elements. During group therapy, the group members and possibly their parents can be helped to look at and evaluate the elements of their social network and, where necessary, to make more effective use of it, expand it, enrich it, or otherwise modify it. The group lends itself to a sharing of a wealth of experiences with community and family extratherapy supports. The experiences will be varied both in degree of usefulness and in perception as to what is helpful. Group members also share with each other how to avoid the potential pitfalls that they have encountered without forsaking the support they might receive. Guided by the group, extratherapy experiences may prevent or at least minimize any negative side effects.

Assessing the Social Network

Before the systematic assessment of the group members' social networks, the group therapist should define the terms *social support, social network,* and *social element* and how these terms apply to the dynamic process of seeking and giving help. Therapists should also orient the group to social network assessment and treatment and discuss the potential problems associated with their use. The group therapist will draw on the members for examples of both effective uses and problems that occurred with use. The group therapist should also be prepared to provide examples and bring in models from previous groups. In the following example, the group therapist brought in a technical school student from the same neighborhood as the youth in the group. He stated,

When I was 15, I used to hang out with a group of guys who smoked dope and shoplifted to pay for the dope. We had a lot of fun. We got into trouble a few times, but usually they just yelled at us and then let us go. I liked doing it. It made you one of the guys. But meanwhile I was flunking out of school, and my parents were furious with me most of the time. The group was doing me in, and I enjoyed every minute of it. My mom tried to get me to sing in the church choir because I had a good voice. Just to get her off my back, I agreed to try it once. The youth minister spent a lot of time with me and got me involved in other group activities and with other kids as well. The guys made fun of me. But gradually I got more involved with the choir, I had less fights with my family, and I started doing better in school. I was also in a group like this. Most of the guys in the old gang eventually did time. None of them have decent jobs or got anywhere. I'm in technical school now, and I'm doing okay, though it's not easy. It's really surprising how much your group affects you.

The group therapist asked the members what kinds of groups the model belonged to and how each group affected him both advantageously and detrimentally. The therapist acknowledged that the gang certainly was fun and exciting. The youth discussed the kind of support the gang afforded him, and then they evaluated the pitfalls. The group then examined in the same way other social units, such as parents, the choir, the school group, and the therapy group, in terms of advantages and disadvantages of continued contact.

An additional way of beginning the assessment process is by having the group members write down all social units that they or others they know are in contact with. They may even include the environment of fictional characters. The group therapist gives them examples from his or her experience of a few categories of groups they might not readily think of themselves. This "brainstormed" list will provide a rich set of possibilities to consider when individuals begin to explore their own unique network.

Once the list of potential social supports has been developed, an effective strategy of obtaining individual information is having members interview each other in pairs. In this way, members play the roles of both interviewer and interviewee. By asking as well as answering questions, they become more sensitive to their own network. An overview of interviewing techniques is provided to them if they have not already been trained in interviewing skills.

Exercise 12.1. Assessing Social Networks

Purpose: By the end of this exercise, each participant will have (a) interviewed at least one person about his or her social network and (b) described and evaluated his or her own social network and shared it with the group.

Individual Task: The members are given an interview schedule (or, better yet, they develop a questionnaire themselves) with such questions as the following:

- Are there any special friends that you would turn to when you needed personal help?
- Which, if any, family members can you turn to in times of stress or trouble?
- Are there any teachers at school who might support you when you got into trouble or were upset?
- What kind of good times do you have with various family members, relatives, and friends?
- Are there any clubs, teams, or interest groups that have provided you with positive experiences? What people in these groups are you comfortable with?
- Are there any friends of your family or relatives or neighbors whom you are comfortable with and would want to have more contact with?
- Is there anyone at school (work) who listens to you or might like to do something with you?
- How critical are all of the above persons with you? How close do you feel with each of the persons mentioned above?
- In what ways are you helpful (unhelpful) to all of the above persons?
- In what ways are the above persons helpful (unhelpful) to you?
- How frequently do you have contact with each of the above persons?

Group Task: In pairs, group members interview each other as to frequency of contact and quality of their social network. The therapist visits each pair throughout the interviewing process, offering guidance as needed. The interviewers are encouraged to probe further and to get recent examples. Once the two interviews are finished, each person is requested to include in the list at least one new idea he or she got from his or her partner. Then, if time permits, each interviewer presents the social network of his or her interviewee to the group.

To evaluate the specific components of the social network in terms of what kind of support youth are receiving and the degree to which they are receiving support and/or interference from the various units of their social network, youth can also fill in and share with each other the form shown in Table 12.1.

The youth are asked to fill in the form, listing all of the people, groups, clubs, or social contacts they have had within the last 3 months or expect to have in the immediate future. (Other forms have been used, such as Barth, 1986, p. 112, and Tracy & Whittaker, 1990.) The youth then are asked to indicate the degree to which these resources could help them to work on the problems addressed in this group or to support them in their own efforts. Because some network elements can also interfere with youth treatment goals, participants should also indicate the degree to which each component is detrimental to the achievement of treatment goals (circling the appropriate number on the form; the higher the number, the higher the degree). Examples of interference are the parent who is constantly criticizing the client and the teacher who is perceived as frequently putting down the client. The members are told that the same people or groups can be both supportive and interfering. They are asked to designate whether the type of support is tangible (T), informational (I), or emotional (E). Finally, they are asked to indicate the circumstances under which the network element provides support. The therapist might draw on the form of a more experienced group member as a model to help the others complete the form (e.g., see Table 12.2).

After the forms are completed, the youth share them with the group. As they read or hear the responses of others, they are told that they should feel free to add to or modify in other ways their own list. They should then discuss which parts of their social network they might turn to in time of need and identify the specific need. Finally, they should discuss which parts of their networks they would clearly avoid and why. The members

TABLE 12.1 Social Support Survey

Name of Member _____ Date _____

Name of Person/ Group	How Supportive[a]	How Interfering[b]	What Kind of Support (T, I, E)[c]	Under What Conditions
	1.2.3.4.5.6.7	1.2.3.4.5.6.7		

a. On a scale of 1 to 7 (1 = least supportive, 7 = most supportive).
b. On a scale of 1 to 7 (1 = least interfering, 7 = most interfering).
c. T = tangible, I = informational, E = emotional.

often suggest to each other sources of support. The purpose of this analysis is to sensitize youth to the various attributes of their social network and to prepare them to expand or delimit the use of the various elements.

In assessment, the therapy group must also be considered as one temporary source of social support and be evaluated by the members in

TABLE 12.2 Social Support Survey for Ralph

Name of Member ____Ralph_____ Date _____9-9_____

Name of Person/ Group	How Supportive[a]	How Interfering[b]	What Kind of Support (T, I, E)[c]	Under What Conditions
Mom	5	5	E	When I'm really down, when I get into trouble
Dillon, Tyrone, Luke (hangout buddies)	7	3	E	When hanging out, getting into trouble, horsing around with the girls
Uncle Jack	7	1	T, I, E	Whenever I have girl trouble
Gym coach at school	3	7	I, E	When I have problems or trouble at school
Therapy group	4	4	I, E	Whatever happens

a. On a scale of 1 to 7 (1 = least supportive, 7 = most supportive).
b. On a scale of 1 to 7 (1 = least interfering, 7 = most interfering).
c. T = tangible, I = informational, E = emotional.

the same way as other sources. The therapy group provides a protected forum for youth to share their concerns without fear of rejection or criticism. It gives all members the opportunity to attend to the needs of others and to demonstrate to themselves their own effectiveness as helpers. The group is also the place where youth can share their experiences of success as well as difficulties in their extragroup activities without fear of being criticized. The group works only if the therapist structures it with rules, models, and limits. Moreover, when treatment ends, the support that the group lends and the opportunity to support one's peers are eliminated. With this ending in mind, the group therapist must help the group members gradually to replace the therapy group with other, individualized sources of support.

Enhancing and Enriching
the Social Network

Once the group and the participants have assessed the scope of each member's social support network, a plan can be developed to enhance the social network by either adding new elements to the network that might give the person more support or eliminating or working with those that hinder their efforts. Usually the therapist or the model will demonstrate a plan for adjusting his or her network and provide the rationale for that adjustment. The youth in pairs develop their own plan. The group therapist serves as consultant in this activity. Then each person reads his or her plan to the group, who evaluate it, reinforce elements of it, and make some suggestions for alternative arrangements.

Perry, age 14, had only a few items on his social network: his mother, who was single and worked full-time; his older brother, who was in the military and rarely home; and his homeroom teacher at school, who was too busy to spend much time with him. His plan was to take drum lessons and get into the school band, where he would get free lessons. Everyone liked the band instructor, who had encouraged him to get involved in the band. All the group members thought that the band was a good idea. Larry said that his brother, Mac, was a drummer and that he would ask him to give Perry some help in learning to read music. Lon suggested that he make use of the free tickets to band concerts available to residents in the day treatment center. Larry said that a lot of the guys in the band were nerds but that some of them were real cool. Some of the older guys had gigs and made a little money. But it was a little early to think of that. Anyway, he would meet guys with musical interests like his, Lon added. Xavier suggested that even if his mom was busy, she'd probably like it if Perry would seek her out sometimes and try to talk to her about what was bothering him. Perry said he liked all the ideas, although he thought it would be difficult to approach his mom now because she had so many problems of her own.

Usually, in developing a plan, extragroup tasks are designed by the group for each individual or for the group as whole. Some extragroup tasks that invigorate the use or the expansion of one's social network are taking field trips to the YMCA to explore the different types of recreational groups available, inviting a speaker from a self-help group relevant to the youth to address the group (e.g., Alcoholics Anonymous), and developing short-term agreements to communicate with new friends or family members. Practicing in the group how to approach individuals associated with these new networks, cognitive restructuring of beliefs that interfere with making further or more positive contacts with some of the significant people in the network, and careful monitoring by another group member promote more effective use and an expansion of one's social network. Often approaching the new networks in pairs provides mutual support. These strategies are discussed elsewhere in relation to other interpersonal targets. In the above example, Perry decided that his task would be to "talk tomorrow to the band director and ask him for information, find out where he could get lessons and for how much, get a book out of the library on drumming, and once during the week at breakfast talk to Mom about the group."

Once a plan is made, each group member, if possible, will monitor the behavior of a partner or even help in facilitating the use of the social contacts in the network. If partner monitoring is not possible, the group member will monitor his or her own activities. The monitors will report back to the group each week as to the progress of their partners, or, in the case of self-monitoring, each person will report back him- or herself.

In the example below, Ralph, age 16, had been sent to Townsville House, a residential treatment center, because of a history of thefts and assault. He was interviewed by Willy. Willy and Ralph filled out the form as shown in Table 12.2.

When Ralph discussed the results of his form with the group, he came to the conclusion that he needed to avoid his "hangout" friends when he got home. The group discussed strategies he could use to avoid them, one of which was to cultivate other people. His cousin, Don, was someone he could turn to for help. His coach in the gym class was another person who could be helpful, although sometimes Ralph felt that the coach gave him unneeded advice. As part of his treatment plan, he decided to get active again in the soccer club at the Y. He had a good friend, Mike, who had never been in trouble with the police and whom he would approach to go with him. He also felt that he could now talk to his mom. He told the group that he wanted to be able to talk to his mom but that he was afraid she would only criticize or nag him. She had been really angry when he was arrested and sent to Townsville and still was upset with him. The members suggested that he prepare for talking with his mother in the group by having the members model and himself rehearse how he would approach her. He also practiced how to deal with her nagging and her criticism without getting angry. Each member of the group reviewed his chart with the group, and in subgroups each developed a similar plan to make better use of his social network. Because Ralph was the first to examine his social network, the therapist enthusiastically complimented him and asked the rest to identify in Ralph's example what they could borrow to include in their own plan.

In the assessment and planning for enhancing the social network, a wide variety of opportunities for playing the teaching or therapist role are provided (as in the above examples): The youth interview each other, brainstorm ideas from which the target person can choose, and monitor each other's performance. These techniques also ensure wide participation and a plethora of opportunities for observing models. Another way of putting youth in teaching or helping roles is through voluntary community service involvement.

Involvement in Community Service Activities

One set of activities with the potential of providing unique support to youth are those services that rely on volunteers from the community to help others. Examples of such projects developed and carried out by the youth and staff of a residential treatment center (Moreau Center, Boysville of Michigan) were the following:

- Youth read to, sang with, and served food to senior citizens at a convalescent center.
- Youth shoveled snow and raked leaves for homes of the elderly in the neighborhood.
- Youth built ramps for wheelchair-bound individuals in the community.
- Youth cleaned up local riverbanks (removing trash, old tires, etc.).
- Youth helped set up props, tables, and chairs for a local charitable group fund-raiser.
- Youth visited the home of another youth in placement and helped with major cleaning and repairs.
- Youth helped with a horseback riding project for local developmentally disabled children.
- Youth earned money (car wash, bake sale, etc.) to raise money for helping a family in need (food baskets, emergency repairs, a new water heater).
- Youth unloaded trucks and put together food packages at local emergency food bank.
- Youth did setup and cleanup jobs for local charitable and service organizations that supported the institution (Knights of Columbus, United Way).
- Youth cleaned local churches.
- Youth helped with providing goods to local disaster victims.
- Youth "adopted a family," low-income senior citizens, and invited them to Boysville for dinner.
- Youth worked at a soup kitchen.

Of course, not all troubled youth are ready for such responsibilities, especially if not supervised. On the other hand, if adequate supervision is available, such an event may be a source of great personal satisfaction and an increased sense of self-efficacy. Yalom (1985, pp. 13-15) described altruism as one of the curative factors in groups. These community projects go beyond the boundaries of the group to provide that altruistic experience and a great deal of prosocial reinforcement of their efforts. For youth who have been largely concerned with meeting their own needs as quickly as possible, a community project represents an opportunity to develop a new value system.

Community service activities have the advantage over other forms of social supports in that, in serving others, youth are involved directly in the helping process in the role of helper rather than as the permanent targets of guidance and other intervention. Preparation for assisting others in these activities is presented not as therapy but as staff training or supervision. The youth are treated as independently functioning helping associates. In the helping role, from our observations, they gain a great deal of self-respect. They demonstrate to others and to themselves that they can do something prosocial. They discover a new source of reinforcement.

Although opportunities for community service may be abundant, successful involvement is dependent on a number of factors. First, the stage of development of the group must be taken into consideration. Only after the youth have had some experience with each other in the group and have developed a working relationship with the group therapist are they willing to try out community service projects.

Second, like most novel ideas, community service is more likely to be acceptable if the ideas come from the youth themselves or a peer model. The group therapist may ask if anyone has participated in such projects and have them tell the group about their experience. If any interest is shown, the therapist may have the group develop a list of potential projects. The therapist may also invite peers who have participated in such projects to tell of their experiences if youth have limited experience in this area. Project representatives or even participants might come to a session and tell about their needs. The group members can assume the responsibility of calling various agencies to discover whether they are interested in a group of volunteers.

Third, success is dependent on whether the youth have adequate interpersonal skills and other technical skills required by their given task or can be readily trained in the skills the project requires. For example, a group of residential youth volunteered to be tutors for younger children at a nearby school. Initially, they had not the slightest idea how the material was to be presented and how they could keep the younger children interested. Only after some training by a teacher from the school in how to present material and how to set limits did the group members feel competent and successful about what they were doing. The group sessions in part were devoted to this training. Therapy gave way to teacher training, which was a more satisfying and therapeutic role.

Fourth, care must be taken in handling the administrative details of organizing a project. Members must be on time, telephone calls must be made, and careful records must be kept of the activities. If money is involved, this must be accounted for. These skills are particularly important because they are skills that youth are required to perform in the outside world to function well in a job or in school. Failure to demonstrate these skills in the project at the appropriate moment may result in failure of the project. Of course, these organizational details can be carried out by the therapist, which will increase the likelihood of success, but the learning potential of the project is enhanced if the youth carry out these functions themselves with minimum supervision.

It is helpful if the sponsoring agency develops a resource list of potential projects with some notes as to each of the community service projects that has worked and any problems associated with a given service. In addition, the level of difficulty and the specific skills required should be attached to service. Group projects are easier to supervise and to organize than individual projects.

Finally, attention should be given to the race, ethnic background, and gender of the youth in selecting projects. Leaders of the projects where the youth are volunteering should be represented by the race, gender, and ethnicity of the youth. If the project involves helping others, they too should be representative of the youth in the group. If helping others is always associated with whites helping African Americans or other ethnic groups, one more unfortunate stereotype is reaffirmed.

Work Experiences

The workplace can be a major source of social support. Success in the real world depends to a large degree on ability to get and keep a job. Many troubled youth have had an erratic employment history. If they get a job, they soon quit or are fired. The therapy group can be a place where the group members are trained in job-hunting and job-maintaining skills in addition to the nitty-gritty skills of coming to work on time, taking only allowable breaks, dressing as the job requires, and following instructions from supervisors. Many of the situations discussed in the modeling chapter refer to stressful or frustrating experiences in the workplace. Modeling is used to teach group members what they could do or say to cope with the multitude of demands and to survive. Youth can be taught how to approach other employees to make new friends and develop other prosocial networks.

Where everyone has a job, the therapy experience can take the form of group supervision in which members bring in the day-to-day real problems of the workplace and share them with the group. The group, after interviewing the target person, may problem-solve how the person might do better. If the person agrees, he or she may be trained in the new skills. Although in some residential settings employed youth are put into a special-interest group that meets on a regular basis, it seems to us that even those without jobs can profit from hearing about the experiences of the employed as they prepared for their jobs. After all, failure in the workplace often is followed by failure in other aspects of community life.

Summary

Focusing solely on the psychological change of the client is usually not sufficient to bring about stable change. The use of prosocial supports outside the therapy group is essential to maintain changes once they are achieved. To use social supports, the group therapist must first help youth to evaluate the components of their individual social network. Later, the group members help each other to add to or modify the existing network. The group therapists or other treatment staff may also directly attempt to facilitate change in the social network where youth cannot do it on their own. Each member of the group develops a plan for enhancing or enriching his or her social network. One particularly useful social support activity may be found in community service projects. These not only provide social support but help the person carry out a series of prosocial behaviors and provide an opportunity for positive recognition, increased self-efficacy, and getting out of the role of patient. Of equal importance is helping youth to get started in and maintain actual work experiences. If youth can be helped to find such jobs, the group may serve to supervise the social components of their jobs and to train members in new skills for dealing with the demands of the workplace.

CHAPTER 13

Integrating Socio-Recreational
Activities Into Therapy

Billy (new resident):   Is that all you do in this group, talk about problems?

Byron (old resident):   Sure, man, we got to talk about what gets us into trouble and situations that are hard for us to deal with. But sometimes we have a good time doing it.

Duane (old resident):   Yeah, we even play all kinds of games, like Scrabble, charades, Monopoly, and computer games. We played soccer lotsa times, but only for a few minutes each time. And we made up our own board game, too. Get what I mean?

Billy: No way, man, not for me. I'll never have any fun doing that. That's kid stuff.

Freddie (old resident):   We put on plays, and we got to videotape one and show it to the other units. It was about kids just like us.

Melvin (old resident):   Don't forget the trip we made to the TV studio. They showed us how the pros do it. And what about that basketball dude from the U. who was trying to show us how to dunk?

Billy: I guess it could be a little fun. But they won't get me to talk that way.

Byron: Well, I guess talk is a big part of it. Most of the fun stuff we do
is at the end of the work part of the meeting. If we do the work,
we get to play. Sometimes the work part is fun, too, like when we
role-played in a circle what we were going to say to a kid who got
in our face.

In the above example, the old residents are orienting Billy, a new
resident, about what happens in the group besides working on problems.
But they do not let him forget that the main purpose of the group is to
learn to cope more effectively with the real world. Homework, modeling,
rehearsal, feedback, exercises, problem solving, relaxation training, and
cognitive restructuring may eventually be fun or at least interesting to
the youth in their own right. But in the beginning, such activities are
often insufficient to motivate consistent interest or even regular attendance in community groups. For this reason, such group activities as
games, sports, dramatics, storytelling, crafts, and photography are incorporated into every session, especially the initial sessions. Initially, only
the last 10 minutes of every session are devoted to socio-recreational
activities. As the group progresses, activities are encouraged that afford
practice in the target behaviors. Wherever possible, activities are selected, such as the social skill board game, in which recreational activities
are fully integrated with treatment activities. Extragroup activities such
as trips may also be planned for as part of the group activities.

The purpose of these activities is multiple. First, as mentioned above,
these activities are used to increase the attraction of the group in the early
phase of therapy. Second, they create a variety of natural problematic or
stressful situations in which the members can reveal or practice their
coping skills. Choosing roles, selecting activities, losing a game, failing
to complete a task, being pressured by one's peers, and making or
receiving demands to cooperate or requests to clean up or put away
equipment are all situations that may require new behavior, such as
following instructions from an adult, assertiveness or other social skills,
self-control, anger management, interviewing, negotiation, problem solving, organizational skills, and decision-making skills. Third, the group
therapist also uses these recreational-interactive situations to monitor the
use of newly learned skills and coach their use in the ongoing group
process. These group activities provide a rich opportunity for staff to
directly observe youth interacting with one another under various stress

levels that duplicate the conditions of the extragroup world. The activities can become a major source of observed behavioral data for assessment and evaluation. Fourth, group activities provide a variety of new roles, including leadership roles, for members to perform. These roles can be coached during the group process and rehearsed either as extragroup tasks or in the therapy part of a group meeting. Group activities may be one of the few contexts in which many of our clients have the opportunity to be a "helper of others," a "star" player in a given sport, a "coach," a referee in a sports event, a teacher of a new activity, or some other attractive social role.

A shared goal often worked toward in groups that are ethnically homogeneous is building ethnic pride. One way of building ethnic pride in groups in which one or more persons are of different ethnic background from the majority is by using high-status models of the same ethnicity as therapists, guests, or even members. When the group is ethnically heterogeneous, it is also useful for each ethnic group to show some positive feature of their culture. The timing is a consideration. It is important to hold some "show and tell" when the members are comfortable with each other and can talk about their similarities and differences. Ethnic stories can be told, ethnic art can be displayed, ethnic food can be cooked and eaten, ethnic music can be listened to, and ethnic games can be played. One or more of these activities can be organized by the members and presented in the institution or agency for the entire membership or for parents and families of the participants. This is more commonly done in institutional groups and even then across the entire agency. But this approach would be equally effective in community groups. Many therapists prefer to incorporate one of these activities each week into the ongoing activities of the group without making it a massive organization. No matter how they are structured, such activities, if well done and well organized, may contribute to self-respect and respect of others of the ethnic minorities.

The purpose of this chapter is to demonstrate the uses of a wide variety of socio-recreational activities and how these are incorporated into the behavioral and cognitive change strategies already described. Wherever possible, we have shared our experiences and noted differences with male and female adolescents, with older and younger adolescents and preadolescents, and with diverse racial and ethnic groups. In general, the differences suggested are based on our experience rather than on any research on the topic.

Types of Program Activities

In this section, we identify the major categories of group activities commonly used in group therapy and some of the conditions under which they can best be implemented. Vinter (1985b) proposed a system for analyzing the components of activities. These include the degree and range of rules that govern conduct, the form and agent of controls, how much physical movement the activity permits, how much competence each activity requires, the degree of interaction the activity permits, and the rewards attached to the activity. Although we have not used the same concepts, where applicable, we have referred to several of these dimensions as we analyze the following activities. These include games (major sports, action, paper/pencil, card, board, social skill), handicrafts and drawing, charades and dramatics, simulated classroom activities, musical activities, photography, storytelling, and field trips.

Games

Games provide an opportunity for such behaviors to occur (and be reinforced) as taking turns, giving feedback, following rules, and learning how to lose and how to win. Most games are highly prescriptive (i.e, governed by many rules), but the control is lodged in the rules rather than in the group therapist. The game format is especially useful with disruptive and resistant adolescents. Although they rarely show initial interest in the work of the group, these adolescents are often swept up in an exciting game, especially if it is of their own choosing. As Cartledge and Milburn (1981) pointed out, "Games provide an opportunity for the youth to learn the consequences of his actions without having to suffer them. In a game mistakes and exposure of ignorance are more tolerated. Games usually encourage laughing and joking, which can be instrumental in relieving anxiety and facilitating involvement" (p. 100).

One can identify a number of categories of games that, though somewhat overlapping, facilitate planning and decision making in the selection of game activities. First on this list are the major sports, such as baseball, basketball, football, and soccer. Second are group action games such as dodgeball or Capture the Flag. Third are paper-and-pencil games such as tic-tac-toe and Hangman, which can be played in a highly confined place with nothing more than a piece of paper and a pencil. Fourth are card games. Fifth are cooperative games in which the rewards do not come from winning at the cost of someone else's losing. Sixth are computer games. In the following subsections, we discuss each of the above game categories in more detail in terms of how each contributes to the therapeutic process or the achievement of treatment goals.

Major Athletic Sports

Many of the youth in our groups have had little success in the major sports. When these games are played in school, many of our clients are customarily assigned to unimportant roles requiring minimal competencies. When they do get a turn because it cannot be avoided, they are often greeted with derogatory remarks about their lack of skill. Nevertheless, the members often initially prefer these games because it is what they know and these games have high peer status. Because of the lack of minimal competencies among many of the youth and because of the extensive time these sports require, they are rarely incorporated into group therapy programs. One advantage of playing these types of games if skill training is carried out is that improvement in these skills has the potential of raising the status of youth with their peer group. Unfortunately, in the short time available in group therapy, there is little likelihood that a given client will make major inroads into skill development. Soccer and basketball appear to be more useful sports than softball in that they permit broader participation, encourage greater cooperation through extensive passing, and require more physical movement. Moreover, a minimal level of competency can be quickly acquired. It is also possible to have a short game of 10 to 15 minutes without the players' becoming angry or upset. Finally, it is possible to modify the rewards by giving points for good passes, effective dribbling, keeping one's position, and good tries. Despite their therapeutic potential, because there are so many problems with major sports and so little time to resolve most of them, group therapists tend to make far greater use of other active games. As mentioned in Chapter 9, a powerful reinforcer can be a volunteer athlete from the local university or college, especially in work with African Americans. The youth ideally would have to earn the right to get lessons from these models.

So these skills can be upgraded, special sessions can be organized that focus solely on instruction in the sports activity. Many members are willing to come an extra session per week because they find such activities useful. A sports education specialist is best qualified to lead such groups, which are not run as group therapy. Such groups provide an opportunity for practicing alternative behaviors to anger and aggression. Because of the time they demand, most often such major sports activities are used in residential treatment programs and coordinated with the therapy program.

Other Active Games

Within the framework of group therapy, it is far easier to squeeze games such as Capture the Flag or dodgeball into the 10 to 15 minutes allotted to activities than softball or soccer. Moreover, the minimal level of competence required to play these games is far lower than in the major sports. Furthermore, the levels of participation are usually more intense and more broadly distributed. As a result, far more frequent reinforcement is possible. The games we have more commonly used and the reasons for using them are described in detail below.

One of the most commonly used games with preadolescents of both genders is Capture the Flag. In this game, two teams with the same number of persons are selected (by the group therapist), and each person on each team is given a number. The group therapist stands between the teams and holds a handkerchief aloft. As he or she calls one or more numbers, he or she drops the handkerchief. The youth with the assigned numbers run up to the handkerchief. The object is to grab the handkerchief and get back to one's own side before being tagged by one's opposite number. A point is given for getting back to a side safely or tagging the opponent with the flag.

Blob (Fluegelman, 1976) is a "new" game that is attractive to preadolescents and adolescents alike and to both genders, although girls take to it more quickly than boys. It starts out like tag, except that the first and all subsequent persons tagged are added on to the person who is "it," forming a "blob." The game is continued until all the members are caught and become a part of the "blob." The time of the game can be limited by restricting the area in which the game takes place. Other tag games, such as Hopping Tag, Three-Legged Tag, and Blindfold Tag, are particularly popular with preadolescents as well.

Indoor track meets consist of the javelin throw (in which a straw is hurled), the discus (a paper plate), and the low jump, which involves crawling under a stick while holding onto a partner who must also get under the stick. The stick is lowered at each successive turn. Another track event is the slow race, which requires consistent forward motion but in which the last person to cover 3 feet wins. In such activities, the poorly coordinated have as much chance to win as the more athletically inclined. These track events can be used by all age and gender groups, although initiating them with adolescent males is likely to be more difficult than with others in the beginning.

As separate activities or as part of the indoor track meet, relays are commonly used in group meetings. Most relays take up very little time and can be readily squeezed into a busy group schedule. Often, more than one can be played at any one group meeting. In most relays, the basic idea is to divide the group into two or more teams with the same number. Each team lines up at a common point. At a given signal, the first person in line on each team begins to carry out a designated activity while progressing to and returning from a designated destination. When the first person on the team returns, he or she tags the second team member, who repeats the activity. A team wins when all the team members have performed the given activity and returned to the team. The most common relays we have used in group therapy sessions are the following:

- *The 40-Yard Swim.* Each team is given a tablespoon of water. The object is to walk to the destination and back without spilling the water. If it spills, the tablespoon is refilled, and the person starts over.

- *Barefoot Marbles.* Two marbles are placed in front of each team. The first player begins by picking up the marbles in his or her bare feet and running to the destination and back without dropping them. If one is dropped, it must be picked up again before the race resumes.

- *Footsie Race.* Each team has a long piece of rope in front of it. Each player is blindfolded and must feel his or her way along the rope until the destination is reached and then return to the team.

- *Shoe Relay.* The shoes for each team are put in a pile across the room. The first person on each team runs across the room and finds his or her shoes, puts them on, runs back, and tags the next person, who does the same.

- *Crab Relay.* Each person leans back on hands and feet and walks like a crab.

- *Balloon Relay.* There are many variations to this relay. One can pass the balloon over one's shoulder to the next person on the team, who passes it under the legs to the next person. The first person can run to a chair and sit on a balloon until it breaks and then run back. The first person can bat the balloon until it hits the wall opposite the team and then bat it back until it is caught by the next team member.

- *Potato Carry Relay.* The first person carries the potato (or a balloon) in a spoon to the destination and back to the next person without dropping it.

Most often, younger adolescents of both genders are interested in these activities.

Cooperative Games

Most of the above games are competitive. It is possible to use games that are designed to be cooperatively played or to make cooperative games out of competitive games by rule changes. The advantages of cooperative games are that they tend to increase group cohesion, reduce interpersonal hostility, and increase cooperative behavior. Because of the norms of most male adolescents, they tend initially to be less popular than competitive games, but once they are played, that resistance seems to disappear. With females, there is greater initial interest. There is a long history of research demonstrating the positive side effects of cooperative games.

CBIGT therapists have used a number of cooperative games in therapy groups. Many of them involve changing the rules of standard games. In One-Basket Basketball, the object is to get everyone to make one basket but not more. After a member gets his or her basket, the member is no longer permitted to shoot but must dribble or pass it off to another group member. One can play without teams, and no body contact is permitted. A similar game has been developed for softball. In this game, there are no teams. Everyone bats until he or she gets a hit. Then the member goes out in the field, and all positions are rotated among the members.

Chinese checkers can be modified to become a cooperative game by making the object the achievement of a tie in getting the marbles to the opposite side. That is, the first person finishes first; on the next move, the second person finishes; and so forth until all players have finished. Everyone seems to help everyone else in this game.

For the reasons mentioned above, cooperative games are usually preferable to competitive ones. However, there are reasons to use competitive games as well. First, achieving skills in competitive games may enhance the client's status at school, where such games are often played. Second, because losing and winning are important parts of these school activities, youth have to learn to deal with both. The group provides a protective setting for these behaviors to occur and an opportunity for youth to receive immediate feedback as to how well they managed these behaviors. The degree of competitiveness and the unfortunate side effects can be reduced by the emphasis the group therapist places on the competition. If rewards are for cooperative plays within the game rather than on winning, the side effects seem to be reduced. Moreover, most activities other than games are noncompetitive. A reliance on these as well as on games tends to deemphasize competition.

Social Skill Board Games

Most board games are extremely popular with youth. Drawing on that interest, CBIGT therapists have made a great deal of use of board games designed to provide practice in or models of specific social skills within the context of a game. It is a way of providing variety to the typical steps of the modeling, rehearsal, coaching, and group feedback routine. There are many variations of social skill games, several of which are discussed in detail below. It is possible to select existing games or to design one's own game, often with the help of the group.

To evaluate, select, or design a social skill game, one should consider the following elements suggested by Heitzmann (1974), which are common to most social skill board games: (a) an aspect of chance, such as can be obtained by throwing dice, drawing a card, or spinning a wheel; (b) elements of surprise or novelty; (c) inherent fun and humor; (d) opportunity for broad participation (everyone has a turn, and everyone's turn is equal); (e) a variety of possible activities; (f) well-defined limits and rules; (g) clearly understood goals as to what is to be learned; and (h) opportunities for immediate and frequent feedback. Figure 13.1 shows a simple format of a social skills board game that has been commonly used with male and female adolescents. It is possible to simplify it for younger adolescents and children or to make it more complicated and dramatic for older adolescents. Let us examine the elements in the game.

There are basically five different kinds of squares. The most important are the role-play squares, which instruct a member to pick a role-play card; in response to this card, the member draws a card from a pile labeled "Role Plays." A list of such role plays is developed for each group. These role-play lists can be taken from any of the role-play tests referred to in Chapter 5.

Simpler instructions are required for preadolescents. The group therapist will provide the additional instructions as required. For youth who

(text continued on page 350)

Start here. If you land here, throw dice again.	Describe your social network and evaluate it. Go to next square if you have done this already.	Pick a role-play card and play the role of the target person. Get group feedback.	Design a home task with the help of neighbor. Group gives feedback.	Do analysis of a situation in which you are dissatisfied with the response.	Pick a problem-solving card and solve systematically with the group.
Brainstorm all possible feeling words with group. Write and summarize.					Pick 2 self-defeating statements and correct them. Group gives feedback.
Pick 2 self-defeating statements and correct them. Group gives feedback.	PUT PROBLEM-SOLVING CARDS HERE				Instruct the group in a short form of relaxation (3 minutes). Group gives feedback.
Pick a problem-solving card and solve problem systematically with the group.	PUT GAME CARDS HERE				Pick a role-play card and play the role of the target person. Get group feedback.
Define a treatment goal and strategies for achieving it. Group gives feedback.	PUT SELF-DEFEATING STATEMENTS HERE				Pick a stress card and tell how you would handle it. Group gives feedback.
Pick a stress card and describe how you would handle it. Group gives feedback.	PUT ROLE-PLAY CARDS HERE				Describe your social network and evaluate it. Go to next square if you have done this already.
Analyze a situation that caused you stress or anger. Get group feedback.	PUT STRESS CARDS HERE				Analyze a situation that caused you stress or anger. Get group feedback.
Define a situational goal and brainstorm strategies for achieving it.	Pick a role-play card and play the role of the target person. Group gives feedback.	Pick 2 self-defeating statements and correct them. Group gives feedback.	Pick a problem-solving card and solve systematically with the group.	Design a relevant home task with help of group.	Pick a game card and play 2 minutes.

Figure 13.1. A Cognitive-Behavioral Board Game

GAME CARDS

Play Hangman for 2 minutes. You choose the word. The others will guess the letter. If a game is already in session, continue that game instead.

Play Rhythm. Number the players. Then clap twice (with hands), clap twice (on lap), snap fingers twice as you say your number, then a number of someone else, who then repeats what you have done except with his number first and then someone else's. If someone makes a mistake, he or she goes to the end of the line. Renumber and start again. Play for 2 minutes.

Play Tangle-Untangle. One person guides all members to hold hands and tries to tie a knot as complicated as possible in one minute without letting go. Then the second minute someone else instructs the group how to untangle.

Play basketball with wadded paper and the paper basket. Play at a distance of 10 feet; second try is 5 feet. Play for 2 minutes, with everyone taking a turn.

Play Simon Says for 2 minutes. You are Simon. The others are the players who obey all commands preceded by "Simon says" but disobey orders that are not preceded by "Simon says." If someone misses, he or she gets a negative point but remains in the game.

Play Detective. One person goes out of the room for 15 seconds and adjusts one item of clothing. The group has 1 minute to determine what it was. Repeat the game one time with a new person. The total time is 2½ minutes.

PROBLEM-SOLVING CARDS

(On all of the following cards, pick a discussion leader; the content of the card is your problem. Add any necessary information to make it your problem. Brainstorm all possible solutions with the group, following the rules of brainstorming. Evaluate and select one set of solutions that you could employ.)

Your roommate plays the stereo too loud while you are studying. You've asked him or her to play it softer once or twice, which helps for a day or two, but then he or she goes back to playing it loud again. Problem-solve with the other players what you should do.

Your teacher gives very picky tests. You don't do well on tests and have been failing her quizzes. What should you do?

You see someone cheating on a test. It is a person who usually gets A's. The course is graded on the curve. You are right on the edge of an A. What should you do?

Figure 13.1. A Cognitive-Behavioral Board Game *(continued)*

You have run out of money. It will be a week before you get your monthly allowance. You want to buy some clothes on sale. None of your friends have a lot of extra cash. What should you do?

MODELING AND REHEARSAL CARDS

You decide to tell your roommate that you will no longer accept his/her playing the stereo so loud when you are studying. Have someone model this for you. Then rehearse it. Then ask for feedback from the group.

You have decided to ask your teacher for the reasons that you got the grade you got. You want to be as tactful as possible, but you want evidence of your doing as poorly as he thinks you are doing. You want to provide him with evidence that you are doing better. It is a course on history. Have someone model what you could say. Then rehearse it. Then get feedback from the group.

Your roommate, who usually plays the stereo too loud, has not done so for 2 days. You want to compliment him/her on it. The roommate dismisses your compliment, and you want to assure him/her that you mean it. Have someone model the situation. You rehearse it. Then get feedback from the group.

You are a member of a therapy group. Some of the members dominate the conversation, while others never say anything. You are particularly annoyed at those who dominate and want to say something in the group about it. Have someone model what you would say, then rehearse it, then ask for and receive feedback from the rest of the group.

Your friend is often putting you down. He/she claims he/she is joking, but you don't like it. You decide to tell him/her how you feel when he/she puts you down and to ask him/her for a change in behavior. Have someone model the behavior, then rehearse it, then get feedback from the group.

STRESSFUL SITUATION CARDS

You must make a presentation in class tomorrow. You are prepared, but you are already frightened. How would you use cognitive procedures to help yourself to handle your fear?

You have to interview for a job tomorrow. You know what to say. But you are still so frightened you don't know whether you can handle it. How would you help yourself (using cognitive techniques) to handle your fear?

Figure 13.1. A Cognitive-Behavioral Board Game *(continued)*

You have been falsely accused of cheating. You will be called before a panel tomorrow to review the accusation. You know you are innocent and even have good proof. But you are frightened to face the board. How would you use cognitive procedures to help yourself to handle your fear?

You are driving in traffic and someone cuts into your lane. You are angry and upset. Analyze how you feel and what you could do or say to yourself to cope with the situation.

You are falsely accused by your teacher of cheating. The teacher will not listen to you. Then someone else provides evidence that you were not involved. The teacher walks away without saying anything. You are extremely upset. What could you do or say to yourself to cope with this situation?

SELF-DEFEATING STATEMENTS

(Pick three of these distortions, tell why they are distortions, and correct them.)

It would be awful if none of the people I know liked me. It would be awful to be a social loser.

I shouldn't make mistakes, especially social mistakes. It would ruin my life.

It's my parents' fault I'm so miserable and I have gotten in so much trouble.

I can't help what I just did; that's just the way I am, and I guess I'll always be this way.

The world should be fair and just.

It's really awful when things do not go my way.

It's better to avoid challenges than to risk failure.

I must conform to what my friends do and want me to do.

I can't stand to be criticized.

Others should always be responsible.

No sense in asking him/her out— he/she won't like me anyway.

A guy I know called me a punk. I'll get even with him.

If you are really smart, you don't have to finish high school to succeed.

The other guys made me do it.

There is nothing I can do to control myself.

I couldn't do anything else. I had to hit him.

When things go wrong, it makes me depressed.

Figure 13.1. A Cognitive-Behavioral Board Game *(continued)*

cannot read, pictures are provided on the cards and on the board. The group therapist will help the youth to interpret the pictures.

A second type of square is the cognitive-affective exercise square (which instructs a member to pick a "think card"; see Figure 13.1). One card might instruct the member to describe some situation and his or her reactions to it, for example, "What's the last situation in which you became angry? Describe the situation, what you thought, and how you felt." Other cards might have the player distinguish between a list of self-defeating and self-enhancing statements.

The third type of square is the "pick a fun card" square. Fun cards instruct the player to do surprise activities, such as singing a song, saying a tongue-twister, or telling a bad joke. The fourth type of square provides game instructions, such as "Start here," "Go back three spaces," or "Rest here." A fifth type of square that is not always used is the reinforcing square: the player who lands on it or passes it receives a raisin, a nut, a piece of candy, or a token. For younger adolescents, this square has made the game highly attractive.

The role of the group therapist is to be a player and a source of constant feedback as to how each group member is doing. He or she is also the regulator of the tempo of the game. The group therapist may adjust the game as it goes along if it does not quite meet the interests of the group members or the goal orientation. The therapist may require the members to respond more quickly or may add new instructions or new cards.

These board games have been used with all ages. Some have been described in detail in the literature. One such board game for emotionally disturbed adolescents, designed by Stermac and Josefowitz (1982), was evaluated for its effectiveness in modifying social skills and "bizarre" behavior. A similar board game developed by Quinsey and Varney (1979) for adult offenders can be used with adolescent offenders.

Cartledge and Milburn (1981) pointed out several important issues in the use of social skill games. The first is that at some point, the connection between what is done for fun in the group and its application to treatment goals needs to be made. There are at least two ways of achieving this. One is through an orientation and discussion after and/or before the game of the relationship between the game and treatment goals. The second is through feedback from the group therapist during the game whenever a connection can be drawn between what a given individual is doing in the game and treatment goals. To further this connection, the design of the game should allow ample opportunity for each member to make specific social responses relevant to his or her targeted problem. The games should be designed or adapted in such a way as to minimize lose-win situations unless the target behaviors are commonly found in competitive situations. Finally, the game should be designed in such a way that no member is eliminated. (This is a good rule for all games.) If a member is excluded, he or she should be given a new start to provide maximum opportunity for continuous participation.

In conclusion, social skill board games are probably one of the most important therapeutic-recreational activities used in group therapy. In some groups, almost no other recreational activity is used. Variation is brought into the program by having the group members continually redesign the game to include new features. Because of the relationship of the social skill games to many therapy goals, this affords a well-integrated socio-recreational treatment program. Therapists who are working with ethnic minorities or who wish to enrich the program with knowledge of other cultures will find interesting alternatives in Bell's (1969) *Board and Table Games From Many Civilizations.*

Resources for Games

There are many excellent resources for games. The book *Play It Again!* (Rice & Yaconelli, 1993) presents more than 200 games specifically for groups of different sizes. It includes inside and outside games, cooperative and competitive games, and active and quiet games. For a few of the better-known books, see Girl Scouts of the U.S.A. (1969) and Boyd (1973), which provide ideas not only for games but for all the other categories of socio-recreational activities mentioned in this chapter.

Handicrafts and Drawing

These arts and crafts activities are often used as a means of increasing manual dexterity and spontaneity. They usually are characterized by a low level of physical movement and interaction among the members unless the group therapist designs the activity in such a way as to increase physical movement and interaction among members. For those youth for whom interaction is anxiety producing, arts and crafts are the ideal starting point, with the gradual addition of more interactive activities, such as subgroup or group projects. Another advantage of arts and crafts is that they can more easily be reduced to 5 to 10 minutes available at the end of the therapy session than active sports and games if they are well organized in terms of the availability of materials and clear instructions.

Arts and crafts activities vary in terms of the degree of minimal competency required. However, there are many activities that require only the lowest levels of competency to participate in and to enjoy. Making simple boats or birdhouses from presawed parts is almost always successful, even with the least handy participants. Similarly, finger paintings and abstract drawings require few initial skills, although most older adolescent males are highly reluctant at first to try these activities. Of course, with increased skill and increased interest, more complicated works can be created. Occasionally, one or two members have special skills in these areas. If these are youth who lack recognition in other areas, they may be encouraged and in fact trained to share their skills with other members of the group.

As we pointed out earlier, the problem of limited interaction among the members while doing crafts can be overcome in the middle and later sessions by using subgroup and group projects. A dramatic example is "making a monster." In this activity, either the entire group or two subgroups are given an assortment of materials (feathers, paste, string, scissors, hair, cloth, paper clips, and whatever the group therapist finds in cleaning out his or her desk). Each person then makes a part of the monster and adds this onto the group monster. Although this activity is in great favor with preadolescents of both genders, we have occasionally used it with adolescents as well, who seem to play it enthusiastically. One of its virtues is that it provides the stimulus conditions for waiting one's turn and for cooperative behavior. Other group projects include a group mural or a group clay sculpture. Once again, because of the adolescent group culture, female adolescents are more likely to be willing to participate in arts and craft activities than adolescent males. Depending on the skills of the therapist, however, youth of all ages and both genders can be eventually stimulated to participate in such activities.

The group can combine crafts with other activities, such as laying out and coloring the prototype of a social skills board game or making scenery for a play. Of course, before one can make scenery for a play, one must develop a play, one of many types of dramatics.

Dramatics

For many youth with few social skills, game skills, or crafts skills, dramatics is the vehicle by which they can accrue status in the group or at least take pleasure in a leisure-time activity. This activity may transfer to the school and have a concurrent effect on their external status. Drama provides a high level of reinforcement for players and stagehands alike. It provides variations in role (not only different kinds of actors, but writers, stagehands, directors, set designers, and so forth). Each of these roles permits the manifestation of a wide variety of skills. This is especially important when not all youth are willing or ready to assume the role of an actor. Drama allows a wide variety of levels of prescriptiveness, from the low level of the spontaneous skit or charades to the high level of the formal play. Dramatics evokes varied stimulus conditions for many different kinds of behaviors. The group therapist, by his or her selection of plays or skits or types of charades, can make it possible for almost every member to act out roles that must be learned for the real world. Dramatics can readily be squeezed into the narrow time limits of the therapy group or can be expanded for special sessions if the demands of therapy require it. For adolescents, it is possible to use primarily dramatics as the vehicle of therapy if youth are using their parts to practice goal-oriented behaviors.

In developing and selecting scripts for youth, it is helpful to consider the following suggestions:

1. Themes should be used that are familiar in the day-to-day life of the youth. Not only are these themes more acceptable, but they permit the acting out by the youth of more goal-oriented behaviors.
2. No one actor should have too long a part or too many lines to memorize. The use of cue cards is also helpful in reducing the demand for memorization.
3. In therapy, quality is not the goal, as it would be in a little theater interest group. However, the quality of the performance must be sufficiently high that the members take some pride in the final product.
4. Employing a narrator is especially helpful in shortening scenes, in reducing memorization, and in adapting an existing script.
5. If one has a particularly large group, the use of choruses and crowd scenes can include those who do not want to memorize their own part or perform in front of an audience all alone.

The play is only one possible form of dramatics. Skits, spontaneous role plays, charades, and other forms of pantomime are even more frequently used than the production of plays. Each has its own particular advantage. For example, skits and spontaneous role plays require no highly prescribed parts. The group therapist or the member can merely sketch out the parts on slips of paper, and the actors can develop the specific content as they go along. The group therapist or an experienced member may serve as a prompter if one is needed. The skit can be audiotaped or videotaped and presented to the parents as an example of what happens in the group and to friends as a means of increasing the status of the members in their peer group. Such taping can also serve as a salient reinforcer for the performance of target behaviors or the completion of behavioral assignments.

Charades are often used as preparation for putting on skits or for eventually doing behavioral rehearsals. However, they are also important activities in their own right with both children and adolescents. Charades is usually a team game, although it can be played as an individual performance. The one team selects a word (theme, movie, TV program) and then secretly works out its dramatization syllable by syllable, word by word, or for the entire subject. As the first team performs the given subject without words, the second team attempts to guess what it is. Many variations are possible, but in most versions the game permits wide participation, requires low to moderate competency to play, provides opportunities for leadership behavior and cooperative behavior, and can be performed in a limited time period and in a limited physical space.

Charades is one type of pantomime—that is, acting without the use of words. A number of other variations commonly used in therapy groups that share most of the advantages described above are described below. In Pantomime This Object, a broom or stick is used as a prop. Each person uses the object to pantomime a guitar, horse, violin, or whatever he or she (or the group therapist) chooses while, as in charades, the members guess what the object is. Then the stick is passed on to another person, who pantomimes a new object. In Occupational Pantomime, different occupations are pantomimed, while the rest of the members guess the occupation. What Kind of Store? is performed in the same way. The group therapist can help the members to achieve educational goals by asking, for each job, what education or training a person must have to get a job like that. Then the charade can be used as a point of departure to discuss members' personal goals and long-term plans to achieve them. This is a particularly good example of linking play and treatment.

The charade activities mentioned above are primarily for all ages and genders. For those with more experience or for older adolescents, Challenge Pantomime offers more possibilities. The group therapist or a team of group members makes up a complex situation that tells a brief story. A pair of volunteers are given the situation, which they then portray for the rest of the group. Those who did not write the scenario try to tell the story when the pair is finished. A prototype of a situation might be the following: "You are at a carnival and are eating ice cream. A friend wants you to go with her on a frightening ride. You don't want to go. Show what happened." (Such situations can later be linked to assertiveness training.) Similarly, the group members can be asked to pantomime stressful situations that the group therapist knows they have actually experienced, such as the following: (a) "You have broken your mother's favorite mug. She comes home and you try to explain" and (b) "Your best friend is playing with a person who always puts you down. You see them together. Show how you would respond." This version lends itself to a discussion and demonstration of nonverbal behavior, with emphasis on its importance in communication. One can also link it to stress management strategies such as relaxation and instructing oneself in anxiety-reducing cognitions. Although there are many opportunities to link dramatics to the work of the group, as in the last example, one of the most effective linking strategies is the use of the simulated school activity.

Simulated School Activity

Because it is often difficult to carry out therapy in the ongoing class, it may be helpful with youth, usually age 13 or under, to simulate the classroom. To create interest in simulated school activities, the members are initially heavily reinforced for the activity. As they are successful in the various goal-oriented activities in the group and in the classroom, the concrete reinforcement is eliminated. During the classroom simulation, the group therapist usually plays the role of the teacher, although a number of group therapists have invited colleagues, older youth, a real teacher, or even one of the members to play the role of the teacher. As the simulation progresses, the "teacher" must attempt to simulate as nearly as possible the atmosphere in the real classroom. The following is an example of such an activity.

The group therapist showed the boys a picture of some men on a boat in the middle of a lake. "This is going to be a writing exercise in which you make up a story about what you see in this picture. You can write anything you want. The only rule is that you keep in your seat. When the timer goes off, anyone in his seat will receive one token, and anyone writing will receive another token. The timer should go off about four times in the next 10 minutes. Any questions?" The boys worked hard all 10 minutes and received the maximum number of tokens. "You guys did a great job. Now comes the hard part. You have to listen to each other while each person reads his report. What does a person who is listening look like?" Following a discussion of the behavioral characteristics of a listener, each boy read his report. The group therapist reinforced them intermittently for giving the appearance of listening. At the end of the exercise, he said, "You fellows are marvelous listeners. What do you say we try that out in class this week? Just hand this listening card to your teacher each day, and she'll check off whether you did a good job of listening. She knows about the card and said she was glad to do it." The group members then discussed the assignment and what they had to do to get the cards checked and back to the group therapist. Everyone agreed it was a good idea.

Musical Activities

Garvin (1987, pp. 127-128) described a number of musical activities that youth have used in groups. These include singing, writing songs, playing musical instruments, and dancing. CBIGT therapists have primarily used the members' own music as a reward for getting the work done. On one occasion, a group prepared a brief musical for the rest of the institution. This required additional sessions and the members' free time to succeed, but it gave them an opportunity to function independently and try out the behaviors learned in the therapy time. It also gave them an opportunity to receive a great deal of approval for prosocial behavior.

Photography

Photography has only been rarely used in CBIGT groups but has been received with enthusiasm by the participating members. It requires some skill on the part of the therapist and considerable interest. Moreover, it is difficult to restrict to the time limits at the end of a session. This activity requires at least one camera or even a homemade pinhole camera, some film, and some understanding of the importance of light and movement in the process of taking pictures. In the beginning, the restrictions of light and movement, the kind of film, and the kind of camera increase somewhat the skill level required. If the group develops an interest, the level of competence can be increased. Because the activity permits but does not require a little interaction, it is an ideal early activity in most groups. Moreover, it requires only a little time to result in a successful experience. We have found it especially useful for economically deprived youth who have never had access to photographic equipment. Of course, if there is only one camera, the time must be carefully negotiated in advance to prevent violent arguments from erupting. If resources are available, the activity can be expanded to include developing and printing as well. Another more sophisticated enhancement of photography would be videotaping if the equipment is available. These activities may be integrated into other activities, such as dramatics, field trips, or role-play simulations. Members might set up an exhibition of photographs that they develop and mount themselves and might publicize and sell tickets for the exhibition. In this as in all projects, the youth who become interested are encouraged to get involved in similar activities in school or the local YMCA/YWCA or youth organization.

Storytelling

Many troubled youth appear never to have had people read to them. Although some are initially bored with the activity, most soon overcome their reluctance. Sitting quietly and listening to others for most troubled youth is not usually a skill that is well developed. The reinforcement of a good story can be used to shape these important school survival skills. Moreover, it can readily be restricted to the 10 minutes at the end of a session. A number of short story books for primarily young people of various ethnic backgrounds are available. One example is *Jump Up and*

Say!, by Goss and Goss (1995), a collection of African stories that are not only interesting stories that capture the imagination of African American youth but also a source of ethnic pride.

Field Trips

These excursions provide the occasion for practicing newly learned skills in the real world and ample reinforcement for a wide variety of different roles and behaviors. Field trips involve group planning, decision making, cooperative behaviors, obtaining information, and teaching others. Because of the great popularity of excursions, they are often used as group contingencies for continued assignment completion.

Most group meetings take place in a highly restricted environment. The excursion dramatically expands the environment in which the youth interact as the transportation system, the shopping mall, the bowling alley, the museum, and the stadium become the vastly enlarged areas of operation. As a result, the youth are confronted with new and often unexpected kinds of experiences. It is an opportunity to try out in the real world the many behaviors learned in the group under the supervision of the group therapist and the other group members. When the group returns from the field trip, one of the important points of the agenda is to review one at a time the achievements of each of the members in demonstrating his or her unique target behaviors.

Some common examples of field trips for preadolescents are visits to the local zoo, a farm, a factory, an elevator in a tall building, a woods, a youth museum or exhibit, a fire station, the police station, the next level of school, the major city library if it is not readily available, a veterinarian's office, a pet shop, or a youth concert. For older adolescents, one might add to the list a visit to the nearby university or technical school campus, concerts, college sports events, an employment office, government offices, a courtroom in session, shopping centers, and a hospital. One can add to this list by brainstorming with youth themselves.

Some field trips can be quite practical. A group of 14-year-olds from lower socioeconomic backgrounds decided to go on a field trip to the kitchens of fast-food restaurants. They had to consider what they would wear, cleanliness, and appearance. They had to call managers to arrange the visits. They discussed the questions they would ask the manager. They decided, too, that they would act as if they eventually wanted jobs at these places and that they would practice going on a job interview. The reinforcers were hamburgers and a soft drink. More important to them was the fact that the managers were sufficiently impressed by their behavior and appearance to ask them to apply when they turned 16.

Although this is the end of our list of activities, many other types of programs for youth can be found in a vast literature available to the group therapist, some of which has been cited in this chapter. The problem is usually not so much finding activities as stimulating interest and helping the group to select activities that are compatible with the attainment of treatment goals.

Selecting Activities

In general, major decisions as to which program activities are to be used at a given meeting are based on a combination of activities' relation to behavior change goals for the members, the interests of the members, and group conditions at a given moment (e.g, the level of group cohesion). Initially, potential activities are reviewed in terms of the criteria discussed earlier in this chapter. Decisions are then made by the group therapist in consultation with the members. In later phases of group development, the members themselves may perform all of these functions, with an occasional reminder from the group therapist as to the criteria.

Throughout this chapter, we have made a distinction between the "work" of the meeting and the "play." In fact, the distinction is arbitrary because both are aimed at facilitating the achievement of therapy goals. "Work" refers primarily to reviewing extragroup tasks and developing new ones, modeling or rehearsing responses to problematic or stressful situations, performing exercises enacting various behaviors in which the group members are deficient, having discussions, and solving problems that occur in the group. The "play" consists of the activities listed in the previous sections. Initially, most meetings consist of the so-called work activities for two thirds of the meeting and the play activities for the remaining third. Depending on the creativity of the group therapist, the boundary between the two becomes increasingly blurred.

During a typical meeting, the group members review the tasks that were carried out since the previous meeting; new problem situations are introduced and systematically analyzed; solutions are proposed, evaluated, modeled, and rehearsed; members receive feedback from each other on their respective performances; an exercise based on a common problem is carried out; new assignments are designed; and then the group plays a game or performs some other activity. Special meetings may occur such as one preparing for a field trip, in which most of the time is devoting to planning and to the group problems that may ensue during the planning process.

Ultimately, the group therapist searches for various ways of integrating the work and play activities. This permits extending the therapy time for each without increasing group time. Ideally, the work and play activities become integrated through such activities as dramatics and social skill board games. Integration can also occur by working in a "playful" fashion. Rehearsals can be done in costumes, problem solving can be carried out in game format, and extragroup tasks can be reviewed in a format like the game of 20 Questions.

Initially, the major input and responsibility for choosing activities belong to the group therapist. At the same time, he or she involves the group members, beginning with the pregroup interview, by asking about games in which they are interested and that they have played or would like to play. The group therapist builds up a group catalogue of common and individual interests from which group activities can later be selected.

Having members make decisions about program activities may be an excellent tool for trying out newly learned decision-making skills. But if decision-making skills are generally deficient or weakly developed in the group, planning may be so chaotic that youth will have an aversive experience without ever deciding on an activity. Therefore, until rudimentary decision-making skills are developed, program activity decisions remain largely guided by the group therapist. At the same time, however, the group therapist gradually shapes independent decision-making skills. For example, the youth might first choose between two possible activities described by the group therapist, such as volleyball or kickball, or between two types of field trips. He or she would raise questions even in this example of how in choosing one activity we make it possible for the minority to realize their interests. Successful decision making by the group at this level may lead to more open choices at subsequent meetings. As has been frequently noted in this chapter, when youth make choices, they must take into consideration therapy goals, just as the group therapist does.

The group must be continually reminded that the activity is a vehicle to change or to modify somewhat behavior, perceptions, and/or values or attitudes. As incidents arise that lend themselves to therapeutic analysis and/or behavioral change, these issues are usually brought to the group for consideration, as shown in the following example:

In a group of eight female adolescents, the members decided to put on a play. One day, Anna failed to get her lines straight, and the others teased her every time she made a mistake. Anna found this so upsetting she decided to quit the play. Gale, the group therapist, stopped the activity and wondered if any of them saw the teasing or the way in which Anna responded to it as a problem. At first, the members began to blame Anna for not ignoring the teasing. The group therapist wondered if the teasers had some responsibility in this as well. This led to a brief discussion of giving and receiving teasing and the decision to spend an entire work session on the subject because giving or receiving teasing was a problem for everyone. In this example, the discussion was brought about by a crisis. If it had not been a crisis, the group therapist might not have stopped the activity but would have brought up the issue in the subsequent "work" portion of the meeting.

Stimulating New Interests

Although a vast array of activities have been suggested in which group members can participate, most clients are characterized by an extremely limited repertoire of socio-recreational skills and interests. The history of failure of many youth in attempting new activities has often discouraged their exploration of new possibilities. For this reason, it is often necessary for the group therapist not only to incorporate activities into the program but also to stimulate interest in new ones. One major procedure for stimulating interest of the youth is the use of a "program table." The materials needed in group activities are placed on the table with books, articles, or pictures illustrating a particular activity in more detail. The group therapist is responsible for keeping the table full at first, but as members gain skill and interest, they are encouraged to add properties and pictures of their own. Similar to this approach is planned observation of an activity on videotape or television. One group decided that each member would make up a commercial for an activity in which he or she was interested. The group therapist also created several commercials. Then, separately or in pairs, the group members presented their commercials with exaggerated fanfare. At the end of the commercials, the group members evaluated each one and selected to perform those new activities in which their interest was awakened.

Other modeling procedures are also used to stimulate interest in and reduce anxiety about new programs. A novel way of stimulating interests has been to have group members observe slightly older peers participating in a new activity. If other groups are readily available, observing the entire group at opportune moments may provide excellent program models. If the groups are not available, having slightly older youth teach a new activity to the group members will also make it more palatable than if it was taught by the adult group therapist. For example, another group therapist and one member of the group who had the necessary skills modeled how to play Scrabble while the group members were waiting for the meeting to begin.

Adolescents may be given recreation books or game books. As an extragroup task, a group therapist may suggest to a pair of youth to learn and practice teaching a new activity within a specified time limit and at a subsequent group meeting. The use of a pair rather than individuals alone has the advantage of increasing opportunities for cooperative planning. In addition, activities introduced by peers tend to be more acceptable than activities introduced by the group therapist.

Another way of stimulating new program activities is "by doing it" (Whittaker, 1976, p. 256). The group therapist merely begins some small handicraft or game and if possible pulls in one or two others. As the other members inquire what he or she is doing, the group therapist asks the active members to explain.

Rejuvenating old standard games or other activities is still another way of stimulating new interests. The game of tag can be spruced up by requiring members to play it in pairs with the inside leg tied together as in a three-legged race or by turning tag into the game of Blob (see p. 342, this volume, for a fuller description). Whittaker (1976) suggested changing the names of the familiar games to make them more contemporary sounding, as in changing the game of Ghost to Rocketship. Common games may be further enhanced by having members play them in costumes, blindfolded, or as comic book superheroes.

With so much from which to choose, the group therapist need not attempt to implement or stimulate activities with which he or she does not feel sufficiently comfortable or skilled. Generally speaking, youth respond best to those activities about which the group therapist is most enthusiastic. Of course, if the group therapist has highly limited program skills, his or her skills in this area should be expanded before he or she runs a group alone. An important procedure that reduces the constant need to stimulate new programs is the use of themes.

Thematic Programming

Initially, program activities are viewed as isolated events tacked onto the end of the meeting as reinforcement for doing the work of therapy. Ideally, activities selected create the stimulus condition for behaviors that need to be worked on in the group. Programming with a general theme or thrust opens up broad opportunities for extending activities to more sessions. For example, in one adolescent group, members expressed the desire to put on a skit. Their first brief try, a one-act play written for young adolescents, was provided by the group therapist. Their initial success stimulated them to do another that they wrote themselves, directed, made props and costumes for, publicized, sold tickets for, and performed twice for the public. This provided rewards for everyone, regardless of his or her interest. But more important, it provided conditions for conflict, cooperation, and the manifestation of all the problem and constructive behavior in the repertoire of the adolescents. For the last 15 minutes of every meeting, the behavior of every individual was observed (on the basis of monitoring done by the group therapist), and, where necessary, therapy plans were drawn up for modifying a given behavior still further.

In the above examples, program planning was relatively simple for a period of five sessions while the thematic program was being carried out. Integration of activities and therapeutic process was to a large degree effectively achieved. Following this play, the focus of the group was primarily on behavior and strategies of transferring what members had learned to home and school.

Another example involved an adolescent group of five girls in a middle school. One of the girls had a camera, and the members decided to monitor the behavior of each other with that camera and the permission of the teacher. They first photographed each other "being good." This had to be defined specifically for each person. The group later decided to give a photography exhibition. They wrote brief stories about each photograph, learned to type these descriptions on a word processor, and then matted these stories with the photographs. As in the previous group, a portion of each meeting was used to look at individual behavioral achievements, interpersonal difficulties inherent in carrying out the complex project, and problem solving or negotiation of conflicting interests.

Several other thematic activities have also been used in therapy groups. In one job-hunting project, older adolescents invited a number of people in different jobs to come to speak to them. This was followed by a series of field trips to their guests' places of employment and to an employment office. They later role-played employment interviews and filled out employment forms. A group of younger adolescents who were particularly interested in outdoor activities organized their entire group program around setting up and planning for a canoe trip. This involved intense sharing behaviors, planning and decision making, examining their own roles and behavior during the inevitable conflicts, resolving group conflicts and interpersonal differences, and carrying out behavioral homework assignments, the completion of which added points to the group thermometer. When filled, the group thermometer indicated that the group had won the canoe trip.

Themes are useful only if there is sufficient group time to permit their completion. When there are fewer than six sessions, it is often difficult to get a given theme started before the group ends. Usually even more sessions are required.

From the above discussion, it should be clear that the theme is merely a vehicle for increasing the enthusiasm for the activity of the group without losing the therapy focus. One of the problems occasionally encountered in the use of themes is that the program becomes more important than the treatment to the youth. Keeping the therapy focus is a relevant issue for all types of programs, but it is not the only remaining issue.

Family Recreational Projects

The use of socio-recreational activities is not restricted to the groups. Youth can teach games and other new activities learned in the group to the family. This may be negotiated with the family as a means of changing the usually coercive pattern in a given family and having the family do planning around a comparatively innocuous topic. The family too can be encouraged to expand their shared leisure-time activities. If the planning breaks down, the process can be looked at by the family therapist or even the group therapist. Youth may first develop a list of activities that they can do with their families in group therapy. Then they can present these activities to their families and/or have them brainstorm any other activities the family can do together. Usually it is helpful to develop a list of at least three acceptable activities and then to develop a plan to rotate their use over a period of time. In this way, everyone gets his or her particular interest met.

Cooking and Food Preparation

Because food is served at most sessions, it is an easy step to preparing pizza or baking cookies. These are cohesion-building activities that usually engender great enthusiasm. Furthermore, food preparation is a useful skill in its own right. As a group project, it often creates some conflict and disagreement that has to be dealt with. Because it cannot be squeezed into the 10 minutes allotted, it can be scattered throughout the session, with one person keeping an eye on the baking or cooking process while the others are working.

Summary

Some group therapists find the addition of socio-recreational activities a luxury for which they have inadequate time. In CBIGT, these activities are considered rich learning opportunities as well as a foundation for a cohesive and well-motivated group and thus are considered worth the investment. This chapter has been devoted to demonstrating how activities can be developed. The major categories of group activities commonly used in group therapy and some of the conditions under which they can best be implemented are described. These activities include games (major sports, action, paper/pencil, card, board, social skill), handicrafts and drawing, storytelling, charades and dramatics, simulated classroom activities, photography, musical activities, and field trips. Considerable attention was devoted to a social skill board game that lends itself particular well to both therapy and recreation. In addition, the principles of stimulating new interests, thematic programming, and integrating recreational activities into the therapy plan were discussed. Finally, the extension of socio-recreational skills learned in the group to family projects was demonstrated.

CHAPTER 14

Intervening in
the Group Process

Every action suggested to the group therapist throughout this book has been discussed in terms of its effect on the group. The group is a dynamic environment in which all action is interaction. Any intervention in the group should be considered as a group procedure, even if the target of that intervention is an individual. A group member sets his or her individual therapy goals in comparison with and with feedback from others in the group. Each member designs an individualized therapy plan within the group context and with broad assistance from fellow members. If the group mutual support system is not working, all of the advantages of group therapy described in Chapter 1 are negated. If the unique attributes of the group are not made use of, the interventions are sorely weakened or ignored. Another reason for positing a group-level concept is that shared opinions, values, and behaviors of group members mediate the behavior of each individual. If Sean arrives late at several meetings of a group in which lateness is the norm, he will make no effort to change. The therapist will first have to facilitate the changing of the norm. Of course, behaviors are also a function of an individual's earlier learning history and patterns of behavior. If Emily has a history of dominating the conversation in most of her interactions with others, she may run into a conflict in her therapy group if the norm of the group is that everyone should have an equal opportunity to participate. Thus, the group can be a powerful tool in changing well-learned nonfunctional behaviors, provided that prosocial norms exist. It may also be a powerful tool against change if agreement on antitherapeutic norms exists in the therapy group. The operation of some of these group-level attributes is illustrated in the following situation.

The youth were noisily running around the room when the group therapist arrived. He settled them down by drawing a cartoon figure and, in a balloon, writing in very small letters, "Time to start." Lex, as was his custom, responded immediately and encouraged the others to sit down as well. The others slowly took their seats. Doug and Gil were the last to take their seats and kept talking loudly. The group therapist sat between them, which calmed them down. He showed the youth the graphed results of the postsession questionnaire from the first 2 weeks. It revealed that the ratings on the satisfaction and self-disclosure items were moderately low but increasing from the first to the second week and that the "mutual helpfulness" item was particularly high in comparison with the rating of the week before.

When the therapist began to review the home tasks, Gil complained that his was too difficult and that he could not do it. The therapist briefly acknowledged that Gil was unable to do the work and went quickly to the others, who had completed theirs. In the discussion, Will, Lex, Casey, Don, Saleem, and Adam presented what they had done and talked to each other. Doug tried to interrupt with a joke, but Lex told him, "Shut up. This is important to some of us at least!" The other four seemed to agree. In general, the five kept the discussion on task and focused on their experiences with their home tasks. Doug and Gil said very little to the others throughout this part of the session but constantly whispered to each other.

In this example, based on only a moment in the history of the group, we can postulate a number of group structural elements. Subgroups seem to be present that distribute the group into active versus less active members. Each subgroup has its own characteristics. In one subgroup, the youth appear to be motivated to work on their problems, but in the other there is less interest. In the first subgroup, there is a moderate level of self-disclosure, but in the other there is none at all. The norm of one subgroup is to keep to the task and get the work done, but the norm of the other subgroup is talking only insofar as it interferes with the work of the group. The task-oriented subgroup appears to be more dominant.

Several member roles are beginning to evolve. Lex is showing some positive leadership by setting limits on off-task behavior of others. Doug is an antisocial leader who tries to undermine the therapeutic process by not cooperating with therapeutic tasks and is clearly followed by his peer. One can surmise from the postsession checklists that the cohesion within the group was low to moderate at the first two meetings, with the cohesion of the subgroups being quite high.

Structure and Process

Group structure and processes play a significant role in group therapy, regardless of whether salient attention is paid to them by the group therapist. There are some data to support the above view. For example, increased group cohesion (Costell & Koran, 1972; Evans & Dion, 1991; Flowers, Hartman, & Booraem, 1981), group self-disclosure and feedback (Dies, 1973; Kirshner, Dies, & Brown, 1978; Ribner, 1974), and group participation (Fielding, 1983) have all been associated with positive therapy outcome. For this reason, the "group" in the CBIGT approach is conceptualized as an active therapy component in itself that operates both as a means and as a context for the achievement of individual and group goals. In this chapter, an overview of the major conceptual aspects of the group and several group frames of reference that can be used to analyze the group structure and group process are presented. These structures and processes often overlap and represent to a large extent different ways of conceptualizing group phenomena. The concepts selected for scrutiny in this chapter are those for which some evidence of relationship to outcome has been established. Our own research with structured groups for young adults with stress concerns (Whitney & Rose, 1989) showed that rates of change were significantly less in groups where group issues were not attended to than in the experimental groups where group issues were dealt with and that the dropout rate was unusually high. This chapter provides the theoretical framework for dealing with group issues and describes the most common strategies used to achieve changes in group structure and processes.

Group Structure Defined

Any structure represents an identifiable arrangement of elements at a given point in time. In a group, the structure contains elements that are interactive in nature or are products of interaction. Some examples of group structure are the arrangement of norms governing the behavior of the participants, the intensity and degree of involvement in self-disclosing, the prevailing emotional state in the group, the distribution of leadership functions among the members, the shared motivational level of the members, the nature and distribution of distinct roles played by the members, and the degree of mutual attractiveness of the members (cohesiveness) at one point in time. In each of these structures, the elements are interactive or mutual phenomena and not the phenomena generated by any one individual. In some cases, the group dimension may be a product of the shared interaction, as in the amount of common work achieved, the amount of mutual assistance given, or the number and quality of group goals or subgoals achieved.

For a given structure to be useful in CBIGT, it must impinge on goal achievement and it must be verifiable. That is, there should be some evidence besides one's intuition that a given phenomenon is occurring; it must be reliably observed and/or measured at some point in time.

Group Process Defined

Group process can be defined as the changes over time of the arrangement of predetermined elements of the interaction of group members as measured at two or more different times in a given session. Structure at the beginning of the group is likely to be quite different from that at the sixth session. Thus, descriptions of a given group structure over time may often provide a more meaningful characterization of the group than a description at one point in time. Process may be considered at multiple points within a given meeting or across meetings. To be useful within a CBIGT framework, group process too must be goal related and observable. To observe group phenomena, one may use a postsession questionnaire to get a weekly picture of the group from the perception of the members and the therapist. One might assign an observer or a cotherapist to rate group phenomena as they occur. It is even possible to count certain interactions at several random periods throughout the group to get a picture of shifts in patterns of interactions or other relevant group attributes.

It is difficult to speak of *the* group process. It is necessary to restrict the picture to one or a few elements, such as the process of group norm development, patterns of relationships over time, or changes in cohesion. One selects those processes to deal with that are most intrusive with respect to goal achievement. For example, in a residential group of adjudicated delinquents, a group norm seemed to exist that one was not to disclose anything about feelings or thoughts. This made therapy quite difficult and warranted attention by the group therapist. In another community group, attendance and satisfaction were low and lateness was high, indicating low cohesion. In this group, the cohesion became the target of concern. In CBIGT, one looks at group process as it contributes to increasing motivation to change, facilitating learning of basic concepts and strategies, and carrying out the cognitive and behavioral interventions that lead to the achievement of the goals. Before achieving individual goals, it may be necessary to achieve process goals (in the terminology of this book, *group goals*), such as increasing the cohesion of the group or establishing protherapy norms in the group. Let us look at some of the specific group phenomena with which we are most concerned in this approach and how these phenomena affect individual learning and goal attainment.

Group Targets of Intervention

In all groups, various patterns of interpersonal behavior can be identified. One can define a group problem as an intragroup interactive event (or series of events) or a product of interactive events that interfere with effective member task performance or goal attainment. The responsibility for achieving a change in group process cannot usually be linked to a change in the behavior of any one member or the group therapist but is linked to interactive changes among all or most members and the therapist. Most groups go through different phases of development. In different phases, different group goals and targets seem to predominate. For example, when the group begins, the therapist attempts to take steps to increase the cohesion of the group as fast as possible. In the final phase of therapy, the therapist encourages the members to join, and increases the attraction of, other prosocial groups in the community.

Group processes can best be dealt with if they are indicated by observed phenomena. They may be subjectively observed by the group therapist, reported on by the members during or following a session, or systematically observed by a nonparticipating observer. Member perceptions are neither more nor less valid than observations of a neutral observer or the perception of the therapist. They merely provide a different perspective. All present different threats to reliability and validity. Many group attributes can be identified. Those that CBIGT therapists have found useful and that seem to have observable referents and hence can be monitored by the therapist, the group, and observers are group cohesion, the communication pattern in the group, group norms, and the distribution of leadership functions. Each of these is examined below.

Group Cohesion

Group cohesion is the degree and intensity to which members are attracted to one another, the program or group task, and the group therapist (Lott & Lott, 1965). It is basically a process variable in that its intensity changes over time (Budman, Soldz, Demby, Davis, & Merry, 1993). Although there have been many definitions since 1965, none seem to improve on the one given here, especially because it readily lends itself to measurement. Cohesion is regarded by all therapists and most theoreticians of practice (see, e.g., Yalom, 1985, pp. 50-51) as an essential attribute of groups because it appears to be correlated with productivity, participation in and out of the group, self-disclosure, risk taking, attendance, and other vital concerns of the group (Evans & Dion, 1991; Stokes, 1983). Despite diverse and fairly vague definitions, most practitioners regard this characteristic as a major group attribute. Yalom (1985, p. 48) asserted that cohesion in group therapy is the analogue of relationship in individual therapy. It seems to reflect the relationship of members not only to the group therapist but also to each other. It appears that cohesion is also related to dependency on the group and a willingness to accept the group's values and norms. As we pointed out earlier, attention to group cohesiveness is essential to keep people coming to the group and to keep them focused on the work to be accomplished. The relationship to work is a complex one. If the goals of the group are agreed on by its members, highly cohesive groups tend to achieve those goals better than low-cohesion groups. Of course, if the members exclude the therapist from the psychological definition of the group, they tend to prefer an implicit non-therapy-oriented goal toward which they appear zealously to strive. For example, a gang group was highly cohesive, but members did not consider their group worker to be one of their group, even though they met in a social agency with him. The interaction in his presence was pleasant but irrelevant to purposes of therapy. This group never got started in therapy until the membership in the group was modified and the therapist was finally accepted.

Usually, as cohesion seems to increase, so do mutual trust and support, self-disclosure, sense of intimacy among group members, and the perception of the group environment as a protected opportunity to test reality. Although cohesion is a group phenomenon, it is most often measured as an average individual phenomenon by asking the members about their attraction to the group and various elements of the group. This particular definition has been selected because it can be readily measured by the questions on a postsession questionnaire and under certain circumstances by the attendance and dropout data (see Chapter 5 for detailed descriptions of these and other group cohesion measures). Though not without limitations, in community groups where attendance is optional, rates of attendance, lateness, and dropouts indicate a group-level dimension as members indicate their attraction to the group behaviorally. The postsession questionnaire yields an average and a distribution of attitudes toward the group that approximate a group-level attribute. Thus, to catch the various dimensions of cohesion, the use of multiple measures is recommended (see Drencher, Burlingame, & Fuhriman, 1985, for a more detailed discussion of these issues).

Changing the Level of Cohesion

When cohesion is too low, the group therapist usually determines the major contributing factors to the low cohesion specific to a given group. When closed groups begin, they are usually low in cohesion. Here, the phase of development is the major contributor. One can do a number of things even before the first session begins to increase the probability that a workable level of cohesion will exist. For example, one can compose the group of youth who show similar problems. Usually it would appear that the greater the similarity, the greater the attraction of the youth to each other. But for such practical reasons as a limited pool of potential members, it is not always possible to have very much similarity. Positive socio-recreational activities also tend to increase cohesion. It is possible to create an early program that is interesting and even "fun" for the members. The opportunity at the end of a session to play interactive games tends to increase the cohesion. The modest use of humor in teaching new techniques and communicating in general with the members seems to be a builder of cohesion. Maximum involvement of the members in their own governance as early as possible has been shown to be a major contributor to cohesion. To achieve this, an exercise in subgroups, each of which has its own leader, is used early in therapy. Because many of the members have a short attention span, a relatively fast tempo keeps the activities attractive. The extensive use of role playing for some groups tends to increase the attraction of the group; so does frequent positive reinforcement.

Other strategies have been used to increase cohesion. In a residential group, the therapist had an extended pop break in which, for the first week, she provided soft drinks and a cookie. During this period, the members had an opportunity to talk informally. The group therapist took advantage of the opportunity to observe the patterns of interaction among the members in this informal activity. Because high levels of reinforcement appear to lead to high cohesion, a commonly used group reinforcement exercise is one in which, one at a time, each person in the group reinforces the person to his or her left for concrete, effective in-group behavior, and then the circle is reversed and each person reinforces the person to the right. Following the use of this exercise, the satisfaction and cohesiveness indicators usually show increases. Sometimes this exercise is labeled by the group as "kid stuff," and the therapist has to postpone it until members feel more comfortable with one another.

It has been noted that some therapists seem to develop in their groups a high level of cohesiveness more quickly than others, despite following the same kind of program. Most often, we have noted that the therapists in highly cohesive groups are judged as less serious and as "more fun" than their low counterparts. These findings seem to be related to personality differences that are not readily accessible through training. Unless the characteristics are extreme, the outcomes of different therapists over the long run do not seem to differ significantly (see Antonuccio, Davis, Lewinsohn, & Breckenridge, 1987).

Thus far, only narrow-range interventions carried out for the most part by the therapist have been suggested. But one way of involving the members in the identification and selection of narrow-range ideas is to use the broad-range intervention strategy of problem solving. In the following example, a modified approach to problem solving was taken to increase the cohesiveness of a group whose data suggested a relatively low level of cohesiveness.

Group Therapist: It seems that the results of the PSQs last week reveal that the satisfaction level and your response to the question about the helpfulness of other members had dropped quite a bit and that a number of you had commented that the meetings were getting somewhat repetitive. I wondered if you still feel that way. I think it's important that we discuss this before we go any further.

Patrick: It was kind of a boring meeting last week. Several of us were talking about it as we left the meeting. Frankly, Al, you did quite a bit of talking about stuff a lot of us didn't understand, that cognitive restructuring stuff. Some of us aren't sure how it affects us.

Group Therapist: I'm really glad you told me this. Anything else of concern?

Charles: Well, I didn't think it was so boring maybe as the others. But I found it confusing, too. And I guess I didn't feel so involved either.

Group Therapist: Well, I see you are all here this week, so the content didn't seem to drive you away. Were you tempted?

Patrick: I thought of it, but I've learned a lot in the group, and you can't expect it to be great every week.

Willy: I wasn't coming back, but my mother said I had to if I wanted to sleep at home tonight.

Group Therapist: I think there is good reason for concern. Let me try to summarize the problem. If I've got it straight, there was too much lecture last week, and there wasn't sufficient clarification or examples. Some people feel that they were not adequately involved. Are these concerns general? Do most of you share them?

Others: (Nod agreement)

Group Therapist: I wonder if we shouldn't see what we can do about it. As we discussed earlier, in a problem such as this one, everyone plays a role. Me, each of you, the group. It might be helpful if each of you writes down anything you can think of that would make the meetings more useful to you. At least one comment for me and at least one comment for the group or for yourself. I'll do it, too. (After a few minutes) You seem to be finished, most of you. What did you write that I might do differently? I'll put it on the board.

(A number of suggestions were made: "Give better examples," "Don't use so much jargon," "Give a few exercises to make sure we understand," "Don't rush so much," "Take at least two sessions to explain difficult ideas," "Don't wait for the people who are late," "Lay off the bad jokes!")

Group Therapist: That's quite a list, all of which I should seriously consider. We'll come back to them later. Now, what did you write that you or the group should do differently?

(The suggestions included "Ask for clarification when I don't understand something," "Try to make examples from our own experience," "Come on time, then maybe I won't be so confused," "Talk more," "Read the handouts, I have to admit I didn't.")

Group Therapist: That's also a thoughtful list. Why don't each of us, including me, decide in particular on as many of these ideas as possible that we will attempt to carry out at this and the following meeting to see whether we can improve the level of satisfaction? Let's do it in pairs. The other person in the pair will serve as consultant. When we're finished, each of us can read our plan to the group. I warn you, though, it's going to be tough for me to lay off the bad jokes.

The major strategy was first to reflect the results of the postsession questionnaire and then to identify the problem in this group. The intervention was to go through the first phase of problem solving. Testifying to the effectiveness was the fact that the level of satisfaction at the end of this meeting showed an increase and that, at the following meeting, all the youth had completed the assignments they had developed. The lack of cohesion seemed to be related to the group therapist's failure to involve the members in discussion and his tendency to overload them conceptually. Without losing the therapy focus of the group, the group therapist helped to increase the cohesion of the group by encouraging the members to talk about their complaints and to design within specified limits their own plan for improvement. It should be noted that he did not get defensive about their criticism but in fact did incorporate their ideas into his approach. There may have been an underlying relationship problem that the therapist did not recognize. If the plan had failed, it would still have been possible to examine his relationship to the group and the members' relationship to each other.

Using tools such as these, the vast majority of groups that CBIGT therapists have worked with are able to achieve quickly a high level of cohesion without problem solving. This may be because the program itself incorporates maximum involvement of the participants, delegates therapist responsibilities, has "enjoyable" activities such as role playing built in, and is basically a positive approach with lots of positive reinforcement and a minimum of critique. As Goldstein, Heller, and Sechrest (1966, pp. 392-430) concluded in a review of the literature, creating a positive climate with a high frequency of reinforcement is an extremely important precondition of high cohesion.

There are two common situations in which the group can be too cohesive. In the first situation, the group invests all its efforts in maintaining the high level of cohesiveness in the group rather than in working toward achieving individual therapy goals. In this situation, it is useful for the therapist to present the evidence that members' present way of relating to each other is interfering with goal achievement and for the therapist to remind them of the group purpose. It is also possible to have the members write what they currently like and dislike about the group and then present their observations to the others. Often the issue of not achieving goals comes out of the discussion that follows.

The second situation occurs as the group moves toward termination. If the group is highly cohesive at this time, members will have major problems in separating from one another. If there are indications of extremely high cohesion, plans should be made to reduce the cohesion relative to the best possible alternatives. The members should be helped to discover other groups and individuals in their lives to replace the therapy group. It is not uncommon for maladaptive behaviors to return as the highly attractive group terminates if there are no equally attractive alternatives.

To avoid this situation, the members are encouraged to bring guests to the last few group sessions (preferably newly made friends), to join new, nontherapeutic interest or friendship groups (see Chapter 15 for more details), and to share their impressions of their new experiences with the others. The group therapist also becomes less reinforcing, trains them in self-reinforcement strategies, and helps them to seek their reinforcement elsewhere. The group therapist may be working in the environment with a family or individual therapist or a recreation specialist to increase the likelihood that reinforcement will continue to occur.

Another situation in which cohesion can be too high is, as noted earlier, when the group therapist is excluded from the members' psychological definition of the group. They feel close to one another but not to the therapist. They experience his or her demands or structure as an imposition on the group experience. They may join together in opposition to the norms represented by the therapist. This may come about as a result of (a) expectations of a different sort of therapy or (b) a leader emerging from a group who successfully competes with the therapist for control of the group. Such a state may lead the group to work solely toward nontherapeutic goals, such as maintenance of the group, enjoying themselves through horseplay and private jokes, sabotaging therapist recommendations, and excluding the therapist from significant interactions. Though not a common feature of short-term structured groups, this phenomenon does occasionally occur, especially in work with gang groups. In general, it is avoided by careful clarification in advance of the goal orientation of the group and the importance of focusing on activities that contribute to that goal. Summarization by the members at the end of each session of what they have learned or achieved and what they are working on also reminds them of the therapy focus. The therapist's making rewarding programs available that are not otherwise available to members, such as driving lessons or the opportunity to make a TV show, may also help redefine the boundaries of the group as the youth begin to find the therapist and the activities that he or she provides attractive. (See the previous chapter for more details.)

Communication Structure

The communication structure in the group comprises the various patterns of interaction among members and the therapist(s) in the group. Although there are many ways to classify communication, the one we have found most useful (because it is readily observable) is to examine the distribution of frequency of the participation of all members and the group therapist in the group and the direction of the communication (toward each other, toward the therapist, toward one member of the group).

A common dysfunctional pattern of communication in group therapy is the situation in which the therapist interviews a member and the member talks directly to the therapist. The rest of the group become observers, as in the following example:

Daron: I saw this guy shoving Pete here, so I went over and shoved him.

Therapist: Then what happened?

Daron: Oh, we got into a fight.

Therapist: And then?

Daron: Mr. Marx came along and took us both to the principal's office, and I got suspended even though it wasn't my fault. No one would listen to me.

Therapist: Pete said he and this other guy were just horsing around. I wonder if you didn't make a mistake.

Daron: Well, maybe.

Therapist: I guess it turned out to be a costly mistake for you. What could you have done differently?

In this situation, the rest of the group are just sitting while the therapist and Daron are doing all the talking. Often the nonparticipants become bored and disruptive during such one-on-one interviews. The therapist needs to establish a pattern in which they are involved in such interviews. At any point in time, he could have involved the other members simply by asking if they had any questions to help them to understand better what was happening. Other questions could have been asked, such as how the others understood what Daron was saying, whether others had had similar experiences and how they dealt with them, or how others would feel in such a situation. Even allowing silences so that the others could respond would be likely to open up the interaction to more members.

Pauly: I always get in trouble with my mom. She's always on my case.

Therapist: (to group) What else do we need to know so we understand better what's going on with Pauly?

Luke: What do you mean by "trouble"? Can you give us an example?

Pauly: For example, last night, my mom said I was late for curfew. Shit, I was only 5 minutes late, so I just walked out again and told her I'd show her what late was.

Mike: What happened then?

Pauly: She wouldn't let me back in the house when I did get home at 12, and this morning she called my parole officer, and I gotta go see him.

Therapist: Anyone here have similar experiences?

Luke: Yeah, that's just what happened to me, except she was mad 'cause I didn't take out the garbage.

Pauly: Did you get in trouble, too?

Luke: I'll say. My dad grounded me for a week and slapped me across the face.

Therapist: Anybody see anything Pauly and Luke were doing to get themselves into trouble?

Alex: Yeah, their big mouths got 'em in serious trouble. Man, sometimes you gotta keep quiet. Like we were talking about last week.

Therapist: What do the rest of you think?

In the above excerpt, the therapist encouraged the other youth to do most of the interviewing. For the most part, she guided the interaction by asking what questions they could ask. As a result, there was a far broader distribution of participation than in the previous example. Of course, this type of interaction takes more time, but the result is usually higher cohesion and greater motivation to work on problems.

Another common problem in discussion groups is the dominance of one or two people and the withdrawal of others in the interaction pattern in the group. To attain individual therapy goals, it is frequently desirable to obtain a broad distribution of communication and participation in discussion and other activities. If some people are describing their problems, giving help and support to others, and generating ideas while others are rarely doing this, the former profit more from the group than the latter. Often the high participators become concerned about how the low participators are judging their disclosures, and the low disclosers become increasingly anxious and reluctant about disclosing. Furthermore, where the discrepancies are large, the cohesion in the group and the reported satisfaction tend to be low. If the group members are to perceive the group as mutually supportive and as a protected setting in which to self-disclose, a rough approximation of balanced mutual communication appears to be essential.

One way of modifying the distribution of interaction is to present the data or the therapist's observations to the group. If they perceive it as a problem as well, the group problem-solving process is initiated. In groups with little experience, the group therapist must serve as the major source of ideas as to what can be done. Some of these ideas are exemplified below.

Group Therapist: As we look over last week's participation data, which I have put on the board, it's clear that John, Everett, and I have done most of the talking, while the rest of you have had little opportunity. I guess we have a group problem, because some of us leap in before others get a chance, and some of us leave long gaps for the rest of us to spring into.

John: I know I do a lot of talking, but I got a lot of concerns.

Emily: That's true, John, and this may sound a little hard, but you might consider the fact that so do the rest of us.

Group Therapist: I'm the therapist, and I'm supposed to give you all an equal chance to talk about your concerns, and as we look at the participation data, I'm forced to admit that I am encroaching on your time.

Gordon: Of course, but you've got a lot to say that's really important.

Group Therapist: That may be so, but you didn't come for a lecture. This is supposed to be participatory learning. What about those of you who haven't been speaking up much?

Anthony: Well, I don't like to speak up in groups, so I'm glad when others do it. But I guess that's one of the reasons I'm in this group. I suppose if I leave it the way it is now, I won't learn anything.

Donna: I have to agree with that for me, too. But what can we do? We all seem to have to do something different about it.

Group Therapist: That's what I think, too. We have to do something together and something on our own. One way to approach it might be for each of us to make a plan for ourselves and then together a plan for the group as a whole.

Group Members: (Nods of agreement)

John: I guess I should just shut up. Is that what you're saying?

Anthony: I'm certainly not saying that. You say some pretty good things. I just need to find a way to hold up my end. I could use a little encouragement.

Group Therapist: I agree that's the direction we need to go in to find ways to increase or decrease, but not eliminate, the participation of all of you so that it's a little more equal. (Nods of agreement)

John: Well, we could sort of brainstorm how each of us could move toward the middle better. Each would sort of suggest things he or she can do for him- or herself?

Group Therapist: Judging by the nods of approval, that seems like a good idea. That being the case, at this very moment, let's write down whatever ideas we have so that we get a chance to say what we think we should do.

Among the ideas that the group generated was the recommendation to ask the observer for more frequent reports of the frequency of their interactions. The observer was asked to report to them how each member was doing after the break as well as at the beginning of the subsequent meeting. Each person on this basis would set a goal for him- or herself and then see whether the data registered movement toward that goal. The "talkers" would remind each other with "Is this statement really necessary?" Using a cognitive approach, the group therapist would request all the members to examine what they said to themselves when they wanted to say something in the group. Persons whose negative self-talk prevented them from speaking would be assisted though cognitive restructuring to change their self-talk from such statements as "I don't have anything important to say" to "My ideas are as good as the next person's and I have the responsibility to share them with others." The members went on to establish individual plans for themselves and a group plan that they monitored weekly to see whether interactional goals were being maintained.

Another way of modifying the distribution of communication within the group was used by a therapist of another group. At the suggestion of one of the members, she provided all of them with a stopwatch and had them monitor themselves. The group then had the task of equalizing the time spoken by dividing the 15-minute period among seven people, including the two therapists. The low participants, however, were coached occasionally by the cotherapist on what to say. The group briefly discussed what could be talked about, and members were encouraged to take notes. A brief practice session then took place, and the group attempted to carry out a discussion of the session agenda for 15 minutes. Reminders were given to individuals when their 2-minute limit was reached. The technique was used amid a great deal of laughter. The content of the discussion was of less interest than the process. A second attempt later in the meeting was more natural. No third trial seemed to be required, even at subsequent meetings.

Another technique occasionally used to decrease participation of the excessive talkers (who don't seem to listen very well) is recapitulation. In this procedure, a given participant must summarize aloud what the person speaking before him or her has just said before being permitted to add something new to the conversation. It is especially effective in curbing dominating individuals who do not seem to listen very well to others. This form of confrontation is less aversive than more direct forms in that most individuals discover for themselves their nonlistening behavior patterns as they attempt in vain to recapitulate their predecessors' remarks. Often, the group therapist is the greatest offender and therefore the best recipient of this procedure.

Normally, this procedure has to be applied for only a short period to get the necessary effect. However, to give youth (and the group therapist) practice in listening and monitoring their listening, repeated trials at various intervals are recommended. If continued for too long a period (more than 15 minutes), the conversation can become stilted, non-task oriented, and aversive. The procedure is more effective if used as a novelty or sporadically. Taping the meeting and replaying the tape for the group is also a useful exercise for presenting youth with their particular pattern of communication. It is helpful to provide or develop with them specific dimensions for them to observe while the tape is playing.

Another procedure is training youth directly in effective listening. They are taught specifically in role plays (modeling and rehearsal) to give appropriate eye contact and other nonverbal recognition of what the others are saying, to repeat key words the speaker has said, and, where appropriate, to show approval of what they have heard, with statements such as "That's interesting," "I think that's useful," and "Yes." Also, they are given practice in how to ask salient questions ("Could you clarify that for me?") and to paraphrase what the speaker has said. These skills not only improve the quality of the communication but are important in their own right.

Another strategy is to present the group with a case similar to the situation in the group. For example, in one therapy group, a description of a fictional group was distributed. The members talked only to the therapist and rarely to each other. The case was first discussed in terms of identifying the thoughts and behaviors of all interacting parties in the example. Then the group members were asked to design a plan in which all the interacting parties had to change something they were doing to improve the communication pattern. The youth then discussed how each person was similar to or different from the actors in the case study. This led to a discussion of the specific situation in their group and to an individualized plan as to ways in which each person in the group could modify his or her behavior to remedy the group problem. When using a case study, a case needs to be designed that is not too similar to the problem in the group but similar enough so that some elements of the group's own problem can be identified in it.

Most of the procedures suggested thus far have been behavioral or problem solving. One cognitive strategy in particular that has been found by some group therapists to be useful is Exercise 14.1.

Exercise 14.1. Redistribution of Participation

Purpose: By the end of this exercise, high and low participants will identify self-defeating statements that seem to impede their participation in the group or excessively enhance it. They will also demonstrate that they can change these cognitions.

Individual Task: Each person should rate him- or herself as a high participant, a moderate participant, or a low participant in the group interaction. If a person doesn't know, he or she should ask a neighbor. Those who are too low should give an example of a situation in the group in which they didn't participate but wanted to or thought they should. High participants should describe a situation in which they thought they talked more than they wanted or should. Finally, each person should describe in writing what he or she was thinking at that moment.

Group Task 1: High and low participants should present their situations to the group and their thoughts before and during the situation. The group members will tell each other whether their thoughts were self-defeating or illogical. Then the group will propose alternative thoughts that each person might employ.

Group Task 2: Each person will cognitively rehearse presenting the group situation, beginning to use his or her distorted cognitions, then stopping him- or herself and replacing the distorted cognitions with coping cognitions.

Dependency on the Therapist

One special case of a problem in communication is when the members direct all their communication, especially requests for help and guidance, toward the therapist. As a result, they depend excessively on the therapist at the rational level of decision making and also emotionally. The consequences of excessive dependency on the therapist is that youth lose the opportunity to make major decisions about their own behavior and to function on their own when the group therapist is no longer available; they rely too heavily on the therapist for decisions and reinforcement; and they do not have to take responsibility for failure. It is as if they are saying, "My group therapist made the decision; it's her fault that I failed."

When these conditions are noted, therapists have employed a variety of interventions in addition to posing the problem to the group for clarification and problem solving. These include a planned fading of the therapist from the interaction. Questions asked of the therapist are thrown back to the group for consideration. If the group becomes anxious or concerned, these reactions are discussed in terms of their implications for learning. When youth are constantly asking for guidance— for example, in the development of extragroup tasks—it is possible to ask subgroups to develop answers to the question. However, as in the example below, the criteria for answering the question are first made explicit by the group. At first, the therapist floats among the subgroups, reminding them of the criteria. Later, the therapist absents him- or herself completely from the process.

Michael: Sheldon, I just can't figure this out. Is this a good way of designing my extragroup task? (He describes his task as he designed it for himself)

Lon: Yeah, I can't either. Nothing goes right. (Describes his plan)

Sheldon: (To the group) I wonder whether we might not first review the criteria we had established last week for a good contract. That might help you to judge whether these assignments are good ones or not.

Lawrence: One point, it should be highly concrete, and stuff like that. You should know exactly what you are supposed to do, and when you are supposed to do it and with whom.

Gary: Didn't we talk about the task being a small step on the way to achieving the goal?

Francis: The thing that was most important to me was that it was something I could do between sessions and it was important to me. It wasn't dumped on me.

Other Group Members: (Continue to elaborate on criteria)

Sheldon: (When the group pauses) To what degree, Michael and Lon, do the tasks you just described meet the criteria? The rest of you can help them.

The occasional request for help does not constitute dependency on the therapist. In fact, complete absence of requests for help from the group therapist may also be a problem. Only if such requests are excessive and the youth have the information or skills to answer the questions themselves can the above request require the group's attention.

Subgroup Structure

In most groups, communication is not distributed equally in direction. That is, youth tend to communicate more frequently with some than with others. They tend to choose to work in teams more with some than with others. These mutual preferences for work or communication lead to subgrouping, or the formation of small groups of persons within the larger therapy groups. Although subgroup influence has not been examined empirically in therapy groups, it has been studied by Gebhardt and

Meyers (1995) in decision-making groups. They concluded that sub-groups' consistency and persistency are related to group outcomes.

Subgrouping is an inevitable part of any group. In the beginning especially, youth have difficulty interacting evenly with everyone else. For some clients, it is only within subgroups that they are comfortable in attempting to make initial social contacts with others. As a result, group therapists usually encourage subgroup activities to get clients to partici-pate at all. More often than not, the subgroup activity enhances rather than detracts from the attainment of most group goals. For example, we have found in some groups that the cohesion level is higher for sessions in which subgroup activities are used than for those in which subgroup activities are not used at all. However, on occasion, the subgroup may be valued by the members so much more than the group as a whole that their relationships tend to disrupt the ongoing group process. Subgroups can become excessively competitive. If such subgroups exist, the struc-ture needs to be modified. Among the narrow-range interventions the therapist might consider are increasing all group activities and reducing or entirely eliminating subgroup activities. The therapist might introduce cooperative games during the recreational 10 minutes at the end of the session. He or she might introduce cooperative extragroup tasks for the members to consider. The group therapist should take responsibility for the structuring of subgroups in formal subgroup activities through the way he or she assigns them. Above all, subgroups should not be estab-lished by the members. Low-status members continually get left out.

All of the above interventions are narrow-range interventions primar-ily introduced and sometimes imposed by the therapist. As with the previous group problems, it is possible to use group problem solving or other group exercises such as those demonstrated above to resolve the problem. In the following brief example, the therapist noted a problem of fixed subgroups.

In a community anger management group of female adoles-cents, the therapist noted a small drop in attendance at sessions. She also noted that everyone seemed to get the same partners every time a subgroup program was announced and that people would rush to sit with their friends at the beginning of the meeting. As a result, some of the members seemed to be working primarily with one or two others, to the exclusion of most of the other members of the group. When the therapist shared her observations with the group, some of them agreed that it was a problem, whereas others were satisfied with the way it was working. After some discussion of the consequences of the present situation, the majority decided to develop a list of things they could do to mix the group a little better. A number of ideas were proposed, but after the group evaluated the ideas, the three they agreed on were that subgrouping activities should not be used for the next four sessions, the seating arrangement should change every week, and members should make an attempt to address people broadly rather than any one or two individuals or the therapist. Those who opposed the changes agreed when the members decided to evaluate whether they were successful by the end of the next month.

In this example, a problem-solving strategy was implemented of presenting the group therapist's observation and available group data to the group and asking for confirmation or rejection of her hypothesis, looking at consequences of the present pattern, developing a list of potential ways of handling the problem, evaluating and selecting several of these, and finally evaluating periodically whether the problem was agreed on. Not all members agreed initially with the plan, as is often the case, but the therapist encouraged them to find a consensus by adding actions that the minority valued.

Group Norms

One set of elements commonly observed in groups is norms or standards. Schopler and Galinsky (1985) defined norms as rules that serve to guide, control, or regulate proper and acceptable behavior of group members. (What is "proper" and "acceptable" depends on a number of factors, such as group expectations, agency policies and procedures, therapist characteristics, presenting problems, and group composition.) The authors also stated that the sanctions, rewards, and penalties that may be applied to members for adherence or nonadherence to the rules help define and maintain the norms.

This definition was expanded by Belfer and Levendusky (1985), who emphasized that norms are behavioral rules that guide the interaction of the group and that norms are established by the ongoing interpersonal process of the group. These authors also stated that group therapists should attempt to build in "appropriate" norms because some norms can be detrimental to positive outcome.

Group norms may be either explicit or implicit. Most common, however, are implicit norms that can be deduced from the shared behavior of the members. One might ask whether the concept of norms is appropriate. Is it not better to talk about the behavior? The reason for the postulation of norms is that the behavior is shared and mutually influenced by the actions of all the members. It is characteristic of the group interaction rather than solely of a given client. In a community group of adolescents referred by the courts and parents for persistent aggressive behavior in school and in the community, the norm in the group seemed to be that one should never talk unless called on and that then one should be as monosyllabic as possible—not atypical behavior for many adolescents in dealing with adults. No one had ever stated this norm. The therapist had ascertained it by observing the common phenomena. Another example of an implicit norm was in a school group of youth who abused drugs. The norm was that members should chat for an hour about their contact with women during the week. They also complained about teachers and the unfairness of parents and shared opinions about various professional sports players and teams. They would get into arguments about extra-group events with peers. Because the therapist had no formal agenda or clear expectations or tasks, the youth found this activity easy, though often boring and unproductive. The content was trivial, and no one seriously self-disclosed. The behavior associated with the norm was mutually reinforced by the members and, in a sense, by the therapist, who remained passive. Norms such as this are particularly relevant because they prevent the real work of the group from occurring.

The Development of Norms

How are norms established in the first place? Sometimes simple rules defined by the therapist are sufficient to establish a given set of norms, provided the rules are accepted by the group. Sometimes a youth with strong charismatic qualities models and is emulated for behaviors that are antithetical to the rules established by the group therapist. In some instances, several people in the group have an established and well-learned pattern of behavior that cannot be overcome by a simple rule. For example, some people tend to be highly critical of others whenever they interact with others, and they continue that behavior in the therapy group despite the rule of "looking first for positives." Others may be so frightened by self-disclosure that despite an expectation to self-disclose about situations that bother them, they are unable to comply. If this fear is shared, the norm is established. The members bring norms from other therapy groups as well. For example, a subgroup of institutionalized adolescents had previously belonged to positive peer culture (PPC) groups. Although they felt that they had been psychologically abused in the PPC groups, they pushed for the norm of mutual confrontation and less structure in the highly structured CBIGT group to which they now belonged.

Some expectations (e.g., expecting adolescent males from a Hispanic cultural background to talk openly about their feelings) may be so foreign to the youth that the expectations may have to be dropped or approximated gradually over time. Deviation from protherapeutic rules established by the therapist may be one way that youth can control the conditions of the group and successfully fight the therapist. It is conceived as a form of resistance and as a group process in its own right.

All groups have norms or informal rules, most of which can be readily identified. A number of group norms have been found to be unproductive or in some way to hinder the achievement of group and individual therapy goals. Some of those we have noted have been excessive criticism of each other or inappropriate criticism or both; inadequate mutually reinforcing or supportive statements; excessive requests to the therapist for help or solutions to problems, indicating therapist dependency; excessive off-task behavior; coming to sessions late or leaving early; inadequate concern for the problems of others; limited self-disclosure; and not doing homework. Most of these norms are negatively formulated. Once the problem norm is identified, the goal should be the achievement of the positively framed norm: for example, everyone sharing his or her problems with others and everyone completing his or her agreed-on home tasks. Each of these problems has been dealt with in a similar way. To illustrate some of these strategies, an excerpt from the meeting of a group of institutionalized adolescents being treated for alcohol and drug abuse is presented. In this group, the prevailing interactive norm seemed to be that "sarcastic criticism is highly valued."

Sara Lee: Walley, you never do your homework. Why do you come if you aren't willing to work?

Others: (Laughter)

Walley: Get off my case. What do you care if I don't do my homework? I'm not the only one.

Sara Lee: We're supposed to be helping each other.

Walley: If your criticism is help, than it's no wonder I'm not getting better. Everybody's idea of help is telling someone what to do. If my mom would let me quit this group, I'd quit tomorrow.

Group Therapist: I guess there is a lot of criticism in this group lately, and it isn't always too helpful. What do the rest of you think?

Charlie: I think it's an exaggeration. Once in a while it gets out of hand maybe. Just maybe.

Biggie: I don't think it's an exaggeration at all. Last week I bet I got 20 put-downs. Frankly, I think that Leah [the group therapist] should be saying something when these kind of put-downs occur.

Sara Lee: Twenty put-downs, speaking of exaggeration.

(The discussion continues in the same tone, with most of the members upset with the high frequency of put-downs and critical statements.)

Mike: Well, how do you learn if we don't criticize one another?

Doran: We sure don't do it in a way that I can learn from.

Several: Yeah, I agree. Me neither. No way!

Group Therapist: I think this is a serious problem, and I'm glad it was brought up so that we can try to do something about it. But first I want to say that to a large degree I feel coresponsible for the emergence of this problem. I have permitted free flow of criticism before we have even discussed, much less practiced, various styles of effective feedback. Does anyone feel that we should do anything about it?

Mike: I for one am going to do what Wayne just did. I'm going to let people know when I feel put down or unfairly or meanly criticized.

(Others agree)

Anita: But even criticism of criticism has got to be handled in a new way. Otherwise everyone will just get defensive, and we'll never break the cycle.

Wayne: I agree with both of you. But I think, Leah [the group therapist], you ought to call it to our attention if we aren't seeing it.

Group Therapist: I'll certainly point it out. But I think it is important that you call each other on it if you experience that the feedback is given in a particularly mean or unhelpful way. I can't always tell.

After this, the group members went right into the selection of a strategy for dealing with the omnipresence of put-downs so that further problem solving initiated by the group therapist was not necessary. However, from then on, Leah carefully monitored the frequency of put-downs or unfair criticism in the group to make sure the plans were working. Furthermore, she built into the next session an exercise on giving and receiving criticism.

In this group, a member complained to the therapist, who, rather than working with the individual alone, encouraged him to bring his complaint into the group at the first opportunity. Not only did this place that person in a leadership position, but it prevented the therapist from taking over the solution process. It is sometimes necessary for the therapist to reflect what he or she perceives is going on in the group, but member perceptions are equally relevant. The problem above is clearly not solved, but the pattern is set for dealing with the problem when it appears again in the future.

Self-Disclosure

One norm that is not naturally occurring in groups is the norm of self-disclosure—the expectation that members will discuss openly with one another their concerns, feelings with respect to situations, and personal conflicts. Assuming conformity to this expectation, it is the norm of self-disclosure. In some groups, the norm exists that members should self-disclose as little as possible. Because of the centrality of self-disclosure to therapy, it is handled here as a separate group attribute. Low levels of self-disclosure, as noted earlier, interfere with assessment and intervention.

One can increase self-disclosure in adolescent groups in the initial phase of therapy by creation of a mutually trusting atmosphere, by the therapist's modeling of self-disclosure, by protection of those who initially display self-disclosure, and by discussion of case studies in which the members note dissimilarities as well as similarities to their own cases. Flowers and Schwartz (1985) reported that self-disclosure in adult groups is increased when members are given as homework the task of writing down and specifying (in depth) the disclosures they might make in the next session. Self-disclosure is even further increased if members are instructed to bring two written disclosures to the next group session, with the alternative of disclosing either, both, or neither, depending on their feelings during that session.

The self-disclosure of group members can also be enhanced by the self-disclosure of the group therapist, as evidenced in studies on the dyadic relationship with adults by Sermat and Smyth (1973). However, too much or too intimate self-disclosure by the group therapist can lead to member distrust or the perception that the therapist is using the group for his or her own therapy. The same is probably true for adolescents. Simonson and Bahr (1974) have shown that to be most effective, self-disclosure by the therapist should be about private matters but not about his or her own personal problems or conflicts. Providing personal examples of various concepts used in therapy is another safe way for the group therapist to self-disclose without frightening the members.

In a CBIGT approach, gradual self-disclosure is advocated to reduce the likelihood of punishment from one's peers for exposing one's feelings or concerns. This would argue against too much self-disclosure, especially in beginning sessions, when cohesion and intimacy have not had ample time to develop. If the member discloses information that provokes intense feelings of embarrassment, and he or she does not get support from the other members, negative results such as emotional "breakdown" may occur, or the person may drop out of therapy in a community group. Several exercises have been developed to enhance self-disclosure. Exercise 3.2, in which the participants discuss a case study of a youth like themselves, seems to serve effectively the purpose of gradually increasing self-disclosure.

In summary, one of the main benefits of self-disclosure seems to be improved assessment and "getting feelings out" while still feeling accepted as a worthwhile human being. A side benefit of others' self-disclosures (in groups) is the discovery that other people share feelings that one assumes are too "terrible" and that one believes are unique to oneself. Moreover, improved verbal skills consequent to practicing self-disclosure and to hearing how others express themselves should be of lasting value. Self-disclosure by reticent members can be enhanced by the self-disclosure of others in the group, including the group therapist. As self-disclosure becomes an established norm of the group, therapists have noted that the cohesion of the group also increases. Sometimes, however, if too satisfying, self-disclosure rather than change of behavior becomes the shared goal of the members. This becomes a signal to deal with the norm.

The Leadership Structure

In therapy groups, informal leaders often arise who command the respect and even the obedience of the group members to a greater extent than the group therapist does.

In the Hawks, a group of 14- to 16-year-old early juvenile offenders who met weekly in a community center, the group therapist encouraged the youth to make many decisions about their activities. After a long discussion, when the final decision was to be made, everyone would look at Gus, who would nod approval or disapproval, and that would become the decision of the group. When the members were running around the room instead of sitting in the group circle and heeding the commands of the group worker, Gus would merely nod his head, and everyone would sit down.

In the above example, it was clear that Gus's informal role was more powerful than the formal role of therapist in influencing the in-group behavior of the members. Natural leaders may serve protherapeutic or antitherapeutic purposes or both. But even if they serve protherapeutic purposes, they exclude others from providing leadership in any way in the group. For this reason, rather than focusing on a leader who arises in the group, it is often more effective for the group therapist to conceptualize the phenomenon in terms of leadership functions that can be distributed among members of the groups. The two major categories of group functions are task and maintenance. Task functions are actions that help the group members to achieve their goals. Maintenance functions are those that serve to keep the group together and enhance interpersonal liking or cohesion. The functions of leadership as opposed to the role of leader can be distributed among all the members. Both maintenance and goal-oriented functions are essential dimensions of group therapy because the group has specific goals, but, at the same time, the members must be attracted to each other and enjoy the experience if they are to use it to attain the therapy goals. To empower the group members, the group therapist usually provides them with the opportunity and even training to perform both kinds of leadership skills. These are social skills in their own right that can enhance the client's status in the group and in his or her extragroup environment.

If the group therapist were the only leader of the group, it would not be necessary to consider the leadership structure. One could merely include leadership behaviors in the sections of this book on interventions. But to empower the group members, it is necessary to search for ways in which they can assume responsibility for functions of leadership and to determine for whom this assumption of responsibility is most appropriate. Initially, in goal-oriented groups, the therapist assumes most of those responsibilities. As the members observe the therapist and as they begin to feel comfortable in the group, they are encouraged to share in the power that was initially lodged in the hands of the therapist. The group therapist works toward a broad distribution of leadership functions in the group.

In therapy groups in which there are many well-defined intervention strategies and a great deal of information available to the members (e.g., in stress management groups), there is a tendency for group therapists to exercise a great deal of control by means of their agendas and their strict adherence to those agendas. Such therapists are often confronted by a high dropout rate that suddenly ensues (see, e.g., Whitney & Rose, 1989).

What is the value of members' performing their own leadership behaviors? First, practice in performing leadership functions that facilitate the attainment of therapy goals often extends the member's area of competence to other social groups in which leadership is usually highly valued. (As a result, leadership skills learned in the therapy group have the opportunity of being reinforced in other groups.) Second, the more the members provide their own leadership, the more likely it is that they themselves will choose to work on problems of central concern and will try out new methods. Third, as we suggested above, members of therapy groups are more likely to be in low-status situations throughout their social world. They experience powerlessness in a wide variety of social situations. The successful performance of leadership activities enhances their perceived power or feeling of self-efficacy in the group. This does not imply that all members become therapists but that they achieve incremental control over their own program and, it is hoped, to an increasing degree over their own lives. If the leadership functions are distributed among the members, it is less likely that the members will become too dependent on the therapist or one particular member of the group.

Of course, there are also dangers in the delegation of responsibilities. The process becomes less efficient. Occasionally, private agendas of the members interfere with goal achievement. Problems may also arise when the therapist abdicates all leadership functions. He or she may find that the most deviant member assumes the reins of power (see Bion, 1959; Redl, 1955) or that someone who has a history of leadership in his or her own gang or has previous group therapeutic experience in another type of group assumes this role, such as Gus in the earlier example. But if the therapist is aware of these potential pitfalls, the advantages far exceed those of a controlling position by the group therapist. Rather than abdication, the most effective approach seems a gradual and planful shift of leadership responsibilities to the members.

For the above reasons, the group therapist is constantly concerned with training all the members in leadership behaviors and transferring his or her responsibilities to them. In fact, by the end of therapy, the members themselves should be helping to clarify problems, suggesting therapy plans, developing contracts for each other, choosing their own tasks, and organizing role plays.

Training in leadership behaviors occurs in the same way as training in all other behaviors that a group therapist attempts to increase. The group discusses what the group therapist specifically does as therapist. The group therapist then asks the members to observe which of these behaviors he or she performs at a given meeting. Subsequently, the members are encouraged, initially by the therapist and later by each other, to perform these behaviors whenever possible. In subsequent meetings, members are given practice in being discussion leaders of the group, with the group therapist acting as either coach or cotherapist. Some group therapists focus directly on extending the members' leadership skills. In these sessions, discussion leading, keeping the group on track, involving others, careful listening, dealing with disagreement, and summarizing are presented and modeled, and opportunities for practice are provided in subgroups. After therapy has terminated, some members may serve as group aides in groups of younger youth, thereby further reinforcing their leadership ability. Obviously, this type of program is limited to youth who are not too restricted by the nature of their problems. For highly stressed youth, this may add just one more burden to their already heavy load. For those who are intellectually challenged, such a program may be beyond their skill level.

In the following example, the problem was initially viewed as exclusively belonging to the two group therapists, who then involved the group in helping them to solve the therapists' problem. As the situation evolved, rather than being solely a case of the therapists talking too much, it appeared to involve the more important, concomitant problem of too little delegation of leadership functions to the youth.

In a social skill training group, according to the observer's data, the two therapists in the group were speaking more than 42% of the time. This obviously left the group members with less than 58% for all seven of them to discuss and practice new social skills. When the data were reviewed, most of the members initially stated that they highly valued the contribution of the therapists and did not want to alter the situation. However, several mentioned that they would like more opportunity to practice. It was also mentioned that sometimes the one therapist repeated with other words what the first therapist had said. (With the help of the therapists, members were, at the moment of the discussion, using their assertiveness skills while the therapists practiced being quiet and carefully listening.)

One of the therapists admitted that he tended to be somewhat competitive and felt that he had to say "smart" things to look good. Maybe he had to have another message for himself, he suggested. The group therapists proposed that perhaps the problem was solely that of the therapists and not of the entire group. ("We talk too much? We interrupt the members too much?" "We do it; we should solve it.") Several youth disagreed. One stated that if they as members were sufficiently involved, the therapists wouldn't have to talk so much. The group therapists asked whether they might be interested in brainstorming observable strategies that the therapists might consider and that the group as a whole might consider. Coming up with a list for the therapists first, the youth decided on the following. Because the therapists tended to amplify unnecessarily each other's statements, the youth established a rule that the group therapists could not talk back to back. The youth agreed that the group would monitor the therapists' adherence to the rule by having one person each week count instances of back-to-back talking by the therapists. They also decided that any lecture that needed to be given would be typed in advance and given as a handout. The members could then ask questions the next week. For the therapist who noted that he had to talk to sound "smart," the members advised, teasingly, that he practice reminding himself that they thought he was smart enough already.

The youth came up with the following recommendations for themselves. They agreed to report the number of back-to-back statements at the beginning of the subsequent session. They agreed to provide the therapists with feedback on how they felt the therapists were doing. They thought it was a good idea for group members to serve as the directors of the modeling-rehearsal role-play sessions. Finally, they offered to do the summarization at the end of the sessions themselves instead of letting the therapists do it.

What is unique in this example is that the therapists used a double brainstorming phase: one for themselves and one for the youth. They also modeled self-disclosure of mistakes they had made and even distorted cognitions. They offered to work on their behavior as a means of resolving an annoying problem. They involved the group in monitoring those changes. They permitted and in fact encouraged the youth to assume leadership functions that the therapists had previously carried out themselves.

Group Development

The term *group development* refers to the ways in which norms, roles, cohesion, communication patterns, subgroups, and leadership shift over time. In that sense, group development is a kind of metaprocess. Common elements seem to run through most paradigms of group development (see, e.g., Corey & Corey, 1997; Forsyth, 1990; Garvin, 1987, pp. 110-111; Sarri & Galinsky, 1985; Tuckman, 1965) that suggest that some phenomena are at least in part a function of time. It is useful for group therapists to be aware of group process insofar as the phase of therapy is one of many conditions that may contribute to the appearance of certain behaviors viewed as obstructionist or constructive. This awareness

TABLE 14.1 Group Development in a Structured Group

Group Phase	Therapist Behavior	Group Processes
Orientation Phase	Orients members to theory and approach Ascertains levels of motivation Orients members to each other Introduces rules Promotes protherapeutic norms Encourages broad participation	Factual communication Limited self-disclosure High mutual anxiety Feedback limited and polite Norms loosely established Leadership functions primarily controlled by therapist
Preliminary Work Phase	Stimulates moderate self-disclosure Examines problem situations Introduces extragroup tasks Trains in effective feedback Teaches basic concepts Initiates brief role plays	Weak subgroups begin to form Cohesion increases somewhat Members focus attention on therapist Feedback is descriptive and positive Mutual seeking of clarification of concepts and strategies Participation increases, distribution broadens
Deterioration or Conflict Phase	Examines nonproductive group processes Becomes more flexible and empathetic Begins to look at consequences of present behavior Initiates discussion of group problems Introduces concept of cognitive distortions Introduces group problem solving	Homework completion rate drops Feedback becomes more negative Anger and withdrawal begin to intensify Cohesion begins to weaken Roles and norms are challenged by members
Resolution Phase	Assists members to assume responsibility for therapy Encourages leadership from members Deals with complex situations Modifies program in accordance with members' suggestions	Feedback to each other constructive Group engages in problem solving Increased and broadened distribution of interaction More task-oriented communication New protherapeutic norms and roles and higher levels of established cohesion

TABLE 14.1 *Continued*

Group Phase	Therapist Behavior	Group Processes
Secondary Work Phase	Reduces own activity	Interaction highly task-oriented
	Reduces frequency of reinforcement	Rate of homework completion high
	Encourages members to work on complex problems	Members assume major leadership functions
		Significant self-disclosure to each other
		Cohesiveness decreases slightly
Termination Phase	Points to principles of generalization	Group is more spontaneous
	Prepares for termination	Cohesion diminishes
	Increases own activity slightly	Group focuses on roles in extragroup social units
	Summarizes progress	Group focuses on future actions
	Helps individuals to plan posttherapy activity	

normalizes the behavior. If conflict persists across phases, the behavior can be viewed in a different light. Unfortunately, the boundaries of phases have not been adequately defined. Clinical judgment and some paradigms provide the basis for the decision that the group is functioning in one phase or another. Wheelan and Hochberger (1996) have demonstrated and checked the validity of a method for assessing development in task groups. Its applicability to therapy groups is uncertain. We have made a preliminary attempt to describe what we have discovered to be common (but not universal) attributes of each of these phases in Table 14.1. We draw heavily on the paradigm developed by Sarri and Galinsky (1985) in our clinical descriptions of the phases and the attendant therapist activities.

In Table 14.1, the phases of development commonly found in CBIGT groups are described in terms of some of the group processes or structures characteristic of a given phase and the therapist's most common behaviors during those phases. We have selected those therapist behaviors that also seem to contribute to a given phase and participate in the evolution of the next phase. Columns 2 and 3 represent only a sample of all possible structures and therapist behaviors. The major phases of closed groups are orientation, preliminary work, conflict, resolution, secondary work, and termination. Each is described in Table 14.1. Failure to allow the youth to be thoroughly oriented to the therapist, the program, and each other in the orientation phase often results in low cohesion and limited cooperation. Entry too early into the preliminary work phase usually results in premature problem solving and superficial discussion of problems. This in turn can trigger the conflict phase, which, when recognized, can be dealt with in the group while facilitating the learning of how to handle conflict. This discussion initiates the resolution phase. Ignoring the conflict phase may result in failure to go beyond the preliminary work phase. It is only when conflict and other deterioration effects have been identified and resolved that the group enters the secondary work phase. It is usually in this phase that important problems are dealt with. As the specified time approaches or, in open-ended groups, as people achieve their major goals for being in the group, the termination phase, in which the focus is on preparation for ending and leaving the group, begins. In open-ended groups, such as one finds in institutions, we have observed the same phases, each of which is characterized by the behavior of the dominant subgroup. Those youth just entering or about to leave the group may have their own subgroup phase that differs from the dominant phase. More research is need on this phenomenon. There is a great deal of literature on phases of group development (see literature cited above), although little of it involves research.

The duration of phases is uneven. It depends in part on experience of the youth in the group, therapist behavior, and the concurrent external events. In some groups, not all the phases can be observed. In other groups, such phases as conflict and revision can be as short as a few minutes or may prevail for a long proportion of the history of the group. If the conflict phase persists for a long time, little can be achieved. If the conflict phase lasts longer than one session, it often results in dropouts. In our experience, if the duration of the group is 7 or fewer weeks, the likelihood of a lengthy conflict phase diminishes. (This may be a function of a therapist's attempting to get through the agenda and failing to deal with important concerns of members.) Groups of more than 12 sessions are likely to repeat the conflict and resolution phases. Also, we have noted that with inexperienced therapists far more often than with experienced therapists, the conflict phase occurs for a longer duration and more frequently. These conclusions are based solely on clinical observations.

Some Final Considerations
About Group Problems

In the initial phase of dealing with group problems, some or all of the group members may expect that the group, on seeing the data, will agree with the therapist's interpretations. Data are often convincing, especially when there are multiple indicators, such as low attendance, low satisfaction, and an uneven distribution of participation. Occasionally, however, for various reasons, the group regards the data as nonproblematic. There may not be enough evidence to convince the group of its problem, or it may be a problem that belongs to the group therapist. In either case, it is usually advisable to leave the problem until more data become available and for the group therapist to examine his or her own stake in the problem. Often, in short-term groups, group therapists will ignore group problems as they arise in order to keep up with the agenda. If a problem is serious, it will persist and function to lessen the effectiveness of the group. Often one will lose more time by ignoring the problem than by handling it. As an intermediate step, some group therapists will take steps on their own without involving the members. For example, in a group in which the interaction among members was directed primarily toward the therapist and not to each other, the group therapist, without consulting the group, asked the members to direct their statements to the group. He also backed a little out of the circle; he would respond with "I wonder what others think" when questions were asked of him. As determined by the data collected on direction of communication, this therapist-initiated solution in this case seemed to work. However, in a similar situation with an anger management group, the therapist's interventions were ineffective in getting broad involvement, and a problem-solving process was begun. The process itself affords an important therapeutic opportunity, often enhancing the relationship of the therapist to the group and increasing the cohesion of the group. But it is a process costly in time. If group problems abound, the group may not get to its other work of learning unique social and cognitive skills for which the clients originally may have been referred to the group. For these reasons, preventative practices are necessary to preserve any possibility of therapy goal attainment. In long-term groups, this may be less necessary. Thus, prevention, though not universally desirable, may represent sound therapy practice in groups that are of short duration and have primarily an educational or a narrow skill training focus.

Basically, strategies of prevention are good intervention approaches. If the attraction of the group is kept high through a balance of effective work and attractive programming with adequate variation and challenge, if group therapists make sure at every meeting that everyone participates and limit those who talk excessively as soon as this occurs, and if group therapists have well-planned meetings with reasonable and achievable agendas, then it is unlikely that many group problems will arise. None of us are perfect, however, and in the absence of that perfection, something is always overlooked or someone is slighted. Group therapists, too, vary in mood, experience, and ability to handle complex group stimuli. And unusually difficult groups and persons can create problems under the most group-hygienic conditions. So problems are inevitable, and an approach to group problem solving is necessary.

It should be noted that many of the problems described above could have been analyzed from one of several perspectives. A norm problem could have been viewed as a communication problem or a communication problem perceived as a question of inappropriate role performance. There is considerable overlapping of the concepts, but in each case it was clear that there was a group problem and that it needed to be dealt with. Strategies of intervention are more dependent on the manifested behavior in the group than on the particular label used to describe the problem.

Summary

In this chapter, we focused on several group processes and structures: cohesion, group communication patterns, group norms, the leadership structure of the group, and group development. These in particular lend themselves to observation or other forms of monitoring. Throughout, emphasis lay on the involvement of the youth in the solution of group problems. The primary means by which this involvement took place in most of the examples presented were presentation of data and other observations indicating a group problem, checking with the group, systematic problem solving, and, especially within the problem-solving approach, techniques of group brainstorming, group evaluation, and ongoing monitoring. It should be clear from the content of this chapter that modification of group structures also involves and has as its purpose the modification of individual behavior. However, if one attempts to modify the behavior of an individual without regard to the level of cohesion in the group, the norms of the group, the communication pattern in the group, and the distribution of leadership functions, the likelihood of success is dramatically reduced. Individual behavior in a group is largely dependent on the behavior of the others in the group. Furthermore, the solving of a shared problem provides an opportunity for firsthand observation of group members' problem-solving skills and excellent modeling of the problem-solving process.

It was also noted that not every group problem needs to be resolved through problem solving. Some problems can be prevented by preventative measures. Others can be dealt with by a change in the therapist's behaviors. It was recognized that group problem solving is time-consuming and needs to be used judiciously.

In this chapter, when the level, distribution, or intensity of any of these attributes interferes with achievement of individual goals, changes in the group process may be called for. Dysfunctional group attributes can arise at any time throughout the history of the group. If they are ignored, they often become a "hidden agenda" that interferes with the work of the group.

Finally, in ascertaining a problem in group process, no one person is forced to assume sole blame for it. On the other hand, no one person in the group can escape at least partial responsibility for the existence of the given problematic process and its eventual remediation. Because blame is not ascribed to any one person and responsibility is attributed to all persons, members are more readily able to participate openly and actively in the process. In the world outside the group, responsibility for most communication problems must also be shared with others if situations are to be improved. Learning to deal with mutual problems is an important task in its own right.

CHAPTER 15

Beyond the Boundaries of the Group

Procedures for Generalization

In therapy groups, youth may readily learn the behaviors appropriate to being good group members. They may learn to role-play coping behaviors and demonstrate in the group their use of sophisticated coping cognitions. They may learn to talk openly in the group about their feelings and cognitions. They may learn how to deal with one another in the group and with the group therapist. But unless they can apply these behaviors and cognitions to situations occurring in the extragroup world and maintain them long after the group has ended, these new behaviors and cognitions will be of little use to them. Throughout this book, a number of principles that enhance generalization of change have been referred to. In this chapter, these principles are summarized and new ones presented for generalizing and maintaining learning beyond the limited but important conditions of the group.

Generalization refers to learning that occurs beyond the boundaries of the therapeutic session in terms of time, behavior, setting, or any combination of these. *Generalization in time* refers to maintenance of what is learned in the group beyond the termination of the clinical experience. Debbie has learned in the group to let her mother know in a matter-of-fact tone of voice when she is upset and what precisely she perceives to have upset her. She will have maintained these skills if, 6 months after the group experience, she continues to address her mother in this way when she feels that her mother has upset her. Relapse prevention falls into this category. Relapse prevention refers to the maintenance of a low level or zero level of addictive behaviors such as alcohol and drug abuse, cigarette smoking, and overeating (Marlatt & Gordon, 1985).

Generalization of behavior refers to the practice of new behaviors similar to but not the same as those already learned in the therapy session. For example, the client who learns to control anger in school may generalize what he has learned to controlling his stress responses in school.

Generalization of setting refers to the application of the behavior learned in one setting to another setting. This is also referred to as *transfer of learning*. For example, the client who learns, in the group session, to refuse attempts of his friends to impose on him learns to apply this same set of behaviors at home when he refuses to let his older brother impose on him.

A combination of all three types of generalization would be demonstrated by the adolescent who, having learned in the group to ask for help from a role-played physician, applies that behavior with her real doctor in the office setting, applies that learning with her teacher from whom she needs help, and continues to demonstrate that help-seeking behavior long after the group has terminated. If therapy is to be considered effective, generalization must have taken place at all three levels.

Principles of Generalization

The most fundamental observation about generalization is that it rarely happens to any significant degree if nothing is done about it (Stokes & Baer, 1977, p. 350). Generalization requires a specific plan that can be implemented. For this reason, in the CBIGT approach, a gradual and systematic program for the generalization of changes from the group to the client's natural environment and beyond the therapy period is planned for and carried out. Once changes begin to be performed on a regular basis in the group, the focus of planning and therapy activities shifts to maintaining these desired changes in the members' lives outside the group and helping them to try out similar behaviors in a variety of settings. Although the emphasis shifts more and more to taking steps that increase the likelihood of generalization, from the first day of group therapy, generalization strategies are increasingly employed.

The group provides a number of advantages over the therapeutic dyad in facilitating generalization. Some of these were already noted in Chapter 1. The group for young people provides an environment that simulates more nearly the real world than the one-to-one relationship; provides multiple models and modeling experiences; provides frequent and varied opportunities for members to assume responsibility for helping others; provides a variety of in-group experiences, situations, and demands; and encourages extragroup experiences that are monitored in the group. As the reader will note in the subsequent sections, each of these circumstances represents an opportunity to apply a unique strategy in the training for generalization. It is possible to identify at least three general categories of strategies of generalization. The first set of strategies involve increasing the multiplicity and variability of experiences and examples used in the treatment program; the second set involve teaching general categories of intervention and general categories of targets; the third set involve preparing the individual in the group for the extragroup experience; and the fourth set involve training directly in the extragroup environment. It should be noted that a firm empirical foundation does not as yet exist for all of these strategies. They are for the most part derived by extrapolation from some modest research, often in nonclinical settings, and from extensive clinical experience.

Many of these principles espoused here overlap. In some of these principles, subprinciples can be determined. Let us discuss these strategies in more detail as to why and how they might be useful and how they are carried out.

Multiple Trials and Variation

The first set of principles focus on providing many varied learning possibilities in the group. These strategies suggest that the group therapist should not only diversify the experience for the group members by providing many different types of examples and intervention program elements but also vary it in such a way as to prepare for uncertainty, to simulate the real world, and to increase the level of difficulty of the training examples.

Provide Multiple Examples

One-trial learning only rarely occurs. One example is even more difficult to learn from. For this reason, many examples are usually introduced into the group for each of the strategies or techniques taught. The therapist not only provides multiple examples in the orientation to a new technique but is constantly asking the group members for examples of topics dealt with from their own experience. Often the therapist will introduce a topic one week, provide examples, and as an extragroup task suggest to the group members that they seek out such examples between sessions.

In the presence of many examples, the parameters of a given strategy can be more clearly delineated, as well as limits of the strategy. Moreover, cues regularly correlated with reinforcement eventually gain control over the associated behaviors with repetition.

Provide Many Modeling and Practice Trials

But learning even from multiple examples is usually not enough. Multiple experiences may be further created by using multiple models for any behavior that is taught and providing the opportunity for multiple rehearsals or practice of the behavior before the client tries it out in the real world. Reinforcement is given on frequent occasions in response to a given situation. One group member noted that after he had role-played how he would respond to his sister when she borrowed his clothes without asking, he responded in his old way by screaming at her until she cried and his mom grounded him. He commented that she did not respond to him in the way that the role player did in the group. The therapist then created a number of opportunities within the program to do it again. Everyone in the group modeled the situation for him. On a board game, the therapist arranged for him to role-play that situation when he landed on the role-play square. Following the modeling demonstration, he rehearsed several variations on the same situation during the session. He even role-played several times with his "buddy" between sessions. He was able to see a total of six models and practice the behavior a total of seven times before he reported success in applying the behavior in the real world.

The more similar the problems of the members of the group, the greater opportunity for both multiple models and multiple rehearsal. One client's rehearsal is frequently a model for other members of the group with the same problem situation and vice versa. But if the group is too similar, there are no effective models in the problem area, and, as we pointed out earlier, it is necessary to bring in models from outside the group. As the problems of the group become more diversified, there are fewer opportunities for multiple trials of relevant situations, but usually the quality of the modeling sessions increases.

The round-robin technique can be used to provide a large number of repetitions of modeling and rehearsals. In this technique, the therapist models a behavior (e.g., refusing to take a drink) for the person on his or her left, who plays the role of the significant other. Then the person on the left repeats the leader's behavior with the person on his or her left, who plays the role of the significant other, until everyone has rehearsed the desired set of behaviors.

Provide Varied Experiences

Multiple trials are not enough. Problem situations in the real world vary a great deal. The significant others do not always act in a consistent way, different significant others initiate stressful interactions, and the environments in which these situations take place change from time to time. To deal with the variation in the real world, the examples used in therapy should also be varied. Variation tends to expand the cues under which the behavior is reinforced (Goldstein et al., 1966). This, in turn, increases the likelihood that a variety of cues, rather than just those associated with the group and the group therapist, will elicit the desired behaviors and hence that the behaviors are more likely to generalize to the natural environment and be maintained over time.

The group therapist may build in variety in a number of ways. Situational analysis generates a pool of relevant and difficult examples that are likely to arise in the client's life. Other situations may be obtained from weekly diaries or logs kept by the members. These situations can then be used as the content of group role plays, as the focus of problem-solving sessions, as cards in a board game, or as themes of group exercises.

Vary the Therapy Media

Role plays and problem situations handled in the group are not the only aspects of the program that can be varied. As the group progresses, variation in the program media through the use of board games, nondirective discussions, diaries, field trips, and different kinds of group exercises are used not only to change the cues of learning but also to increase the members' interest in the group and the group cohesion. Most individuals have unique learning patterns. Reliance on one medium such as role plays or cognitive restructuring may not be suitable or useful to some clients. A variety of learning contexts increases the likelihood that something will work with everyone. It is also our experience that groups that adhere too rigidly to one type of intervention, such as modeling, tend to reduce the level of attraction for members. Although all meetings have some common elements, such as a review of extragroup tasks and a summary of the data from the previous week, each session introduces increasingly new and different program components.

Vary the Level of Difficulty

It is not sufficient to vary the role plays, group exercises, games, examples, and problems dealt with in therapy; all of these should also grow more difficult as therapy progresses. To achieve early success, the client should be prepared for and involved in relative simple tasks. Success is one of the most powerful reinforcers of behavior. But the demands of the real world are often far more complex and exacting. To prepare youth to eventually deal with complex problems, they must gradually be presented with successively more difficult and longer tasks.

In a group of youth, all of whom were characterized by anxiety, social skill deficits, and isolation, the initial task in the group was to learn the names of the other people in the group. The extragroup task was to call one of the other members and discuss the group. The telephone call was rehearsed in the group. The later in-group tasks were to observe and comment on a role play by the therapists. It was not until the third session that the members themselves role-played a single response to a situation in which the antagonists were played by the therapists. In the fifth session, the members were playing both roles in simulated situations that were of concern to them. In the sixth session, they agreed to try out the newly learned behaviors in the real world before the seventh session. They discussed their experiences with each other at the seventh session. The real-world assignments not only were increasingly more difficult but also increased the degree of unpredictability.

Vary in Such a Way as to Simulate More and More Closely the Conditions of the Real World

As in the above example, one should vary the examples so as to simulate more and more closely the conditions of the outside world. All other structural elements should also move in the direction of duplicating as nearly as possible the conditions of the real world. A modest way of simulating the real world is to use props in role playing, longer role plays, and multiperson role plays. Using people who are similar to the real antagonists is also helpful. Some groups meet in living rooms or in cafes, especially during the last meetings.

Another way of simulating the real world is fading therapy cues. Reinforcement schedules are thinned. Real-world reinforcement schedules are intermittent at best. Therapist instructions are reduced in frequency. Responsibility for therapy planning, as noted in one of the above strategies, is delegated to the members. Conflict in the group is eventually left to the members to resolve.

Vary the Degree of Predictability

The natural environment is often very uncertain; thus, it becomes necessary to structure increased unpredictability of situations practiced in the group setting as well. One way to prepare for uncertainty is to bring in situations with entirely new cues attached to them, to which the clients are required to respond without any prior preparation. After initial successful experiences, these unprepared-for situations may be introduced. The danger in the early sessions is that the clients may feel overwhelmed and the procedure may become aversive. For this reason, the use of spontaneous role plays is usually restricted to the later sessions, when members have had a great deal of role-play experience and the relationship to the therapist as reinforcing person has been established.

An example of a spontaneous role play would be for the group therapist to state, suddenly in the middle of a session, that he is the neighbor with whom Pete has told the group he has had frequent arguments. "Your ball is on his lawn, you go to get it, and he says, 'Punk, get the hell off my property or I'll call the police,' " the therapist tells Pete. "Okay, handle it." Another interesting example of this principle was demonstrated by a group therapist who wore a sign that read "Mrs. Williams" (the teacher whom the group members had complained about). When the young women entered the room, she said to the last one who came in, "Elizabeth, you're late again! I should send you to the principal," and awaited her response. She wore a different sign from time to time, representing significant others with whom the group members interacted.

Review Periodically What Has Been Learned

In reviewing what one has learned and the principles involved in learning it, one increases the likelihood that the behavior and associated principles will be maintained. This is also an excellent technique for increasing the number of trials, cognitively, of what someone has been working on. As a matter of course, review occurs at the end of each session. Initially, the review is performed by the therapist, but as the group progresses, the members assume the task, first with coaching and later without.

Keep a Diary of Successes and Difficulties

As a regular part of treatment activities, group members are encouraged to keep a diary of their successes in dealing with situations that are stress or anger inducing. Following treatment, this procedure becomes a generalization strategy because, if it is successful, it keeps the client aware of what he or she is doing well and where help is needed. Diary keeping is a form of self-monitoring that occurs on a regular basis and as such adds to the many in-group practices and the variety of treatment media.

Selecting Target Behaviors That
Mediate Generalization in the Real World

Some behaviors not only are important skills in their own right but can be used to mediate generalization in the real world. These include self-management skills, problem-solving skills, skills that modify one's lifestyle, and learning of general principles behind the specific skills that are learned. In the later phase of therapy, these skills are taught following the teaching of other specific targets, such as expression of alternatives to aggression in stressful situations or to talking back to teachers and parents, improved study behaviors, and increased job-seeking behaviors.

Teach Self-Management Skills

Rehm and Rokke (1988) specifically designated self-management as a generalization strategy designed to extend the client's new behaviors into the client's daily life under his or her own direction or control. Rather than being taught only new behaviors or cognitions, youth are also taught to apply the principles of learning to whatever situations they believe they need to change or maintain. In the group, youth are taught how to reinforce themselves and when it is efficacious to do so, how to manage their own environment to obtain a desired outcome, how to instruct themselves in effective coping behaviors, and how to prepare themselves with covert modeling. All of the procedures for applying these self-management techniques have been discussed elsewhere (see Chapter 10). As a potential extragroup task, the members are encouraged to try out these procedures on their own without prestructuring or guidance from the group. They are then provided with the opportunity in the therapy group to describe successful application of these skills in their day-to-day experiences.

Teach the Skills of Systematic Problem Solving

As has been pointed out throughout this book, problem solving is an essential mediating set of cognitive skills for learning new and more effective strategies for coping with difficult situations. If the skills of problem solving are sufficiently well learned, this strategy can mediate solutions to newly observed problems outside the group. To train persons to use their problem-solving skills in this way, one exercise requests that clients observe and record new problems that occur between sessions and describe how they used their problem-solving skills to deal with these previously undiscussed events. This exercise has been used either between several of later sessions (e.g., between the 11th and 14th sessions) or between the last regular session and a booster session, because an extended period of time is usually necessary to carry out this assignment. (For more details on problem solving, see Chapter 7.)

Select Target Behaviors
That Change the Lifestyle

Changing the lifestyle of the client is probably one of the more important ways of attaining maintenance and preventing relapse (Marlatt & Gordon, 1985, p. 280). Usually the undesirable behaviors are associated with a given lifestyle, especially when the problem behaviors are related to alcohol and drug abuse, violent behavior, and smoking. Modifying the social network is one step in changing the lifestyle of the client. However, a number of other interventions are equally important. Among the new behaviors learned are incorporating regular exercise into one's life, using relaxation or meditation on a daily basis, and changing one's eating habits—for example, by eating regularly.

Lifestyle changes might involve the client's getting involved with music or theater instead of "hanging out." They might include expanding academic interests and activities. The therapist must usually build on interests that already exist or have existed and then create opportunities and encourage further development of these interests.

In a community group for former and younger members of an adolescent gang group, the group therapist noted an interest in and skill in gymnastics. He was able to obtain scholarships for the members to take lessons and even found volunteers to transport the youth to these lessons. The therapist found old journals on gymnastics and used books that he shared with the members at the therapy sessions. Part of the time in the sessions was spent on reviewing the achievements of gymnastic sports stars. Several of the youth who were not as skilled nevertheless developed an interest and were coached by the more skilled members.

The group can help particularly in the development of these new lifestyles by planning together what each member might do, listening to the accounts of trying out the plan, and supporting each other in the initial changes. These are immense changes and cannot be readily achieved without the initial help of the group. It is particularly supportive to know that everyone in the group is working on similar lifestyle changes. Learning these skills is described in more detail in Chapter 13 and in Marlatt and Gordon (1985).

Teach the General Principle

As the group approaches termination, most youth will have learned a number of behaviors to be applied in a number of highly specific situations. It becomes crucial for the members to draw patterns for themselves as to when procedures they have learned are applicable and to develop for themselves general strategies that guide them in the determination of what they can do when new problems arise. One general principle already suggested is the use of systematic problem solving when the members do not know what to do in an anger- or stress-producing situation. Youth can learn many other general principles demonstrated in CBIGT to guide their behavior in these situations without going through all the problem-solving steps. The following is an example.

Vick had learned to handle a situation in which he thought he had been unfairly criticized by his mother. He disagreed with her in a matter-of-fact tone of voice and presented reasons for that disagreement. He then listened carefully to her reasons. This was in contrast to his screaming defiantly or running out of the house. The group therapist asked the others what they thought might be the "message" learned for all of them in this situation. Several group members responded that it rarely pays off to "lose your cool" when you are criticized. You are more likely to be listened to if you respond in a calm and factual manner. The therapist wondered if Vick ever lost his cool in other situations. Vick mentioned that he once had gotten kicked out of school for a couple of days because of it. The therapist reviewed the situation and noted the similarities between the two situations. The therapist continued to use this and similar examples to illustrate the importance of learning the general principle. The general task was negotiated with the group, as Stokes and Baer (1977, p. 361) recommended, that those with the problem of losing their cool try out generalized behaviors in the real world and report back to the group the next session as to their experience.

Before the individual works on generalized behaviors, it is necessary for him or her to identify general patterns of the behavior. These patterns include the range of people and other environmental conditions in which the behavior is manifested. Training to identify these general patterns can be carried out in a group exercise (Exercise 15.1). This exercise is handed out to the members the week before its use so that they can prepare in advance. They are encouraged to work with their buddies in preparing to carry out this exercise in the therapy group.

Exercise 15.1. Seeing the Larger Pattern

Purpose: By the end of this session, each member will be able to describe (a) patterns of situations each finds difficult or stressful and (b) cognitive, affective, and behavioral patterns of responses to stressful or otherwise difficult interpersonal situations.

Steps in the Exercise:

1. The group therapist will present the reasons that determining general patterns is important and open up his or her presentation to discussion. He or she will also provide an example of someone who succeeded in determining a general pattern (see above example).

2. Each participant will briefly present the review to the group and will note (a) patterns in the type of situations that he or she finds difficult or stressful and (b) patterns in response (cognitive, emotional, and/or behavioral) across several situations.

3. Other group members and the group therapist may suggest to the member additional patterns, as well as newly developing changes in earlier patterns.

4. The group will focus on the general strategies that seem to be guiding the successes each participant is having in the real world.

5. Each member will serve as discussion leader for another member.

6. At the end of the exercise, the therapist or a group member will summarize all the "patterns" that were noted and the process used to determine the pattern.

In-Group Preparation for Out-of-Group Experiences

Thus far, we have discussed what the group therapist does within the structure of the group to facilitate the generalization of change or response prevention. Effective generalization, however, can occur only with difficulty unless the group therapist prepares members directly for interacting in the natural environment. Modeling is one way of preparing them. Several other strategies that prepare directly for extragroup experiences are available. These include preparing members to do extragroup tasks, preparing them for an unsympathetic response to their new behavioral patterns, preparing them to modify their social networks, and preparing them for the possibility of relapse. Although the implementation of these behaviors occurs outside the group, preparation for implementation usually occurs within the group.

Prepare for Extragroup Tasks

As we discussed in Chapter 11, the use of extragroup tasks is one of the major strategies of generalization from the therapy setting to situations in the real world because most tasks require practice in the external environment of new behaviors learned in the group. Because this strategy has already been thoroughly dealt with in Chapter 11, many of the other extragroup strategies of generalization will be dealt with in greater detail below. Preparation for extragroup tasks is an intervention employed in every session and is the only generalization strategy that is used in every group.

Prepare for an
Unsympathetic Environment

One element in the real world that is often unpredictable is the degree of acceptance by others of real changes that were realized in the group. Because clients often expect the world to be enthusiastic about their changed behavior, they are often deeply disappointed and even offended when those expectations are not realized. For this reason, role plays of unexpected responses of significant others are presented to the client to deal with, and these are discussed in the group. Former members of similar groups are often an excellent source of rich anecdotal accounts of unsympathetic responses they received when they returned to the community or to their families and friends following therapy.

Examples of unsympathetic responses related by youth to the group have been "You used to be lots more fun before you got therapy," "Hey, I thought you had therapy, you should do better than that," "You can't tell me you really changed, I know what you're really thinking. Once a bum always a bum," and "Come on, one drink won't hurt you." It is possible to do spontaneous role plays with these unsympathetic statements.

Modify the Social Network

Often the abuse is so great from persons in the client's social network that it is necessary to help him or her change his or her network. One way of dealing with this is to examine the client's social networks in the group in terms of the needs it is serving and to problem-solve ways of modifying that network. Following this pattern, one group therapist working with aggressive youth took the social network analysis (see Chapter 12) that the members had done and had each member add at least one social unit (a group, friend, family member) to his list who was not likely to put him down for the changes he had manifested. In one case, group members chose getting involved with some relatives in a nearby town, becoming a Little League coach, volunteering at a food kitchen, getting involved in a community dramatic program, or making new school friends who were not in trouble all the time. The new people had no history and thus no expectations. The new behaviors were totally acceptable. Chapter 12 describes this intervention in more detail.

Prepare for Post-Therapy Relapse

In addition to maintaining positive behaviors, it is also necessary to prevent the recurrence of negative behaviors once these have been inhibited or reduced in frequency. Examples of such behaviors that readily recur are excessive drinking, use of drugs, aggressive behaviors, sexual abuse, agoraphobia, bulimia, and compulsive gambling. Most of the strategies advocated for relapse prevention are the same as those for maintenance of positive behaviors, but some specific strategies are especially suited to the prevention of negative responses rather than the maintenance of positive ones. One technique in particular is to identify the risk factors with a high probability of leading to relapse. If youth can be trained to identify those conditions and can be prepared to avoid or deal with them when they occur, the actual relapse may be prevented (Marlatt & Gordon, 1985). Such a procedure particularly lends itself to group training. For example, in a group of recovering drug abusers, several members pointed out that in the past they had relapsed when the pressure at school became too great, when they were put under pressure by their peers, or when their parents made what they thought were unfair demands. When asked by the therapist if they could give concrete examples of pressure, the group members described situations in which they felt they had too much homework or the homework was too difficult. Pressure from peers was experienced when the group members were criticized by them and as a result felt unsure of the relationship or rejected. To decrease the likelihood of relapse in the face of criticism, members learned to use this feeling of uncertainty as a cue to say to themselves that they worked hard at coping with the pressures of the world, that no one could be or needed to be perfect, and that criticism was one way of learning and growing on the job. They also learned how to receive the criticism through both overt and covert modeling-rehearsal sequences in which they both observed and practiced responding to criticism from each of the members of the group. To help them handle the pressure induced by homework, the members were also helped to get a special tutor whom they indicated they liked. Finally, the members learned to identify the physiological cues that preceded relapse (e.g., breathing changes, headaches, getting intensely angry, sweating). They learned to respond to such cues with one of the above coping strategies.

In varying the problems presented to the members, the group therapist introduces some situations in which a relapse might take place despite the steps taken to avoid it. Relapses are such a common occurrence, especially in the treatment of addictive behaviors, that they become one of the regular topics to be dealt with in the last few sessions of the group. One of the most common procedures is the use of case studies of how other people handled relapse. The following is an example of a case study that was used in a group of recovering alcoholic teenagers.

In the group, the therapist introduced an example of an individual who had quit drinking but who one day began to feel overwhelmed by the stressors in her life. She dropped out of the group, claiming, when called, that she was a failure and would never amount to anything. In both groups, the members discussed how they would feel in such a situation and brainstormed what one could do about it. Then each group member had to imagine what a relapse for him or her might be and how he or she might respond to such a setback. In addition to case studies, former clients can be brought in to discuss relapses they experienced and the strategies they employed to get back into active self-control. If any of the group members have ever relapsed, they too are encouraged to share their experiences with the group.

Mathews, Gelder, and Johnston (1981), using the concept of "setback" instead of "relapse," used an individualized setback list for each agoraphobic patient in their groups. Such a list contained instructions on what to do in case of a setback. The strategies outlined were to go back to the anxiety-producing situation as soon as possible, to take one step back in practice and rehearse that step often, to brush up on the coping instructions, and to remind oneself of previous gains.

Another set of strategies involves changing the evaluation of relapses. Although youth are encouraged and prepared to take whatever steps are necessary to avoid relapses, their occurrence should be evaluated as part of the therapy. All too often, youth who relapse are viewed and view themselves as the helpless victims of circumstances beyond their control (p. 31). In contrast, the group therapist introduces the idea that relapses are a "fork in the road" and that one can learn from the road signs how to handle such situations in the future without relapse. Each client's relapses are viewed as objects of careful study by the rest of the group to determine the conditions of those relapses. These conditions eventually become the cues for coping behavior. A group agreement is established as part of therapy in which potential setback situations or actual setbacks are to be brought to the group if it is still in session and to the therapist if it is not.

In summary, there are four strategies for preparation for setbacks or relapses, all of which can be used in the group: case studies, the use of models who have handled setbacks before, the use of a relapse list, and changing the evaluation of relapses. These same principles apply to highly anxious or aggressive youth, who often have relapses as well.

Training Directly Outside the Group

In the previous section, we focused on the principles involved in preparing youth for community experiences. The following are a set of principles about providing or encouraging therapeutic experiences directly in the community while the group is ongoing or after it has ended.

Make Booster Sessions and
Maintenance Groups Available

The major extragroup strategy for improving the probability of maintenance and generalization after the group has terminated is the organization of booster sessions, usually outside the clinical setting. These meetings create an opportunity for review, updating on successes and failures, and keeping members accountable for changes or lack thereof for an extended period beyond the series of regular meetings. New problems may be dealt with as well. Booster sessions are often organized to be held 1 month, 2 months, and 4 to 6 months after therapy. Usually, because of dropouts during that period, the members of several similar groups may need to be combined. The attendance increases at booster sessions if the members are involved in planning for it. They share the responsibility of providing refreshments, mailing notices of the sessions or calling, and planning an agenda.

It appears that once the group has ended, the booster session represents one more tie to the values inculcated in therapy. It is a source of continued support in a difficult and stressful world. It permits fading the therapy rather than dropping it dramatically. The limited research on booster sessions with children has been encouraging. Kazdin (1982) demonstrated the efficacy of the use of booster sessions with children in maintaining and even increasing gains occurring in the group. In our own clinical experience, the use of booster sessions has been essential to obtain maintenance. On occasion, one or even two booster sessions may not be enough to maintain new behavior or show continuing gains. One way to remedy this situation is to organize an extended series of sessions called a maintenance group.

The maintenance group is usually organized on the basis of the strategies established in the first part of this chapter. The maintenance group meets less frequently than an ongoing therapy group, usually once a month. The maintenance group is far less structured than a therapy group. The group therapist acts as consultant to the group. The members serve as discussion leaders. The members determine for the most part their own agendas, although problem situations continue to be discussed. These are for the most part more complex than those discussed in the regular therapy group. The maintenance group tends to be larger than the therapy group, but there is less of a need to individualize. Each member must do that for him- or herself. The group is composed of youth from various groups who are not yet prepared to sever ties with the program or who cannot find support in their present environment for their newly learned lifestyle.

Some group therapists have referred youth to existing groups, such as Teens Anonymous or even Batterers Anonymous, as maintenance groups. Though the philosophy of these groups is often different, they provide needed ongoing support from youth with similar problems. It is especially important, if possible, to make the referral while youth are still in the therapy group so as to help them to make the transition.

A special kind of follow-up is the individual contact. Gambrill (1983) recommended such contacts after individual therapy has terminated. She reasoned that, just as in booster group sessions, "Anticipation of this meeting may serve as a reminder to use skills that have been learned and as support for their use" (p. 387). In our groups, we have found it difficult to obtain as many as 50% of the original membership at a given booster session. With individual follow-up, a larger percentage of the membership can be reached. The ideal solution is to organize a set of booster sessions at the last session of the group. When telephone calls go out to remind people of the booster session, this may also serve as an individual follow-up interview if the members are willing.

In a day treatment center for adjudicated delinquents, such a plan was carried out. The family worker visited the clients and their families sporadically or called them on a planned basis. In some cases at least, this kept the clients from relapsing and saw them through receiving their high school diploma. In a school after the aggression management group terminated, a similar contact was instituted by the social workers, who stopped by after class or continued to have informal contacts in the school. Such contacts make it possible to evaluate the long-term effects of therapy if systematic observations are made or standardized questions are asked. Following residential treatment, the staff noted that many youth returned to see their residential staff as a way of creating their own booster session.

Encourage Membership in
Recreational-Educational Groups

Another variation of the maintenance group is to encourage membership in existing groups that do not have a therapeutic focus. Sociorecreational groups that members have joined just before termination have been dance classes, bowling clubs, friendship groups, art groups, and practically everything else a community center has to offer. The strategy of joining just before termination is extremely important to prevent failures or even difficulties that the clients are unable to handle without help. Also, in the therapy group, the adolescents find support and encouragement for attempting to find new friends and prosocial activities. This is not a trivial intervention. One of the major contributors to delinquency is peer group pressure. If alternative peer groups can be found, for many this may be a major source of prevention of relapse as well as an opportunity to practice and receive reinforcement for recently learned prosocial behaviors.

One exercise used in the groups to enhance the process of finding new groups is the following. The members are instructed to interview peers at schools to find at least 10 activity groups for young people their age. They can also go to the Y's, community centers, and nearby churches. In the group, practical matters related to obtaining this information, such as transportation to these places, are discussed. To provide each other support, group members usually go in pairs. Once they obtain their 10 names, they eliminate the duplications and place the names on a large poster. Then, as in problem solving, the members systematically evaluate each of the activities on the list. The criteria are interest, skill level, shared interest with one other member in the group, cost, and availability. Following the evaluation, they choose two of the activities they might want to join and get more information about each of them. The members then decide on the activity they wish to join and do so. In the final of four sessions in a row, they describe to the other group members their initial experiences in the activity. If the initial experiences are successful, membership in the recreational groups will usually continue after termination from group therapy.

Provide Opportunities for Youth to Teach Others

One way of becoming committed to an approach is by teaching others. By participating in subgroups, members get an opportunity to review and teach others any new technique or procedure that is being worked on. In addition, some members who are comfortable in describing their experiences are used as models in beginning groups and have the opportunity to do supervised teaching in this capacity. Whenever a client has knowledge in a given area relevant to the group, the therapist will encourage him or her to share the information or skill or experience with the rest of the members. Members are also encouraged to teach what they have learned in the group to their parents or other family members, especially systematic problem solving and negotiation. In at least one session, teaching skills and problems of teaching others are discussed.

Hold Training Sessions in the Real World

It is far easier to transfer learning from the therapeutic setting to the real world if the therapy actually occurs in the real world. For practical reasons, this is not always possible. Occasionally, group sessions are held in restaurants, in community centers, in bowling alleys, in bars, at dances, and in other locations where the actual problem takes place. If, as we assume, the learning is associated with the cues under which the behavior is learned, such practices will increase the variety of cues under which the behavior is learned. When therapy is in the outside community, the therapist is present only for a part of the meeting or for the entire meeting but in the role of consultant. In this way, increased responsibility is given the clients to practice handling their own problems as preparation for when the group has terminated.

Working with the family appears to be an excellent strategy for improving generalization. In a recent case study by Nangle, Carr-Nangle, and Hansen (1994), the authors demonstrated the importance of family problem solving as a means of obtaining generalization of change in a 15-year-old severely conduct-disordered youth. In working with three youth and their families in a clinical setting on their communication skills, Serna, Schumaker, Sherman, and Sheldon (1991) did not obtain generalization until they actually shifted the training to the homes. Though difficult in groups, training in the setting to which change should be generalized seems to be a powerful enhancement of generalization.

Use Self-Help Literature

There is an abundance of self-help literature that fits the style of many youth and is compatible with the approach advocated in CBIGT. Not all youth can use self-help manuals. Their use implies an average level of intelligence and a high degree of motivation. Usually such manuals are introduced and reviewed at one of the last sessions. Members are encouraged to borrow and browse through them and decide whether they might be helpful. Santrock's (1994) *The Authoritative Guide to Self-Help Books* presented a survey of more than 1,000 self-help books, along with ratings by professionals of each of the books, that the group therapist can draw on for any given population.

Employ Client Advocacy

All of the principles discussed above are related to helping youth to do something either in or out of the group. In many groups, the therapist may have to advocate on behalf of the clients to other social agencies or organizations or the family. Though not a group intervention, advocacy is often a way of making it possible for youth to transfer to the community what they have learned in the group or to make use of the other principles mentioned above. In many situations, clients may be able to advocate for themselves, and the group can train them in that activity. But often this is not possible without preliminary intervention by the therapist. Some examples are as follows.

In one community anger management group, the therapist advocated to the school principal on behalf of a youth for readmission of the given youth to the school from which he had been expelled. The therapist told the principal about the group, the youth's gains, and the strong desire of the youth to finish school. He reviewed the various tasks that the youth had already completed. The therapist stated that he could not guarantee the cessation of aggressive behavior but thought it was highly likely. The therapist recommended that even if the principal was willing, it would be important for the youth to ask for readmission himself and give his reasons and assurances and his plan to prevent relapse to his former way of behaving.

A young woman in a similar group had a history of petty thefts that had stopped since her entry into the group. She had been arrested several months earlier for the last theft before the group had actually begun. The therapist testified on her behalf at a presentencing hearing before the client's testifying on her own behalf as to what she had learned in the group and how the group might keep her from repeating the offense.

In the same group, one young woman wanted to return home from a foster home. Her parents would not even talk to her. The therapist talked to the parents on her behalf, noting important changes in behavior and attitudes and encouraging them to see for themselves. They agreed at least to listen to her and, as in the earlier example, agreed that the daughter would first plead her own case before they would let her back. In this as in the above examples, the target person had several of the other members model, and then she herself rehearsed several times, the interaction with the significant others. In none of these examples did the therapist guarantee maintenance of the new lifestyle of the client, but the therapist did describe what the client in each case had been doing, how he or she had been successful, and how the group might continue to help and gave a prediction of what was likely to occur in the future. Over time, if the predictions prove to be correct, the power of the therapist to influence these other organizations and families increases.

Putting It All Together

One way to put all the above strategies together is, as the group approaches termination, to make a list of all the strategies presented in the course of the group. Some new strategies may be introduced. After all the strategies are briefly reviewed, the group members are asked to carry out Exercise 15.2.

Exercise 15.2. Transfer and Maintenance of Change

Purpose: By the end of this exercise, all participants will have devised a personal plan for the generalization of what they have learned in the group.

Individual Task 1: Review the following principles, which have already been discussed in the group, and note which ones have already been used.

1. Practice many situations with different levels of difficulty.

2. Provide many examples, observe many models, and practice many times.

3. Vary the situations and level of difficulty.

4. Periodically review the techniques you have learned.

5. Keep a diary of successes and problem areas after the group has terminated.

6. Do extragroup tasks every week of gradually increasing difficulty.

7. Learn problem solving and apply it to a problem situation without the help of the group.

8. Expand your social network to include more time spent with people compatible with the new behavior.

9. Develop a new lifestyle that includes exercise, relaxation, meditation, and/or a sports activity on a regular basis.

10. Make a setback list, and prepare in the group for setbacks or relapses in the real world.

11. Attend booster sessions and maintenance groups if available.

12. Seek opportunities to teach others.

13. Plan follow-up contacts with buddies or staff.

14. Join recreational-educational and self-help groups.

15. Use self-help literature.

Group Task 1: Discuss the principles that have already been in operation in the group.

Individual Task 2: Each participant develops a realistic generalization plan that includes as many as possible of the principles listed in Individual Task 1, with specific examples.

Group Task 2: In pairs, each participant describes a plan and suggests other ideas to his or her partner, who may include the suggestions in the plan. In the full group, each person presents his or her partner's plan, which is evaluated in terms of its completeness, its realism, and its practicality. Then the group members discuss how the group can help each participant to maintain change.

Some plans developed during this exercise in a group for alcohol-abusing adolescents were the following:

The members noted that they already had multiple role plays, did lots of homework assignments, practiced many situations at very different levels of difficulty, and practiced repeatedly with varied examples. They noted, too, that they reviewed all the things that they had learned at the end of each session. For the new plan, each person designed a setback list for him- or herself in which he or she first described the high-risk situations and what he or she would do if such situations occurred. He or she rehearsed coping responses to the potential setback situations with a partner outside the group. Three persons decided as a lifestyle change to do tai chi at a class in their neighborhood twice a week, one decided to take a course in meditation, and the rest planned to do relaxation on a regular basis, which they would monitor in pairs. They all agreed to contact each other once a week to tell each other how they were doing. In emergencies, or if setbacks actually occurred, they agreed to call the group therapist or their buddy. All decided to adjust their social support network by spending more time with a sympathetic and nondrinking friend, and one decided to reduce time spent with overanxious family members who seem to create more rather than less stress. All joined socio-recreational groups at the Y. Each person developed his plan in writing and gave copies of it to the therapist and to a parent. Members agreed to examine what they had done at the booster session the following month.

Preparing for Termination

In contrast with many other forms of group therapy, the attention in preparing youth for termination focuses primarily on planning how they will continue to carry out target behavior and cognitions when the group terminates. It has been noted that often members become extremely attached to the group experience and the other group members, even in short-term groups. For some, termination from the group can be a painful experience, especially if the cohesion has been high. For others, the discomfort may be due to a history of difficult separations from families and friends. Behaviors occasionally seen as the group approaches termination may be a recurrence of previously maladaptive coping behaviors, a sudden increase in dependency on the group therapist, new complex problems arising when there is not sufficient time to deal with them, and a focus on social activities. For most participants in CBIGT groups, however, no serious concern has been noted.

For those clients for whom termination is problematic, it is possible to look at the distorted cognitions that seem to evoke these coping behaviors and teach alternative ways of coping with the ending of relationships. Often, dependency can be avoided completely by ensuring that the group members receive much more responsibility for the group activities and for planning their own individualized therapy as the group develops. The therapist reduces gradually his or her activity level and helps the members to establish and strengthen social networks in the community and to broaden their interactions with persons not in the group. The generalization strategy of encouraging membership in socio-recreational groups and helping the clients to increase their attraction to such groups also reduces the anxiety associated with termination. Another strategy commonly used to weaken bonds with members of the group is to have each person invite a nonmember to the group and explain to the guests what the group is all about. To maintain confidentiality, only general issues and strategies are discussed rather than each person telling about his or her unique problems. If the prosocial relationships outside the group have become as strong as or stronger than those within the group, the therapist has done his or her task with respect to termination.

Summary

The foremost principle of generalization is that the therapist must plan for it. It rarely occurs spontaneously. In this chapter on developing a plan, a battery of principles for enhancing generalization of what members have learned in the group to the world and specific techniques have been recommended. We have outlined the major strategies and principles that guide group planning around issues of generalization. Although these strategies and principles related to them are discussed toward the end of this book, this does not lessen their importance and their omnipresence in all phases of the group history. Some generalization strategies are initiated in the very first session, and new ones are continuously incorporated into the ongoing therapeutic process. Because the success of a group is measured by its members' success in altering their behavior and cognitions in problematic situations in the natural environment, attention to the principles established in this chapter should be a part of every treatment plan.

PART IV

Applications of Cognitive-Behavioral Interactional Group Therapy

CHAPTER 16

Group Strategies for Reducing
Anger and Aggression

One of the major concerns of society today is adolescent aggression. Adolescent crime rates are rapidly mounting. According to Guerra, Tolan, and Hammond (1994, p. 383), there has been a dramatic rise in violent behavior in the United States over the last four decades. This rise has been accompanied by a decrease in the modal age for violent offenses. Both self-report and arrest data reveal that the majority of antisocial and criminal acts of violence are committed by teenagers and young adults. Though violent crime rates in general are decreasing, violent crime rates for this age group are rising. Parents are complaining in increasing numbers about their out-of-control adolescent children (Pepler & Slaby, 1994). Newspaper reports of adolescent destruction and violence are daily events throughout the country. The number of referrals to social agencies, residential treatment facilities, and private practitioners appears to be mounting dramatically. Aggressiveness, antisocial behavior, and conduct disorders comprise one third to one half of youth clinical referrals (Kazdin & Frame, 1984). The relevance of this phenomenon to this book is that many of these aggres-

---

AUTHORS' NOTE: This chapter was coauthored by Sheldon D. Rose and Martin D. Martsch.

sive adolescents are being treated in groups in both residential and community settings.

Many causal factors for the increase in youth aggression have been postulated: an increase in poverty, violence on television and movies that serves to model the unwanted behavior, and the breakdown of the family, to name only a few. But behavioral and psychological factors cannot be ignored. Several psychological theories of aggression have been proposed as well. Cognitive-behavioral theories take into consideration environmental factors but in addition suggest that anger and aggression are to a large extent mediated by a set of cognitive variables in response to environmental events impinging on the individual. The individual's cognitive resources, which are thought to be measurable, influence or mediate these external events that can eventually lead to antisocial behavior (Guerra & Slaby, 1990). What adolescents believe about people (e.g., "They are all out to get me") and about themselves (e.g., "I can't do any better than this") and how they appraise a situation (e.g., "There is no way out of this except fighting") to a large extent determine whether an aggressive response will occur. Aggressive behavior is often reinforced by observers and victims of aggression. This is the main point of Patterson's (1982) coercion theory. For many, aggression serves as an effective way to control others (Finkelhor, Gelles, Hotaling, & Straus, 1990). For still others, impression management is the goal of aggressive behavior (Toch, 1969). Most peer groups, so important to the adolescent, strongly approve of the aggressive behavior, and alternative behaviors to aggression are often viewed as "uncool." Some parents even will express their approval, at least of males who fight when imposed on by others. Other parents model aggressive behaviors toward each other and their children. The peer group and sometimes the parents are the object of control and the audience to be impressed.

As DiGiuseppe, Tafrate, and Eckhardt (1994) pointed out, anger and aggression are two separate phenomena. Anger is the emotion most strongly associated with aggression (although Berkowitz, 1993, argued that other emotions, such as sadness, fear, frustration, and self-loathing, can also lead to aggression), and aggression is the behavior. According to Berkowitz (1993), "Anger as an experience does not directly instigate aggression but usually only accompanies the inclination to attack a target" (p. 296). It is aggression that gets the client in trouble and with which adults are most concerned. Aggression has been defined by Berkowitz (1993) as some kind of behavior, either physical or symbolic, that is carried out with the intention to harm someone. Anger often accompanies aggression but does not inevitably lead to aggression. One can express one's anger in many ways. Some are destructive to oneself, some are destructive to others, and some, although rarely, lead to effective social interaction. Some of the various ways of dealing with anger are discussed in the subsequent sections of this chapter.

Hudley (1994) showed that aggression can be differentiated into instrumental or proactive aggression (behavior directed toward obtaining objects, privileges, positions, or activities) and reactive, retaliatory, or hostile aggression (behavior provoked by the actions of others). It is the latter aggression on which most anger treatment paradigms are based. However, because many of our clients also manifest considerable proactive aggression, often no substantial anger can be identified. Depending on the assessment of the type of aggression, the treatment will differ in part.

Reactive and proactive aggression manifested by youth can be further differentiated into physical and verbal aggression. Researchers have found that physical aggression diminishes in importance as children grow into adolescents. Most aggression of adolescents is verbal aggression, which includes threats, threatening gestures, insults, swearing, and other verbal behaviors that provoke others. Treatment strategies for both overlap but are not quite the same, as shall be demonstrated later.

Aggressive adolescents are difficult clients. They do not perceive that they have a problem with anger or aggression. Most often, they blame others or their situation as the cause of their antisocial behavior. Youth often do not see that their aggression is damaging to themselves as well as others. They do not recognize that any other behavioral response might be more appropriate. Often, they manifest a kind of self-righteousness about their behavior. Finally, many seem to believe that getting rid of their anger through aggression is a cathartic expression, a necessary psychological release. Another reason that aggression is so difficult to treat is that it is highly stable over time (Huesmann, Eron, Lefkowitz, & Walder, 1984). In Huesmann et al.'s study spanning 22 years, the stability of aggression was shown to be very similar to that of intellectual competence.

What aggressive youth fail to recognize or view as undesirable are the side effects of persistent and even occasional aggression, such as reciprocation of the aggressive behavior, pain and suffering for all parties, damaged relationships, avoidance, rejection, and even hatred. More specifically, when the targets of the aggression are authority figures such as teachers or parents, the side effects, such as being suspended or expelled from school, arrested, adjudicated, or placed in a psychiatric or correctional institution, may be even more devastating to the youth. The reinforcing effects of peer approval appear to be more powerful than the threat of these dire consequences. Thus, to function in society, a treatment program must be established that both makes use of peer pressure and effectively offsets street group peer pressure to perform aggressive acts. The program must at the same time teach the clients new strategies for coping with situations that lead to aggression. One such program developed and evaluated in recent years is anger management. Although not without limitations, anger management is a useful tool for training in alternative behaviors. There is considerable empirical research to demonstrate that youth can be taught in groups to deal more effectively with situations that induce anger (see, e.g., Dupper & Krishef, 1993; Etscheidt, 1991; Feindler et al., 1984, 1986; Guerra & Slaby, 1990; Hawkins et al., 1991; Lochman et al., 1984; Lochman & Curry, 1986). A summary of this research is to be found in Chapter 1. Although the treatment program in all of these studies occurred in groups, little mention was explicitly made of any group dimension or group problem in any of the above studies. Ignoring the group does not make it go away. Group problems are endemic in work with youth in a group context. It seems that a program could be developed that would draw on the empirically supported technologies of these studies and could be readily combined with greater awareness of the group and the inclusion of various group strategies to build a more powerful clinical interventive approach.

In particular, one could borrow from Guerra and Slaby (1990) a focus on correcting social problem-solving skill deficits and changing beliefs that supported the use of aggression. From Feindler et al. (1984), one could borrow the analysis of provocation cues and anger responses, the provision of alternative responses to provoking stimuli, and the use of other strategies (such as self-monitoring, self-imposed "time-out" from anger-producing stimuli, and relaxation, assertiveness, and problem solving) to control one's own provocative behaviors. The therapist, as in the Feindler et al. (1984) study, could provide didactic instruction and make use of modeling, behavioral rehearsal, and negotiated homework assignments as training procedures. To add a greater focus on the group, the therapist would take steps to enhance group cohesion and maximally involve members in providing each other with ideas and help in decision making and in resolving any group problems as they arose. The major steps in the program as it has evolved are described below.

The Steps in Anger and Aggression Management

In the above literature on anger and aggression management, a number of steps stand out. Each of these steps has already been described in detail in earlier chapters, but in this chapter all of them come together in a multicomponent package for the treatment of inappropriate anger and aggression. Basically, anger and aggression management involves the following activities when the aggression is reactive. The steps are not always in the same order.

1. Describing the anger- and aggression-inducing situations
2. Describing the internal events: beliefs, self-evaluations, and other cognitions related to the behavior or strong emotions
3. Observing one's physiological arousal (awareness of the arousal process: early identification, knowledge of its course)
4. Assessing the nature of the aggressive response directed toward others or oneself
5. Examining and "rubbing in" the consequences of the aggressive response
6. Preparing to implement alternative cognitive control strategies
7. Preparing to perform alternative behavioral responses
8. Getting ready for the real world

When the aggression is proactive, Step 1 also includes looking at the client's motivation for aggression, Step 3 (observing one's physiological arousal) gets less attention, and Steps 2 and 4 get far greater emphasis. Steps 5, 6, 7, and 8 get equal attention in both types of aggression. Sometimes the distinction between reactive and proactive cannot be made until one reaches Step 2.

In the following subsections, we present each of these steps in more detail and provide examples of how the group is employed in carrying out each step.

Describing the Anger-Inducing Situations

Most youth believe that external events cause their anger. The group therapist seeks to demonstrate how the external events elicit cognitions such as beliefs or expectations and self-defeating self-descriptions, which in turn elicit the anger and aggression. The group therapist orients the members to the concepts, providing personal examples and a list of examples from other youth, having them keep a diary of such events, and evaluating the examples of others in the group. As has often been noted, adolescents are extremely reluctant to self-disclose. Yet many are more willing to do so when they disclose as part of an exercise that makes self-disclosure less personal and when each step is handled independently. Adolescents have also stated that they feel more comfortable in a group where everyone is self-disclosing. Finally, many youth initially perceive that, in describing the aggression-provoking conditions, they are describing the cause of their problem and that they are safely blaming others for their aggression. As they examine their cognitions and other aspects of the situation, they become aware that the causes are not as simple as they originally assumed. In the early phase of treatment, the therapist avoids confronting the client with the noncausal nature of the situation and the subsequent aggression. The goal is to make it possible for the client to arrive at this conclusion him- or herself.

The first step in the process is to present the members with a set of situations that seem to evoke anger and aggression from youth their age and to ask them to respond to each item in terms of the degree to which each item provokes them to anger or aggression. A 5-point scale is used (not at all, a little, some/not much, much, and very much). This can be administered as a pretest, posttest, and follow-up to evaluate the degree to which members perceive a reduction in the perception of anger- or stress-provoking situations. Hall and Fortney (1994) provided an inventory modified from Novaco's (1975) Anger Inventory for application with adolescent alcohol and drug abusers. It asks about responses to the following situations:

1. Being singled out for correction while the actions of others go unnoticed.
2. Being called a liar.
3. You are in the midst of a dispute, and the other person calls you a "stupid jerk."

4. Someone borrows your car, uses half a tank of gas, and doesn't replace it or pay you for the gas.

5. People who think that they are always right.

6. Watching someone bully another person who is physically smaller than he is.

7. Teachers who refuse to listen to your point of view.

8. You have hung up your clothes, but someone knocks them to the floor and does not pick them up.

9. You are talking to someone, and he doesn't answer you.

10. You have made arrangements to go somewhere with a person who backs off at the last minute and leaves you hanging.

11. Being pushed or shoved by someone in an argument.

12. You accidentally make the wrong kind of a turn in a parking lot. As you get out of your car, someone yells at you, "Where did you learn to drive?"

13. Someone makes a mistake and blames it on you.

14. You are trying to concentrate, and a person near you is tapping his foot.

15. When you are criticized in front of others for something that you have done.

16. You lend someone something important, and they fail to return it.

17. Being forced to do something in a way that someone else thinks it should be done.

18. People who constantly brag about themselves.

19. Being joked about or teased.

20. Being forced to do something that you don't want to do.

21. Someone making fun of the clothes you are wearing.

22. Someone sticking their nose into an argument between you and someone else.

23. Being talked about behind your back.

24. You have just cleaned up an area and organized things in it, but someone comes along and messes it up.

25. You are involved in watching a TV program, and someone (friend or relative) comes along and switches the channel.

26. Being told by a teacher or employer that you have done poor work.

27. Being mocked by a small group of people as you pass them.

28. You are in a movie ticket line, and someone cuts in front of you.

29. Being falsely accused of cheating.

The group members are then asked to describe in detail the items that they rated as "much" and "very much." If time is available, they are also asked to relate a recent situation that occurred in which the theme was present. For example, one member stated as an example of a situation of "being singled out for correction while the actions of others go unnoticed" a time when the principal yelled at him and pulled him out of class. "All I was doing was horsing around a little bit like lots of other kids when he walked into the room." At first, such descriptions and the placement of blame are taken at face value. Eventually, the therapist and group examine whether the client stimulated the situation in the first place by his provocative behavior. "What happened just before he pulled you out of class?" "Could you tell us a little more about this horsing around?" The entire chain of events ultimately needs to be examined. In our experience, it is better to take one step at a time.

The following excerpt takes place at about 10 minutes into the third session. The group therapist has already reviewed last session's data from the postsession questionnaire and the characteristics of events that evoke or "trigger" anger and aggression. The trigger concept is suggested by Feindler et al. (1984), who differentiate "external" and "internal" triggers: External triggers are the actual events, and internal triggers are the individual's subsequent thoughts about the situation that continue to make him or her more angry.

Group Therapist: Last week, we talked about using "triggers," or events, that make us angry. I want each of you to write down one example of an event triggering anger that you experienced since the last session. You can take it from your diary if you would like. I see some blank faces. Anybody remember what a triggering event is?

Byron: Yeah, that's easy, when someone does something to make you mad. It sorta triggers it.

Derrick: What about something happens that keeps you from doing something you really want to do, like your car breaks down? That might really blow you away.

Deron: And if you see someone doing something to a friend?

Group Therapist: You all have it. Okay, everyone, now write down an example. Give us some detail on what happened, who was involved, and where and when it occurred. You can look at your neighbor's paper, or you can ask him to help you to get ideas. (pause) Okay, here's what I wrote down. My friend and I were supposed to meet last Saturday at 6:00 at a restaurant. He's often late. I waited until 6:30, when he sauntered in. Not even an apology. That really triggered my anger. And I told him in a loud and angry voice that he had no consideration for his friends and wouldn't even let him explain. Okay, what did the rest of you write down? Derrick, you seem ready.

Derrick: Last night, Gary told me to get out of the recliner chair in the lounge, like it was his chair. What a lot of bullshit. That really got to me.

Group Therapist: Good example, huh, guys? (Nods of approval) What else?

Randy: Like when Arnie (residential staff), walking through our room last week, told me my bed was a mess, and it only had a few wrinkles in it. Nobody asked him. It really pissed me off. Is that a trigger?

Group Therapist: I see everyone is nodding. You've got the idea, too. Who else?

Deron: Man, this is easy. When someone does something that keeps me from doing what I am doing?

Group Therapist: Could you give us an example?

Deron: Sure, that's easy, too. Last weekend I was watching TV, and my sister changed the program. I won't tell you what happened next. That was a first-class trigger because I was watching the football game.

(The members continue until everyone but Barney gives an example)

Group Therapist: Say, Barney, you have one?

Barney: (sullenly) Naw.

Randy: (sarcastically) Nothin' makes Barney mad?

Others: (laugh)

Group Therapist: What's so funny?

Deron: Barney's mad all the time. Everything makes him mad.

Group Therapist: Barney's not ready to talk about specific events. When he's ready, he'll tell us. (Protects Barney, then provides him a canned situation) For the moment, though, so that you can do the rest of the exercise, Barney, why don't you let your trigger be that situation you told us about last week, when you went home and your mom blamed you for something your younger brother did? You really got steamed about that.

Barney: (reluctantly) Oh, I guess I did. Okay, I'll use that.

Group Therapist: You can change it any time you want, Barney, but meanwhile we all have situations now that we can examine further.

Once the youth have practiced identifying a wide range of anger- and aggression-provoking situations, they are encouraged to keep track of all situations in which anger or aggression is elicited. They may also agree to monitor each other if they go to the same school or live in the same unit. They are encouraged to describe the event in detail in their diaries, answering the questions of what happened, where it happened, who was involved, when it happened, and their response. Later, as they learn the following terms, these should also be included in the diary: their emotional arousal (feelings) and their cognitions at the critical moment. (If the demand for recording is too great, they will not cooperate; wherever possible, we contract with them for sometimes as few as one or two examples a week and then gradually increase the demand as they find it useful.) As discussed earlier, each client is encouraged to present to the group each week one example of a situation that triggered anger, whether or not he or she was successful in controlling the anger or aggression. To handle all the situations, clients present the situations to the other group members in pairs or triads rather than to the group as a whole. Later, as they master the criteria, more events can be dealt with.

When the aggression is proactive, the trigger is the mere presence of something the client wants. For example, he sees someone with a jacket he would like, or she wants to control someone or expand her power in general. Sometimes the trigger for aggression is interpersonal conflict. In the group session, it is necessary to get the facts about the conflict as completely as possible. Often, the careful description of the event in a matter-of-fact way is helpful to the client for finding ways of remediating the conflict.

Evaluating Beliefs and Other Cognitions

At the critical moment, the situation seems to elicit cognitions that in turn provoke the anger. Some of these cognitions appear to elicit aggression and keep it going. There are a number of overlapping categories of cognitive statements that serve to control the response. One of the main ways an individual maintains his or her aggressive pattern of behavior is through a system of beliefs and expectations that supports and encourages his or her aggression. Some of these beliefs were revealed in the above examples: "It's not my fault; my sister was giving me a hard time. She made me do it," "You got to show people who's boss," "They'll laugh at me if I back down," "If someone puts you down, you've got to show them you don't take it," and "He asked for it." Sometimes these statements are made overtly. At other times one must extrapolate these beliefs from the behavior of the individual. Some of these beliefs take the form of unrealistic expectations: "Everyone should treat me well," "Nobody has the right to tell me anything I don't want to hear," "I'll never be able to follow the rules," and "I rarely get a fair shake." Thus, the next step in treatment is looking at commonly held beliefs and expectations, as in the following example.

Group Therapist: Most of us believe that the event that happened caused us to get angry (Everyone nods), but let's look and see if that's really true. When my friend was late, I thought to myself, "That's a lack of respect. No one has the right to make me wait so long." And then I got mad. You see that how I evaluated the situation and what I believed and what I said to myself seemed to cause the anger. We call those evaluations, beliefs, or thoughts the "internal" triggers. (Writes it on the flip chart to give emphasis) Here are several external triggers and the internal triggers that some people have in situations like these. (He draws the following outline on the flip chart) Now let's each look at our examples and write down what we were thinking or what we might have been thinking when we experienced the triggering event.

External Trigger	*Internal Trigger*
You were criticized in front of others for something that you didn't do.	I'll get even with him for embarrassing me.
You lent someone something important and they failed to return it.	He doesn't have any respect for me.

You were forced to make your bed in the way that the counselor thought was best. You liked to do it another way.

Nobody can boss me around. I won't make it at all.

The guy said to you, "What do you do to someone who calls you a punk, punk?"

The guys'll laugh at me if I back down. I'll smash his teeth in. I'll show 'em.

Group Therapist: Are there any questions? (pause) Okay, what are some of the internal triggers that you had or might have had in the situations you described earlier?

Then each member describes his or her thoughts at the critical moment in his or her situation. If someone is too vague, the group therapist or another member asks for more concrete examples. Sometimes a client cannot distinguish between a cognition and a behavioral response or between the cognitions and the description of the situation. The group members are encouraged to clarify these thoughts for each other. In each situation, youth are asked to determine, with the help of the group, the contribution of the thoughts as well as the situation to their anger or aggression.

The therapist will then summarize the relationship of the situation to the cognition and of the cognition to the aggressive act. At this point, the group therapist suggests, as an extragroup task, self-monitoring the cognitions (what the person actually said or might have expressed to him- or herself). This would be added to the task of describing the problematic situation, psychological arousal, and aggressive response. (See Chapter 10 for other types of cognitions and strategies for monitoring them.)

Observing One's Physiological Arousal

Physiological arousal is the bodily sensations experienced at the critical moment before and during the aggressive response. At first, all the (reactive) aggressors can think of is that they are angry or upset. Other arousal indicators include fist tightening, sweating, headaches, stomach pains, sweaty palms, clenched teeth, flared nostrils, and forced breathing. Once the individual identifies his or her unique physiological responses, these can become cues for using a calming response or a problem-solving response, either of which may be incompatible with the aggressive response. One of the main reasons for spending time identifying the cues for arousal is that it has become apparent to us that no real cognitive solutions can be used while the client is aroused because this arousal interferes with any rational problem solving or thinking of alternatives. Once the physiological arousal has subsided, the process of dealing with the problem or trigger can be undertaken. In this way, the two processes are separate: First, manage anger, then address the situation or provocation. Some youth are more skilled than others in recognizing their physiological arousal, but training, as demonstrated below, is helpful in increasing the percentage of those capable of identifying their physiological arousal cues. The group therapist begins by orienting the group members to the phenomenon.

Group Therapist: Sometimes we don't know we're really angry until we're screaming at or pushing or hitting someone, and then it's too late. If we can recognize what our body is telling us immediately before showing our anger or our aggression, we might be able to do something about it. What kind of body sensations (how do you feel and where in your body is it felt) do you experience just as you get mad? You need to catch your anger early to manage it successfully; it's easy to put out a small fire but almost impossible to control a large blaze. Like a fire anger starts small and grows according to how much fuel or wind is encouraging it. Anyone can put out a match. But if you wait too long when it is clear to everyone that you are angry (big fire), then it's sometimes too late, and the anger is very difficult to control.

Let's go back to the signs of arousal. Here are some examples. (He puts them up on a flip chart)

- My hands tighten up.
- I begin to sweat.
- My stomach tightens.
- My stomach hurts.
- My head hurts.
- My teeth clench.
- My breathing gets fast.
- I hold my breath.

Do you have any examples to add?

After the examples are added, the group therapist continues by reporting his or her own physiological responses and then has the group attempt to examine their responses to their respective situations. (A "canned" situation can also be used.)

Group Therapist: Let's look at your situations one at a time and see what kind of body sensations you experience just before and while you are angry. As is my custom, I'll go first. When I got mad at my friend for being late, I could feel my breathing get fast and shallow. I felt hot like I had a fever. I began to sweat. My mouth tightened. Then I was breathing fast and laboriously. Now what about the rest of you?

Then each group member presents his or her situation to the whole group or in pairs and examines his or her particular form of arousal. When they are finished, the group therapist either summarizes the arousal experienced by all the group members or asks one of the more experienced members to summarize. Then he or she reminds them that they can use these emotions, as soon as they experience them, as cues to give themselves alternative instructions. Now self-monitoring will be suggested as a task to be performed between sessions. Self-monitoring will include the identification of at least one anger-inducing situation and a description of the concomitant physiological arousal.

Assessing the Aggressive Behavioral Response

Anger, the emotion, usually precedes (reactive) aggression, the behavior. Although therapists commonly treat angry behavior or aggression, not the emotion of anger, it is possible to treat the emotion of anger at the same time. The aggressive behavior is usually performed as part of a long chain of events and usually follows a given event in the chain. It is the aggressive behavior that is most likely to create a hostile or aggressive response from others or to damage the relationship with others.

In the group, we look primarily but not exclusively at the reactive aggression of each person to the situation that evoked it. The group helps each member to recognize the unique characteristics of his or her responses. The same strategies are used in training youth to identify aggressive behavior as in training them in the previous concepts. These strategies are illustrated in the following excerpt.

Group Therapist: The question now is, What do we do or say to others when we feel angry and blame them for it? Remember my example of my friend being late. When he finally arrived, I started yelling at him without waiting to find out why he was late. I criticized him and pointed to a general pattern of being late. It was verbal aggression. What about the rest of you? How did you express your anger? Write it down first. (Pause a minute while they write) Okay, what did you write? It looks like everyone wants to tell us. Let's start with Randy.

Randy: When Arnie told me my bed was a mess, and it only had a few wrinkles in it, I told him he was full of shit and gave him a little push.

Group Therapist: How did you tell him?

Randy: I yelled at him, and I stuck my face into his.

Group Therapist: That's a good description of how you were aggressive. You yelled, you stuck your face into his, and you swore at him. Yelling and swearing were verbal aggression, and sticking your face into his was physical aggression. And shoving him was physical aggression too. Your anger led to verbal aggression, and your verbal aggression seemed to lead to physical aggression. Hey, Derrick, you really look eager to share your example.

Derrick: Yeah, when Gary told me to get out of the chair in the lounge, I told him I didn't see his name on it and that it's no wonder his mom kicked him out of the house. He probably told her he owned it. Then he . . .

Group Therapist: Hold it, we'll get into that later. Okay, you were sarcastic and you put him down with something you knew he was sensitive about. What kind of aggression is that?

Derrick: That's verbal aggression, I guess.

The group therapist continued asking about each person's aggressive responses until everyone had given examples. At the end, he summarized the different ways people in the group had been aggressive. There was some discussion about whether some behavior was really aggressive or just "horsing around." In this way, youth usually become aware of the wide variety of behavioral manifestations of anger and aggression. In group discussion, the group members "rub in" the fact of each other's aggression toward significant others. Often, adolescents do not realize that they are being aggressive until it is pointed out in such discussions. In most instances, the initial response is verbal, although in some cases the verbal aggression escalates into physical aggression. A distinction is made because physical aggression usually has more serious side effects than verbal aggression. If one cannot catch one's aggressiveness at the point of feeling angry, perhaps control may be more readily attained at the inciting of the verbal aggression.

In subsequent analyses of aggressive behavior, the group therapist begins to examine how general certain aggressive behaviors are. In the above example, if it had been a later meeting, he would have asked Randy if sticking his face into someone else's face was something he did often. The group will assist in revealing whether that is indeed the case. In this approach, the therapist helps the group to look for general patterns.

Examining the Consequences
of the Aggressive Response

Recognizing that one is being aggressive is only part of the equation. It is also necessary for youth to become skilled in recognizing the consequences of that aggression. At this point in the treatment process, the aggressive response of the adolescent is examined in terms of its inevitable short- and long-term consequences. The consequences determine whether the aggression is worth working on and could eventually be the motivation for finding alternative strategies of responding to the triggering events. Both immediate and long-term consequences should be looked at because short-term consequences, such as getting control of the other person, are in some cases highly reinforcing.

Just as many youth do not perceive their behavior as aggressive, many do not see beyond the aggressive behavior to its consequences. In an exercise, the therapist first looks at consequences in his or her own example, then looks at the range of exercises in a "canned" situation, and finally helps the group look at the consequences of each of their own sets of aggressive behavior.

Group Therapist: What were the consequences of my getting angry at my friend for being late? As I said earlier, I started yelling at him without listening to his reasons for being late. What do you think?

Deron: I would imagine that yelling would upset how you guys got along with each other, at least for a little while.

Randy: I bet he got really angry with you. It would have pissed me off.

Derrick: Hey, my guess is that you ended up not eating with each other as you had planned.

Group Therapist: All of those things are true. Besides, later, I was quite embarrassed that I had let it get to me. Probably the worst part of it was that once I told him off, I was madder than ever. My whole day was ruined. I sulked around and didn't enjoy anything that day. The funny thing was that his being late wasn't all that important to me. It just got out of hand.

Supposing you do get angry and become aggressive, what are the possible results or consequences of that anger? Let us look first at an example that several of you mentioned earlier: when your teacher criticizes you aloud in class. (The group therapist can provide some models such as the following or allow the group to make the list. If the therapist provides them, he or she puts them on an overhead transparency or flip chart.)

- I could get kicked out of class.
- I could get sent to the principal's office.
- I could get kicked out of school.
- I could get a bad grade.
- The teacher might get mad at me.
- I'd be upset all day long and mad at everyone.
- I could be sent back to Hill Center (the correctional institution).
- The guys would think I'm really tough.
- She'd know better than to mess with me the next time.

The last two consequences are reinforcing of the aggressive behavior. So it is necessary to look at the long-term consequences and determine whether the aggression is worth the long-term outcome.

Group Therapist: We got a great list, but it isn't complete. Now write down what the consequences were of your being aggressive in your situation. I already told you mine. (Pause a few minutes.) Okay, what did you write?

Deron: Remember, I told you that last Friday night when I was home, I was watching TV and my sister changed the program. She didn't even ask. So I bent her wrist back just a little. Anyway, she went screaming off to my old man, who came after me with a strap, and I ran out of the house. When I finally came home, he was asleep. But I was lucky that time. Usually he'd have beat the hell out of me whenever he caught me. It was my sister's fault. She shouldn't have changed the TV channel.

Group Therapist: (Ignores the blaming for the moment) Okay, it seems that aggression gets more aggression in return, and you never did get to see the program you wanted. Your dad came after you with a strap and would have beat you if he caught you. And I'll bet your sister was pretty mad at you, too. Anybody else got an example of where aggression gets aggression multiplied many times?

Randy: When Arnie (residential staff) told me my bed was a mess and I told him in his face to fuck off, he yelled at me and gave me five demerits, which meant I couldn't go home this weekend. Listen, if he can get mad, I can get mad.

Deron: Not if your getting mad gets out of control all over the place. That's one of the reasons most of us are here.

Group Therapist: Some of the rest of you seem to be nodding agreement. Let's go on. Derrick?

Derrick: Remember when Gary told me to get out of his special chair in the lounge? I told him I didn't see his name on it and that it's no surprise his mom threw him out of the house like she did. So he smashed me in the face. Staff broke up the fight before it got really started, and then they had the group circle up and we had to talk about it. I think that was the worst. Anyway, I guess I'm not getting out of here as soon as I thought. But it was worth it.

Group Therapist: Well take a look at that later.

Even as the members are recognizing the consequences of their behavior, several still are blaming the other person for his or her aggression toward them (e.g., Randy) or are cognitively self-reinforcing their aggressive behavior (e.g., Derrick). Examining the consequences is only a beginning in getting youth to accept their responsibility for the aggressive behavior.

After discussing the consequences of the aggression of each of the individuals, the therapist summarizes the discussion. In the summary, he begins to deal with the issue of who has the responsibility for the aggressive behavior.

Group Therapist: Okay, in most cases we have seen clearly that aggression gets aggression from others, and then the whole thing escalates. Some of you said you didn't care. Some said you had to teach them not to mess with you. But in the long run, their education was expensive for you. Some of you felt that the actions of others are what triggered your anger and aggression. They "pushed your button"; therefore it was their fault. But for many of you, that's an easy button to push. It seems like they are really getting control of you. Almost everyone knows how to push some of your buttons. I understand that control may be difficult under some of the conditions you mentioned in your situations, but you are the one who suffers the consequences. Therefore, you have to be the one who shows the control.

Preparing to Implement Alternative Cognitive Control Strategies

Breaking the Anger Cycle

Often the conflict is part of an anger behavior cycle (Feindler et al., 1986). That is, one person's response becomes the trigger for another person's anger and aggression, which in turn becomes the trigger for the first person's anger or aggression. It is a cycle of events and responses that keeps going around, and each time around it gets bigger and the responses get worse until it culminates in someone's getting hurt or getting in trouble (or both). The only way for it to end without such an unfavorable outcome is if someone "jumps" off the cycle. Ways of jumping off the cycle before it gets out of hand are brainstormed and discussed. The anger behavior cycle is one of the more dangerous consequences of being aggressive with people in authority, friends, and family.

To teach the group to identify and break anger behavior cycles, the therapist provides a definition and a number of examples. Then the members present their own escalated situations. Ways of breaking the cycle are brainstormed with the group members, and once a decision is made, overt and covert modeling followed by rehearsal is employed, as demonstrated in the following example.

Group Therapist: I'm glad you guys recognize the cycle, but who's going to break it?

Anthony: Someone has to do it. I guess in the cycle I described it was up to me. It's not so easy. You don't want to look like a pushover.

Group Therapist: How can he break the cycle in this case without looking like a pushover? Why don't all of you write down any ideas you have. (Pauses for 1 minute while they write) Arnie has been done for a long time.

Arnie: Maybe he should say, "I don't need this" and then walk away.

Billy: What about saying, "Listen, this is going nowhere. Let's just stop."

Deron: Why don't you call it an anger cycle, and ask the guy what both of you can do to break it?

Reg: I might say, "You're not worth my getting kicked out of school for," and then walk away.

Gonzales: Why not just say, "This ain't cool, man"?

Group Therapist: Hey, you guys have some great ideas. Anthony, do you think you can use any of them? Let's take a look at what might happen with each of them and compare that with what is happening now.

After Anthony had evaluated the various ideas, he chose what he found best and, following modeled demonstration, practiced them in a covert rehearsal.

Learning Cognitive Control

Because cognitions are able to evoke and maintain anger and aggression in response to some situations, cognitions may also be able to change or at least reduce the intensity and frequency of aggression. Feindler et al. (1984) referred to these cognitions as "reminders": These are the things one tells oneself so as to think about the situation in a less provocative way. A number of overlapping categories of cognitive control or reminders exist. In the first category are statements establishing prosocial beliefs. Such statements as "You don't always have to be right," "A little criticism is not the end of the world," "Backing down may save your life," and "I don't have to show my anger every time I feel it" might be able to replace the proaggression self-statements commonly used in such situations.

In the second category are statements reminding oneself of the consequences of aggressive behavior. The client might learn to make use of "if-then" statements, such as "If I lose it, then I'll get in trouble," "If I push it to a fight, I'll get kicked out of school," and "If I yell at my mom, she'll ground me for a month." Considerable training time is invested in teaching the members how to look at consequences of their behavior (as in the earlier example) and to include these in their self-talk at the critical moment following an anger-inducing situation. The training involves comparing future contingencies for the aggressive and the alternative behavior.

In the third category are statements and questions involving self-evaluation. The youth are taught to recognize when they have succeeded or failed at controlling their anger or using some of the other cognitive control strategies mentioned above. At the end of every situation in which anger is experienced, they practice asking themselves how they did.

In the fourth category are statements of self-instruction. The youth are taught to tell themselves to perform the alternative behavior. As one youth said to himself, "Just ignore his wisecracks." The youth are taught to instruct themselves to deal directly with the physiological arousal response by telling themselves to be calm, to relax, to breathe deeply and slowly, or to focus their thoughts on a target expression (meditation). In almost every situation, they are advised to make a statement such as "Relax, take a deep breath, and let it out slowly." Before the use of such statements, the skills of calming, relaxation, breathing, and meditation will have already been taught.

Actually, all of the categories above at one level involve self-instruction (see Chapter 10 for more details on self-instructional training).

After explaining the importance of finding alternative cognitions and providing examples of each of the categories, the group therapist helps the group to develop a list of them that might be appropriate, first in a "canned" situation and then in a real situation of their own. Below is an example of how this process worked in one group.

Group Therapist: Jerry really got ticked off when the teacher accused him of not paying attention and then added that he never paid attention. He noted that his breathing was forced. His eyes felt like they were pushing out of his head, and his teeth clenched so hard he thought they would break. He told himself he didn't care who it was, nobody could tell him he wasn't paying attention. He told himself she was always picking on him. Then he started screaming swear words at her. What things could Jerry have said to himself in this situation before he told the teacher off? Write them down. Don't forget the five categories. (Pause for a couple of minutes) Okay, read them aloud to all of us, and I'll write them down on the flip chart. Deron?

Deron: Well, you could tell yourself, "Cool it, it's not that important."

Randy: He might tell himself, "Take a deep breath and relax," like we did in that exercise last week.

Tyrone: He could remind himself of what would happen to him if he blew up at the teacher.

Group Therapist: Give me a concrete example of a consequence.

Derrick: For example, "If I tell her off, I'll get myself kicked out of school."

Randy: Yeah, I got another one. I'd tell myself, "Even teachers make mistakes."

Jerome: When I was finished, I could tell myself I was really cool if I did any of those things.

Group Therapist: These are all possibilities. Any more? We're doing great.

Deron: I got one. "She has sometimes said good things to me."

Randy: I guess Jerry could say to himself, "I'm not the only person she accused of not paying attention, so I shouldn't take it personally."

Group Therapist: That's a great list. Okay, everyone look carefully at the list and pick three or four that you could use in your own situation that we looked at last week. You don't have to rely on the list. Remember, choose statements that you really believe. If you want it to work, it has to be something you can buy. First tell your partner. You can make suggestions to one another.

The first time the group does this exercise, the therapist may provide the list of alternative cognitions. Members often do not have the vocabulary. In open-ended groups where the more senior members are revisiting the exercise, they can develop the list together with the therapist. At this point, the group members will meet in pairs, and each member will come up with a list appropriate to his or her situation. Then the therapist instructs them to tell everyone in the group what their coping statements might be.

Group Therapist: Let's look at our various coping cognitions. Since we know each other's situation pretty well now, just use a few words to remind us. Okay, let's go around the room, and I'll start. My friend was late. When I felt myself getting angry, I could just say, "Cool it, Sheldon, just relax, and at least just ask why he was late." I could remind myself that being late is not the end of the world. I could tell myself, "Getting mad may lose me my friend." (Turns to Jerry)

Jerry: The teacher says I never pay attention in class. When I start to get mad, I could say, "Take it easy. If I get mad, I get kicked out of class." I could remind myself that sometimes I don't pay attention.

Group Therapist: Do you believe what you're saying?

Jerry: Oh yeah.

Group Therapist: (Nods to Derrick, who is sitting next to Jerry)

Derrick: Gary told me to get out of his special chair in the lounge. When I start to get pissed, I could think, "Take a deep breath" and, let's see, oh yeah, "It's no big deal." I could just laugh and act like he was kidding.

When all of the members have provided examples of the various coping cognitions they could use, the therapist once again summarizes what they have used and notes both similarities and differences. If necessary, they can use cognitive modeling and rehearsal (see Chapter

10) to practice it. Because it may take a considerable amount of time to prepare the cognitive rehearsal and to get it organized, it is possible to divide the group into subgroups of three or four to help one another and provide an opportunity for everyone to practice. Once the members can do it quickly, they repeat it in the entire group. It should be noted that in this way each client has numerous models for many different situations and several opportunities to practice his or her new cognitive responses. This entire sequence usually takes several sessions to complete. This exercise needs to be repeated periodically throughout treatment as often as time permits, so as to provide as much learning as possible. But the therapist must vary the form of presentation to keep the adolescents from becoming bored. One can use role playing by means of the round-robin procedure shown above, practice in subgroups of varying sizes, and play the board game described in Chapter 13 as an alternative form of practice. Extragroup tasks that could be suggested to the group members include self-monitoring of anger-inducing situations and alternative cognitions that were or could have been used in the situation.

Preparing to Perform
Alternative Behavioral Responses

Using several of the above strategies of cognitive control may not be sufficient to prepare the individual to respond to anger-inducing situations effectively. Most cognitions are instructions to do or say something. These overt behaviors must be elicited, evaluated, taught, demonstrated, and practiced in the group before they can be performed in the real world. These often involve some of the steps of problem solving, in which the group brainstorms the best verbal statements and behavioral actions a person can take to avoid the consequences of being aggressive. The specific solution is the statement or action decided on by the target client. Sometimes the self-instruction is sufficient for the client to perform the desired behavior. More frequently, however, the major means of teaching this behavior is the modeling sequence or social skill training discussed in Chapter 9 or the relaxation and deep breathing training discussed in Chapter 10. For example, in a situation in which a client who frequently jumps to unjustified conclusions feels he or she is being unfairly criticized, he or she has agreed to the self-instruction of listening carefully to what the other person is saying. The client will have to indicate aloud that he or she is at least interested in what other people present have to say. Listening responses can be modeled by other members of the group and practiced by the target client in a role play. If the self-instruction is to relax, that can be learned through relaxation training. Let us examine how this might occur in the following excerpt.

Group Therapist: We all are experts now in what we say to ourselves. We have begun to change the way we evaluated the anger-inducing situation or we have changed our beliefs about the meaning of the situation or our expectations from that situation. Usually we must also change what we do and say in the situation. In fact, some of our new cognitions are self-instructions to do or say something differently. For example, last week I told you about my friend being late. My new cognition the next time someone is over 15 minutes late is to take a deep breath and let it out slowly, remind myself that he might have a good reason, and then tell him, "I was getting worried and wondered what happened to you." I would then wait for a response. Let's review each of your situations and see what you can do or say differently. Who wants to go first? Okay, Tabitha.

Tabitha: My dad was drunk and began to put me down by telling me what a slut I was. After I told myself to cool it, I would say to him that I would talk to him in the morning.

Group Therapist: Just say it like you would say it to him. I'll be your dad. (slurred) You slut, you no-good kid. I ought to have you locked up. I ought to kick you out of the house.

Tabitha: (In a matter-of-fact tone of voice) Okay, Dad, I'll talk to you about it in the morning.

Group Therapist: That's great. Now do the silent part in a loud whisper, and then do the other part aloud, the part that you say to him.

Tabitha: Okay, I think I have it.

Group Therapist: (slurred) You slut, you no-good kid. I ought to have you locked up. I ought to kick you out of the house.

Tabitha: (whispers) Cool it, he's drunk. Whatever I say will be wrong. He'll be better in the morning. (aloud) Dad, I'll talk to you about it in the morning.

Group Therapist: Okay, everyone can do this with their situation, but let's do it in small groups of four people, and I'll float between them.

Tabitha might have had someone model the situation for her first and then practiced what she would think and say. Note that this involves a combination of cognitive and overt rehearsal. Because of time constraints, the group therapist instructed them to practice the new cognitions and verbal behavior appropriate to their situations in subgroups of three or four persons.

Sometimes it is difficult for someone to come up with effective responses on his or her own. In this case, the group therapist might ask the group to brainstorm all the expressions they could think of as to what the target person could think and say and then let the target person evaluate and select the most suitable set.

At this point in the sequence, the group therapist has each person review, first with a partner and then for the group, the characteristics of the type of situation that seemed to provoke the anger and aggressive responses, the cognitions that it elicited, the responses to the situation, the consequences of those responses, the characteristics of the anger arousal, the coping cognitions, and the coping behaviors. This multiple review provides many models and a clearer understanding of the sequence by the members.

Getting Ready for the Real World

Feindler et al. (1986) advocated, as part of preparation for transferring what the youth have learned to the real world, the use of the "barb technique," in which the therapist and group members provide increasingly difficult provocations with decreased warnings or prompts to each of the group members. One of the dangers of this technique is that if it is used either too long or too frequently, it changes the group climate to basically a hostile one or at least reduces the cohesion of the group, even though it is clear that the provocations are merely simulations. To be most effective, the barb technique has each person build up a list of situations that he or she has practiced coping with in the group and some additional ones for which he or she has had no training. The group members divide up the situations for the target person and at one session spring several of the situations on the given target client at various times throughout the session. At the end of the session, the interaction is processed, and the responses of the client are evaluated with the help of the group.

In this phase of treatment, some of the pitfalls of performing these prosocial responses instead of the more common responses in members' neighborhoods are discussed as well. The group looks at the likely responses, which in some cases will be their peers' labeling them as "dorks." The members are asked to compare the fallout or negative consequences of the responses learned in the group and the more commonly used responses in the real world. After all, responses that are acceptable in groups of adolescents protected from heavy judgments of their peers may be totally unacceptable in the community or in the family.

Working With Families

If the client is going back to his or her family or is to return to another family situation, it is necessary to work with the family to prepare them for that return. In addition, parents in some families may inadvertently play a role in the reinforcement of coercive and aggressive behaviors.

Patterson (1986) pointed out that coercive interaction patterns often play a central role in promoting aggressive child behavior. Coercion refers to situations in which aggression by the client directed toward a parent may be reinforced when the parent gives in or complies. The reinforcement trap is that the parent may give in to the client's aversive behavior in the short run as a way of stopping the coercive behavior but ends up increasing the probability that the behavior will recur because the client's aversive behavior is reinforced too. By submitting to the client's pressure, parents end up escalating the coercive behaviors.

Kazdin (1987) advocated the use of parent management training so that parents learn those skills necessary to alter the pattern of interchanges between parent and child. In the new way, prosocial rather than coercive behavior is directly reinforced and supported within the family. This requires developing several parenting behaviors, such as establishing the rules for the client to follow, providing positive reinforcement for appropriate behavior, delivering mild forms of punishment such as time-out to suppress behavior, and negotiating compromises.

Further help to the family may be necessary to improve communications skills. These include listening to each other, negotiating decisions with each other, praising each other, and decreasing verbal abuse of each other.

Summary

In this chapter, a theory of anger and aggression was proposed in which a distinction was made between anger (the emotion) and aggression (the behavior). Different kinds of aggression suggesting different types of treatment were also examined. The unique steps required to treat anger and aggression were outlined and exemplified. These included having group members describe the anger- and aggression-provoking situations; evaluate beliefs, self-evaluations, and other cognitions related to the behavior; observe their physiological arousal; assess their aggressive response; examine and "rub in" the consequences of the aggressive responses; prepare to implement alternative cognitive control strategies; and prepare for performing alternative behavioral responses. The final step was preparing youth for the complexities of the real world, or generalization. The pros and cons of the "barb" technique as a way of teaching youth to handle unusual or difficult situations were presented. The "barb technique" involves confronting youth with various anger- and aggression-inducing situations without an opportunity to prepare for them.

Of course, working with the client is clearly not enough. If possible, working with the family, in which the aggressive behavior may be constantly modeled, is also advocated. Parents may also need help on how to understand and handle aggressive behavior of their children.

CHAPTER 17

Staff Training and Supervision for Cognitive-Behavioral Interactive Group Therapy

CBIGT requires competency in a complex set of leadership, motivational, cognitive-behavioral, and small group intervention skills. One can learn about these competencies by exploring the relevant literature (e.g., this text and Rose, 1989), doing on-the-job observation, and assisting a more experienced person with the leadership of a group. Some formal training in the form of ongoing in-service training, workshops, or classes should dramatically enhance the process of learning. Training should ideally involve conceptual presentations, opportunity to observe models, occasions to practice new group leadership skills, constructive feedback on one's leadership skills from peers, and the chance to try out in the real world what one has learned in the training sessions. Training for CBIGT readily lends itself to simulation in small training groups because the same leadership skills demonstrated in the training program must be carried out in small therapy groups by the group therapist.

The Simulated Training Model

The simulated training model is one in which the trainee participates both as a member and as a "therapist" in a training group that is similar to a real therapy group but is carried out under the supervision of the trainer. The emphasis in the simulated group is on giving the trainee an accurate picture of the leadership skills required in leading a therapy group and the response of participants to the application of those skills. Simulated group therapy experiences can be readily created by involving the participants in a set of exercises similar to those used in therapy groups. Among the advantages of a simulated training model are the following:

1. It affords the trainees the opportunity to perform a variety of leadership activities, all of which can be directly observed and supervised by the trainer and peer group.

2. Trainees and trainer provide a rich source of feedback to each of the learners in their roles of leader and member. (However, the stringent rules of feedback discussed in Chapter 9 must be followed to prevent the situation from becoming too aversive.)

3. The small groups provide a laboratory for examining group process in vivo and how it influences behavioral and cognitive outcomes.

4. The training program provides structured practice in a wide range of intervention strategies.

5. Observations of the trainee provide a basis for determining his or her relative level of initial competency.

In this chapter, a training program will be presented that has been used with numerous staff members interested in learning the approach in hundreds of workshops, formal classes, and in-service training programs throughout the world. This program represents one model of training group therapists and other helping staff primarily through the use of continuous simulated groups of six to eight people within the larger workshop, in-service training, or class. Stress management, as a central theme for these simulation groups, appears to be appropriate for most trainees because it is a rare practitioner or student who does not suffer sometimes from excessive stress. Moreover, all the relevant strategies for coping skill training in groups can be found in a stress management model. A realistic simulation makes the training group more relevant to participants. In addition, the stress model is quite similar in structure to the anger and aggression management model commonly used with youth in institutional and community settings. Let us first examine the structure of training sessions.

The Structure of Training Sessions

There are three types of programs: in-service training, workshops, and courses. The agency training programs in which CBIGT has been taught have varied in size from 7 to 100 participants. The number depends on the size of the agency and the relevance of small treatment groups to their practice. Workshops vary in size from 24 to 150. Regardless of the size of the program, the participants are divided into subgroups of five to seven members. Larger subgroups limit the number of opportunities for each person to be leader of the group and reduce each person's time available for participation. A subgroup size of four persons or fewer limits the diversity of patterns of interaction and, in the case of absences, makes it difficult to perform the work. The staff trainer or workshop leader floats among the various subgroups and then summarizes his or her observations at the end of each exercise. An opportunity is given to the participants to make their observations on the techniques being taught and on the group process, to voice their concerns about applicability in their setting, and to have their questions addressed about definitions and applicability of any procedures used.

As has been demonstrated throughout this book, CBIGT is a structured approach that can be readily replicated in training programs for the participants. In the following subsections, the building blocks of training are described: the structure of sessions, the simulated groups, the exercises carried out in the simulated groups, the use of extragroup tasks, and the role of the discussion leaders in the simulated groups.

Most in-service training programs for CBIGT consist of six to twenty-four 2-hour sessions. The mean number of sessions in workshops is usually eight. In a class, the mean number of sessions is 15. Training sessions involve the trainees in a set of one to three topics per session.

An example of a topic would be the use of modeling in groups. After a topic is handled, it is followed by the performance of an exercise related to the topic. (See below for titles and an example. The specific modeling exercise is found on p. 249, this volume.) Each topic is initiated by the trainer with a theoretical presentation that is limited to 5 minutes. The basic assumptions of the topic are presented, and questions are answered. Usually, the therapist will model the use of any assessment or intervention procedure and then present diverse examples. The trainees are also asked for examples from their own experience.

In many agencies, two to four additional sessions are increasingly being provided for "booster" experiences to enhance generalization. The additional sessions also extend the opportunity for necessary repetition and "overlearning" and for trying out all the procedures as extragroup tasks and allow time to report back to the group on what and how well the participants were doing.

Group Exercises

The information and skills to be taught are summarized in *A Training Program for Leaders of Coping Skill Training Groups: A Book of Exercises* (Rose, 1997). A number of these exercises have been presented throughout this text. (A complete list of exercises in this book is on p. vii.) The participant can further his or her understanding of the material by reading the introduction either before or after performing a given exercise or by reading related material in this or earlier books by the author (see, e.g., Rose, 1989; Rose & Edleson, 1987). There are two types of exercises. The first are written in such a way that they can also be used by the trainee directly with his or her own group members. The second group of exercises are relevant to the trainees in their role as group therapists and would not be useful to employ directly with youth.

All the exercises are included in the leader's guide (Rose, 1997). The exercises in the guide that are for only training purposes and not for the trainees to use with youth are the following:

- Organizing the Group
- Building Cohesion
- Measuring With Self-Rating Scales and Inventories
- Identifying Resources for Treatment

- Ascertaining Barriers to Treatment
- Refining Assessment With Role Plays

The exercises in this book that can be used both in the training program and with youth are the following:

- Getting Acquainted
- A Case Study
- Defining a Behavioral Response
- Looking at Cognitions
- Defining Feeling Words
- Looking at Feelings in Situations
- Identifying the Critical Moment
- Identifying the Consequences
- Situational Analysis
- Identifying Resources and Barriers
- Goal Formulation
- Systematic Problem Solving
- Reinforcing Others
- The Modeling Sequence
- Dealing With Racial, Ethnic, Homophobic, and Gender Put-Downs
- Irrational Thoughts
- Identifying Thinking Errors
- Replacing Thinking Errors With Coping Thoughts
- Self-Instructional Training
- Increasing the Probability of Task Completion
- Assessing Social Networks
- Redistribution of Participation
- Seeing the Larger Pattern
- Transfer and Maintenance of Change

Each exercise (in Rose, 1997) contains the rationale for the exercise, the purposes of the exercise, the individual tasks to be performed either before or during the session, the small group tasks, potential extragroup tasks, and instructions for evaluation. (The rationale for each exercise described in this book is found in the text.)

Not all the earlier mentioned exercises are presented in every training program, workshop, or course. On occasion, new topics not on the list are also introduced to meet the unique demands of a given population. Also, the order of the exercises is somewhat arbitrary. Usually, assessment exercises are in the beginning, intervention exercises in the middle, and generalization strategies at the end. However, because the goal of treatment is ultimately generalized change, the generalization exercises have been recently moved up to an earlier time slot. Because the participants have all the exercises available to them at the beginning of training, in ongoing training programs it may also be possible for them to negotiate which exercises they prefer and when they want to do them.

Small Group Discussion Leaders

In the course of a 2-hour session, two or three small group exercises are carried out under the leadership of one of the small group members, for whom clear instructions are provided. The instructions include the amount of time available for the exercise, specific expectations from the participants, and specific leadership tasks to be performed by the discussion leader. Leaders are assigned to subgroups on a rotating basis. The members can then observe each in turn and provide feedback on the leadership skills of their peers. In particular, they are observed for their skill in encouraging broad participation, keeping within reasonable time limits, setting limits on dominating speakers, identifying group problems, keeping the proceedings at a reasonable tempo, and maintaining the cohesion of the group. The workshop or course instructor who briefly observes each subgroup in turn also provides feedback.

At the end of a given set of exercises, the instructor leads a discussion of how the same exercises can be used with youth. The participants present any problems they perceive in the application as well as strategies for dealing with those problems. For example, one participant noted that her group members of poorly educated juvenile offenders were unable to use the cognitive strategies presented in the in-service training. The participants then brainstormed what strategies she might employ to help them verbalize cognitions and, if necessary, change them. The participants suggested that she simplify the language and make it less technical, that she use examples from other youth groups whose members were more accepting of the approach, that she invite models from other groups to explain the material, and that she practice her orientation speech with the training group the next week. Having evaluated the suggestions in terms of potential effectiveness, her value system, her competency level, and the group's competency level, she selected almost all of the strategies and agreed to try them out at the next session of her group.

Extrasession Tasks

Extrasession tasks (like extragroup tasks) are sets of self-negotiated tasks to be performed between sessions. The purpose of extrasession tasks is twofold. First, these tasks provide the participants with understanding of the demands and difficulties of using such tasks with clients, and second, like extragroup tasks, extrasession tasks extend the training program into the real world. Tasks are negotiated with the participants in the course of ongoing training programs and usually consist of the trainees' trying out the various procedures with their groups and the family workers' trying them out with their clients in families. In workshops that meet only 1 or 2 days back to back, extrasession tasks are not possible because the groups do not come together again. Some trainers have found it useful to give 2-day workshops 1 day at a time, 1 month apart, just to give the trainees a chance to do these tasks, which are designed on the first day, carried out between sessions, and monitored on the second day of training. Where the trainer comes from a long distance, this is not feasible for financial reasons. Usually, in the case of the 1- or 2-day workshop, the trainer will have the participants develop extrasession tasks in their work groups *as if* they were returning the next week. These tasks are evaluated by the group in terms of how well they meet the criteria of effective tasks (see pp. 314-316, this volume). Examples of extrasession tasks developed by participants were the following: to develop a treatment contract with the group with whom they were working; to use the modeling sequence with the group; and to discuss a persistent group problem with the group and systematically problem-solve with the members concerning what could be done about it. A number of persons videotaped their sessions when they used coping skill training methods, and these were reviewed by the trainer and feedback given to the instructor. In some cases, these tapes could be used with the leaders' and participants' permission as training material for the entire workshop or for future workshops. The participant then received additional feedback from the group as to what he or she did well and what he or she might consider doing differently.

In courses and ongoing in-service training, readings may be assigned (from this text and from Rose, 1989) as extrasession tasks and discussed at subsequent sessions. The same readings may also be recommended to participants in the workshops and in other noncontinuous training programs, but reading cannot be monitored through discussion at subsequent sessions. Attempts to require reading in advance of the workshop have only rarely succeeded.

Participants

Almost all participants in the workshops and in-service programs have had a minimum of a bachelor's degree, and many have had a master's degree, a PhD in psychology, social work, counseling, or a similar field, or an MD in psychiatry. Almost all have had clinical experience, and some have had extensive small group experience as well. This level is not required, but the BA is usually the lowest educational level of a person who does group therapy, and the norm is usually a master's degree or higher. The heterogeneity in experience and education appear to contribute to the quality of the discussions. In-service training programs have included group therapists, family workers, and residential staff as a way of orienting the entire treatment staff to the approach. Classes tend to be more homogeneous than either in-service training or workshops. The participants in classes are usually taking the course for credit toward a common degree. However, the amount of experience among the participants usually varies dramatically.

Teaching Functions

The workshop leader, instructor, or trainer performs a number of different functions, many of which are discussed in the following sections. These include lecturing, modeling the group leadership skills, involving the participants in small group discussion, and building the cohesion of the group.

Lecturing/Discussion Leading

Lecturing is held to an absolute minimum. The instructor never lectures for more than 10 minutes at a time. Most lecturing precedes the exercise and prepares the participants to do the exercises by explaining the concepts associated with them and giving examples of how the concepts can be applied. Even in the brief lecture, overhead transparencies and other audiovisual aids are used to illustrate concepts clearly and to maintain interest. The lecturer also provides a few minutes for answering questions following the brief lecture. Following the exercise, there is a brief review of what the participants have done. A more extended opportunity for questions and general discussion follows. Whenever a basic group principle has been demonstrated in the exercise, the trainer points this out or asks the participants what they perceive as the underlying principle.

Modeling

This is the most commonly used educational strategy. In the presentation of all the exercises, the workshop leader, the instructor, or the trainer usually models what is expected from the participants. In the above exercise, the trainer will make a list of all activities, interests, or socio-recreational skills that he or she enjoys now or has enjoyed in the past year before asking the group to do this. Similarly, in the exercise on identifying self-defeating statements (see p. 269), the trainer will provide an example of a self-defeating statement that he or she has been known to make. Wherever role-played modeling is called for, the trainer will usually role-play the type of situation demanded of the participants first. By modeling this kind of self-disclosure and willingness to make oneself vulnerable, the trainer increases the likelihood and intensity of self-disclosure and the openness of the group members.

Involving the Participants

The structure of the small group and the use of exercises lend themselves to broad participation. In the early training sessions, whenever the trainer asks a question about member experiences, he or she asks the members to write down their answers before permitting anyone to answer the question. This prevents the fast reactors from always dominating the question-and-answer periods. It is also a technique that the participants should be emulating in their own groups. In later sessions, as the participants have developed more respect for each other, the writing requirement may be dropped.

The sharing of leadership is also a way of maximizing the trainees' participation at all levels. The trainer is careful to protect them by providing a great deal of structure in the early exercises and by giving specific instructions as to how long the exercises should be and their specific function in the overall format of the course or workshop.

Building the Cohesion of the Training Groups

Several principles are involved in keeping the cohesion of the small groups high. They include keeping the tempo of the group program fast, providing variety in the program, and creating opportunities for physical movement. Providing maximum opportunities for broad participation and autonomous functioning in the groups, which has already been discussed, is also important for building cohesion. Other principles, not discussed further, are keeping the lectures brief, providing opportunities for discussing the experiences, modest use of humor, and, as in all groups, the intermittent availability of food and beverages.

Tempo of the Program. The trainer is also responsible for keeping the tempo of the training program fast to maintain the participants' interest. Using time limits, encouraging the discussion leaders to keep track of time, and frequently changing activities all contribute to tempo.

Variety. If the program of the workshop or training sessions is too repetitious, participants quickly become bored. The use of very brief lecture with the help of audiovisual aids, demonstrations by the trainer, brief discussions of issues, opportunities for questions, many different kinds of exercises, and opportunities for role playing contributes to that variation.

Physical Movement. One also needs variety in physical situations. Although the subgroups in which the participants are situated remain fixed, the trainer makes sure that the participants change seating positions from time to time in the groups. One can move whole groups to another part of the room. When pairs are used in the exercises, the composition of the pairs should change with every exercise so that no one gets "stuck" with the same person. In role playing, wherever feasible, the role players should move about, open doors, sit down, and stand up as part of role play. Physical movement is especially important in all-day workshops.

Frequent Summarization

Not only should the trainer make use of frequent summarization of the techniques used or the principles applied, but he or she should encourage the discussion leaders to do the same thing in their subgroups. One of the principles noted for achieving generalization is overlearning. Summarization provides an opportunity to revisit principles and encourage overlearning through repetition. After an initial demonstration, the participants are asked to summarize at the end of each session.

Evaluation

Evaluation is an essential component of every training program for making relevant improvements in the program as it progresses on the basis of trainees' experience and changing the development of the program for future use. Two objects of evaluation are used: the exercises as they are employed and a final overview of the entire workshop or other training program. Toward the end of every session, the group evaluate in writing and give positive feedback to the discussion leader on what he or she did well, and, if the group members feel they are ready, they can make suggestions as to what the leader might have done differently. (Such critical feedback is not permitted until the exercise in giving critical feedback has been completed.) At the very end of the session also, a post-session questionnaire, similar to the one given in the therapy groups with youth, is given to the participants in which the experience and group processes are evaluated. Open-ended questions are also posed. "What did you find useful?" and "What would you like to see changed?" are added to the rating scales or are substituted for them. The results of the post-session questionnaire and open-ended questions are analyzed and reviewed by the participants at the beginning of the next session. In 1-day workshops, this is not possible because there is insufficient time available.

The final evaluation at the end of the program provides information about overall consumer satisfaction with the course or workshop, aspects of the program found to be most useful, and participants' opinions about the impact or potential impact of the program on their work. Participants also provide their opinions as to the effectiveness of the administration and organization of the workshop. This evaluation simulates the evaluation requested from the clients. In general, we have found that the instruments must be kept brief if the cooperation of the trainees or students is to be maintained. Otherwise, the evaluation instruments become too intrusive and disruptive and a source of resistance.

The following questions (postsession questionnaire) can be used at the end of a morning or afternoon session in a workshop or at the end of a 2- or 3-hour session in a class or ongoing in-service training program.

1. How useful was this session in helping you to achieve your learning goals?

1	2	3	4	5	6	7	8	9
not at all		very little		somewhat		quite a bit		extremely

2. How well did you enjoy the group in this session?

1	2	3	4	5	6	7	8	9
not at all		very little		somewhat		quite a bit		extremely

3. How much were you involved in this session?

1	2	3	4	5	6	7	8	9
not at all		very little		somewhat		quite a bit		extremely

4. How independently (of the instructor or trainer) were you able to work during this session?

1	2	3	4	5	6	7	8	9
not at all		very little		somewhat		quite a bit		extremely

5. What specifically did you find most useful or interesting during this session?

6. What would you like to change about this session?

The data collected from the above questionnaires are summarized and presented at a subsequent session to the participants in ongoing training programs or courses. In workshops, there is not enough time to do the collating of the data. One problem in using this questionnaire so frequently is that the participants begin to tire of filling out the forms. For this reason, the questionnaires are kept extremely short, and their importance in the process is emphasized. For the final evaluation, the following questions are often asked.

1. How useful was the workshop for you in preparing you to do your work more effectively?

1	2	3	4	5	6	7	8	9
not at all		very little		somewhat		quite a bit		extremely

2. How well organized was the workshop?

1	2	3	4	5	6	7	8	9
not at all		very little		somewhat		quite a bit		extremely

3. (Look at list of exercises.) Which exercises did you find most useful? Least useful?

4. What did you find particularly useful in this workshop or training program? (Be specific.)

5. What changes in the program would you have found to be particularly helpful?

6. What do you perceive you learned in this training program? (Provide as much detail as time permits.)

The data collected from the above questionnaire are used to evaluate consumer satisfaction with the training program as a whole and some of the elements of that program.

Recently, a 6-month to 1-year follow-up questionnaire similar to the above questionnaire has been distributed as a means of determining whether there have been any long-term effects. Although the return rate has been less than 60%, a number of excellent suggestions for adaptations of the program have been noted.

Training Is Not Enough

No matter how effective the course, the ongoing in-service training, or the workshop, the participants may not be successful in implementing such a group program in their respective agencies. The agency must provide organizational supports for the newly trained staff. Among those supports are supervision and future training.

Postworkshop training or parallel supervision is often conducted by agency supervisory personnel who have been trained in the approach. Because of the similarity to the context of therapy, group supervision is the preferable mode. Where no one is already trained and experienced in working with CBIGT, often peer group supervision is used. The supervision involves review of tapes, agendas, extragroup tasks, assessment, goals, interventive strategies, group problems, and steps taken to achieve generalization. Usually each person brings one situation or one issue to the supervisory session. Problem solving is used to deal with problems presented by the trainees.

In addition, a program of reading is established. The group discusses the agreed-on literature and its applicability to the groups the participants are conducting. The group may also develop new exercises that are appropriate to members' client populations, and these are tried out in the supervisory sessions.

Where peer group supervision is used, at the end of the session, the person serving as supervisor gets positive feedback from the others. If the supervisor feels comfortable, he or she can ask for suggestions as to what the supervisor might consider doing differently. Also, periodically it is helpful for the group to consider the overall structure and to consider temporary or even permanent termination when the group seems to be wearing out its usefulness.

Summary

One model of training staff for CBIGT has been presented. Adaptations of this program can be used in in-service training, workshops, and formal courses. It appears to be applicable to diverse populations of learners and levels of competence. The results from the evaluation of training suggest that the model offers an effective strategy for training persons in the skills required to develop and organize CBIGT groups, provided they have adequate agency support.

Basically, the model proposed here involves carrying out a set of exercises in small groups under the guidance of the trainer or instructor. These exercises replicate those used with the client population, many of which have been illustrated throughout this book. They cover most of the assessment and intervention strategies used in CBIGT. The trainees are given the opportunity to lead the small groups and to receive feedback on their leadership from the other participants. The trainer or instructor models the skills that the participants must learn to implement CBIGT. The strengths of the model include the active involvement of the learner in the process, the similarity of the training model to the practice model, and the enthusiasm generated among the participants.

References

Achenbach, T. M. (1991). *Manual for the child behavior checklist/4-18 and 1991 profile.* Burlington: University of Vermont, Department of Psychiatry.

Achenbach, T. M., & Edelbrock, C. S. (1986). *Manual for the child behavior checklist and the revised child behavior profile.* Burlington, VT: University Associates in Psychiatry.

Anthony, E. J. (1968). Reflection on twenty-five years of group psychotherapy. *International Journal of Group Psychotherapy, 18,* 277-301.

Antonucci, T. C., & Israel, B. (1986). Veridicality of social support: A comparison of principal and network members' responses. *Journal of Consulting and Clinical Psychology, 54,* 432-437.

Antonuccio, D. O., Davis, C., Lewinsohn, P. M., & Breckenridge, J. S. (1987). Therapist variables related to cohesiveness in a group treatment for depression. *Small Group Behavior, 18,* 557-564.

Arbuthnot, J., & Gordon, D. A. (1986). Behavioral and cognitive effects of a moral reasoning development intervention for high-risk behavior-disordered adolescents. *Journal of Consulting and Clinical Psychology, 54,* 208-216.

Ausubel, D. P. (1963). *The psychology of meaningful verbal learning.* New York: Grune & Stratton.

Azrin, N. H., & Besale, V. A. (1980). *Job club counselor's manual: A behavioral approach to vocational counseling.* Baltimore: University Park Press.

Bandura, A. (1969). *Principles of behavior modification.* New York: Holt, Rinehart & Winston.

Bandura, A. (1973). *Aggression: A social learning analysis.* Englewood Cliffs, NJ: Prentice Hall.

Bandura, A. (1975). Generalizing change through participant modeling with self-directed mastery. *Behaviour Research and Therapy, 13,* 141-152.

Bandura, A. (1977a). Self-efficacy: Toward a unifying theory of behavioral change. *Psychological Review, 84,* 191-215.

Bandura, A. (1977b). *Social learning theory.* Englewood Cliffs, NJ: Prentice Hall.

Barrera, M. (1981). Social support in the adjustment of pregnant adolescents: Assessment issues. In B. H. Gottlieb (Ed.), *Social networks and social support* (pp. 69-96). Beverly Hills, CA: Sage.

Barrera, M., & Baca, L. M. (1990). Recipient reactions to social support: Contributions of enacted support, conflicted support and network orientation. *Journal of Social and Personal Relationships, 7,* 541-551.

Barth, R. P. (1986). *Social and cognitive treatment of children and adolescents.* San Francisco: Jossey-Bass.

Beck, A. T. (1976). *Cognitive therapy and emotional disorders.* New York: International Universities Press.

Beck, A. T., & Emery, G. (1985). *Anxiety disorders and phobias.* New York: Basic Books.

Bednar, R. L., & Moeschl, M. J. (1981). Conceptual and methodological considerations in the evaluation of group psychotherapies. *Advances in Psychological Assessment, 5,* 393-423. San Francisco: Jossey-Bass.

Belfer, P. L., & Levendusky, P. (1985). Long-term behavioral group psychotherapy: An integrative model. In D. Upper & S. M. Ross (Eds.), *Handbook of behavioral group therapy* (pp. 119-144). New York: Plenum.

Bell, R. C. (1969). *Board and table games from many civilizations.* London: Oxford University Press.

Bellack, A. S., Hersen, M., & Turner, S. M. (1978). Roleplay tests for assessing social skill: Are they valid? *Behavior Therapy, 9,* 448-461.

Belsher, G., & Wilkes, T. C. R. (1994). The middle phase of cognitive therapy: Intervention techniques for five steps in the therapeutic process. In T. C. R. Wilkes, G. Belsher, A. J. Rush, & E. Frank (Eds.), *Cognitive therapy for depressed adolescents* (pp. 132-143). New York: Guilford.

Berkowitz, L. (1993). *Aggression: Its causes, consequences, and control.* New York: McGraw-Hill.

Bernstein, D. A., & Borkovec, T. D. (1973). *Progressive relaxation training: A manual for the helping professions.* Champaign, IL: Research Press.

Bion, W. P. (1959). *Experiences in groups.* New York: Basic Books.

Borkovec, T. D., Mathews, A. M., Chambers, A., & Ebrahimi, S. (1987). The effects of relaxation training with cognitive or nondirective therapy and the role of relaxation-induced anxiety in the treatment of generalized anxiety. *Journal of Consulting and Clinical Psychology, 55,* 883-888.

Boyd, N. L. (1973). *Handbook of recreational games.* New York: Dover.

Brierton, D., Rose, S. D., & Flanagan, J. (1975). A behavioral approach to corrections counseling. *Law in American Society, 4,* 10-16.

Budman, S. H., Soldz, S., Demby, A., Davis, M., & Merry, J. (1993). What is cohesiveness: An empirical examination. *Small Group Research, 2,* 199-216.

Cardillo, J. E. (1994). Goal setting, follow-up, and goal monitoring. In T. J. Kiresuk, A. Smith, & J. E. Cardillo (Eds.), *Goal attainment scaling: Applications, theory, and measurement.* Hillsdale, NJ: Lawrence Erlbaum.

Carrington, P. (1978). *Learning to meditate: Clinically standardized meditation (CSM): Course workbook.* Kendall Park, NJ: Pace Educational Systems.

Cartledge, G., & Milburn, J. F. (1981). *Teaching social skills to children.* Elmsford, NY: Pergamon.

Cautela, J. R., & Groden, J. (1978). *Relaxation: A comprehensive manual for adults, children, and children with special needs.* Champaign, IL: Research Press.

Comas-Diaz, L., & Duncan, J. W. (1985). The cultural context: A factor in assertiveness training with mainland Puerto Rican women. *Psychology of Women Quarterly, 9,* 463-475.

Conners, C. K. (1990). *Conners' rating scales manual, Conners' teacher rating scales, Conners' parent rating scales: Instruments for use with children and adolescents.* North Tonawanda, NY: Multi-Health Systems.

Corey, M. S., & Corey, G. (1997). *Groups process and practice* (5th ed.). Pacific Grove, CA: Brooks/Cole.

Cormier, W. H., & Cormier, L. S. (1991). *Interviewing strategies for helpers: Fundamental skills and cognitive behavioral interventions* (3rd ed.). Monterey, CA: Brooks/Cole.

Costell, R., & Koran, L. (1972). Compatibility and cohesiveness in group psychotherapy. *Journal of Nervous and Mental Disease, 155,* 99-104.

D'Alelio, W. A., & Murray, E. J. (1981). Cognitive therapy for test anxiety. *Cognitive Therapy and Research, 5,* 299-307.

Deffenbacher, J. L., Lynch, R. S., & Oetting, E. R. (1996). Anger reduction in early adolescents. *Journal of Counseling Psychology, 43,* 149-157.

DeLange, J. M., Lanham, S. L., & Barton, J. A. (1981). Social skills training for juvenile delinquents: Behavioral skill training and cognitive techniques. In D. Upper & S. M. Ross (Eds.), *Behavior group therapy.* Champaign, IL: Research Press.

Dies, R. (1973). Group therapists' self-disclosure: An evaluation by clients. *Journal of Counseling Psychology, 20,* 344-348.

DiGiuseppe, R., Tafrate, R., & Eckhardt, C. (1994). Critical issues in the treatment of anger. *Cognitive and Behavioral Practice, 1,* 111-132.

Dinkmeyer, D. (1973). *Developing Understanding of Self and Others (DUSO).* Circle Pines, MN: American Guidance Service.

Drencher, S., Burlingame, G., & Fuhriman, A. (1985). An odyssey in empirical understanding. *Small Group Behavior, 16*(1), 3-30.

Dupper, D. R., & Krishef, C. H. (1993). School-based social-cognitive skills training for middle school students with school behavior problems. *Children and Youth Services Review, 15*(2), 131-142.

D'Zurilla, T. J. (1986). *Problem-solving therapy: Social competence approach to clinical intervention.* New York: Springer.

Edleson, J. L., & Rose, S. D. (1981). Investigations into the efficacy of short term group social skill training for socially isolated children. *Child Behavior Therapy, 3*(2), 1-16.

Elie, D. (1977). An analysis of Wagner's Hand Test and its capacity to predict. *Crime and Punishment, 3,* 221-224.

Ellis, A. (1973). *Humanistic psychotherapy.* New York: McGraw-Hill.

Erikson, E. (1963). *Childhood and society.* New York: Norton.

Etscheidt, S. (1991). Reducing aggressive behavior and improving self-control: A cognitive-behavioral training program for behaviorally disordered adolescents. *Behavioral Disorders, 16,* 107-115.

Evans, C. R., & Dion, K. L. (1991). Group cohesion and performance: A meta-analysis. *Small Group Research, 22,* 175-186.

Everly, G. S., & Rosenfeld, R. (1981). *The nature and treatment of the stress response: A practical guide for clinicians.* New York: Plenum.

Ewart, C. K., Harris, W. L., Iwata, M. M., & Coates, T. J. (1987). Feasibility and effectiveness of school-based relaxation lowering blood pressure. *Health Psychology, 6,* 399-416.

Eyberg, S. M. (1980). Child Behavior Inventory. *Journal of Clinical Child Psychology, 9,* 29.

Eyberg, S. M., & Robinson, E. A. (1983). Conduct problem behavior: Standardization of a behavioral rating scale with adolescents. *Journal of Clinical Child Psychology, 12,* 347-354.

Feindler, E. L., Ecton, R. B., Kingsley, D., & Dubey, D. R. (1986). Group anger-control training for institutionalized psychiatric male adolescents. *Behavior Therapy, 17,* 109-123.

Feindler, E. L., Marriott, S. A., & Iwata, M. (1984). Group anger-control training for junior high school delinquents. *Cognitive Therapy and Research, 8,* 299-311.

Ferster, C. B., & Skinner, B. F. (1957). *Schedules of reinforcement*. East Norwalk, CT: Appleton-Century-Crofts.

Fielding, J. (1983). Verbal participation and group therapy outcome. *British Journal of Psychiatry, 142*, 524-528.

Finkelhor, D., Gelles, R. J., Hotaling, G. T., & Straus, M. A. (1990). *Physical violence in American families: Risk factors and adaptations to violence in 8,145 families*. New Brunswick, NJ: Transaction.

Flowers, J. V., Hartman, K. A., & Booraem, C. D. (1981). Problems as a function of group cohesiveness. *Psychotherapy: Theory, Research, and Practice, 18*, 246.

Flowers, J. V., & Schwartz, B. (1985). Behavioral group therapy with clients with homogeneous problems. In S. Ross & D. Upper (Eds.), *Handbook of behavioral group therapy*. New York: Plenum.

Fluegelman, A. (1976). *The new games book*. Garden City, NY: Doubleday.

Fodor, I. G. (1988). Cognitive behavior therapy: Evaluation of theory and practice for addressing women's issues. In M. A. Dutton-Douglas & L. E. Walker (Eds.), *Feminist psychotherapies: Integration of therapeutic and feminist systems* (pp. 91-117). Norwood, NJ: Ablex.

Forman, S. G. (1993). *Coping skills interventions for children and adolescents*. San Francisco: Jossey-Bass.

Forsyth, D. R. (1990). *Group dynamics* (2nd ed.). Pacific Grove, CA: Brooks/Cole.

Foster, S. L., & Ritchey, W. L. (1979). Issues in the assessment of social competence in children. *Journal of Applied Behavior Analysis, 12*, 625-638.

Freedman, B. J. (1974). *A socio-behavioral analysis of skill deficits in delinquent and nondelinquent adolescent boys*. Unpublished doctoral dissertation, University of Wisconsin-Madison.

Gambrill, E. D. (1977). *Behavior modification: Handbook of assessment, intervention, and evaluation*. San Francisco: Jossey-Bass.

Gambrill, E. D. (1983). *Casework: A competency-based approach*. Englewood Cliffs, NJ: Prentice Hall.

Garvin, C. (1987). *Contemporary group work*. Englewood Cliffs, NJ: Prentice Hall.

Gebhardt, L. J., & Meyers, R. A. (1995). Subgroup influence in decision-making groups: Examining consistency from a communication perspective. *Small Group Research, 26*, 147-168.

Girl Scouts of the U.S.A. (1969). *Games for Girl Scouts*. New York: Author.

Goldfried, M. R., & D'Zurilla, T. J. (1969). A behavioral-analytic model for assessing competence. In C. D. Spielberger (Ed.), *Current topics in clinical community psychology*. New York: Academic Press.

Goldstein, A. P., Carr, E. G., Davidson, W. S., II, & Wehr, P. (1981). *In response to aggression*. Elmsford, NY: Pergamon.

Goldstein, A. P., Heller, K., & Sechrest, L. B. (1966). *Psychotherapy and the psychology of behavior change*. New York: John Wiley.

Goldstein, A. P., & Kanfer, F. H. (1979). *Maximizing treatment gains: Transfer enhancement in psychotherapy*. New York: Academic Press.

Goldstein, A. P., & Keller, H. (1987). *Aggressive behavior assessment and intervention*. New York: Pergamon.

Goss, L., & Goss, C. (1995). *Jump up and say!* New York: Simon & Schuster.

Gottman, J., Gonso, J., & Schuler, P. (1976). Teaching social skills to isolated children. *Journal of Abnormal Child Psychology, 4*, 179-197.

Groveman, A. M., Richards, C. S., & Caple, R. B. (1975). *Literature skills counseling and behavioral self-control approaches to improving study behavior* [Abstract, Journal Supplement Abstract Service, Ms. No. 1128]. New York: American Psychological Association.

Guerra, N. G., & Slaby, R. G. (1990). Cognitive mediators of aggression in adolescent offenders. *Developmental Psychology, 26*, 269-277.

Guerra, N. G., Tolan, P. H., & Hammond, W. R. (1994). Prevention and treatment of adolescent violence. In L. D. Eron, J. H. Gentry, & P. Schlegel (Eds.), *Reason to hope: A psychosocial perspective on violence and youth* (pp. 383-403). Washington, DC: American Psychological Association.

Gwynn, C. A., & Brantley, H. T. (1987). Effect of a divorce group intervention for elementary school children. *Psychology in the Schools, 24*, 161-164.

Haaga, D. A. F., & Davison, G. C. (1991). Cognitive change methods. In F. H. Kanfer & A. P. Goldstein (Eds.), *Helping people change* (4th ed., pp. 248-304). Elmsford, NY: Pergamon.

Hall, J. A., & Fortney, M. A. (1994). *The Problem Situation Inventory for Teens: A role play test for social skills.* Unpublished manuscript, University of Iowa.

Hansen, J. C., Warner, R. W., & Smith, E. J. (1980). *Group counseling: Theory and practice* (2nd ed.). Skokie, IL: Rand McNally.

Hawkins, J. D., Jenson, J. M., Catalano, R. F., & Wells, E. A. (1991). Effects of a skills training intervention with juvenile delinquents. *Research on Social Work Practice, 1*, 107-121.

Heide, F. J., & Borkovec, T. D. (1983). Relaxation-induced anxiety: Paradoxical anxiety enhancement due to relaxation training. *Journal of Consulting and Clinical Psychology, 51*, 171-182.

Heitzmann, W. R. (1974). *Educational games and simulations.* Washington, DC: National Education Association.

Henggeler, S. W., Melton, G. B., & Smith, L. A. (1992). Family preservation using multisystemic therapy: An effective alternative to incarcerating serious juvenile offenders. *Journal of Consulting and Clinical Psychology, 60*, 953-961.

Hepler, J., & Rose, S. D. (1988). Evaluation of a multi-component group approach for improving the social skills of elementary school children. *Journal of Social Service Research, 11*(4), 1-18.

Hepler, J. B. (1994). Evaluating the effectiveness of a social skills program for preadolescents. *Research on Social Work Practice, 4*, 411-435.

Hill, W. F. (1977). Hill Interaction Matrix. *Journal of Personnel and Guidance, 49*, 617-623.

Hillenberg, J. B., & Collins, F. L., Jr. (1982). A procedural analysis and review of relaxation training research. *Behaviour Research and Therapy, 20*, 251-260.

Hillenberg, J. B., & Collins, F. L. (1986). The contribution of progressive relaxation and cognitive coping training in stress management programs. *Behavior Therapist, 9*, 147-149.

Hoehn-Saric, R., Frank, J. D., Imber, S. D., Nash, E. H., Stone, A. R., & Battle, C. C. (1964). Systematic preparation of patients for psychotherapy: I. Effects on therapy behavior and outcome. *Journal of Psychiatric Research, 2*, 267-281.

Hops, H., & Lewin, L. (1984). Peer sociometric forms. In T. H. Ollendick & M. Hersen (Eds.), *Child behavioral assessment* (pp. 124-147). New York: Pergamon.

Hops, H., Tildesley, E., Lichtenstein, E., & Ary, D. (1990). Parent-adolescent problem-solving interactions and drug use. *American Journal of Drug and Alcohol Abuse, 16*, 239-258.

Hudley, C. (1994). Perceptions of intentionality, feelings of anger, and reactive aggression. In M. Furlong & D. C. Smith (Eds.), *Anger, hostility and aggression.* Brandon, VT: Clinical Psychology Publishing.

Hudson, W. W. (1982). *The clinical measurement package.* Homewood, IL: Dorsey.

Huesmann, L. R., Eron, L. D., Lefkowitz, M. M., & Walder, L. O. (1984). Stability of aggression over time and generations. *Developmental Psychology, 20*, 1120-1134.

Huey, W. C., & Rank, R. C. (1984). Effects of counselor and peer-led group assertive training on black adolescent aggression. *Journal of Counseling Psychology, 31*, 95-98.

Humphrey, L. L. (1982). Children's and teachers' perspectives on children's self-control: The development of two rating scales. *Journal of Consulting and Clinical Psychology, 50*, 624-633.

Jacobsen, E. (1929). *Progressive relaxation.* Chicago: University of Chicago Press.

Jacobsen, E. (1978). *You must relax.* New York: McGraw-Hill.

Jesness, C. F. (1972). *The Jesness Inventory: Manual.* Palo Alto, CA: Consulting Psychologists Press.

Kamerman, S. B., & Kahn, A. J. (1982). *Helping America's families.* Philadelphia: Temple University Press.

Kanfer, F. H., & Busemeyer, J. P. (1982). The use of problem-solving and decision-making in behavior therapy. *Clinical Psychology Review, 2*, 239-266.

Kazdin, A. E. (1982). Symptom substitution, generalization, and response covariation: Implications for psychotherapy outcome. *Psychological Bulletin, 91*, 349-365.

Kazdin, A. E. (1987). *Conduct disorder in childhood and adolescence.* Newbury Park, CA: Sage.

Kazdin, A. E. (1989). *Behavior modification in applied settings* (4th ed.). Pacific Grove, CA: Brooks/Cole.

Kazdin, A. E. (1992). *Research design in clinical psychology* (2nd ed.). New York: Macmillan.

Kazdin, A. E., Esveldt-Dawson, K., French, N. H., & Unis, A. S. (1987a). Effects of parent management training and problem-solving skills training combined in the treatment of antisocial child behavior. *Journal of the American Academy of Child and Adolescent Psychiatry, 26*, 416-424.

Kazdin, A. E., Esveldt-Dawson, K., French, N. H., & Unis, A. S. (1987b). Problem-solving skills training and relationship therapy in the treatment of antisocial child behavior. *Journal of Consulting and Clinical Psychology, 55*, 76-85.

Kazdin, A. E., & Frame, C. (1984). Aggressive behavior and conduct disorder. In R. J. Morris & T. R. Kratochwill (Eds.), *The practice of child therapy* (pp. 167-192). New York: Pergamon.

Kelly, G. A. (1955). *The psychology of personal constructs.* New York: Norton.

Kelly, J. A., Wildman, B. G., & Berler, E. S. (1980). Small group behavioral training to improve the job interview skills repertoire of mildly retarded adolescents. *Journal of Applied Behavior Analysis, 13*, 461-471.

Kendall, P. C., & Braswell, L. (1985). *Cognitive-behavioral therapy for impulsive children.* New York: Guilford.

Kendall, P. C., & Finch, A. J. (1976). A cognitive-behavioral treatment for impulse control: A case study. *Journal of Consulting and Clinical Psychology, 44*, 852-857.

Kendall, P. C., & Finch, A. J. (1978). A cognitive-behavioral treatment for impulsivity: A group comparison study. *Journal of Consulting and Clinical Psychology, 49*, 110-118.

Kiresuk, T. J., Smith, A., & Cardillo, J. E. (Eds.). (1994). *Goal attainment scaling: Applications, theory, and measurement.* Hillsdale, NJ: Lawrence Erlbaum.

Kirshner, B., Dies, R., & Brown, A. (1978). Effects of experimental manipulation of self-disclosure on group cohesiveness. *Journal of Consulting and Clinical Psychology, 46*, 1171-1177.

Klein, A. (1972). *Effective group work.* New York: Association Press.

Kovacs, M. (1981). Rating scales to assess depression in school-aged children. *Acta Paedopsychiatrica, 46*, 305-315.

LaFromboise, T., & Rowe, W. (1983). Skills training for bicultural competence: Rationale and application. *Journal of Counseling Psychology, 30*, 589-595.

Larson, J. D. (1992). Anger and aggression management techniques through the *Think First* curriculum. *Journal of Offender Rehabilitation, 18*, 101-117.

Lazarus, R. S. (1966). *Psychological stress and the coping process.* New York: McGraw-Hill.

LeCroy, C. W. (1983). Social skills training with adolescents: A review. In C. W. LeCroy (Ed.), *Social skills training with children and youth.* New York: Haworth.

LeCroy, C. W., & Rose, S. D. (1986). Evaluation of preventive intervention for enhancing social competence in adolescents. *Social Work Research and Abstracts, 22,* 8-17.

Linahan, M. M., Walker, R. O., Bronheim, S., Haynes, K. F., & Yezeroff, H. (1979). Group versus individual assertion training. *Journal of Consulting and Clinical Psychology, 47,* 1000-1002.

Lochman, J. E. (1985). Effects of different treatment lengths in cognitive behavioral interventions with aggressive boys. *Child Psychiatry and Human Development, 16,* 45-56.

Lochman, J. E., Burch, P. R., Curry, J. F., & Lampron, L. B. (1984). Treatment and generalization effects of cognitive-behavioral and goal-setting interventions with aggressive boys. *Journal of Consulting and Clinical Psychology, 52,* 915-916.

Lochman, J. E., & Curry, J. F. (1986). Effects of social problem-solving training and self-instruction training with aggressive boys. *Journal of Clinical Child Psychology, 15,* 159-164.

Lochman, J. E., & Lampron, L. B. (1986). Situational social problem-solving skills and self-esteem of aggressive and nonaggressive boys. *Journal of Abnormal Psychology, 13,* 527-538.

Lochman, J. E., Nelson, W. M., & Sims, J. P. (1981). A cognitive behavioral program for use with aggressive children. *Journal of Clinical Child Psychology, 10,* 146-148.

Locke, E. A., Frederick, E., Buckner, E., & Bobko, P. (1984). Effect of previously assigned goals on self-set goals and performance. *Journal of Applied Psychology, 69,* 694-699.

Locke, E. A., Shaw, K. N., Saari, L. M., & Latham, G. P. (1981). Goal setting and task performance: 1969-1980. *Psychological Bulletin, 90,* 125-152.

Lott, A. J., & Lott, B. E. (1965). Group cohesiveness as interpersonal attraction: A review of relationships with antecedent and consequent variables. *Psychological Bulletin, 64,* 259-309.

Magen, R., & Rose, S. D. (1994). Parents in groups: Problem solving versus behavioral skills training. *Research on Social Work Practice, 4,* 172-179.

Maher, C. A. (1987). Involving behaviorally disordered adolescents in instructional planning: Effectiveness of the goal procedure. *Child and Adolescent Psychotherapy, 4,* 185-189.

Marlatt, G. A. (1985). Life style modification. In G. A. Marlatt & J. R. Gordon (Eds.), *Relapse prevention.* New York: Guilford.

Marlatt, G. A., & Gordon, J. R. (Eds.). (1985). *Relapse prevention.* New York: Guilford.

Mathews, A. M., Gelder, M. G., & Johnston, D. W. (1981). *Agoraphobia: Nature and treatment.* New York: Guilford.

Matson, J. L., Rotatori, A. F., & Helsel, W. J. (1983). Development of a rating scale to measure social skills in children: The Matson Evaluation of Social Skills with Youngsters (MESSY). *Behaviour Research and Therapy, 21,* 335-340.

Maultsby, M. (1971). Systematic written homework in psychotherapy. *Rational Living, 6,* 17-23.

McFall, R. M., & Marston, A. R. (1970). An experimental investigation of behavioral rehearsal in assertion training. *Journal of Abnormal Psychology, 76,* 295-303.

Meichenbaum, D. H. (1974). *Therapist manual for cognitive behavior modification.* Unpublished manuscript, University of Waterloo, Waterloo, Ontario, Canada.

Meichenbaum, D. (1977). *Cognitive-behavior modification: An integrated approach.* New York: Plenum.

Meichenbaum, D. H., & Genest, M. (1980). Cognitive behavior modification: An integration of cognitive and behavioral methods. In F. H. Kanfer & A. P. Goldstein (Eds.), *Helping people change* (2nd ed.). New York: Pergamon.

Miller, W. R., & Rollnick, S. (1991). *Motivational interviewing.* New York: Guilford.

Mischel, W. (1973). Toward a cognitive social learning reconceptualization of personality. *Psychological Review, 80,* 252-283.

Mooney, K. C. (1984). Child behavior checklist. In D. J. Keyser & R. C. Sweetland (Eds.), *Test critiques* (Vol. 1, pp. 168-184). Kansas City, MO: Test Corporation of America.

Nangle, D. W., Carr-Nangle, R. E., & Hansen, D. J. (1994). Enhancing generalization of a contingency-management intervention through the use of family problem-solving training: Evaluation with a severely conduct-disordered adolescent. *Child and Family Behavior Therapy, 16*(2), 65-76.

Nelson, W. M., & Birkimer, J. (1978). Role of self-instruction and self-reinforcement in the modification of impulsivity. *Journal of Consulting and Clinical Psychology, 46,* 183.

Nelson, W. M., & Finch, A. J. (1978). *The Children's Inventory of Anger.* Unpublished manuscript, Xavier University.

Nemeroff, C. J., & Karoly, P. (1991). Operant methods. In F. H. Kanfer & A. P. Goldstein (Eds.), *Helping people change* (4th ed., pp. 122-160). New York: Pergamon.

Novaco, R. W. (1975). *Anger control: The development and evaluation of an experimental treatment.* Lexington, MA: D. C. Heath.

Nowicki, S., Jr., & Strickland, B. R. (1973). A locus of control scale for children. *Journal of Consulting and Clinical Psychology, 40,* 148-154.

Patterson, G. R. (1982). *Coercive family process.* Eugene, OR: Castalia.

Patterson, G. R. (1986). Performance models for antisocial boys. *American Psychologist, 41,* 432-444.

Pepler, D. J., & Slaby, R. G. (1994). Theoretical and developmental perspectives on youth and violence. In L. D. Eron, J. H. Gentry, & P. Schlegel (Eds.), *Reason to hope: A psychosocial perspective on violence and youth* (pp. 27-58). Washington, DC: American Psychological Association.

Phillips, E. L. (1968). Achievement Place: Token reinforcement procedures in a home-style rehabilitation setting for "pre-delinquent" boys. *Journal of Applied Behavior Analysis, 1,* 213-223.

Piacentini, J. (1993). Checklists and rating scales. In T. H. Ollendick & M. Hersen (Eds.), *Handbook of child and adolescent assessment.* Boston: Allyn & Bacon.

Piper, W. E., Montvila, R. M., & McGihon, A. L. (1979). Process analysis in therapy groups: A behavior sampling technique with many potential uses. In D. Upper & S. M. Ross (Eds.), *Behavioral group therapy.* Champaign, IL: Research Press.

Quay, H. C., & Peterson, D. R. (1987). *Manual for the Revised Behavior Problem Checklist.* Available from H. C. Quay, Ph.D., Department of Psychology, University of Miami, Coral Gables, FL 33124.

Quinsey, V. L., & Varney, G. W. (1979). Social skills game: A general method for the modeling and practice of adaptive behaviors. *Behavior Therapy, 8,* 279-281.

Redl, F. (1955). Group emotion and leadership. In P. Hare, E. Borgotta, & R. Bales (Eds.), *Small groups: Studies in social interaction.* New York: Knopf.

Rehm, L. P., & Rokke, P. (1988). Self-management therapies. In K. S. Dobson (Ed.), *Handbook of cognitive-behavioral therapies.* New York: Guilford.

Reid, W. J. (1978). *The task centered system*. New York: Columbia University Press.

Reinecke, M. A., Dattilio, F. M., & Freeman, A. (Eds.). (1996). *Cognitive therapy with children and adolescents*. New York: Guilford.

Reynolds, W. M. (1985). Depression in childhood and adolescence: Diagnosis, assessment, intervention strategies and research. In T. R. Kratochwill (Ed.), *Advances in school psychology* (1st ed., pp. 133-189). Hillsdale, NJ: Lawrence Erlbaum.

Reynolds, W. M. (1993). Self-report methodology. In T. H. Ollendick & M. Hersen (Eds.), *Handbook of child and adolescent assessment*. Boston: Allyn & Bacon.

Reynolds, W. M., & Coats, K. I. (1986). A comparison of cognitive-behavioral therapy and relaxation training for the treatment of depression in adolescents. *Journal of Consulting and Clinical Psychology, 54*, 653-660.

Ribner, N. G. (1974). Effects of an explicit group contract on self-disclosure and group cohesiveness. *Journal of Counseling Psychology, 21*, 116-120.

Rice, W., & Yaconelli, M. (Eds.). (1993). *Play it again! More great games for groups*. Grand Rapids, MI: Zondervan.

Rook, K. S. (1992). Detrimental aspects of social relationships: Taking stock of an emerging literature. In H. O. F. Veiel & U. Baumann (Eds.), *The meaning and measurement of social support* (pp. 157-169). New York: Hemisphere.

Rose, S. D. (1978). The effect of contingency contracting on the completion rate of behavioral assignments in assertion training groups. *Journal of Social Service Research, 1*, 299-306.

Rose, S. D. (1981). Assessment in groups. *Social Work Research and Abstracts, 17*, 29-37.

Rose, S. D. (1989). *Working with adults in groups: A multimethod approach*. San Francisco: Jossey-Bass.

Rose, S. D. (1997). *A training program for leaders of coping skill training groups: A book of exercises*. Madison: University of Wisconsin-Madison, School of Social Work.

Rose, S. D., Duby, P., Olenick, C., & Weston, T. (1996). Integrating family, group and residential treatment: A cognitive-behavioral approach. *Social Work With Groups, 19*(2), 35-49.

Rose, S. D., & Edleson, J. L. (1987). *Working with children and adolescents in groups: A multimethod approach*. San Francisco: Jossey-Bass.

Rose, S. D., Sundel, M., DeLange, J., Corwin, L., & Palumbo, A. (1971). The Hartwig Project: A behavioral approach to the treatment of juvenile offenders. In E. Ulrich, T. Stachnic, & J. Mabry (Eds.), *The control of human behavior* (Vol. 2). Glenview, IL: Scott, Foresman.

Rosenberg, R. P., & Beck, S. (1986). Preferred assessment methods and treatment modalities for hyperactive children among clinical child and school psychologists. *Journal of Clinical Child Psychology, 15*, 142-147.

Rosenthal, L. (1978). *The development and evaluation of the Problem Inventory for Adolescent Girls*. Unpublished dissertation, University of Wisconsin-Madison.

Ross, A. L., & Bernstein, N. B. (1976). A framework for the therapeutic use of group activities. *Child Welfare, 56*, 776-786.

Rutter, M. (1981). Stress, coping, and development: Some issues and some questions. *Journal of Child Psychology and Psychiatry, 22*, 323-356.

Santrock, J. W. (1994). *The authoritative guide to self-help books: Based on the highly acclaimed national survey of more than 500 mental health professionals' ratings of 1,000 self-help books*. New York: Guilford.

Sarason, I. G., & Ganzer, V. J. (1969). Developing appropriate social behaviors of juvenile delinquents. In J. D. Krumboltz & C. E. Thoresen (Eds.), *Behavioral counseling: Cases and techniques*. New York: Holt, Rinehart & Winston.

Sarri, R. L., & Galinsky, M. J. (1985). A conceptual framework for group development. In M. Sundel, P. Glasser, R. Sarri, & R. Vinter (Eds.), *Individual change through small groups* (pp. 70-86). New York: Macmillan.

Schinke, S. T., Blythe, B. J., & Gilchrist, L. D. (1981). Cognitive-behavioral prevention of adolescent pregnancy. *Journal of Counseling Psychology, 28,* 451-454.

Schopler, J. H., & Galinsky, M. J. (1985). The open-ended group. In M. Sundel, P. Glasser, R. Sarri, & R. Vinter (Eds.), *Individual change through small groups* (2nd ed.). New York: Free Press.

Schradle, S. B., & Dougher, M. J. (1985). Social support as a mediator of stress: Theoretical and empirical issues. *Clinical Psychology Review, 5,* 641-662.

Seaberg, J., & Gillespie, D. (1977). Goal attainment scaling: A critique. *Social Work Research and Abstracts, 13,* 4-11.

Sermat, V., & Smyth, M. (1973). Content analysis of verbal communication in the development of a relationship: Conditions influencing self-disclosure. *Journal of Personality and Social Psychology, 26,* 332-346.

Serna, L. A., Schumaker, J. B., Sherman, J. A., & Sheldon, J. B. (1991). In-home generalization of social interactions in families of adolescents with behavior problems. *Journal of Applied Behavior Analysis, 24,* 733-746.

Shapiro, D. H. (1982). Overview: Clinical and physiological comparison of meditation with other self-control strategies. *American Journal of Psychiatry, 139,* 267-272.

Shapiro, E. S., & Coles, C. L. (1993). In T. H. Ollendick & M. Hersen (Eds.), *Handbook of child and adolescent assessment* (pp. 124-139). Needham Heights, ME: Simon & Schuster.

Shelton, J. L., & Ackerman, J. M. (1974). *Homework in counseling and psychotherapy.* Springfield, IL: Charles C Thomas.

Shelton, J. L., & Levy, R. L. (1981). *Behavioral assignments and treatment compliance: A handbook of clinical strategies.* Champaign, IL: Research Press.

Simonson, N., & Bahr, S. (1974). Self-disclosure by the professional and paraprofessional therapist. *Journal of Consulting and Clinical Psychology, 42,* 359-363.

Spivack, G., Platt, V. V., & Shure, M. B. (1976). *The problem solving approach to adjustment.* San Francisco: Jossey-Bass.

Spivack, G., & Shure, M. B. (1974). *Social adjustment of young children: A cognitive approach to activating real life problems.* San Francisco: Jossey-Bass.

Stermac, L., & Josefowitz, N. (1982). *Social skills board game: Enhancing social competence in emotionally disturbed adolescents.* Los Angeles: Association for the Advancement of Behavior Therapy.

Stokes, J. P. (1983). Components of group cohesion: Intermember attraction, instrumental value, and risk taking. *Small Group Behavior, 14,* 163-173.

Stokes, T. F., & Baer, D. M. (1977). An implicit technology of generalization. *Journal of Applied Behavior Analysis, 10,* 349-367.

Taussig, I. M. (1987). Comparative responses of Mexican-Americans and Anglo-Americans to early goal setting in a public mental health clinic. *Journal of Counseling Psychology, 34,* 214-217.

Teri, L., & Lewinsohn, P. M. (1985). Group intervention for unipolar depression. *Behavior Therapist, 8,* 109-111.

Thoits, P. A. (1986). Social support as coping assistance. *Journal of Consulting and Clinical Psychology, 54,* 416-423.

Tisdelle, D. A., & St. Lawrence, J. S. (1988). Adolescent interpersonal problem-solving skill training: Social validation and generalization. *Behavior Therapy, 19,* 171-182.

Toch, H. (1969). *Violent men.* Chicago: Aldine.

Toseland, R. W ., & Siporin, M. (1986). When to recommend group treatment: A review of the clinical and the research literature. *International Journal of Group Psychotherapy, 36,* 191-206.

Tracy, E. M., & Whittaker, J. K. (1990). The social network map: Assessing social support in clinical practice. *Families in Society, 71,* 461-470.

Tuckman, B. (1965). Developmental sequence in small groups. *Psychological Bulletin, 63,* 384-399.

Tyler, V. O., & Brown, G. D. (1967). The use of swift, brief isolation as a group control device for institutionalized delinquents. *Behavior Research and Therapy, 5,* 1-9.

Vanderhoof, L. (1980). *The effects of a simple relaxation technique on stress during pelvic examinations.* Unpublished master's thesis, University of Maryland, School of Nursing.

Vinter, R. D. (1985a). The essential components of group work practice. In M. Sundel, P. Glasser, R. Sarri, & R. Vinter (Eds.), *Individual change through small groups* (pp. 11-35). New York: Free Press.

Vinter, R. D. (1985b). Program activities: An analysis of the effects on participant behavior. In M. Sundel, P. Glasser, R. Sarri, & R. Vinter (Eds.), *Individual change through small groups* (pp. 226-236). New York: Free Press.

Walker, H. M. (1970). *Walker problem behavior checklist.* Los Angeles, CA: Western Psychological Services.

Waters, V. (1981). The living school. *RET Work, 1,* 1-6.

Wheelan, S. A., & Hochberger, J. M. (1996). Validation studies of the group development questionnaire. *Small Group Research, 27,*(1), 143-170.

Whitney, D., & Rose, S. D. (1989). The effect of process and structural content on outcome in stress management groups. *Journal of Social Service Research, 13,* 89-104.

Whittaker, V. K. (1976). Differential use of program activities in child treatment groups. *Child Welfare, 55,* 450-468.

Wilkes, T. C. R., Belsher, G., Rush, A. J., & Frank, E. (Eds.). (1994). *Cognitive therapy for depressed adolescents.* New York: Guilford.

Wolfe, J. L. (1987). Cognitive behavioral group therapy for women. In C. M. Brody (Ed.), *Women's therapy groups: Paradigms of feminist treatment* (pp. 163-173). New York: Springer.

Wortman, C. B., & Lehman, D. R. (1985). Reactions to victims of life crises: Support attempts that fail. In I. G. Sarason & B. R. Sarason (Eds.), *Social support: Theory, research and applications* (pp. 463-489). Dordrecht: Martinus Nijhoff.

Yalom, I. D. (1985). *The theory and practice of group psychotherapy.* New York: Basic Books.

Zarb, J. M. (1992). *Cognitive-behavioral assessment and therapy with adolescents.* New York: Brunner/Mazel.

Name Index

486

Subject Index

About the Author

Sheldon D. Rose is Professor of Social Work at the University of Wisconsin-Madison. He received his Ph.D. from the University of Amsterdam (Holland) in social psychology and his master's degree in social work from Washington University in St. Louis. He has carried out extensive research on the effectiveness of various family and group approaches to the treatment of both children and adults in groups. He has written numerous articles in this area as well as eight books, including *Working With Children and Adolescents in Groups* (with Jeffrey Edelson, 1987); *Group Therapy: A Behavioral Approach* (1977); *Casebook in Group Therapy* (1980); and *Working With Adults in Groups* (1989). He is the author of training manuals for family therapists, leaders of children's groups, stress management groups, assertiveness training groups, and pain management groups. He serves on the editorial board of many journals in psychology and social work. His present research is on "damaging group experiences." He has given numerous workshops and lectures throughout the United States, Canada, Europe, and Asia, on the topics of group work and group therapy from a cognitive-behavioral perspective, children and adolescents in groups, group therapy for adults, parent training in groups, family therapy, stress management training in groups, and integration of group and family methods. He has lived and taught abroad for many years, including ten in Holland and one in India as a Fulbright professor.

About the Contributors

Martin D. Martsch is a Ph.D. candidate in social welfare at the University of Wisconsin-Madison. He received his B.A. degree in social work from Boise State University, Boise, Idaho (1985), and his M.S.W. degree from Florida State University (1987). He has extensive clinical experience working with adolescents and families in community and residential settings. His research interests involve delinquent adolescents and their families and working with adolescents in groups. His dissertation research is a comparison of two group treatments to address adolescent aggression.

Katherine P. Reardon is the Military Director of the Behavioral Science Family Practice Residency Program, Scott Air Force Base, Belleville, Illinois, and a clinical faculty member at St. Louis University Family Practice Residency Program, St. Louis. She received her Ph.D. in social welfare from the University of Wisconsin-Madison and her M.S.W. from the School of Social Work at Louisiana State University-Baton Rouge. She holds a diplomate conferred by the National Association of Social Workers and is certified by the Academy of Certified Social Workers. She conducts and supervises health and social research and teaches mental health diagnostics and treatment interventions. Her primary research interest is in the area of social support. She has published educational materials and devised prevention programs.